FOLK MUSIC

A Regional Exploration

Recent title in
Greenwood Guides to American Roots Music

Jazz: A Regional Exploration
Scott Yanow

GREENWOOD GUIDES TO
AMERICAN ROOTS MUSIC

FOLK MUSIC

A Regional Exploration

Norm Cohen

GREENWOOD PRESS
Westport, Connecticut • London

Library of Congress Cataloging-in-Publication Data

Cohen, Norm, 1936–
  Folk music : a regional exploration / Norm Cohen.
    p. cm. — (Greenwood guides to American roots music, ISSN 1551–0271)
  Includes bibliographical references and indexes.
  ISBN 0–313–32872–2 (alk. paper)
  1. Folk songs, English—United States—History and criticism. 2. Folk music—
United States—History and criticism. I. Title. II. Series.
ML3551.C56 2005
781.62'00973—dc22   2004017425

British Library Cataloguing in Publication Data is available.

Library of Congress Catalog Card Number: 2004017425
ISBN: 0–313–32872–2
ISSN: 1551–0271

First published in 2005

Greenwood Press, 88 Post Road West, Westport, CT 06881
An imprint of Greenwood Publishing Group, Inc.
www.greenwood.com

Printed in the United States of America

The paper used in this book complies with the
Permanent Paper Standard issued by the National
Information Standards Organization (Z39.48–1984).

10 9 8 7 6 5 4 3 2 1

Copyright Acknowledgment

Every reasonable effort has been made to trace the owners of copyright materials in
this book, but in some instances this has proven impossible. The author and publisher
will be glad to receive information leading to more complete acknowledgments in
subsequent printings of the book, and in the meantime extend their apologies for any
omissions.

Contents

Series Foreword

If present trends are any indication, soon anyone with access to the Internet will be able to tune in to music from any part of the world. When that happens, listeners may well find Kentucky bluegrass bands playing Tex-Mex music along with banjo tunes and gospel favorites, while musicians in India may intersperse elements of American rap music with their own native raga traditions.

It's difficult to predict right now, but even to understand the significance of this revolution requires an appreciation for the fact that until recently all musical genres, like every aspect of human activity, were associated with relatively compact geographic regions, bounded not only by national boundaries but also by the more limiting barriers of language, religion, geography, and cultural heritage. In the United States, regional boundaries might enclose an area as large as the vast Southwest or as small as the immediate environs of Galax, Virginia.

This series of musical studies seeks to describe American musical traditions that are, or once were, associated with geographic regions smaller than the nation as a whole. These musical varieties include jazz, blues, country music, Hispanic American music, Irish American music, polka music, Franco-American music (including Cajun and Zydeco), Native American music, and traditional folk music. Jazz music originated in New Orleans and other cities along the lower Mississippi River in the early 1900s, but by midcentury it was equally at home in New York and San Francisco as in New Orleans or Memphis. Jazz was in turn heavily influenced by blues music, an African American creation born in the broader regions of the Deep South.

Country music of recent decades is a merger of two regional Anglo-American musical traditions, one from the Appalachians and other southeastern states, and the other from the southwestern plains. Its earlier name of country-western music reflects more clearly that parentage. Irish American music, brought to these shores mainly in the 1840s and later by emigrants from the Ireland, flourished best in the big cities where the Irish made their new homes: Boston, New York, Philadelphia, and Chicago.

Hispanic (Latino, Tex Mex) music migrated north from Mexico and other Latin American countries. In the early 1900s it could be heard only in Texas, New Mexico, and California; a century later, Spanish language radio stations reach almost everywhere in the lower forty-eight. Polka music was brought to the New World by musicians from Central Europe—Germany, Switzerland, and what used to be Czechoslovakia. It was fruitfully transplanted to the Midwestern states from Texas north to Nebraska and the Dakotas.

The music of First Nations (Native Americans) was spread across the continent in varieties associated with particular groups of peoples, but as a result of ethnocentric federal policies that forced their relocation to "Indian Reservations," was subsequently located in regions that were often at great distances from the original homelands. Traditional folk music, the product of evolved music of European American and African American immigrants, had developed distinct regional characteristics in the New World by the eighteenth and nineteenth centuries, but as a result of internal, primarily western migrations, had changed considerably by the early twentieth century.

Four of these musical styles—jazz, blues, country, and traditional folk—are treated in separate volumes; the other "ethnic" traditions (Hispanic, Cajun/Zydeco, Polka, Irish, and Native American) are presented together in a fifth volume.

American music continues to evolve. Readers of these volumes can doubtless think of changes in music that have taken place in their own lifetimes. The many musical heritages of the nineteenth and twentieth centuries laid the foundations for today's music. The advent and growth of national media—radio, television, digital recordings, Internet—exert powerful forces on the nature of musical genres that were once regional. Ironically, national media permit two contradictory phenomena. At first, they introduce listeners to the regional musical forms that a wider audience otherwise might never have known about. Eventually, though, they provide the mechanism for the scrambling and cross-pollination of what were once distinct styles.

This does not mean that American musical regionalism is gone forever, doomed to a homogeneous culture that is the same in Key West, Florida, as in the San Juan Islands of Washington. If the past is any guide, new regional styles will continually emerge, gradually to become part of the national mix. As long as immigration to these shores continues, the influx of new musical styles will contribute to and invigorate the old. It is an exciting prospect.

Norm Cohen
Portland Community College, Oregon
Series Editor

Preface

Interest in American folk music has waxed and waned for over a century. This is true for both those who perform it and those who study it. Students and scholars from different disciplines have been intrigued by folk music for different reasons. Social historians see a wealth of documents that display public attitudes and sentiments at a level very different from the public media. Musicologists find unusual tunes and musical styles from a bygone era that somehow survive in spite of the changes in contemporary musical genres. Educators seek songs, ballads, and tunes that can readily be adapted for teaching purposes with various age level students. Literature students find ballad texts of wonderful elegance that preserve narrative styles of two centuries ago or more. Performers relish songs with more content than popular music and are at the same time more singable and "audience friendly." Finally, anthropologists and folklorists see keys to social patterns in the music of a community.

Since each of these audiences has its own interests, no text of manageable length can fully satisfy them all. The presumed reader of this volume is a high school student or adult who has little or no formal knowledge of traditional American music, who may have heard some recordings or seen one of the several recent films and videos that describe or make use of traditional music, and who wants to learn more about the subject. To avoid overly technical discussions of music, the emphasis is definitely on the textual rather than on the musical aspects of folk song.

The aim is to present an overview of the field of American folk music that stresses breadth rather than depth. Many particular topics have been explored more fully elsewhere, and I have tried to include useful references to those works. In particular, I have omitted detailed analysis of any particular song or ballad or tune, even though such studies can provide the most engaging and most penetrating insights into the nature of folk song and its place in its society. Case studies—in-depth analyses of a particular song or group of songs—often exhibit folk song scholarship at its best.

To many, reading a descriptive book on folk music will be no more satisfying to the appetite than reading a provocative restaurant menu. One must proceed from here to the music, itself; and to that end, I have provided numerous references to recordings that, hopefully, will be available for some time to come.

Acknowledgments

This book represents a blending of the writings and ideas of many folk music scholars. In the text I have tried to acknowledge borrowings directly by means of citations to specific published works. However, over the years I have assimilated unconsciously many more insights, the sources of which I have long since forgotten. The late Ed Kahn was the only person from whom I learned about folklore and folk song in the formal context of a classroom, but our exchange of ideas and collegiality continued long after those two semesters more than forty years ago. D. K. Wilgus urged me to write my first academic paper on the subject of folk music in 1964 and was a source of information from our first meeting until his death in 1989. Archie Green, more than anyone else, has been a constant source of inspiration for four decades; we have visited together in cities across the continent, have done fieldwork together, and have exchanged ideas regularly. No one has had more of an impact on my own views about folk music. David Cohen offered many suggestions regarding musical aspects of the subject, as is appropriate since our interests in folk music began together almost a half century ago. If other individuals find traces of their own work embedded in mine and without the courtesy of acknowledgment, I deeply apologize.

The process of gathering illustrations for this book involved a different coterie of individuals. I am particularly grateful to Paul F. Wells and Lucinda Cockrell at the Center for Popular Music at Middle Tennessee State University, to Steve Weiss at the Southern Folklife Collection at the University of North Carolina (and to Dan and Beverly Patterson for hosting my visit there), and to Jennifer A. Cutting and Judith A. Gray at the Archive for Folk Culture at the Library of Congress. They all facilitated what proved to be one of the more challenging aspects of pulling this book together.

To Jane McGraw and her colleagues at Capital City Press, my warm thanks for a sympathetic and sensible handling of the conversion from typescript to book.

To my wife, Verni Greenfield, I am especially grateful for advice and encouragement and for just being a willing audience for my periodic grumblings and complaints during the completion of this project.

Chronology

1565	First Spanish colony on North American continent founded at St. Augustine.
1568	Georgia sea islands settled and claimed by Spain.
1598	New Mexico settled by Spanish.
1603	First permanent French settlement in New World.
1607	Jamestown founded by British in Virginia.
1619	First African slaves to New World brought to Jamestown, Virginia.
1620	Pilgrims land at Plymouth in Massachusetts.
1624	New Amsterdam (later New York) founded by Dutch.
1638	New Sweden established on Delaware River.
1664	New Netherland forcibly absorbed into English colonies.
1680s	German immigration to America begins; becomes the Pennsylvania "Dutch."
1699	Settlement of Louisiana.
1716	First permanent settlement of Texas by Spanish.
1736	First known fiddle contest, Hanover, Virginia.
1755	French Acadians deported by British; eventually settle in Louisiana.

1761	Death of Timothy Myrick in Connecticut, memorialized in ballad, "Springfield Mountain."
1770s	First reports of banjo/fiddle music by African American plantation slaves. Colonial settlers cross Appalachians into Tennessee and Kentucky.
1808	Jonathan Lewis accused of murder of Naomi "Omie" Wise in North Carolina; ballads written about the event. Importation of slaves outlawed by Congress.
1814	American officer James Bird executed for desertion during War of 1812; Charles Miner publishes ballad on event.
1819	First descriptions of African elements in American religious singing. Spain cedes Florida to the United States.
1822	Textile mills established at Lowell, Massachussetts, on the Merrimack River.
ca. 1828	Actor Thomas D. "Daddy" Rice witnesses an African American boy doing a little dance that he imitates and presents as the "Jim Crow" dance.
1828	The Baltimore & Ohio becomes the first chartered American railroad.
1833	Frankie Silver hanged for the murder of her husband in North Carolina; inspires numerous folk legends and songs.
1834	"Zip Coon" published.
1836	Texas General Sam Houston defeats Mexican General Santa Anna at the Battle of San Jacinto; inspires the song, "Yellow Rose of Texas."
1843	Four entertainers (Billy Whitlock, banjo; Dan Emmett, fiddle; Dick Pelham, tambourine; and Frank Brower, bones) put on first burnt-cork show in New York and call themselves The Virginia Minstrels, the beginning of minstrel shows. Dan Emmett's "Old Dan Tucker." Seba Smith publishes "A Corpse Going to a Ball," later popular as "Young Charlotte."
1844	First edition of influential shaped note hymnbook, *The Sacred Harp*, published.
1845–1850s	Major Irish immigration following potato famine in Ireland.
1846–1848	War between the United States and Mexico ends with Mexico ceding a large portion of the Southwest to the Unitd States.
1848–1850s	Major German immigration following revolution of 1848.
1848	Stephen Foster's "Oh! Susanna."

1849   Gold discovered in California leads to gold rush.

1850   Stephen C. Foster publishes "Camptown Ladies."

1852   "Row Row Row Your Boat" published.

1853   Stephen Foster's "My Old Kentucky Home."

1853?   "Pop Goes the Weasel" published.

1856   B. R. Hanby publishes "Darling Nellie Gray."

1858   "Sweet Betsy from Pike" published by John Stone in his *Put's Golden Songster*.

1860   Stephen Foster's "Old Black Joe" published. Gold rush in Idaho.

1860–
1864   Civil War inspires numerous ballads and songs.

1862   Gold rush in Montana. Julia Ward Howe publishes words to the "Battle Hymn of the Republic." Civil War naval battle between the *Cumberland* and the *Merrimac*, soon memorialized in ballad.

1865   "Faded Coat of Blue" published by J. H. McNaughton.

1866   "Goober Peas" published, credited pseudonymously to "A. Pindar" and "P. Nutt." "When You and I Were Young, Maggie" written by Johnson and Butterfield. Thomas Dula of North Carolina murders sweetheart, Laura Foster; ballad written about the event.

1867   William F. Allen, Charles P. Ware, and Lucy McKim Garrison publish *Slave Songs of the United States*. Route of the Chisholm cattle trail is laid out.

1868   Collision between the *Persian* and the schooner *E. B. Allen* in Lake Huron; memorialized in ballad by Patrick Fennell.

1869   First transcontinental railroad completed.

1870   "Package of Old Letters" (or "Little Rosewood Casket") published by White and Goullaud.

ca. 1872 Effie I. Crockett (under the pseudonym Effie Canning) publishes now standard version of "Rock-a-Bye Baby," first published in *Mother Goose's Melody* in 1765.

1873   Temperance song, "Little Blossom," published by Margaret Bidwell. "Home on the Range" first published by Dr. Brewster Higley under the title "Western Home."

1876   "Streets of Laredo" written by Francis Henry Maynard under the title "Cowboy's Lament."

1879   "Golden Slippers" written by African American James Bland.

1881   "Polly Wolly Doodle" published.

1882   Outlaw Jesse James, living in St. Joseph, Missouri, under name of Thomas Howard shot in the back by his cousin, Robert Ford.

1882–   Harvard scholar Francis James Child publishes his monumental *The*
1898   *English and Scottish Popular Ballads.*

1884   Music to "Clementine" published (words, 1863).

1889   "The Cowboy's Dance Song" was written by James Barton Adams.

1890   Harry Duncan murders policeman James Brady in St. Louis saloon,
         the basis for the ballad "Duncan and Brady."

1890s   Professionally written and published sentimental ballads and songs
         reach height of popularity; many become traditional folk songs.

1892   "After the Ball" (Charles K. Harris).

1893   "After the Roundup," by D. J. O'Malley, published in *Stock Growers'*
         Journal, later titled "When the Work's All Done this Fall."

1894   "I've Been Working on the Railroad" published.

1895   "Roll On Little Dogies" published by Will Croft Barnes. Stack Lee
         shoots William "Billy" Lyons in St. Louis saloon, the basis for the
         ballad "Stackolee"/"Stagolee."

1896   "In the Baggage Coach Ahead," by Gussie L. Davis, published. Pearl
         Bryan of Greencastle, Indiana, murdered by her lover, Scott Jackson,
         and Jackson's roommate, Alonzo Walling; event memorialized in
         several ballads.

1898   "Lightning Express" published by J. Fred Helf and E. P. Moran under
         the title "Please, Mr. Conductor, Don't Put Me Off the Train."

1899   Frankie Baker shoots her lover, Allen Britt, in St. Louis, the basis for
         the ballad "Frankie and Johnny." Words to "She'll Be Coming Round
         the Mountain" published (music published in 1927).

1900   Casey Jones wrecks an Illinois Central train near Vaughan, Mississippi;
         ballads written about the event.

ca. 1900 Logging becomes established in the Northwest. First references to
         new African American popular song style, the blues.

1902   Explosion at Fraterville mine at Coal Creek, Tennessee; possible
         source of song, "Shut Up in Coal Creek Mine."

1903   J. B. Marcum shot to death in the doorway of the Breathitt County
         Court House, Kentucky; memorialized in feud ballad. Number 97,
         fast mail train on the Southern Railway from Washington, D.C.,
         to Atlanta, Georgia, wrecks, inspiring ballad by Fred Lewey and
         others.

1908   N. Howard "Jack" Thorp publishes first book of traditional cowboy
         songs, *Songs of the Cowboys.*

1909   "Casey Jones" published by vaudevillians T. Lawrence Seibert and
         Eddie Newton.

1910   Publication of *Cowboy Songs and Other Frontier Ballads* by John A. Lomax.

1910–   "Casey Jones, the Union Scab" written by Joe Hill.
1911

1911   Tragedy in Cross Mountain mine, Tennessee; another possible source of the song "Shut Up in Coal Creek Mine."

1912   First published blues songs by W. C. Handy ("Memphis Blues") and Hart Wand ("Dallas Blues"). *Titanic* sinks, inspiring many songs and poems.

1914   "St. Louis Blues" by W. C. Handy published. "Yellow Dog Blues" by W. C. Handy published.

1914–   English folk song collector Cecil Sharp comes to the United States to
1918   collect folk songs in the Appalachians; selection of his fieldwork published as *English Folk-Songs from the Southern Appalachians* (1932).

1915   "Joe Turner's Blues" by W. C. Handy published. "Hesitating Blues" by W. C. Handy published. "The Strawberry Roan" by Curley W. Fletcher published under the title "The Outlaw Broncho." "The Dying Mine Brakeman" written by West Virginia miner-composer Orville Jenks.

1917   "Beale Street Blues" by W. C. Handy published.

1922   Alexander "Eck" Robertson becomes first traditional fiddler to make commercial recordings.

1924   First recording of "John Henry" (based on events of the 1870s–1880s) by Fiddlin' John Carson. Vernon Dalhart's recording of "The Prisoner's Song"/"Wreck of the Old 97" becomes first million selling country music record.

1925   First commercial recordings of traditional cowboy songs by Carl T. Sprague. Explorer Floyd Collins trapped and perishes in cave in Kentucky; "The Death of Floyd Collins" written by Andy Jenkins and recorded by Vernon Dalhart.

1927   First recordings by Jimmie Rodgers and the Carter Family. Carl Sandburg's *The American Songbag* published; first major popular folk song collection for a general audience.

1928   Archive of Folk Song established at Library of Congress with Robert W. Gordon named as its first director.

1934   *American Ballads and Folk Songs* by John A. Lomax and Alan Lomax published; first collection published from their extensive fieldwork across the country. First National Folk Festival held.

1941   Pete Seeger and Lee Hays form the Almanac Singers. Bonneville Power Administration hires Woody Guthrie to write songs for a public information film about BPA.

1945   First recordings by Bill Monroe and his Blue Grass Boys issued. Pete Seeger and Lee Hays form the Weavers.

1946–   Vance Randolph's decades of folk song collecting culminates in the
1950   publication of *Ozark Folk-Songs*.

1950   First recording by the Weavers, "Tzena" and "Around the World," sells over one million copies.

1951   Weavers' recording of "On Top of Old Smokey"/"The Wide Missouri" ("Shenandoah") becomes their second million seller.

1952   Folkways Records issues an *Anthology of American Folk Music*, edited by Harry Smith; introduces many traditional blues and country recordings to urban revival singers.

1958   Kingston Trio recording of "Tom Dooley" becomes a million seller.

1959   First Newport Folk Festival held.

1961   Peter, Paul and Mary begin coffeehouse appearances together. Joan Baez's first, eponymous album released.

1962   Peter, Paul and Mary's first, eponymous album hits charts. Bob Dylan's first, eponymous album released.

1963   Peter, Paul and Mary's third album, *In the Wind*, hits number one on the charts.

1967   Smithsonian Institution inaugurates Festival of American Folklife on The Mall in Washington, D.C.

1969   *The Erotic Muse*, by Ed Cray, published; first scholarly collection of traditional American bawdy songs.

Introduction

The subject of this book is the music and songs of the United States and, to some extent, Canada that flourishes outside of, but may not be completely separate from, the mainstreams of mass media music (popular or "pop") or high culture music (classical). The guiding theme is the search for music that has some regional specificity. In this case, the term "regional" can be applied to a small mountain community in the Ozarks or to the entire Southwestern United States. The chronological range is in principle from the date of the first European and African immigrants to the New World, but in practical terms there is little to offer beyond general speculation for the pre-Revolutionary period. True, some texts exist from that period, but no recordings, few direct transcriptions, and not enough stylistic descriptions to permit any regional characterizations with certainty.

The musical traditions Old World immigrants brought with them since the seventeenth century are also surveyed, and the evolution of those traditions as settlers established cultural roots in America is examined. The discussion also includes commercial musical genres that are derived from traditional folk music and are still fairly close to it, but as those genres move away from their folk roots with the passage of time, as almost all of them did, they figure less prominently in the text. What is considered, however, are the interactions between traditional folk music and the commercial traditions, such as minstrel show, hillbilly, gospel, blues, and nineteenth-century pop music. In these cases, there has been an important flow of song lore in one or both directions. The folk music "revival" in this country is also discussed, examining its social and musical relationships to the traditional musical cultures whence it took inspiration.

Sooner or later, books on classical, jazz, swing, or country music have to address the definition of the music under discussion. It is often difficult to produce a concise, accurate description of any of these musical styles; still, there is general agreement on just what is or is not that particular type of music. In the case of folk music, the problem runs considerably deeper: opinions of what is American folk music not only differ sharply, but they are often mutually inconsistent.

In Britain, interest in what are now referred to as folk songs began in the late seventeenth and early eighteenth centuries. At that time, scholars turned their attentions to the popular ballads and songs printed by local presses in broadsides and chapbooks and distributed on the streets to the common folk. Decidedly different from literary ballads and poems, some were the product of contemporary hacks; a few were cranked out by men of letters writing anonymously or under a pseudonym, just as today some noted authors write potboiler mysteries for a quick penny. Others were older songs and ballads from the sixteenth and seventeenth centuries, or perhaps earlier, whose origins were lost to general knowledge. These were the pieces that attracted the most attention when academics began to collect broadsides. It was soon discovered that many of these songs could be heard on the lips of milkmaids, chimney sweeps, farmers, and shepherds. Collectors, whose interest was primarily antiquarian, began to gather up broadsides much as later collectors acquired picture postcards or baseball cards.

Just when the term "folk song" was first applied to this material is not known. Nineteenth-century dictionaries stressed the nature of "folk song" as something originating among the common people, for example: "A song of the people; a song based on a legendary or historical event, or some incident of common life, the words and generally the music of which have originated among the common people, and are extensively used by them."[1]

If a folk song is a song of the common people, however that group may be defined, what are its characteristics? How do we recognize it, if we hear it from people who are not readily identifiable as "common?" Presumably, something about these songs marks them as a class, apart from the mere identity of their bearers. Later writers tried to define folk songs by their properties. Through the years, a half-dozen different criteria were proposed for delimiting folk songs: by origin (who wrote it), possession (in whose repertoire is it now), internal stylistic characteristics, method of transmission, subject matter, and social function (under what circumstances it is sung). In the first decades of the twentieth century, transmission and possession were the most common criteria applied.

A more useful approach is to define folk music as the music that survives without complete dependence on commercial media. Often the term "traditional music" is taken as synonymous with "folk music." Traditional, or folk, suggests music that is performed in family or community settings rather than in commercial contexts—that is, the performer is not doing it for pay. But what happens when a singer is paid? In the last century in America, the available media can thrust any traditional musician into a commercial setting (a concert, folk festival, coffeehouse, radio show, audio recording, video documentary, and so on). Merely moving a folk performer into the limelight does not by itself invalidate calling him or her a folksinger or folk musician, or the material folk songs or folk music. Nevertheless, it seems to be that when performers who had been used to performing for members of their own community in an informal setting are repeatedly put on a stage, they start thinking of themselves and their songs in a different way: "Is this what my audience wants to hear? Should I change this song? Last night they got really restless when I sang those hymns. Should I make that fiddle tune a little flashier?" As a result, changes start to creep in that might not have appeared if the performer had not been placed in commercial situations.

Since most modern listeners do not live in communities where folk music originates, many people are able to hear folk music only thanks to the commercial media. Does that mean we aren't really hearing folk music? Although some purists might argue so, this is such a restrictive approach that it is self-defeating. While it is possible that folk music is accessible via commercial media, it is important to be aware of the fact that some compromises might have been made along the way. Keeping this in mind, it is clear that there are the purely non-commercial performers of folk music: those who grew up with the music and perform it in an unself-conscious way, who's work is available only because some enterprising song collector heard and recorded them; and folk music interpret-ers, who deliberately set out to make it available to wider audiences (and perhaps earn a living thereby). In either case (and in between), there are some performers who faithfully sing or play songs as they learned them, while there are others who deliberately change songs, combine different versions, put lyrics to a differ-ent tune, and so on.

The definition just given makes unnecessary some of the criteria that earlier writers used to decide whether particular items were folk songs. An early hallmark of a folk song for many decades was the notion that it was transmitted orally (that is, learned by word of mouth through direct contact between one singer and another) rather than by means of printed sources. While this seems like a rather trivial distinction, a century ago it was often tied up with rather prejudicial views about peasant and working-class society, illiteracy, and lack of education. What was often implied in the assertion that folk songs are orally learned was the elitist notion that folk songs are the lore of lower (that is, inferior) social classes. But setting such ideas aside, there are some instructive things in the process of oral transmission: if a song is learned by word of mouth, this is of itself proof that its survival is not entirely dependent on commercial media. More importantly, it suggests that the nature of the song makes it easy for the singer to learn and remember it. How many schoolchildren extract their playground ditties from books? However, while some groups may learn a certain song orally, in other social circles the same song may be known only thanks to published media.

Another characteristic folk song collectors and scholars of the early twentieth century noted was that different versions of the same song exhibited extensive differences in text and/or tune. This is in contrast to a piece of popular or classical music, which was regarded as unchanging throughout its life. These are not necessarily changes that can be accounted for by faulty memory. The ballad "The Unquiet Grave" has been widely found in Britain and America.

It would be impossible to say that one of these was the original and the other an imperfectly remembered rendition. Neither one is poetically inferior; neither one is clearly the source for the other.

Variation or change, then, are hallmarks of traditional folk song. The factors that account for alterations include accidental as well as intentional ones. In the first category are both faulty memory and misunderstanding or mishearing. The latter can occur when words have fallen out of use or meanings have been forgotten or altered as the language itself changes. Readers may be familiar with the parlor game "telephone" in which each participant whispers a phrase into the ear of the next person in the chain, the object being to see how much (or how hilariously) the phrase changes in the course of transmission. Much the same can happen with folk song, though the venue is not a parlor and the time scale not a matter of minutes. After the round of telephone has been played, the players can conduct a postmortem and repeat the process out loud, thereby seeing just exactly where changes occurred. Unfortunately it is rare to have such an opportunity when studying a folk song.

The results of faulty song transmission are sometimes called "mondegreens," a term coined by Sylvia Wright, who had misheard an old English ballad with the line, "They had slain the Earl of Moray and laid him on the green," to be "… and Lady Mondegreen."[2] An oft-quoted misheard hymn is, "Gladly, the Cross-Eyed Bear" instead of "Gladly the Cross I'd Bear." Some changes occur because a word or phrase no longer makes sense to the singer. In the Ozarks in the early twentieth century, the ballad of "Lady Margaret" often was sung "Liddy Margaret" or "Lydia Margaret"; the title "Lady" was unfamiliar to the singers.[3]

"The Unquiet Grave"

A Shepton Beauchamp, England, version:

The wind blows cold today, sweetheart,
Cold falling drops of rain.
I never, never knew but one sweetheart
And in green 'ood she is lain.

A singer from Sussex, England, begins:

How cold the wind do blow, dear love!
How heavy fall the drops of rain!
I never had but one true love,
And in the greenwoods he was slain.

Also, there are the changes that some singers introduce deliberately; perhaps they disapprove of the message of a song or feel something doesn't fit right. When North Carolina singer/songwriter Dave McCarn (1905–1964) recorded "Everyday Dirt" in 1930, his version of an old Anglo-American broadside ballad "Will the Weaver," he added his own stanzas to help even the score in favor of the cuckolded husband because he felt the unfaithful wife shouldn't have gotten the better of him, as happened in the older lyrics.[4]

Sexually suggestive lyrics or displays of excessive violence may induce a modest singer to bowdlerize or "clean up" a text for a particular audience. Many singers are sufficiently creative to modify their texts accordingly. Helen Harness Flanders collected two different versions of "Captain Wedderburn's Courtship" at an interval of seventeen days from the same singer. After singing the second, substantially different and slightly risqué version, the woman claimed she never even knew the earlier one.[5]

Variability always exists in live musical performance, even in classical music. Variability must always be evaluated in a framework of what is considered meaningful variation within its idiom. Generally, we expect variation on a much coarser scale in folk music than in classical but do not always find it. Indeed, if there is variation, it often is an indication of oral tradition but not invariably. A century ago it seemed to be permissible for pop songwriters to rewrite someone else's song, changing words and tune slightly, and then copyright it themselves. In folk music of the 1920s and 1930s, one finds many instances of pop songs entering oral tradition and changing extensively from the sheet music original in the interval of a few decades.

It is not surprising that such transformations occur. Lack of a reference text— a "correct" version—removes an important brake on meandering transmission; more importantly, without a conscious sense of the song being the commercial property of a legal author, there is no obligation or need to rein in textual drift. A singer/musician who feels it important to retain a song intact will not allow it to slip out of memory. When the song is not commercial—that is, if it is not identified as someone else's property and, therefore, is as much the singer's own song as anyone else's—why take the trouble? In other words, faulty memory will account for changes only when it is not important to resist changes.

It used to be taken for granted that a folk song is anonymous. When sense of an author is lost, the song is not regarded as commercial property, though it may not always be obvious which came first. At any rate, if a careful search fails to disclose an author, which is true of a great many folk songs, it suggests that the song has survived through noncommercial means.

Antiquity of at least a hundred years used to be considered a requirement for a piece to be labeled a folk song, but it certainly is not proof. In any society, commercial music has some normal range of lifetime. That range is largely determined by the nature of the disseminating media. Some classical compositions remain in the concert repertoire for centuries, but most do not. Pop music today has a much shorter lifetime than it had a century ago. Coupled with other appropriate characteristics, antiquity can be evidence for a noncommercial survival, but by itself, it is not sufficient.

One of the most striking features of folk songs is the use of traditional patterns, stock language, and familiar situations. Most noncommercial composers/writers write in patterns familiar to them. They borrow unhesitatingly from older compositions because they are unencumbered by notions of plagiarism, copying, unoriginality, and so on. For example, when Charles Guiteau was hanged in 1882 for the assassination of President James A. Garfield, a poet wrote a ballad about it in the style of a criminal's "last goodnight." This was a once widespread type of song, written as if it were the last confessional words of the criminal about to be executed. The author had borrowed from a ballad printed (without author credits) in 1858 about another murderer, executed in New York in that year.[6]

> **"The Lamentation of James Rodgers"**
>
> The opening stanza reads:
>
> My name is Charles Guiteau, my name I'll never deny,
> I leave my aged parents in sorrow for the die;
> But little did they think, while in my youthful bloom,
> I'd be taken to the scaffold to meet my earthly doom.
>
> Whereas the earlier version reads:
>
> My name is James Rodgers—the same I ne'er denied,
> Which leaves my aged parents in sorrow for to cry;
> It's little ever they thought, all in my youth and bloom,
> I came into New York for to meet my fatal doom.

The author of the Guiteau ballad felt no reluctance to use an earlier work because it was regarded more or less as public property. The borrowings may be as extensive as the example just given, or as simple as two or three words, such as "milk white steed" or "long yellow hair," descriptions that are used in many old ballad texts. It is unlikely that folk poets would borrow freely from compositions that they knew were commercial property, except for purposes of parody. Some scholars have argued that stock words, phrases, or whole stanzas were reused in traditional folk songs because they aided the memory in the case of oral transmission.[7] More likely, those songs that use stock words and phrases have a better chance both of entering oral tradition and of surviving. In general, songs can enter oral tradition when they imitate the characteristics of that tradition.

Folk music, then, is music that has survived without the necessity of commercial media. A particular performance is folk music if the above is true, and it is in a noncommercial context. A singer/musician is a folk performer if his or her material comes to him through noncommercial media. It is possible for one rendition of a song to be a folk performance and another not; a performer can be a folk performer for some material but not others.

FOLK MUSIC, CULTURE, AND MIGRATION

The seeds of America's musical culture were planted by the immigrants who came here starting in 1620 and continuing to the present. At first, the major flow came from the British Isles, and it proceeded in four distinct waves.[8]

1629 to 1640. Immigration, numbering 21,000, was from southern and southeastern counties of England, in particular, East Anglia, and primarily to Massachusetts and greater New England. The immigrants came mostly in families (90 percent), belonged to the Protestant sect known as Congregationalists, settled in cities (65 percent), and were mostly artisans (54 percent) and farmers (33 percent) by occupation. Their literacy was high (80 percent for males, 50 percent for females). Their speech became the northern American dialect.

1642 to 1675. Some 45,000 immigrants came from the south and west of England, settling in Virginia and the tidewater South (the coastal plains between the Atlantic and the mountains). About 42 percent of Virginia's population came from London, Gloucester, and Kent. Primarily Anglicans, they were mainly farmers by occupation (60 percent), with only 30 percent artisans, and therefore a smaller urban settlement (35 percent) than the earlier group. Few came in families (20 percent); most were single males (83 percent), and 70 percent were in the fifteen-year-old to twenty-four-year-old age group. Their literacy was lower than the earlier group: 50 percent for males and 25 percent for females. Their speech became the south coastal American dialect.

1675 to 1715. Some 23,000 immigrated from the north and north midlands of England and settled in the Delaware Valley (New Jersey, Pennsylvania, Delaware, and north Maryland). They were mostly Friends (commonly known as Quakers), equally divided between farmers and artisans, and about 30 percent settled in cities. Their literacy was in between the two previous groups' rates: 65 percent for males and 33 percent for females. Their speech became the midland American dialect.

1717 to 1775. During this long period, approximately 250,000 emigrated from England's borderlands (including Scotland) and settled in the southern highlands (Appalachians and Ozarks) of America. Mostly Presbyterians and Anglicans, they became primarily farmers (60 percent). From their speech evolved the southern highland dialect. One should note especially the presence of the Scotch-Irish, or Ulster Irish. These were originally lowlands Scots who were driven out of Scotland in the seventeenth century by the English, settled in Ireland, and later immigrated to the New World. By 1790, Scots and Scotch-Irish constituted 24 and 28 percent of the population of North Carolina and South Carolina, respectively, and 25 and 27 percent of the populations of what would become Kentucky and Tennessee. Literacy rates in this region varied widely, according to wealth and rank rather than location. Based on who could sign their names to documents and who used "marks," male Lowland Scots were 50 percent literate, and Highland Scots were 70 to 80 percent literate.

Though these four migrations originally constituted somewhat distinct cultural groups, they rapidly blended with each other to create a uniquely American culture. This has been noted in our main regional dialects but is also true of other aspects of culture.

Other European countries founded colonies, some of which contributed significantly to our musical patchwork. These include primarily Dutch immigration to New York (1610s), Germans to Pennsylvania and New York (1710s), and French and Spanish to Louisiana and the far Southeast (1740s to 1770s). Much later, in the nineteenth century, great influxes from other regions made their mark: the Irish in the 1840s, the Chinese in the mid-nineteenth century, more Germans and Scandinavians in the 1860s to 1890s, and Italians, Russians, and Austro-Hungarians in the 1890s to 1920s. Other ethnic groups immigrated in smaller numbers, but some had a cultural (especially musical) impact well out of proportion to their quantitative representations.

We could not understand American musical culture at all if we did not acknowledge the major contributions from America's unwilling immigrants, namely the African slaves and their descendants. In 1790 there were 697,000 slaves in the United States out of a total population of 3,170,000. Of these, 136,000 resided in the Deep South, 521,000 in the upper South, and 40,000 in the North. In the North lived another 60,000 free blacks. Students of the development of blues music, which was originally an African American creation, have tried to relate its musical characteristics to those of the regions of the western African hinterlands whence the slaves came.

The dates of the migrations from England would lead us to expect that New England, settled earliest, would have some of the oldest folk songs, which might be scarcer in the southern highlands. However, there are some other factors to consider. Most important is a cultural phenomenon sometimes referred to as "archaism of the fringe"; that is, culture out at the fringes of the culture area changes more slowly than it does in the cultural centers. The cultural centers, generally cities, are the sources of innovation and change most rapidly. The settlers who peopled the southern mountains came from what were cultural backwaters of Britain relative to London and other major cities; they were already "old-fashioned" when they first arrived in America. Once they arrived here and migrated into the relatively inaccessible Appalachian and Ozark mountain regions, they became somewhat isolated from further contact. New England and the southern tidewater region, on the other hand, were in continuous contact, thanks to their seaports. In the ballad repertoires found in New England and the southern highlands, both regions preserved ballads from the seventeenth and eighteenth centuries; however, New England has proven much richer in imported ballads from the post-Revolutionary period.

Once it is recognized that folk music is but one aspect of culture, it is then possible to draw some useful information from the studies in other cultural fields, in particular, language. For example, British linguistic changes up to the middle of the eighteenth century, or perhaps even until the Revolutionary War, were generally mirrored in the American colonies as well, though some isolated southern mountain regions retained the older pronunciations.[9] By the late eighteenth century, colonies began to assert their independence culturally if not yet politically. By now, inland America was sufficiently removed from contact with England that the older pronunciation was retained, but near the Atlantic coast, these changes were adopted.[10]

Regional dialecticians have recorded an abundance of Elizabethan survivals in the speech of the southern mountains, but extrapolations shouldn't be made too extravagantly from this observation as was formerly done by some wide-eyed travelers. Even a century ago, there were no remote "hollers" wholly untouched by the passage of time, but it was true that many expressions and pronunciations long abandoned in other parts of the country (and even in the British Isles) could be recorded in the Appalachians and Ozarks.

Whatever songs, ballads, and tunes were brought west by trans-Atlantic passengers, once here they tended to spread across the continent. This occurred either by transfer from person to person or as cultural baggage as they migrated westward. The relative increased mobility of Americans (compared to their Old World ancestors) has, almost from the earliest years of the nation, contributed to the blurring of cultural boundaries.

Observing language patterns provides some expectation with regard to musical lore, but the speculations must not be carried too far. Virtually everyone is a language bearer, and language being our primary means of communication, there is necessarily a considerable consistency in the language of a region. Musical lore is inessential culture, and the driving force toward homogeneity is weaker. Furthermore, musical traditions may be carried by only a small fraction of the population; it may not be reliable to look to statistical differences as the sources for cultural differences. Small numbers of singers or musicians can exert a disproportionate effect on the traditions of their regions by virtue of their personalities rather than their numbers.

What should these discussions of language lead the listener to expect when turning back to music? Most importantly, it is common to find ballads, songs, tunes, singing styles, and playing styles traceable back to the seventeenth or eighteenth century that have long since disappeared in the regions of origin. Also, late nineteenth-century popular songs that had faded from favor in American urban centers by the jazz age were still sung in the Southeastern regions well into the mid-twentieth century. There might be some direct lines of transmission from particular regions of Britain to particular regions of America—some studies have shown that certain ballads found in the southern highlands have definite sources among the Lowland Scots and Scotch-Irish—but there were not too many. Internal migrations of the population starting soon after their arrival in the New World and the exposure of musicians to other musicians of different ancestry within a relatively short time tended to blur those lines of transmission.

In antebellum America, regional cultures were very distinct even though their origins were somewhat complicated. Later, other more efficient means of passing a song from one person to the next gradually began the process of blurring regional culture boundaries. These include various mass media: the stage, traveling shows and performers, broadsides, songsters and songbooks, sheet music, phonograph records, radio, audiotapes, television, videotapes, and digital compact disc recordings (CDs).

FOLK MUSIC IN ITS COMMUNITY: ORIGINS, FUNCTIONS, AND MEANINGS

In preparation for looking at folk music, it is important to examine its relation to society. Immediately a host of questions flutter to mind: What is the function of folk music in its own natural setting? What role(s) does it play in society? Are time and region independent of that role? What do folk songs mean to their singers? How can that be determined? Is the meaning invariant over time? Can cultural outsiders understand the folk songs? What is the role of the singers and musicians in changing and preserving the songs? Are they passive transmitters of culture? Where do folk songs originate? What are our sources of information for folk music?

There are many different reasons for making music. Some music is made privately, with no other audience in mind. The purpose of religious music is to appease, persuade, or glorify deities. "Prayer-song" might be a better term for this category. Ceremonial music, such as patriotic songs, songs at football games, or protest or political songs, try to influence or alter the public's mood. Some music is made to achieve a goal, such as work songs, lullabies, and commercial musical jingles. Some music is made to entertain others for compensation: dance music, pop music, classical music. Finally, there is music made to communicate informally to one's immediate social circle. Communicating includes entertaining, comforting, admonishing, and so on. This would include not only many songs we generally call folk songs but also pieces sung by only one individual or that have a very short lifetime, such as children's songs, fraternity songs, and most folk music. These categories do not exhaust all possibilities nor are they non-overlapping. Many musical performances might satisfy more than one purpose. More importantly, a song or tune may at different times be performed in different venues for very different purposes; that is, the reason for the performance is not always the same. The purpose is thus identified by the performance setting, not the music itself.

Although folk music's purpose is most often for social communication, it is certainly an important component of religious music as well. Most writers consider some types of religious music—spirituals, hymns, gospel songs, carols, religious ballads—as qualifying as folk music at least some of the time. Some writers, as well, would not consider financial compensation as necessarily disqualifying the performance as folk music. For example, when a fiddler sitting by his hearth entertains his family with fiddle tunes, most people would agree the musician is making folk music. When the village fiddler saunters to the schoolhouse on Saturday night to play for a community dance and receives free drinks or money in exchange, most would still say the fiddler is making folk music.

One of the reasons for the difficulty outsiders have in settling on a definition of folk music is that insiders (within the community where the music is taking place) often do not use the term among themselves. In the last half century, when meetings of outsider collectors with performers became increasingly common, astute performers learned to accept—or at least, understand—what the collector wanted and meant by a "folk song." Some became quite adept at recontextualizing, that is, conjuring up a false source for, their music so that it would fit the collectors' prejudices of what constituted a folk song: "Here's an old song I learned from my grandmother" rather than, "I found this song in John Lomax's book, *Cowboy Songs*." Beyond this, most of the classification schemes of the scholars and collectors ("Child ballad" versus "broadside ballad," "work song" versus "occupational song," "lyric song" versus "ballad") were outside the knowledge of the typical performer. According to one anecdote, Chicago bluesman Bill Broonzy, a major artist during the 1920s and then again during the folk revival of the 1950s, was asked if the songs he sang were folk songs. He responded with something like: "They weren't sung by horses."

Putting aside temporarily the question of what is and what isn't folk music, there is another problem: how to understand the meanings of folk songs and ballads. Usually, there is no ambiguity. In some cases, a listener who did not grow up in the same community as the singer and therefore doesn't know the local slang, the proverbs, and other communication conventions may not fully appreciate the text's message. Most of us have had the experience of reading a literary work from a different era (such as Shakespeare) or culture (such as Cervantes) and not getting the point without extensive footnotes explaining conventions that contemporary readers understood but we may not.

Many African American work songs and early blues tunes contain the line, "I asked my captain for the time of day / He said he threwed his watch away."[11] The singer isn't describing a ne'er-do-well supervisor who can't keep track of his timepiece; rather, the exchange is between a work-weary laborer yearning for day's end and a boss who tells him it's none of his concern; get back to work.

Many popular African American antebellum spirituals seem to deal with the ancient people of Israel and their condition of servitude in Egypt under the Pharaoh, as in, "When Israel was in Egypt land, / Let my people go." It is now understood that the real concern of the singers is not the children of Israel but rather their own release from bondage, a sentiment slaves could not express openly in the presence of their white owners.

Sometimes the ambiguity or erroneous interpretation is a result of phrases, events, or concepts whose meaning has become forgotten with the passage of time. Folksinger Buell Kazee's recording of the old Anglo-American ballad "Lady Gay" contains the stanza:

It was just about Old Christmas time,
The night being cold and clear,
She looked and she saw her three little babes
Come running home to her.

"Old Christmas" is an allusion to the calendar discrepancy that existed before the adoption of the Gregorian calendar reform. In 1582, Pope Gregory deleted ten days to bring the calendar year into agreement with the solar year: the day after October 4 was decreed to be October 15. While Catholic countries accepted the reform immediately, England and its colonies didn't until 1752. Thus, Christmas, "old style," would have fallen eleven days later—on January 5 on the Gregorian calendar. Many communities in the American southern highlands refused to accept the reform and continued to celebrate Christmas according to the older calendar. Kazee, a native of Kentucky, sang the song as he learned it and as many other singers from the southern mountains recorded it. But more recent listeners have not always understood the meaning; in at least one text transcription, Kazee's stanza was rendered as "It was just about, oh Christmas time."

Sometimes, without further information, it is impossible to determine whether the words of a song express the singer's or the writer's own feelings. In 1925 in Dayton, Tennessee, the high school science teacher, John Scopes, was tried in court for teaching evolution in violation of the state's recently passed law. The events prompted several songs, which were written and recorded in the months following. Vernon Dalhart, a prolific hillbilly recording artist of the day, concluded his recording, "The John T. Scopes Trial," with,

> Oh, you must not doubt the word that is written by the Lord,
> For if you do your house will surely fall;
> And Mr. Scopes will learn that wherever he may turn
> The old religion's better after all.

In another recording of that year, "The Death of William Jennings Bryan," Charles Oaks sang,

> [William Jennings Bryan] fought the evolutions and infidel men, fools,
> Who are trying to ruin the minds of children in our schools;
> By teaching we came from monkeys, and other things absurd,
> Denying the works of our Savior and God's own holy word.

These songs have similar messages; but whose messages are they—the singer's, the songwriter's, or the audience's? Oaks was a blind minstrel singer from Richmond, Kentucky, several of whose songs were disseminated on broadsides or phonograph records and later turned up in local oral tradition. He himself wrote the Bryan song that he recorded. Although no one ever interviewed Oaks to ask his opinions, his background and other songs provide justification for assuming that he was indeed expressing his own sentiments and expected his local audience would respond sympathetically. On the other hand, Dalhart's song was written by his longtime partner, Carson J. Robison, who, though a native Kansan, lived much of his life in New York and was a professional performer and writer of many songs, most intended for the regional "hillbilly" market but others with wider appeal. He turned out ballads in abundance in response to local tragedies and other newsworthy events specifically for the purpose of immediate recordings. He knew who his audience would be, and he was adept at expressing his songs in language and sentiments familiar to that southern audience. We cannot, therefore, assume that he and singer Dalhart were expressing their own sentiments.

Social historians have often used folk song texts as evidence for popular beliefs or attitudes on the grounds that the anonymous songs are the products of the community as a whole and represent the viewpoint of the community. But folk song scholarship has become more sophisticated, learning more about the origins of individual songs and their authors. When there is specific information about the circumstances of a song's origin and dissemination it may alter the conclusion that the song conveys the singer's own point of view.

Folk songs are rich in metaphor (often sexually suggestive) that outsiders may often fail to recognize. The Anglo-American ballad "The Nightingale" describes an amorous encounter between a fiddling soldier and a young maid. After walking together and talking for a while,

> Now they had been there an hour or two
> When out from his satchel a violin he drew.
> Sang the old concordance and he made his fiddle ring,
> Then they watched the water gliding, and they heard a nightingale sing.

Many folk song scholars accept that the phrase in the second line is a double entendre, with one meaning being risqué or off-color. But Ozark folksinger Almeda ("Granny") Riddle (1898–1986) sang the version with the above stanza and insisted there was nothing suggestive about it. "Now, dirty minds may have made dirty ballads around this 'Nightingale' song, but actually that began as a classic.... Personally, I've never been able to see anything unclean in the 'Nightingale' song, and I've sung it to some pretty big audiences."[12]

Interpretations of folk song lyrics are limited only by the bounds of our own imagination and ingenuity, and, in truth, it is a credit to the author(s) of a song text if its language is rich enough to support an abundance of interpretations. Each listener is free to explore his or her own understandings, but we must be careful not to attribute our own interpretations to the singer or writer without direct verification from those persons themselves.[13]

Granny Riddle was very specific on this point. She said,

> Of course, "folklore," the word was not even known then [in my
> youth]. Nobody knew anything about that, which probably was a
> very happy situation. I think so, because maybe if we didn't try to go
> so deeply, I think maybe we might enjoy what we have more. We're

becoming entirely too technical in this thing. We're trying to pick it apart. I really believe that. And I think that folk songs are meant more or less like children: you're not meant to try to understand them or analyze them, just to enjoy them.[14]

As a check on the tendency to over-interpret song lyrics—to tease out subtle nuances from particular choices of wordings—it does well to remember the great numbers of verses in collected song texts that make no sense at all. Many singers would not sing a song that they couldn't understand, but not all are so fussy. A classic example is "I'll Twine 'Mid the Ringlets," written in 1860 by Maude Irving and J. P. Webster. Never mind that no one has been able to figure out what the aronatus was. But as recorded in 1927 by the Carter Family (under the title "Wildwood Flower")—and subsequently copied by numerous singers who learned from them—it became something entirely different.

As incoherent a mixture of words as it is, no instructions for finding a buried treasure are here; there is simply an accumulation of mis-hearings of words and phrases that are not idiomatic—at least not in the communities where this song has remained in oral tradition for a century and a half.

"I'll Twine 'Mid the Ringlets"

The Irving and Webster version:

I'll twine 'mid the ringlets of my raven black hair
The lilies so pale and the roses so fair;
The myrtle so bright with an emerald hue
And the pale aronatus with eyes of bright blue.

The Carter Family version:

Oh, I'll twine with my mingles and waving black hair
With the roses so red and the lilies so fair
And the myrtle so bright with the emerald dew
The pale and the leader and eyes look like blue.

Many of the prior examples contain quotations from the texts of commercial recordings of the 1920s, genres that were marketed specifically to Southeastern Anglo-American audiences and rural or inner-city African Americans and were called respectively "hillbilly" and "blues" music. Yet earlier, we noted the distinction between folk music and the folk-derived commercial traditions such as hillbilly and blues music. Many folk-derived commercial genres began as reliable reflections of older folk traditions. Only as the genres matured and were increasingly commercialized did they turn from older material to fresh material written either by the artists themselves or, generally later, by a separate bevy of commercial writers. In this progression, the music tended to move further away from folk roots, and it became a less accurate reflection of those folk roots. Early blues and hillbilly recordings can be regarded as folk music, but as blues evolved into rhythm and blues, and hillbilly music into country and western, they became less relevant to the discussions of this book.

Where, then, is folk music found? Naturally, the primary source is from folk musicians themselves. Field recordings and field transcriptions—that is, songs

Old Songs That Men Have Sung

Devoted to outdoor songs, preferably hitherto unprinted—songs of the sea, the lumber-camps, Great Lakes, the West, old canal days, the negro, mountains, the pioneers, etc. Send in what you have or find, so that all may share in them.

Although conducted primarily for the collection and preservation of old songs, the editor will give information about modern ones when he can do so and IF all requests are accompanied with self-addressed envelop and reply postage (NOT attached). Write to Mr. Gordon direct, NOT to the magazine.

Conducted by R. W. GORDON, 4 Conant Hall, Cambridge, Mass.

ONE of the most valuable recent contributions to the department was made the other day by Mr. A. S. White of Ontario; a group of eight songs learned in Canada, mainly from lumberjacks, about 1900. Two of these I print below, exactly as they came to me with the exception of a few changes in the punctuation.

The first, "Willie and Mary," is better known under the title "The Drowsy Sleeper." The text is one of the most perfect I have yet seen.

Willie and Mary
(Text of A. S. W. "as sung in lumber camps north of Massey to Ste. St. Marie, 1900-3.")

"Wake, awake! you drowsy sleeper,
   Wake and listen unto me!
There's some one at your bedroom window,
   A-weeping there so bitterly."

"Oh who is at my bedroom (window)
   A-weeping there so bitterly?"
"Oh it is I, your dearest Willie,
   A-weeping there so bitterly.

"Oh, Mary dear, go and ask your mother
   If you my wedded bride might be;
If she says no, then come and tell me,
   And I'll no longer trouble thee."

"Oh, Willie dear, I dare not ask her
   If I your wedded bride might be,
But go and court some other lady
   Who yet your bride might be."

"Then, Mary dear, go and ask your father
   If you my wedded bride might be;
If he says no, then come and tell me,
   And I'll no longer trouble thee."

"Oh, Willie dear, I dare not ask him
   If I your wedded bride might be,
For by his side lies a silver dagger
   To pierce the heart so true to me."

"I can climb the highest tree, love,
   I can rob the richest nest,
I can court the gayest lady,
   But not the one that I love best!"

Then Willie seized a shining dagger,
   Pierced it through his manly heart,
Saying, "Farewell, Mary, farewell, Mary,
   It's here we both shall never part."

Then Mary seized the silver dagger,
   Pierced it through her lily-white breast,
"Farewell, father; farewell, mother;
   It's here we both shall be at rest."

Of the second, Mr. White says: "This is one of the real old-timers sung by all classes of men. Heard it in Montreal in 1900. It was an old song at that time." This song goes under various names: "The Jealous Lover," "Lorella," "Florilla," "Flora Ella," etc. Although I believe that the "flow Ella" is merely a corruption, I keep to the text as sent to me.

Flow Ella
(Text of A. S. W.—Ontario.)

Down by yon weeping willows
   Where the violets sadly bloom,
There lies one, fair flow Ella,
   Lies sadly in her tomb.

She died not broken hearted,
   No sickness on her fell;
But in one moment parting
   From whom all she loved so well.

The moon was shining gaily,
   Shone over hill and dale,
When to her lonely cottage
   Her jealous lover came.

"Oh, Ellen, let us wander
   Down by yon meadows gay,
And let us talk and ponder,
   All on our wedding day."

"Oh, Edward, I am tired
   Of wandering here alone.
Oh, Edward, I am weary;
   I pray you'll take me home."

"Oh, you have not the wings of an angel
   Or far from me you would fly!
Oh, Ellen, you've deceived me;
   This night you must instantly die!"

Down on her knees she bended,
   And begging for her life,
But into her snow-white bosom
   He thrust that fatal knife.

"Oh fare you well, fond parents,
   This is my dying breath;
I pray you will forgive me
   When my eyes are closed in death.

"And fare you well, you Edward,
   Far from you I must go.
May God forgive you, Edward,
   And all your vows prove true."

Down on his knees he bended,
   Crying out, "What have I done?
I've murdered my flow Ella,
   As true as the rising sun!"

A sample page from Robert W. Gordon's song column in *Adventure Magazine* (May 30, 1924). *Author's collection.*

obtained in the singers' own communities as distinct from those recorded in the artificial setting of a recording studio—published in many collections in the twentieth century are accurate representations of the oral tradition of the time and place reflected. Between about 1910 and 1960, an abundance of material of this type was gathered so that we have a robust body of songs and tunes at our disposal. In the 1960s and 1970s, thanks to the resurgence of interest in folk music, a younger generation of song collectors and record company proprietors went into the field and recorded, for subsequent publication on commercial LP recordings, the music of traditional singers and musicians. This, also, is a valid body of folk music in spite of the fact that they were recorded for commercial purposes. Prior to the early 1900s, however, there are no recordings nor, for Anglo-American music, any field transcriptions of significance. What, then, are the sources for the folk music of nineteenth-century America?

In the first place, there is material from Britain dating back to the seventeenth century. These sources include field transcriptions (mostly late nineteenth century and later), cheap print publications of songs that we believe came from oral sources, and manuscript collections of traditional materials. A connection between these as an ultimate source for American folk song and the products that were found in the twentieth century can clearly be seen, and the intermediaries can be confidently assumed. Attempts to find threads of connectivity between African American music and its African antecedents have met with only modest success.

Second, there is a variety of print and manuscript sources in eighteenth- and nineteenth-century America—a resource that has not yet been explored fully. For example, sometimes manuscript collections of song texts and poems written a century or more ago turn up. On the basis of internal evidence and sometimes other supporting information, we can decide whether the writer took material from contemporary oral or written sources.

Newspapers and magazines have often run columns of old songs and poems. Some of these were conducted by folk song collectors who used them not only to induce readers to send songs that they knew but also as vehicles for locating potential informants who they might later visit in person. Out West a number of newspapers and cattlemen's journals published occasional songs or poems that were made into songs. Many literary magazines in the late nineteenth century ran feature articles on slave songs, spirituals, Revolutionary War songs, and other types that include traditional material.

By far the most extensive potential source for old songs is the category of cheap print, which includes chapbooks, songsters, and broadsides, that were forms of inexpensive literature that published words, but generally not the music, to older favorites or currently popular songs. Most important among these were the *Forget Me Not Songster* and the *American Songster*, both of which were published in numerous editions between the 1830s and 1850s.

OCCUPATIONS

Most of the occupations in this country that gave birth to rich troves of documented musical folklore reached their zenith in the nineteenth and early twentieth centuries. If there were any existing earlier, they have been stingy in the lore they left behind. More recently, increasing mechanization as well as changes in the way Americans entertain themselves (as a result of greater dependence on commercial media) have resulted in fewer occupational songs being written and disseminated.

Folklorists have found that folklore thrives with particular vigor when men and women live under conditions of hardship, danger, or even just uncertainty. The lore takes many different forms: it can be ballads and songs, that are the focus of this book, but it can also include tales, sayings and proverbs, superstitions, and customs. An air force pilot may value a certain scarf that he always wears, without which he would feel more likely to face an accident. A miner may carry a lock of his sweetheart's hair in his wallet, where it serves not only as a reminder of his true love but also as a talisman that affords protection. Soldiers at the front during World War I and World War II believed it was bad luck to light three cigarettes (for three different soldiers) from the same match. Actors are dismayed by wishes of "good luck" before a performance and send each other off with "break a leg."

Among the songs and ballads of cowboys, miners, lumberjacks, and others, recurring subjects are the potential threats that the workers face: stampedes among cowboys, explosions or cave-ins among miners, logjams among lumberjacks, and so on. It would be wrong to conclude from this that a morbid interest in death and tragedy as such flourished. Some of these ballads and songs have a basis in historical events; their purpose was at least in part to memorialize the dead and injured comrades. But others are completely fictional, suggesting that perhaps the singers and their audiences felt that by verbalizing their fears they would be protecting themselves against the dangers actually happening—or, at least, distributing the fear among the community as a whole.

THE COLLECTORS AND THEIR CRITERIA

For many folk song and tune collectors the primary criterion for deciding whether to notate or record a particular selection was that it had been reported by a previous collector. This tendency of the biases and interests of collectors to persist from generation to generation is almost as tenacious as the persistence of the folk songs themselves. One of the guiding beacons used by almost all collectors was the monumental collection of ballads published by Harvard scholar Francis James Child as *The English and Scottish Popular Ballads* (1882 to 1898). More about this work is covered later, but suffice it to note for now that the 305 ballads enumerated by Child were especially sought after by American collectors from the 1890s onward and always displayed with pride in any publication.

Cecil Sharp, an English folk song collector who visited the southern high-lands in 1914 to 1918 when the World War prevented his fieldwork in Britain, was particularly interested in American versions of the songs he and other English collectors had previously recovered in the British Isles. Some important collectors have shown more willingness to include a broader range of material: John Lomax, in the early 1900s, was one of the first cowboy song collectors, a genre in which almost no scholarly collecting had been done previously. New England collector Phillips Barry recognized the importance of the British contribution to American folk song but soon came to champion the songs and ballads that originated on American soil, even though some scholars belittled their significance. Vance Randolph, whose four-volume collection of Ozark folk songs is one of the best regional collections available, was innovative in including songs that first appeared on, and were later learned from, hillbilly recordings of the 1920s. Many of his contemporaries scorned material that was so close to popular media. Additionally, many collectors didn't bother with songs that were so ubiquitous they seemed uninteresting, for example, "Happy Birthday" and "Jingle Bells."

In sum, the definitions of folk song proposed or accepted by those early collectors had a great influence on when later collectors chose to turn their tape recorders on or off.

FOLK MUSIC AND COMMERCIAL MEDIA

Chapter 7 explores in some detail the relationship between American folk music, urban centers, and several important commercial media of the last century and a half. This book uses a definition of folk music that makes commercial media an important consideration. Folk music survives without the necessity of commercial media, but it is not wholly divorced from it. Romanticized depictions aside, no region of the United States since the Civil War (and perhaps since the Revolutionary War) has been untouched by the commercial media of the day.

In different periods, different commercial media played roles in the dissemination of folk song. Unlike a popular song or a work of elite music, though, a folk song did not die out when it was no longer commercial; to the contrary, that is when it achieved its status as folk song regardless of its origins. This interplay between commercial and other media has resulted in particular songs passing back and forth more than once between the domains of folk and pop song.

The interrelationship between folk and pop music is illustrated by two different, widely known ballads: "Barbara Allen" and "Casey Jones." The British ballad "Barbara Allen" was first mentioned in the diary of Samuel Pepys in 1666. Three centuries later it had become the imported ballad most often collected in North America. The details of its origins and migrations are obscure: Did it begin life in cheap print, or was it circulated first orally? In the seventeenth and eighteenth centuries it appeared frequently in cheap print, but it also was recovered from oral sources with sufficient variation to assure us that print was not the ballad's only means of survival. In nineteenth-century America, the ballad was printed in songsters and broadsides whose texts were copied from British models. By the twentieth century, numerous variants had been collected, some clearly learned from printed sources but others so divergent that they must have passed through several generations of oral transmission. By the middle of the twentieth century, the song was fading from commercial media but continued to be collected in the field. Thus, the details of transmissions of "Barbara Allen" are vague, but both oral and written sources have played a role (see Chapter 7 for the song text).

John Luther "Casey" Jones was a railroad engineer killed in a wreck on the Illinois Central's *Cannonball Express* on April 30, 1900, near Vaughan, Mississippi. One of Jones's friends, an African American engine wiper named Wallace (Wash) Sa(u)nders at the Canton, Mississippi, railroad yards made up some verses about him, borrowing from older traditional songs about other engineers, hoboes, ramblers, and trains. Saunders's song gained some local currency, until somehow it came to the attention of two traveling professional vaudevillians, Eddie Newton and T. Lawrence Siebert. Sensing commercial potential, they extensively revised Saunders's piece and presented their own song on stage, where its enthusiastic reception led to sheet music publication and several highly successful recordings in 1911. This sheet music song became so popular that by the 1930s folk song collectors were recording it from traditional folksingers. Thus, the song "Casey Jones" has passed from folk song to pop song and back again to folk song.

Understanding the background of "Casey Jones" is clearer than for "Barbara Allen" because more is known about the role of the commercial media in the twentieth century than in the eighteenth. Examining folk songs and ballads current in the eighteenth century and earlier, it can be speculated that the relations between commercial and non-commercial processes have not changed qualitatively. However, our definition of "folk song" may not be as apt for the seventeenth century as it is for the twentieth.

THE FOLK MUSIC REVIVAL

In the middle of the twentieth century, interest in folk songs grew enormously as singing groups such as the Weavers, the Kingston Trio, and Peter, Paul and Mary introduced folk songs to a wide urban audience—for many listeners, their first exposure to folk song. In this folk song revival, many urban singers searched out old folk songs from published and recorded sources to present them in their own public commercial performances. With row after row of bins in music stores labeled "folk," the question of what belongs in those bins is a practical one rather than just an argument among scholars. Should the term be confined to the relatively simple music generally passed from generation to generation or person to person by word of mouth and performed nonprofessionally in small groups or communities? Or should it be broadened to include the more recent commercial styles that deliberately emulate the characteristics of that music? Some writers use the adjective "traditional" to refer exclusively to the first type, and the broader term "folk" (or "folk-derived" or "folk-like") to designate primarily the second type. Others prefer to call these latter artists "folk song singers" or "revivalists" to distinguish them from the "tradition bearers"—performers who grew up with the music as part of their own culture. Nevertheless, in most commercial record and bookstores of the late twentieth and early twenty-first centuries, it is primarily this latter material that is labeled "folk music." Some writers see the distinctions as meaningless (or, at least, fruitless) and decline to distinguish between them.

In this volume, unless specifically stated otherwise, both "folk" and "traditional" will refer to the first, narrower, category. After exploring that earlier music, the nature of the later music of the folk song revival (in Chapter 7) will be easier to understand. Brief synopses of some songs are included in the Appendix.

REGIONAL DIFFERENCES

America's folk music is determined by two main factors. The first is the ethnic background of its people, which (at least initially) greatly determines the particular songs and tunes as well as the types of music, both vocal and instrumental, that establish a foothold. The second is the circumstances in which the people found themselves where they settled, which influenced the themes and contents of particular songs and ballads.

To a European visitor, one of the most remarkable facts about the United States is the relative homogeneity of our culture. Except for recent immigrants, almost all of the country's 300 million residents, spread over a geographic region the size of all Europe, speak—or at least understand—a single language. It certainly was not always this way. Seventeenth-century explorers who landed on these shores encountered a diverse native population that spoke hundreds of different languages. Immigrants who came in the eighteenth and nineteenth centuries brought dozens of different languages with them. While the tactics that led to it are regrettable and the cultural losses that resulted from it lamentable, the settlers from the British Isles managed to impose their language and culture as the dominant and nearly ubiquitous one across more three million square miles of widely varied territory.

By the latter half of the nineteenth century, two broad, regional folk music styles had been established in the United States: northern and southern. Probably they were established before the Civil War, but the documentary evidence is too scanty to say with certainty.[15] The factors mostly responsible for the differences were the population characteristics: the North consisted mainly of English settlers, complemented by French Canadian and Irish in the first half of the nineteenth century; the South was settled by a greater proportion of Scots and Scotch-Irish, overlaid by African slaves and their descendants. A considerable difference in literacy rates between the two regions may have played a secondary distinguishing role.

The results of these factors were that, in the North, English songs and musical styles dominated, long texts and other signs of the influence of print persisted, melodies tended to be in the conventional major scale, ballad singing was generally unaccompanied, and singing style was very plain, metrically regular, without any vocal decorations, syncopations, or swinging rhythms. Fiddle music showed evidence not only of the original English sources but also of the later Irish and French Canadian immigrants, both of which had vibrant instrumental musical traditions.

In the South, ballads sung to instrumental accompaniment—fiddle and banjo in the nineteenth century, guitar starting in the twentieth—were much more common, pentatonic melodies predominated, singing was more rhythmic, and vocal decorations were common. The African penchant for polyrhythms manifested itself both vocally and instrumentally in the freer use of rhythms and in syncopation, which is, in a way, a form of polyrhythm: one irregular melodic rhythm played against another regular, background rhythm. Scottish and Scotch-Irish fiddle tunes were predominant, which meant greater use of drones, double stops (playing two strings at once), and pentatonic melodies.

These differences were not invariable but are reliable as broad generalizations. Unfortunately, when looking only at printed texts, some easily heard distinctions are not apparent. Folk songs are, after all, meant to be sung, and many characteristics are not captured on paper when they are written down. Texts that do not scan well or look awkward or dull when read can leave a completely different impression when sung by a traditional singer.

As pioneers moved westward, settling first the Great Lakes states and the Midwest and then the Far West, they brought with them the music of their respective Northeast or Southeast regions. As lifestyles and occupations in the different regions pursued different courses determined by climate, geography, crops, and so forth, different song topics naturally emerged. There is no major difference in the styles of these other regions except what developed because of geographic differences.

The following chapters explore the traditional music of some distinctive regional groups. To some extent, there will be a common underlayer of broadly distributed ballads, songs, and tunes, such as were discussed earlier. Nevertheless, there are localized songs in each region that are not likely to be found far from their places of origin. It bears repeating, though, that just as the rise of nationwide marketing chains, construction corporations, and financial institutions tend to make all parts of the country visually similar to one another, similarly, the steady growth of mass communication media made possible by technological changes has gradually eroded the distinctive regional musical cultures that used to be the norm.

The musical traditions of some other groups that, for other reasons, are distinct from the mainstream of American musical culture also deserve at least brief mention. These traditions and their bearers are set apart by some circumstance that defines them as what folklorists and anthropologists call a "folk community"—an enclave within the dominant culture that has a shared, somewhat exclusive, culture of its own. That culture is not private because of any attempt to create artificial secret societies but rather as a consequence of the lifestyle of its own community. Ancestral heritage, language, and religion are certainly sources of a folk community's identity, but just as important are identities established because of occupations, associations, and recreational lifestyles.

Broadly speaking, the purposes in this volume are to understand America's regional musical forms, their history and evolution, and to learn from them whatever possible about the lives, beliefs, and concerns of the people who make or listen to that music. These explorations will provide background for the other volumes in this series: *Country Music*, *Blues Music*, *Jazz*, and *Ethnic/Border Traditions*.

NOTES

1. *Century Dictionary*, 1889, quoted in Cecil Sharp, *English Folk Song: Some Conclusions*, 4th revised ed. (1907; repr., Yorkshire, UK: EP Publishing, Ltd., 1972), p. 3.

2. Sylvia Wright, in a 1954 article in *Atlantic* magazine. Steven Pinker, *The Language Instinct* (New York: William Morrow and Co., 1994), p. 160. In his book, Pinker used the term "oronymns" to apply to strings of sound that can be divided into words in different ways—a linguist's explanation of at least some mondegreens.

3. "Lady Margaret," quoted in Francis James Child, *The English and Scottish Popular Ballads*, 5 vols. (1882–1898; repr., New York: Dover, 2003), No. 74. Throughout this book, ballads that appear in Child's *The English and Scottish Popular Ballads* are indicated by including in parentheses his name and the number he assigned to it. Brief synopses of the ballads mentioned are in the Appendix.

4. Patrick Huber, "Cain't Make a Living at a Cotton Mill: The Life and Hillbilly Songs of Dave McCarn," *North Carolina Historical Review* 70 (July 2003): 297–333. Huber argues that McCarn's recomposition reflected his own deep distrust of women and his unsatisfactory relationships with them.

5. Helen Hartness Flanders, *Ancient Ballads Traditionally Sung in New England*, vol. 1 (Philadelphia: University of Pennsylvania Press, 1960–1965), p. 17.

6. From an uncredited broadside, "The Lamentation of James Rodgers," printed by H. DeMarsan of New York. The fragment of the "Charles Guiteau" ballad was printed by Louise Pound in *American Ballads and Songs*, New York: Scribners, 1922, p. 146. Other nineteenth-century murder ballads used the same stanza.

7. Fleming G. Anderson, "Technique, Text, and Context: Formulaic Narrative Mode and the Question of Genre," in *The Ballad and Oral Literature*, ed. Joseph Harris (Cambridge: Harvard University Press, 1991), pp. 18–39. Another reason proposed for the use of commonplaces (see Glossary for definition) in ballads is to avoid distraction from the narrative itself: see M. J. C. Hodgart, *The Ballads* (1950; repr., London: Hutchison University Library, 1962), p. 3.

8. This discussion borrows from David Hackett Fischer's presentation in *Albion's Seed: Four British Folkways in America* (New York and Oxford: Oxford University Press, 1989).

9. Examples of eighteenth-century pronunciation changes adopted in the colonies are the "ea" sound of sea, peak, lead, and so on, which used to rhyme with "day," and the "oi" vowel combination, formerly pronounced as a long "i"—"bile," "ile," "pis'n."

10. Two important pronunciation changes in late eighteenth-century England not adopted in the colonies, except along the seacoast, were the loss of preconsonantal and final "r" ("Hahvahd," "fahthah") and the shift from the flat "a" in words such as "can't" (with the same vowel sound as in "man") to a broad "a" (as in the word "father").

11. For example, Charley Lincoln's "Chain Gang Trouble," recorded 1927.

12. Roger D. Abrahams, ed., *A Singer and Her Songs: Almeda Riddle's Book of Ballads* (Baton Rouge: Louisiana State University Press, 1970), pp. 23–25. The topic has been discussed at length by Barre Toelken in his study, *Morning Dew and Roses: Nuance, Metaphor, and Meaning in Folk Songs* (Urbana, IL: University of Illinois Press, 1995).

13. This is reminiscent of the abundant analyses of 1960s rock music songs that sought esoteric references to drugs in the lyrics. Many researchers insisted that the Beatles's "Lucy in the Sky with Diamonds" was a coded reference to the recreational drug, LSD, in spite of writers Paul McCartney's and John Lennon's vigorous denials.

14. Roger D. Abrahams, ed., *A Singer and Her Songs: Almeda Riddle's Book of Ballads* (Baton Rouge: Louisiana State University Press, 1970), p. 132.

15. We have available a small handful of manuscript collections from the mid-nineteenth century or earlier, but they are all from northerners. They show what is expected: a consistency with the older folk songs of England and with the songlore of the American Northeast in the twentieth century. Unfortunately, we have no comparable manuscripts written by southerners, so we can't date the beginnings of the southern style.

1

Types of American Folk Music: Ballads and Songs

No convenient way exists to look at a song text or tune and decide whether it is a folk song or not. It makes more sense to define folk music in terms either of its social role or its means of dissemination rather than its intrinsic characteristics (such as language, verse form, subject matter, tune, accompaniment, and so on). Some useful generalizations, however, can be made by narrowing the focus and considering individual types of song and music, at least as descriptions if not definitions. In this chapter, different categories of folk songs are described; the following chapter considers musical aspects.

NARRATIVE SONGS

Folk songs can be categorized by their narrative content—that is, whether there is a story being told or not. If a song is to tell a story effectively, it must have narrative continuity from stanza to stanza. Even though alternative versions of the same ballad can have great differences, there is still the same story line, which exerts some control over the permissible range of variations in the text. Non-narrative songs have no such constraint; consequently, not only lines but entire stanzas move from one song to another, restrained only by the musical or metrical requirements.

Outside the subject of folk music, the term "ballad" has different meanings. In the nineteenth century, the term referred to any romantic or sentimental song, usually a narrative, as distinguished from the more raucous songs of the minstrel or vaudeville stage (or, in England, the music hall). In the twentieth century, the term meant a slow love song, as distinguished from the novelty song. In the context of folk music, a ballad is a poem set to music that tells a story, is divided into stanzas of consistent length and rhyme scheme, and is sung to a repeating melody. The story can be told in first person or in third person. It can also be presented as a dialog—a characteristic of many of the oldest ballads.

A story has a beginning, a middle, and an end. This means that there must be a sequence of events of sufficient consequence that the story line could not simply continue with further similar happenings; the "end" is a state of affairs that is irreversibly different from the way matters were at the "beginning." This excludes an important part of almost all folk song traditions: cumulative songs, in which each stanza adds a line to the preceding stanza ("The House That Jack Built"); sequential songs, in which only a number or obvious word changes ("Ninety-Nine Bottles of Beer"); and cyclical songs, in which each stanza is simply linked to its predecessor ("The Farmer in the Dell").[1] After these types are excluded, some examples still have a narrative thread that is so weak that it is difficult to say whether a story is present or not.

In particular, opinions differ on how to classify a song that in itself has little story line but happens to be a fragmentary version of a more complete ballad found elsewhere. This refers not only to the casual loss of stanzas through faulty memory or careless transmission but also to the cases where certain stanzas of a ballad take on a life of their own as a non-narrative song. Two good examples are "I Gave My Love a Cherry," a detached fragment of the ballad "Captain Wedderburn's Courtship" (for synopses, see Appendix), and "Who's Going to Shoe Your Pretty Little Feet," derived from "The Lass of Roch Royal." It also happens in popular song: "The Man on the Flying Trapeze" is a ballad telling a complete story, but all most people remember now is the chorus: "He flies through the air with the greatest of ease, / The daring young man on the flying trapeze."

Minstrel Ballads

In the English-language tradition in North America, at least six ballad styles can be characterized. They differ partly in historical period and partly in such stylistic details as the presence or absence of editorializing or moralizing, use of rhetorical devices, and whether the plot unfolds chronologically.

The oldest type is minstrel ballads, which originated in late medieval European literature and generally told stories about courtly figures, knights, lords, and ladies. Written by poets, bards, or minstrels associated with the courts of nobility, minstrel ballads often had analogs in other forms of medieval literature. They typically began with a call to get the audience's attention: "Come listen a while, you gentlemen all" ("Robin Hood Newly Revived") or "Lyth and listen, gentlemen, / That's come of high born blood" ("Robin Hood and the Beggar II"). The vocabulary includes many words of Norman French, which

"Robin Hood's Birth, Breeding, Valor, and Marriage"	"King Estmere"
Kind gentlemen, will you be patient awhile? Ay, and then you shall hear anon, A very good ballad of bold Robin Hood, And of his man, brave little John. .... Now out, alas! I had forgotten to tell ye That marryd they were with a ring; And so will Nan Knight, or be buried a maiden, And now let us pray for the king: That he may get children, and they may get more, To govern and do us some good; And then I'll make ballads in Robin Hood's bower And sing 'em in merry Sherwood.*	And you shal be a harper, brother, Out of the north countrye, And I'le be your boy, soe faine of fighte, And beare your harpe by your knee. And you shal be the best harper That ever tooke harpe in hand, And I wil be the best singer That ever sung in this lande.**

*"A new ballad of bold Robin Hood, shewing his Birth, Breeding, Valour and Marriage" (Child, No. 149, version A).
**"King Estmere" (Child, No. 60); taken from Bishop Thomas Percy's seventeenth-century manuscript.

once was characteristic of the language of the English nobility, and the text shows a preference for alliteration (words with the same vowel sound, such as "with/give" or "bird/girl") rather than rhymes. (Alliteration works particularly well in oral poetry or song, where there is a tendency to elide, or omit, the final consonants.) Minstrel ballads express great interest in armor and jewels and in details about jousting and hunting. Many of these traits were shared with medieval romances (long adventure poems that were not sung) and with Anglo-Saxon poetry in general. Occasionally, the minstrel poet interjects a stanza that suggests he needs to hold his audience's attention in the face of such distractions as jugglers, side shows, mouth-watering dishes, and itinerant merchants.[2]

The opening and closing stanzas from "Robin Hood's Birth, Breeding, Valor, and Marriage" give the mood of these old stories. Stanzas from "King Estmere" make heroes out of the musician and his page—hints that the courtly minstrels are engaged in a little immodest self-promotion.

In North America, minstrel ballads are now only of historical interest because little survives of this genre. A few minstrel ballads were collected from oral tradition in the twentieth century (such as "King John and the Bishop," "Andrew Barton," and some of the Robin Hood ballads) but mostly without the details that identify them as being of minstrel origin.

Popular ("Child") Ballads

The cornerstone of Anglo-American ballad classification is the canon, or accepted standard, that ballad scholar Francis James Child established at the end of the nineteenth century. Child set for himself the task of gathering together all the surviving remnants of what he called the "popular" or "traditional" folk ballads of the British peoples, a ballad style that flourished in the fifteenth century through the eighteenth century. He published his results between 1882 and 1898 as *The English and Scottish Popular Ballads*. Though he reported some 1,660 variants of the 305 ballads, scarcely thirty examples came from North America. As far as he was concerned, the survival of his ballads in the New World was negligible. Child himself was not a field collector but relied mainly on manuscripts, broadsides, and published British collections. Unfortunately, he never published a clear statement of his principles for inclusion and exclusion, and the collection itself reveals neither clues to his criteria nor signs of consistency. Some ballads in his collection bear few, if any, of the characteristics that are generally associated with the traditional ballads of the popular type. On the other hand, only a half dozen British ballads have been found since the 1880s that Child would (or should) have included had he known about them. Among the 125 or so of Child's collection that have been recovered in North America, there is more stylistic consistency than in the entire 305.

The ballads in Child's compilation originated in Britain mostly between the fifteenth and seventeenth centuries and dealt with pre-industrial themes: romance (the dominant topic in the most widespread ballads) and family conflicts in pastoral or courtly settings; historical ballads, mostly dealing with local events; and a handful of comic or tragic stories derived from the older international stock of European folk tales and songs. In spite of the lack of consistency in style, as a class they all focus on a single incident, tend to be presented dramatically, often beginning near the height of action (*in media res*, or in the middle of things), with little attention to character development or setting and no editorializing or moralizing. More than one-fourth depend heavily on the use of dialog to advance the plot. Language is used very economically.

Often, verses are repeated with minor modifications that advance the plot dramatically, a trait called "incremental repetition." For example, a Scottish version of "Sir Patrick Spens," a ballad in which the hero, Sir Patrick, dies at sea while on a mission for his king, concludes with two stanzas that are structured similarly but with significant changes in the wording.

The device is used even more dramatically in "The Braes O Yarrow," in which a maid's lover goes to battle with rival suitors and is treacherously slain by her brother. In the fourth stanza, she bids him farewell:

> She kissd his cheek, she kaimd his hair,
> As she had done before, O;

"Sir Patrick Spens"

Lang, lang may our ladies wait,
Wi' the tear blinding their ee,
Afore they see Sir Patrick's ships
Come sailing oer the sea.

Lang, lang my our ladies wait,
Wi' their babies in their hands,
Afore they see Sir Patrick Spence
Come sailing to Leith Sands.*

*"Sir Patrick Spence" (Child, version B); from David Herd's manuscript, ca. 1776.

She belted on his noble brand,
An he's awa to Yarrow.

But after his death:

She kissd his cheek, she kaimd his hair,
As oft she did before, O;
She drank the red blood frae him ran,
On the dowy houms o Yarrow.[3]

Sometimes the device is used to repeat the dialog with an action. A Virginia text of "Sir Patrick Spens" recounts the sailors' vain attempts to battle the storm.

The device of incremental repetition can advance the plot with remarkably dramatic effectiveness; it is also less taxing on the singer's memory than completely different phrasing would be. Another common ballad device is the tendency to jump abruptly from scene to scene (called "leaping and lingering"), a technique familiar to modern moviegoers. The in-between events, perhaps somewhat useful to the narrative but mostly inessential extra verbiage, are omitted.

Popular ballads commonly have a refrain— one or two lines that are repeated as a part of each stanza. Refrains can be internal, falling between a rhymed couplet, or they can be external, in which case they follow the usual four-line stanza. Kilby Snow's "Wind and Rain," a version of the ballad, "The Two Sisters," illustrates the internal refrain:

> **"Sir Patrick Spens"**
>
> Go fetch me a bolt of the silken cloth
> And another of flaxen twine,
> And wrap them into my good ship's sides
> To let not the sea come in.
>
> They fetched up a bolt of silken cloth
> And another of flaxen twine,
> And wrapped them into the good ship's sides,
> But still the sea came in.*
>
> *"Sir Patrick Spens," sung by George H. Tucker of Norfolk, VA. Published by John Powell in *Southern Folklore Quarterly* 1 (1937): 10.

It was early one morning in the month of May,
Oh, the wind and rain;
Two lovers went fishing on a hot summer day,
Crying the dreadful wind and rain.

The second and fourth lines repeat in each stanza. Some ballads have a combination of internal and external refrains, as in other versions of the same ballad. In the example sung by McCord reprinted here, the internal refrain (second and fourth lines) and the external ones (last two lines) occur unchanged in each successive stanza. Sometimes the refrain consists of nonsense syllables or words with questionable meaning, as in a common version of "The Elfin Knight":

Are you going to Scarborough Fair?
Parsley, sage, rosemary, and thyme;

Remember me to one who lives there,
And she will be a true lover of mine.

Variants have been collected in which the refrain became "rozz-marrow and time" (Arkansas), "Rose de Marian Time" (North Carolina), "Save rosemary and thyme" (Florida), "Sing ivy leaf, sweet william, and thyme" (England), "Every rose grows merry in time" (Vermont), and "So sav'ry was said come marry in time" (North Carolina). This ballad was widely popularized in a beautiful rendition, "Scarborough Fair/ Canticle," by Simon & Garfunkel in 1967.

As in these examples, the refrain doesn't always contribute to the story's narrative. The origins of such refrains are unknown; various explanations, ranging from magical incantations to dance instructions have been suggested. It is safe to say that to singers of recent decades, the refrains are just nonsense lines, meaning no more than "Hi ho the dario" in "The Farmer in the Dell."

> **"The Two Sisters"**
>
> There was an old lord by the northern sea,
> Bow-wee down;
> There was an old lord by the northern sea,
> Bow and balance to me.
> There was an old lord by the northern sea,
> And he had daughters, one, two, three,
> I'll be true to my love
> If my love will be true to me.*
>
> *"The Two Sisters," sung by May Kennedy McCord. Published by Vance Randolph in *Ozark Folk Songs*, vol. 1 (1946), pp. 60–62.

Ballad language in the popular ballads also makes extensive use of what are called commonplaces: stock vocabulary, or clichés, that range from single adjectives to entire stanzas. For example, a disproportionate number of popular ballad horses are milk-white:

Childe Watters in his stable stoode,
And stroaket his milke-white steed …[4]

Lord Lovel he stood at his castle wall
Combing his milk-white steed …[5]

She called to her stable groom,
To saddle her milk-white steed.[6]

Upon a bonny milk white steed
That drank out of the Tyne …[7]

A bonny boy him behind,
Dressing a milk-white steed.[8]

Coming to the castle or cottage door, the traveler (especially if Scottish) is most likely to "tirl at the pin," that is, rattle the part of the door fastening which lifts the latch, as in the following three examples:

Then he's on to Maisry's bower-door / And tirled at the pin.[9]

But he's awa to his sister's bower, / He's tirled at the pin.[10]

O he has run to Darlinton, / And tirled at the pin.[11]

"Lady Margaret"

Lady Margaret was buried in the new churchyard,
Young William was buried in the choir;
Out of her bosom there sprang a red rose,
And out of William's a briar.

They grew and they grew to the church steeple top,
Until they could grow no higher;

They tied themselves in a true lovers' knot,
For all true love to admire.*

*Version collected in 1916 in Virginia and published by Arthur Kyle Davis Jr., *Traditional Ballads of Virginia* (Charlottesville: University Press of Virginia, 1929), pp. 232–235.

A more extended commonplace consists of two entire stanzas about the intertwining of two plants that spring from the graves of the buried lovers and express their eternal mutual love ("Lady Margaret"). The plants represent the souls of the two lovers. This motif, or thematic element, of the twining plants occurs in several old ballads:

"Barbara Allen"

"Lord Lovel"

"Lady Margaret"

"George Collins"

"Earl Brand"

"Lord Thomas and Fair Annet"

"Lass of Roch Royal"

Early versions of ballads were full of folklore, superstitions, and supernatural beings: talking birds, fairies and elves, revenants (the dead returned—more corporeal in appearance than the modern "ghost") (see Glossary), humans (especially deceased lovers) transformed into (or reincarnated as) animals, and other magical persons. Herbs and plants were associated with magical properties (in later years these were exchanged for medicinal beliefs). Sometimes, even when a printed original did not have it, later popular versions incorporated supernatural elements, as we will see in the case of "The House Carpenter." These traits, abundant in British (particularly Scottish) versions of ballads from the eighteenth century and earlier, tended to disappear with transatlantic passage and also, to some extent, with time in Britain. When they do turn up in American versions, they often indicate that the ballad was recently transplanted from Scotland and had not been growing long on American soil.

Certain language traits, some enumerated in the preceding paragraph, occur repeatedly in different popular ballads. Usually, when one finds a number of texts with such stylistic similarity, one suspects a single author behind them, but clearly a single author could not have written so many ballads found in widely different places and times. At first, it was proposed that ballads were composed by a community as a whole (the process was labeled "communal composition"), which would account for the consistent stylistic features. It is difficult to envision, however, how so many great ballads could have been written as if by committee; a likelier view is that there was an individual original author, whose source work was subjected to the continued process of recomposition, consciously and unconsciously, by a community of singers who shared a narrow range of aesthetic standards and a mental source book of commonplace expressions, descriptions, and sentiments.

The process was "communal recomposition" rather than "communal composition." In other words, whether the ballad started out as the polished poem or song of a professional writer or as the awkward verses of an unsophisticated folk poet, successive generations of singers smoothed out the rough edges, replacing unusual phrases with more familiar ones, deleting unnecessary details that burdened the memory, and forgetting details that jarred the aesthetic sense or violated moral or social standards. The end products are more similar to the ballad body of work as a whole than the originals were, regardless at which end of the continuum between very rough and very polished the ballad commenced life. As a result, in a singing community with a data bank of songs in collective memory, not only do individual songs persist for generations, but more importantly, song styles persist. This is the essence of traditional balladry.

As a class, popular ballads are of unknown authorship, though a handful can be reliably attributed. British broadside ballad writers Laurence Price and Martin Parker may have written a couple in the seventeenth century, and the novelist Sir Walter Scott has been credited with at least rewriting, and possibly originating, one or two others. Among the authors of some of the others must have been professional poets, songwriters, and minstrels of the fifteenth to seventeenth centuries. It may seem strange to us today that an author's name became irrevocably detached from his creations, but there is more at work here than just the loss of original signed/dated publications. Until the middle of the nineteenth century, men of leisure who wrote literature had little need or interest in receiving public credit for their writings. They were not necessarily done for profit, and they cared little whether anyone beyond an immediate circle of associates knew of their authorship.

In North America, these ballads have been widely distributed, but they have been reported most often in the Appalachians, Ozarks, New England, south coastal states, and Canadian maritime provinces. Of course, this may reflect the selectiveness of collectors as much as actual differences in currency. Until the mid-twentieth century, the ballads were most often sung unaccompanied or with simple accompaniment on a single banjo or fiddle. More recently, musicians have worked out string-band accompaniments—often something of a challenge musically since many of the ballads are sung in non-major (i.e., modal or gapped) scales (see Chapter 2).

Most Often Collected Popular "Child" Ballads

United States	Canada
"Barbara Allen"	"Barbara Allen"
"The House Carpenter"	"The Golden Vanity"
"Lord Thomas and Fair Ellender"	"Lady Isabel and the Elf Knight"
"The Gypsy Davy"	"Lord Bateman"
"The Golden Vanity"	"The Cruel Mother"
"Lord Randal"	"Little Musgrave and Lady Barnard"
"Lady Isabel and the Elf Knight"	
"The Maid Freed from the Gallows" or "Hangman"	
"The Two Sisters"	
"Fair Margaret and Sweet William"	

In the twentieth century, more than 4,300 versions of ballads from Child's canon were reported from the United States and over 500 more from Canada. The ballads most often recovered in oral tradition, in order of frequency are listed here (for brief synopses of the stories of these ballads, see the Appendix).[12]

Ballad characteristics and evolution can best be understood by comparing different texts of the same ballad. A good example is "The House Carpenter," two versions of which are given here. The popularity of this ballad in the Southeastern parts of the United States is far greater than in the Northeast or in the British Isles. The first version, "A Warning for Married Men," is from an undated broadside circa 1660. The original sheet was decorated with two woodcuts (a woman's bust and a ship) following the heading and above the text itself. Good evidence suggests the original of this ballad is a broadside published in London in 1657 and written by a prolific ballad writer named Laurence Price. Having a real author's identity revealed is useful in that it undermines the contention of some ballad scholars who believed that the popular ballads did not have a single identifiable author but were written by the community as a whole. The second text, "The House Carpenter," was recorded three centuries later by Clarence Ashley at the 1964 Newport Folk Festival (see Chapter 7).

These two texts illustrate many features of the older popular ballads in Britain and in America in general, as well as about this very widespread ballad in particular. The first text is full of the typical features of the broadside style: long and rambling, awkward lines that seemed forced in achieving a rhyme, stern moralizing at the end, and a beckoning call to the audience (see the seventh stanza)—a common feature of the older minstrel ballads. The length and stilted language would pose a challenge to memorization and oral transmission. There is a supernatural element: the returning James Harris is a revenant, not a proper living human.

J. H. JOHNSON, SONG PUBLISHER, STATIONER AND PRINTER,
No. 7 N. Tenth Street, 3 doors above Market, Philadelphia, Pa.

HOUSE CARPENTER.

"Well met, well met, my own true love,
Well met, well met," cried he—
"For I've just returned from the Salt Sea,
All for the love of thee."

"I might have married the King's daughter, dear,"
"You might have married her," cried she—
"For I am married to a House Carpenter,
And a fine young man is he."

"If you will forsake your House Carpenter
And go along with me.
I will take you where the grass grows high,
On the banks of old Tennessee."

"If I forsake my House Carpenter,
And go along with thee,—
What have you got to keep me upon,
And keep me from misery."

Says he, "I've got six ships at sea,
All sailing to dry land,
One hundred and ten of your own countrymen,
Love, they shall be at your command."

She took her babe upon her knee,
And kissed it one, two, or three,
Saying, "stay at home, my darling sweet babe,
And keep your father's company."

They had not sailed four weeks or more,
Four weeks or scarcely three,
When she thought of her darling sweet babe at home,
And she wept most bitterly.

Says he, "Are you weeping for gold, my love,
Or are you weeping for fear,
Or are you weeping for your House Carpenter,
That you left and followed me."

"I am not weeping for gold," she replied,
"Nor am I weeping for fear,
But I am weeping alone for my sweet little babe,
That I left with my House Carpenter."

"Oh! dry up your tears my own true love,
And cease your weeping," cried he,
"For soon you'll see your own happy home,
On the bank of old Tennessee."

They had not sailed five weeks or more,
Five weeks, or scarcely four,
When the ship struck a rock and sprung a leak,
And they were never seen any more.

A curse be on the sea-faring men,
Oh, cursed be their lives,
For while they're robbing the House Carpenter,
And coaxing away their wives.

☞Cards, Circulars, Billheads, Hand-Bills, Labels, Ball, Raffle, Party
and Excursion Tickets, Programmes, Ladies' Invitations, Checks,
&c., neatly Printed, with accuracy and despatch, and 25
per cent. cheaper than any other Printer in the City.

A broadside for "The House Carpenter" (ID: CPM, 001340-Broad). *Courtesy of the Kenneth S. Goldstein Collection, Center for Popular Music, Middle Tennessee State University.*

"A Warning for Married Men"

There dwelt a fair Maid in the West
of worthy Birth and Fame
Neer unto Plimouth stately Town,
Jane Reynolds was her name.

This damsel dearly was belov'd
by many a proper youth:
And what of her is to be said,
is known for very truth.

Among the rest a Seaman brave
unto her a wooing came,
A comely proper youth he was,
James Harris, call'd by Name.

The Maid and Young man was agreed,
as time did them allow,
And to each other secretly
they made a solemn vow.

That they would ever faithful be,
whilst Heaven afforded life,
He was to be her husband kind,
and she his faithful Wife.

A day appointed was also,
when they were to be married,
But before these things were brought to pass
matters were strangely carried.

All you that faithful Lovers be,
give ear and hearken well,
And what of them became at last,
I will directly tell.

The Young man he was prest to Sea,
and forced was to go,
His sweetheart she must stay behind
whether she would or no.

And after he was from her gone,
she three years for him staid,
Expecting of his coming home,
and kept her self a Maid.

At last news came that he was dead,
within a Foreign Land,
And how that he was buried,
she well did understand.

"The House Carpenter"

"Well met, well met," said an old true love,
"Well met, well met," said he;
"I'm just returning from the salt, salt sea,
And it's all for the love thee."

"Come in, come in, my old true love,
And have a seat by me;
It's been three fourths of a long long year,
Since together we have been."

"I can't come in or I can't sit down,
For I haven't but a moment's time;
They say you are married to a house carpenter,
And your heart can never be mine."

Said it's "I could a married a king's daughter dear,
I'm sure she'd a married me;
But I've forsaken her crowns of gold,
And it's all for the love of thee."

"Will you forsaken your house carpenter,
And go along with me?
I will take you where the grass grows green,
On the banks of the deep blue sea."

Well it's she picked up her little babe,
And kisses she gave it three;
Says "stay right here, my darling little babe
And keep your papa company."

Said it's she jumped on the snow white steed,
And him on the dapple grey;
They rode till they come to the banks of the sea,
Three hours before it came day.

Hadn't been on the ship but about two weeks,
I'm sure it was not three;
Till his true love begin to weep and to mourn,
And she weeped most bitterly.

Says it's "are you weeping for my silver or my gold"
Says it's "are you weeping for my store?
Are you a-weeping for that house carpenter,
Whose face you'll never see any more?"

Says, it's "I'm not a weeping for your silver or your gold,
Or neither for your store;
I am a weeping for my darling little babe,
Whose face I'll never see anymore."

continued

For whose sweet sake the maiden she,
lamented many a day:
And never was she known at all,
the wanton for to play.

A Carpenter that liv'd hard by,
when he heard of the same,
Like as the other had done before,
to her a wooing came.

But when that he had gain'd her love,
they married were with speed,
[A]nd four years space (being man & wife)
they lovingly agreed.

Three pritty Children in this time,
this lovely couple had.
Which made their Fathers heart rejoyce
and Mother wondrous glad.

But as occassion serv'd one time,
the good man took his way,
Some three days journey from his home
intending not to stay.

But whilst that he was gone away,
a spirit in the night,
Came to the window of his Wife,
and did her sorely fright.

Which Spirit spake like to a man,
and unto her did say,
My dear and only love (quoth he)
prepare and come away.

James Harris is my name (quoth he)
whom thou didst love so dear,
And I have travel'd for thy sake,
at least this seven year.

And now I am return'd again
to take thee to my wife,
And thou with me shalt go to Sea,
to end all further Strife.

O tempt me not sweet *James* (quoth she)
with thee away to go,
If I should leave my children small,
alas what would they do?

My Husband is a Carpenter,
a Carpenter of great fame,
I would not for five hundred pounds,
the he should know the same.

Hadn't been on the ship but about three weeks,
I'm sure it was not four;
Till it sprung a leak in the bottom of the ship,
And it sink for to rise no more.**

I might have had a King's Daughte[r]
and she would have married me,
But I forsook her Golden Crown
and for the love of thee.

Therefore if thou'lt thy husband forsake
and they children three also
I will forgive thee what is past
if thou wilt with me go.

If I forsake my husband and
my little Children three,
What means hast thou to bring me to,
if I should go with thee.

I have seven Ships upon the Sea
when they are come to Land.
Both Marriners and Merchandise
shall be at thy command.

The ship wherein my love shal sail,
is glorious to behold,
The sails shall be of finest silk,
and the mast of shining gold.

When he had told her these fair tales,
to love him she began,
Because he was in humane shape,
much like unto a man.

And so together away they went,
from off the English shore,
And since that time the Woman-kind,
was never seen no more.

But when her Husband he came home,
and found his Wife was gone,
And left her three sweet pretty babes,
within the house alone.

He beat his breast, he tore his hair,
the tears fell from his eyes.
And in the open streets he run,
with heavy doleful cries.

And in this sad distracted case,
he Hang'd himself for Woe,
Upon a tree, near to the place,
the truth of all is so.

13

continued

The children now are fatherless,
and left without a guide,
But yet no doubt the heavenly Powers,
will for them well provide.*

*"A Warning for Married Men. Being an Example of *Mrs. Jane Reynolds* (a West-country-Woman) born near *Plimouth*, who having plighted her troth to a Seaman, was afterwards married to a Carpenter, and at last carried away by a Spirit, the manner how shall presently be recited. Printed for W. Thackeray, and T. Poffinger; To a west-country Tune, called, *The Fair Maid of Bristol: Bateman,* or, *John True*." Reprinted in Robert Latham, ed. *Catalogue of the Pepys Library at Magdalene College, Cambridge. The Pepys Ballads, Facsimile Volume I* (Cambridge: D. S. Brewer, 1987), p. 101. Parentheses are in the original; brackets mark missing or illegible letters.
**"House Carpenter," as sung by Clarence Ashley accompanying himself on banjo at the Newport Folk Festival, Newport, RI, 1964. Recording: Vanguard, LP VRS 9147.

Clarence Ashley, singer of the second version, was a popular hillbilly entertainer who had recorded the ballad—learned from his family—earlier in his career (1930) on a commercial 78-rpm disc. The dramatic intensity has been heightened, partly by the sense of urgency we get from the visitor's refusal to sit down and pass the time (the second and third stanzas). The text has been shortened to manageable length, with all the inessentials stripped away but enough details and incremental repetition to maintain the build-up of tension.

Broadside Ballads

The third type of ballads has been called "broadside," "stall," "vulgar" (meaning ordinary, not obscene), or "come-all-ye" ballads. The first term comes from their frequent origin and dissemination in cheap street literature such as broadsides, the second from the stalls on streets and at local fairs where they were sold, the third because critics considered them poetically inferior to the Child ballads. The last term reflects a common beginning: a call to an audience to listen (an "incipit"), a trait that was also widespread among the older minstrel ballads.

Broadside ballads originated mostly in the late seventeenth, eighteenth, and early nineteenth centuries, probably at the hands of hack writers and poets. They were disseminated initially through cheap print (broadsides and chapbooks), then entered oral tradition. Except for some of the oldest, the style tends to be more stilted than Child ballads. Longer texts, introductory verses, more details, moralizing tone (see, for example, the ballad "Little Blossom" in the section on religious songs in this chapter), and the retention of some supernatural elements are characteristic.

Some 300 such ballads have been recovered in North America that are identifiably of British origin; of those that can be dated, most are from the eighteenth and early nineteenth centuries. Favorite themes are of soldiers and war, sailors and the sea, crime and criminals, family opposition to lovers, lovers'

Most Widespread Broadside Ballads and Their Themes

Murdered pregnant sweethearts:	"Pretty Polly"
	"Knoxville Girl"
	"Oxford City"
Wayward young men:	"Boston Burglar"
	"Rake and a Rambling Boy"
Unrequited love:	"Sailor Boy"
	"The Drowsy Sleeper"
Unfaithful lovers:	"The Girl I Left Behind"
	"Rich Irish Lady"
Lovers reunited:	"Jack Monroe"
	"Pretty Fair Maid in the Garden"

disguises and tricks, and faithful or unfaithful lovers. G. Malcolm Laws Jr. provides a descriptive summary as well as a thematic catalog with references in *American Balladry from British Broadsides: A Guide for Students and Collectors of Traditional Song*,[13] useful for identifying any imported ballad of the broadside era. His catalog numbers are given after ballad titles wherever appropriate. (A summary of the complete catalog is given in the Appendix.)

In the twentieth century, nearly 5,000 versions of these imported ballads were reported in the United States and almost 1,500 in Canada. Compared to Child ballads, these figures suggest that later ballads have survived better in Canada than in the United States. A regional breakdown would show that the repertoire in the northern parts of the United States is more like that in Canada than that of the southern states.

Broadside ballads are usually performed with instrumental accompaniment, and as they generally represent a more recent era of music than the Child ballads, they are not so often rendered in modal or gapped scales. This reflects the gradual percolation down of musical practices that were new during Europe's emergence from the medieval period and the adoption of newer principles of harmony.

Two different broadsides, both widely known in the United States, are presented here, each with a comparative version from cheap print. The first set of song versions is best known in America as the "Story of the Knoxville Girl"; a typical American version was sung by Bill and Earl Bolick of North Carolina in 1937. It is descended from a British broadside ballad, "The Berkshire Tragedy."

Nothing is known about the author of this ballad, when it was penned, whether it was based on a true incident, and what the original text was like, but the British broadside version is probably very close to the original. It bears all the attributes of the cheap press of the period: stilted language, an abundance of details, numerous expressions of regret and anguish on the part of the narrator (especially after he was convicted), stress on the shame to his family, and a closing moral addressed to the listeners and readers.

Bill and Earl Bolick of the Blue Sky Boys (1960s). *Author's collection.*

The short version of two centuries later shows how oral transmission—in a community that has many models of this type of story in its collective repertoire—can reduce the unwieldy original to a compact ballad that focuses directly on the essentials. Although the forty-four couplets have been reduced very efficiently to twelve, there is no doubt that the earlier text is the predecessor of the later one. The original motive—the girl's pregnancy and the narrator's unwillingness to marry her—are absent from the North Carolina version. This is characteristic of murdered girl ballads in America as contrasted to the British versions. In the latter, lurid details of sex, violence, and betrayal are not spared. Prudish American sentiments (or some other reason) furnished the scalpel to pare away these details. As a result, the motive for the murder is altogether puzzling if the listener isn't familiar with the old ballad story.

When the Bolick brothers sang this ballad in 1965 at a University of California at Los Angeles folk festival for an urban college audience, there were many snickers at the recital of the bloody beating, brutal manhandling, and then drowning. Unperturbed, Bill Bolick commented that, although he might see how some folks could take this unreal recitation of violence upon violence as verging on the comical, that was certainly not the response the ballad drew in his native North Carolina. What also often puzzles urban northern audiences is the singer's recital of these acts of violence and lust

"The Berkshire Tragedy" or "The Wittam Miller, with an Account of His Murdering His Sweetheart, &c."

Young men and maidens all give ear, unto what I
shall now relate;
Mark you well, and you shall hear of my unhappy fate.
Near famous Oxford Town, I first did draw my
breath,
Oh! that I had been cast away in an untimely birth.

My tender parents brought me up, provided for
me well
And in the town of WITTAM then, they plac'd me
in a Mill.
By chance upon an Oxford lass, I cast a wanton eye,
And promis'd I would marry her, if she would with
me lie.

But to the world I do declare, with sorrow, grief
and woe:
This folly brought us in a snare, and wrought our
overthrow.
For the damsel came to me, and said by you i am
with child:
I hope dear John you'll marry me, for you have me
defil'd.

Soon after that, her mother came, as you shall
understand,
And oftentimes did me persuade to wed her out
of hand.
And thus perplex't on every side, I could no
comfort find
So to make away this creature, a thought came in
my mind.

About a month since Christmas last, oh! cursed be
the day,
the devil then did me persuade, to take her
life away.
I call'd her from her sisters door, at eight o'clock
at night;
Poor creature she did little dream I ow'd her any
spight.

I told her, if she'd walk with me aside a little way:
We both together would agree about our
wedding-day.
Thus I deluded her again in to a private place:
Then took a stick out of the hedge, and struck her
in the face.

"Story of the Knoxville Girl"

I met a little girl in Knoxville, a town we all
know well;
And every Sunday evening out in her home
I'd dwell.
We went to take an evenin' walk about a mile
from town,
I picked a stick up off the ground and knocked that
fair girl down.

She fell down on her bended knees, for mercy she
did cry;
"Oh, Willie dear, don't kill me here, I'm
unprepared to die."
She never spoke another word, I only beat
her more,
Until the ground around me within her blood
did flow.

I taken her by her golden curls, I drug her round
and round,
Throwing her into the river that flows through
Knoxville town.
"Go there, go there, you Knoxville girl, got dark
and rolling eyes,
Go there, go there, you Knoxville girl, you can
never be my bride."

Starting back to Knoxville, got there about
midnight,
My mother she was worried, and woke up in a
fright;
Saying, "Son, oh son, what have you done to
bloody your clothes so?"
I told my anxious mother had been bleeding at
my nose.

"Call for me a candle to light myself to bed,
Call for me a handkerchief to bind my aching
head."
Roll and tumbled the whole night through as
trouble were for me,
Like flames of hell around my bed and in my eyes
could see.

They carried me down to Knoxville, they put me in
a cell
My friends all tried to get me out but none could go
my bail.

continued

But she fell on her bended knee, and did for
mercy cry,
For heaven's sake don't murder me, I am not fit
to die.
But I on her no pity took, but wounded her full sore,
Until her life away I took, which I can ne'er
restore.

With many grievous shrieks and cries, she did
resign her breath,
And in inhuman and barbarous sort, I put my love
to death.
And when I took her by the hair to cover this
foul sin:
And drag'd her to the river side, then threw her
body in.

Thus in the blood of innocence, my hands were
deeply dy'd,
And shined in her purple gore, that should have
been my bride.
Then home unto my Mill I ran, but sopely was
amaz'd,
My man he thought I had mischief done, and
strangely on me gaz'd.

Oh! what's the matter then said he? you look as pail
as death:
What makes you shake, and tremble so, as though
you had lost your breath.
How came you by that blood upon your trembling
hands and cloaths?
I presently to him reply'd, by bleeding at
the nose.

I wishfully upon him look'd, but little to him said,
But snatch'd the candle from his hand, and went
unto my bed.
Where I lay trembling all the night, for I could take
no rest,
And perfect flames of Hell did flash wishing [print
blurred] my guilty fate.

Next day the damsel being missed, and no where to
be found,
Then I was apprehended soon, and to the Assizes
bound.
Her sister did against me swear, she reason had no
doubt,
That I had made away with her because I call'd
her out.

I'm here to waste my life away down in this dirty
old jail
Because I murdered that Knoxville girl, the girl
I loved so well.**

But Satan did me still persuade, I stiffly should
    deny:
Quoth he, there is no witness can against thee
    testify.
Now when her mother did her cry, I scoffingly
    did say,
On purpose then to frighten me, she sent her child
    away.

I publish'd in the Post-boy then, my wickedness to
    blind,
Five guineas any one should have, that could her
    body find.
But Heaven had a watchful eye, and brought it so
    about:
That though I stifly did deny, this murder would
    come out.

The very day before, the Assize her body it was
    found,
Floating before her Father's door, at Hindley Ferry
    Town,
So I the second time was siez'd, to Oxford brought
    with speed,
And there examined again about the bloody deed.

Now the Coroner and Jury both together did agree,
That this damsel was made away, and murdered
    by me.
The Justice too perceiv'd the guilt, no longer would
    take bail:
But the next morning I was sent away to Reading
    Goal.

When I was brought before the Judge, my Man did
    testify,
That blood upon my hands and cloaths that night
    he did espy.
The Judge he told the Jury then, the circumstance
    is plain,
Look on the Prisoner at the bar, he hath this
    creature slain.

About the murder at the first the Jury did divide:
But when they brought their Verdict in all of them
    guilty cry'd.
The Jailor took and bound me strait, as soon as
    I was cast:
And then within the Prison strong he there did lay
    me fast.

continued

With fetters strong then I was bound, and
  shin-bolted was I,
Yet I the Murder would not own, but did it
  still deny.
My Father did on me prevail, my kindred all
  likewise,
To own the Murder, which I did to them with
  watery eyes.

My father then he did me blame, saying, my Son,
  oh! why
Has You thus brought yourself to shame and all
  Your Family?
Father, I own the crime I did, I guilty am indeed,
Which cruel fact I must confess, doth make my
  heart to bleed.

The worst of deaths I do deserve, my crime it is so base,
For I no mercy shew'd to her, most wretched is
  my case.
Lord grant me grace while I do stay that I may now
  repent:
Before I from this wicked world, most shamefully
  am sent.

Young men take warning by any fall all filthy
  lusts deny;
By giving way to wickedness alas! this day I die,
Lord, with my hateful sins awy, which have been
  manifold,
Have mercy on me I thee pray, and Christ receive
  my soul.*

*"The Berkshire Tragedy," or, "The Wittam Miller, with an Account of His Murdering His Sweetheart, &c.," probably
England, early eighteenth century. From the eleventh to the middle of the twentieth stanza, the text is in italic type. Under
the title is a woodcut showing a man with a club and a woman before him on bended knee; off to one side is a man hanging
from a gibbet, and at the other side, a body floating in the water.
**"Story of the Knoxville Girl," as sung by Bill and Earl Bolick (The Blue Sky Boys) with guitar/mandolin accompaniment,
North Carolina, 1937. Recording: Bluebird, B7755. Reissue: Blue Tone Records, BSR CD 1003/4, *Within the Circle/Who
Wouldn't Be Lonely.*

with no betrayal of emotion at all; city folk expect to hear the singer, whether
of pop or classical, match voice to content with changes in tempo, volume,
vibrato, gestures, and facial expression to be consistent with the story. Traditional
singers, on the other hand, appear to be totally emotionless, letting the story
carry its own emotions. Inwardly, however, they feel the emotions as pro-
foundly as anyone else.[14]

A second good example of the evolution of a broadside ballad is often titled
"The Girl I Left Behind." No original text of this ballad survives, but it probably

Fred Price (fiddle), Clint Howard (center), and Doc Watson at Carnegie Hall (December 1962). *Photographer, Dan Seeger; courtesy of the Southern Folklife Collection, University of North Carolina.*

was written in the first half of the nineteenth century, and "Margaret Walker," from an English broadside printed in the 1840s, may be close to the original. The second version, "Maggie Walker Blues," is from Clint Howard, a North Carolina singer/guitarist, recorded in 1961. Some of his lines are difficult to understand, and the corresponding lines from other versions are included here.

Unlike "The House Carpenter" or "Knoxville Girl," the "Maggie Walker" ballad has no simple central theme. Consequently, as it passes from singer to singer, details that are not held in check by the necessity of a story line are forgotten or confused. In the British version, the girl left behind proves unfaithful; in the American text, though, it appears that the narrator is the unfaithful party. The word "blues" in the title is rather arresting, since by most definitions nothing about the ballad, either structurally, musically, or stylistically, justifies calling it a blues song. Perhaps the singer used the term because the story was a sad one. Characteristically, all the place names have been localized to the United States. The text also shows signs of faulty memory in transmission. For example, the first stanza is two stanzas combined into one.

Indigenous Popular Ballads

Four hundred or so folk ballads originated in the New World, some dating back to Colonial and Revolutionary days, but most are from the nineteenth and early twentieth centuries. These used to be called "native American

"Margaret Walker"

My parents reared me tenderly,
Having no child but me,
My mind being bent for rambling,
With them could not agree,

When I became a courtier,
Which after grieved me sore,
I left my aged parents,
And I never saw them more.

There lived a wealthy farmer,
In the country hard by,
He had a handsome daughter,
On her I cast my eye.

I asked her was she satisfied,
That I should cross the main,
Or if she would be true to me,
Till I returned again.

She told me that she would be true,
Till death should prove unkind,
So we kissed, shook hands, and parted,
And I left her far behind.

First when I left old Ireland,
For Scotland I was bound,
When I set off to Glasgow,
To view that pleasant town,

One evening when I quit my work,
I roved by George's square,
The mail coach just arriving,
The post he met me there,

He handed me a letter,
Which gave me to understand,
That the girl I left behind me,
Was wed to another man.

The further I proceeded,
I found the news too true,
I turned myself around,
Not knowing what to do,

Says I hard labour I'll resign,
Her company I'll resign,
I'll rove about from town to town.
For the girl I left behind.

Then I set off to New York,
Strange faces for to see,
Then handsome Peggy Walker,
She fell in love with me,

"Maggie Walker Blues"

My parents raised me tenderly, they had no child
    but me,
My mind being placed on rambling, with them
    I couldn't agree,
Just to leave my aged parents and them no more
    to see.

There was a wealthy gentleman who lived there
    very near by,
He had a beautiful daughter, on her I cast my eye;
She was so tall and slender, so pretty and so fair,
There never was a girl in this wide world with her
    I could compare.

I asked her if it differed if I crossed over the plain,
She said, "It makes no difference if you never return
    again." [or, "as long as you return again"]
We two shook hands and parted, and I left my girl
    behind.

I started out in this wide world strange faces for
    to see,
I met little Maggie Walker and she fell in love
    with me;
Her pockets all lined with greenback and her labor
    I'll grow old [or, your pockets shall be lined with
    silver, and labor you'll give o'er.]
"Now if you'll consent to marry me I'll say I'll roam
    no more."

I traveled out one morning, to the salt works I were
    bound, [to Salt Lake City]
And when I reached the salt works I viewed the
    city all around;
Work and money were plentiful and the girls all
    kind to me,
But the only object to my heart was a girl in
    Tennessee.

I traveled out one morning down on the market
    square,
The mail train being on arrival, I met the carrier
    there;
He handed me a letter so's I could understand
That the girl I left in Tennessee had married
    another man.

I drove on down a little further and I found out it
    was true,
I turned my horse and buggy around, but I didn't
    know what to do;

My pockets being empty,
I thought it was full time,
To stop with her and think no more,
Of the girl I left behind.

One day I sat condoling,
Says she, don't grieve my boy,
For I have money plenty,
If you will wed with I.

If I should consent to wed with you,
I would be much to blame,
Besides my lovely sweetheart,
Would laugh at me with shame.

For Peggy is the mistress of my heart,
She is loving and she's kind,
And I'll never forget the perjured vows,
Of the girl I left behind.*

I turned all around and about there; bad company
   I'll resign;
I'll drive all about from town to town for the girl
   I left behind.**

*"Margaret Walker," from a broadside printed by Samuel Russell of Birmingham, England, 1841–1850. Typographical errors have been corrected. In the original, there are no breaks between stanzas.
**"Maggie Walker Blues," sung by Clint Howard, North Carolina, 1961. Recording: Smithsonian/Folkways, CD SF 40029/30, *Doc Watson & Clarence Ashley—The Original Folkways Recordings*, 1994.

ballads" before "Native American" came to be reserved for ethnic groups native to the New World; they will henceforth be called "indigenous popular ballads," meaning English-language ballads originating in North America in the repertoires of Canadians, Anglo-Americans, or African Americans.

A catalog of most of these is given by G. Malcolm Laws Jr. in *Native American Balladry: A Descriptive Study and a Bibliographical Syllabus*.[15] This syllabus, however, has some flaws. For example, Laws excluded many ballads from his catalog on the grounds that they had appeared only once in folk song collections and thus were of "doubtful currency in tradition." Subsequent collections often have provided that missing evidence. Second, Laws excluded ballads recovered only from manuscript or from print, ballads not reported from traditional singing since 1920, and ballads of professional Tin Pan Alley authorship, the commercial songwriting establishment centered in New York City (1870s to 1920s).

Last, some ballads in this catalog have since been found to have British antecedents and therefore belong in the companion catalog of imported ballads. This also raises the question of how to categorize an American recomposition of a British ballad: how much change is required before we recognize it as a different (and therefore indigenous) ballad? However, as with his broadside ballad catalog, Laws's syllabus is an immensely useful tool. (The ballads mentioned in his book are summarized in the Appendix.)

Indigenous ballads are found in all parts of the United States. The ones that survived in more recent eras, late enough to be collected or recorded, originated mostly in the nineteenth and early twentieth centuries. The authors of many have been identified. They include well-known popular songwriters whose compositions later entered oral tradition, such as Henry Clay Work's "The Ship That Never Returned," and folk poets who were well known locally in their day, such as Larry Gorman in New England and Canada, Joe Scott in Maine, and Andy Jenkins in Atlanta. Most indigenous ballads from the nineteenth century or earlier appear to have been disseminated only by word of mouth—at least, printed texts have not survived.

> **Most Often Collected Indigenous Popular Ballads**
>
> "Texas Rangers"
> "Jesse James"
> "The Jealous Lover"
> "Poor Omie"/"Naomi Wise"
> "Poor Ellen Smith"
> "Wreck of the Old 97"
> "Wreck on the C. & O."
> "Casey Jones"
> "Fair Charlotte"
> "The Jam on Gerry's Rock"
> "The Dying Cowboy"
> "Joe Bowers"
> "Twenty-One Years"
> "Streets of Laredo"
> "The Ship That Never Returned"
> "Thy Dying Hobo"
> "The Roving Gambler"
> "Wild and Reckless Hobo"
> "The Little Mohea"

The majority of these indigenous popular ballads concern identifiable historical (or supposedly factual) events: wars, maritime incidents, cowboy and lumberjack stories, outlaws and/or murders, and disasters of some sort or another—mining accidents, train wrecks, fires, floods, earthquakes, and so on. Many are stylistically similar to British broadside ballads, others have much simpler language. The ballads often reuse older tunes, are devoid of supernatural elements, and puritanically suppress details of pregnancy, illicit sex, and such. They are usually performed with instrumental accompaniment. The oldest still preserve some pentatonic melodies, but those originating in the twentieth century tend to be in the major scale.

Unless these ballads are about common topics, for which the singing community has well-known ballad patterns, they tend not to change extensively with time—at least, not during the century or so for which we have representative samples. Nevertheless, it does happen that stanzas are dropped or created anew. The latter is usually evidence of deliberate recomposition by a singer, and in some cases, we have the testimony of the recomposer to that effect.

Several ballads associated with particular occupations and regions are discussed in subsequent chapters. One tragedy ballad, though, has been popular throughout the country: "Young Charlotte," called "Young Carlotta" by Ozark folksinger Almeda Riddle.

Under the title "A Corpse Going to a Ball," the ballad was first published by Seba Smith (1792–1868) in a journal he edited, *The Rover*.[16] Smith was born in Portland, Maine, and wrote many pieces that enjoyed popularity in his day. His poem was in none of the styles we have already identified. Yet its simple, direct language and suspenseful telling, together with the innately (possibly morbidly) interesting plot made many listeners want to add it to their repertoires; it would have been a superb piece for declaiming at a public gathering—a popular pastime in the nineteenth century.

In spite of the remarkably well-preserved state of the ballad as it was sung by Almeda Riddle—a singer who had a profound interest in old ballads and often searched among friends and neighbors to get the best version she could—the hand of at least one folk recomposer is evident in her two final stanzas, which were not in Smith's original. Whoever wrote them was skillful in matching Smith's style and also in adding an element of narrative irony that was lacking from the original. Other recorded versions have still two more stanzas that were not in Smith's original:

They bore her out into the sleigh,
And Charles with her rode home.
And when they reached her cottage door,
Oh, how her parents mourned!

Almeda Riddle of Heber Springs, Arkansas (ca. 1963). *Photographer, Robert Yellin; jacket photo from Vanguard LP.*

They mourned for the loss of their daughter dear,
And Charles mourned o'er his bride,
Until at length his heart did break
And they slumber side by side.[17]

Blues Ballads

The blues ballad (not to be confused with blues songs, which are discussed later) seems to have evolved from an amalgamation of Anglo-American narrative song with African American song styles. Of all the ballad types, it has the weakest narrative line. The event concerned is assumed to be familiar to the listeners so that most of the text deals with the responses and attitudes of the participants and their community. The blues ballad arose first among African American singers in the Southeastern states, probably between the 1880s and 1890s. By the early twentieth century, the style was common among Anglo-American singers as well. Favorite topics are murders, disasters, and local criminals.

"Young Carlotta"

Young Carlotta lived on a mountain side,
A wild and a lonely spot,
There were no dwellings for many miles around
Except her father's cot.

And yet on many a winter night,
Young swains would gather there;
Her father kept a social board,
And she was very fair.

One New Year's Eve as the sun went down,
Far looked her wishful eye;
Out from the frosty windowpanes,
As merry sleighs dashed by.

At the village fifteen miles away,
Was to be a ball that night;
And though the air was freezing cold,
Her heart was warm and bright.

How brightly beamed her laughing eye,
As a well-known voice she heard;
And as she looked to the cottage door,
Her lover's sleigh appeared.

"Oh daughter dear, O daughter dear,
This blanket around you fold;
For it's an awful night outside,
You'll catch your death of cold."

"Oh nay, nay, nay," Young Carlotta cried,
And she laughed like a gypsy queen;
To ride in blankets muffled up,
I never will be seen.

"My silken coat is quite enough,
You know it's lined throughout;
And there's my silken scarf
To twine my head and neck about."

Her bonnet and her gloves are on,
She jumped into the sleigh;
And swiftly sped down the mountainside
And over the hills away.

With muffled beats so silently
Five miles at length were passed;
When Charles with a few and shivering words
The silence broke at last.

"Such a dreadful night I've never seen,
My reins I scarce can hold";
Young Carlotta faintly then replied,
"Oh I am very cold."

He cracked his whip, he urged his steed,
Much faster than before;
And thus five other weary miles,
In silence they passed o'er.

Spoke Charles then, "How fast the ice
Is freezing on my brow";
Carlotta still more faintly said,
"I'm getting warmer now."

Thus on they rode through the frosty air,
And the blustering cold afright;
Until at last the village lamps
And the ballroom came in sight.

They reached the door, young Charles sprang out,
He held his hand to her,
"Why sit you like a monument
That hath no power to stir?"

He called her once, he called her twice,
She answered not a word;
He asked her for her hand again,
But still she never stirred.

He took her hand in his—'twas cold,
'Twas hard as any stone;
He tore the mantle from her face,
The cold stars on it shown.

Then quickly to the lighted hall
Her lifeless form he bore;
Young Carlotta's eyes had closed in death,
Her voice was heard no more.

And there he set down by her side,
His bitter tears did flow;
He cried, "My own, my charming bride,
You never more will know."

He twined his arms about her form,
And kissed her marble brow;
His thoughts went back to when she said,
"I'm getting warmer now."*

*"Young Carlotta," sung by Almeda Riddle, Arkansas, 1964. Recording: Vanguard, LP VRS 9158. Written by Seba Smith, "A Corpse Going to a Ball," *The Rover*, no. 15 (December 28, 1843): 2:225.

The best known is "John Henry." In the version reproduced here, the last line of each stanza is repeated by the singer.

The ballad about John Henry has been the most oft-recorded American folk song, with over 500 versions since it was first commercially recorded in 1924. Although no unambiguous references are made to John Henry prior to 1909, either the man or the song, in the 1920s two folk song collectors, Guy Johnson and Louis Chappell, seemed to establish that the ballad dealt with events of 1870–1872 in Summers County, West Virginia, when the C&O Railroad was con-

> **Most Widespread Blues Ballads**
>
> "Frankie and Johnny"
> "Casey Jones"
> "Stackolee"
> "Ella Speed"
> "Railroad Bill"
> "Little Sadie" (or "Bad Lee Brown")
> "Whitehouse Blues"
> "John Hardy"
> "John Henry"

structing the Great Bend Tunnel near the Greenbriar River. More recent research suggests that the story is based on fact but that its locale was on the C&W Railroad in Alabama from 1887 to 1888.[18]

In those days, human muscle was required to drill holes in solid granite for planting explosives to blast out rock. When a new invention was brought forward—a mechanical, steam-driven device, to do the drilling—it was controversially received; many contended that dumb steam and steel could never replace muscle and bone. A contest was arranged between the steam contraption and the best of the steel drivers: an African American named John Henry. Upon its outcome depended the livelihoods of countless manual laborers. John Henry bested the machine, drilling fourteen feet to its nine, but his superhuman exertion proved fatal, and he died shortly afterward.

"John Henry"

John Henry said to his captain,
"A man ain't nothin' but a man;
Before I let your steel drill beat me down,
Why I'll die with my hammer in my hand."

John Henry said to his shaker,
"Now man, why don't you sing;
I'm shaking twelve pounds from my hip
  on down,
Man, don't you hear that cold steel ring."

John Henry hammered on the mountain,
And the mountain was so high;
And the last words that I heard that poor boy say,
"Will you gimme a cool drink of water before I die."

John Henry found that railroad track,
With a twelve pound hammer by his side;
Yes, he went down that track but he never came
  back,
Because he laid down his hammer and he died.

John Henry had a little woman,
And the dress that she wore was red;
And the last word that I heard that little girl say,
She say, "I'm goin' where John Henry fell dead."*

*"John Henry" (Laws, I 1), sung by Bill Broonzy in a concert broadcast over WFMT, Chicago, 1956. Recording: Smithsonian/Folkways, CD SF 40023 (1989). The repeated lines are not precisely the same each time.

The earliest song references to John Henry are from the early 1900s, but it is reasonable to assume a ballad can circulate for a decade or two before leaving any traceable footprints. True or not, the story has endured for over a century in both Anglo-American and African American tradition. Its theme has also inspired stories and legends, novels and movies, sculpture and painting. Its popularity can be attributed to many factors: a lively, rousing tune serving as vehicle to a compelling action drama; the satisfying tale of human supremacy over machine, but with the covert warning that progress both in the factory and the office continually threatens job security; and the sexual innuendo of the big man driving home hard steel.

Bill Broonzy, singer of the above text, recorded "John Henry" several times, and his texts were different each time, sometimes adding or deleting stanzas, sometimes changing their order. The stanzas reprinted here can easily be rear-ranged without damaging the already weak narrative, which does not make much sense to a listener who doesn't already know the basic story. In this regard, the performance is typical of most blues ballads.

Although "John Henry" is sung in a four-line verse similar to the other ballad styles discussed earlier, some blues ballads are in a different stanza form: a rhymed couplet (sometimes one line, repeated) followed by a refrain (AA'R or AAR):

Railroad Bill, Railroad Bill,
He never worked and he never will,
It's ride, Railroad Bill

or:

De first time I seen de boll weevil,
He was a-settin' on de square,
De next time that I seen de boll weevil,
He had all of his family dere,
Jus' a-lookin' for a home,
Jus' a-lookin' for a home.[19]

In all of the last three ballad styles—broadside, indigenous, and blues ballad—singers or composers tend to reuse stock phrases and even entire stanzas from older ballads. The concept of originality in folk balladry is different from that in formal poetry; borrowing phrases and stanzas from earlier works is no more plagiarism than it would be for a literary poet to hunt for words in a thesaurus.

Sentimental Ballads

The final English-language ballad type is the sentimental ballad, which flourished in the last half of the nineteenth century and usually originated from the hands of professional songsmiths of Tin Pan Alley. Almost all were published as sheet music. Many examples have turned up of different sheet music publications of the same ballad within a few years of each other but with slight differences in text or tune and with different authors or compos-ers credited. Such borrowings never prompted lawsuits or accusations of plagiarism. Evidently, there were different standards for such a concept in the nineteenth century. Either that, or writers were indifferent to the potential competition.

Unlike the older imported British ballads, sentimental ballads and songs recount little action. Events have already occurred, and the ballad text focuses on responses to that action. It is more a bal-lad of feelings or emotions than of action. The hero or heroine is the passive object (sometimes even victim) of events that are outside of his or her control. If some response is made, it is by way of speech rather than action.

This style disappeared from pop music in the early 1900s, but the style was influ-ential enough to provide the model for many hillbilly ballads or ballad-like pieces (i.e., similar language and themes but a very minimal story line) written during the 1920s and 1930s expressly for commercial recordings. Many of these (such as "Mother, the Queen of My Heart," by Rodgers and Bryant, 1932; "Hobo Bill's Last Ride," by O'Neal, 1929; and "They Cut Down the Old Pine Tree," by Raskin, Brown, and Elison, 1929) ultimately found their way into oral tradition.

> **Well-Known Sentimental Ballads**
>
> "In the Baggage Coach Ahead" (G. L. Davis, 1896)
> "After the Ball" (C. K. Harris, 1892)
> "Package of Old Letters" or "Little Rosewood Casket" (White & Goullaud, 1870)
> "Lightning Express" (Helf and Moran, 1898)
> "The Blind Child" (Anonymous)
> "The Drunkard's Doom" (Anonymous)
> "The Hell-Bound Train" (Anonymous)
> "Little Blossom" (Bidwell, 1873)

A classic example of the turn-of-the-century sentimental ballad was "In the Baggage Coach Ahead," an 1896 hit by African American songsmith Gussie L. Davis (1863–1899). Davis, whose résumé included a stint as a Pullman porter prior to his education at the Nelson Musical College in Cincinnati, reportedly based the ballad on personal experience, but he very likely borrowed the theme from older poems and/or songs.

Sentimental ballads are often criticized on the grounds that they portray artificial situations contrived to make the listener weep in sympathy. This a problematic criticism. Even if the story of the casket in the baggage coach really were based on a true incident, that would not make it any less of a sentimental tale. What generally prompts us to label a ballad as "sentimental" isn't its verac-ity, nor the story itself, but the way the story is told. The language contrasts with the passionless objectivity of the older traditional ballads. Very likely, readers of different backgrounds will not react the same way to these ballads— just as some audiences are moved to tears by the Blue Sky Boys' "Knoxville Girl," while others are forced to laugh. When modern audiences hear or read them, their reactions are more likely amusement rather than empathy.

Popular as these sentimental ballads were, the genre faded away in the first quarter of the twentieth century. Snappy ragtime songs, dance tunes, and light

An ad for Columbia New Process Records from *The Talking Machine World* (1924). Ernest Thompson is in the upper right portion of the picture. *Author's collection.*

"In the Baggage Coach Ahead"

On a dark stormy night as the train rattled on,
All the passengers all gone to bed,
Except a young man with a babe in his arms,
Who sat with a bowed-down head.

The innocent one began crying just then,
As though its poor heart would break;
An angry man said, "Make that child stop
    its noise,
For it's keeping us all awake."

"Take it out," said another, "don't keep it
    in here,
We've paid for our berths and want rest";
But never a word said the man with the child,
As he fondled it close to his breast.

"Oh, where is its mother? Go take it to her,"
A lady then softly said;
"I wish that I could," was the man's sad reply,
"She's dead in the coach ahead."

Every eye filled with tears as his story he told,
Of a wife who's so faithful and true;
He told how he had saved up his earnings
    for years,
Just to build up a home for two.

How heaven had sent them a sweet little babe,
Their young happy lives to bless;
His heart seemed to break when he mentioned
    her name,
And in tears tried to tell the rest.

Every woman arose to assist with the child,
There were mothers and wives on that train;
And soon the little one was sleeping in peace,
Without any thought, sorrow, or pain;

Next morning at the station he bade them goodbye,
"God bless you," he softly said;
Each one had a story to tell in their homes,
Of the baggage coach ahead.

CHORUS:
As the train rolled on and on a husband sat in tears,
Thinking of the happiness of just a few short years;
For the baby's face brings pictures of the cherished
    hope that's dead,
But baby's cries can't waken her in the baggage
    coach ahead.*

*Gussie L. Davis, "In the Baggage Coach Ahead," sung by Ernest Thompson, recorded in North Carolina, 1924. Recording: Columbia, 216-D.

novelty verses edged them off the musical stage. Through the rest of the twentieth century, one rarely encountered such sentimentality in a professionally composed popular song. Their decline was due to the changing role of popular music as the twentieth century wore on. Popular songs of the late nineteenth century were written to be sung by nonprofessionals around the parlor piano at home as well as on the public stage. The advent of the phonograph and radio gradually but inexorably eroded the American custom of singing for our own entertainment.

Furthermore, by the post–World War II years, the vendors of popular music had emptied their shelves of sheet music sold to audiences in their twenties or older and restocked them with sound recordings intended for consumers in their teens or younger. The dissimilarity in age and life experiences contributed to the diminished interest in songs that lingered lovingly over life's bleakest moments.

NON-NARRATIVE SONGS

Non-narrative songs are more varied in structure than the ballads that have been discussed so far. Whereas ballads are divided into subtypes on the basis of their narrative style, most non-narrative songs are categorized by the song's function (work songs, religious songs, dance songs). The last group (lyric folk songs) is identified by neither form nor function but rather by the mood or feeling of the song—a result of its poetic style.

Work Songs

The term "occupational song" denotes one in which descriptions of work, work conditions, or attitudes toward work form a significant textual element. A "work song" is actually sung during the work process. Unfortunately, it is not always known whether a particular song was sung to accompany work. Given this difficulty, the term will be applied to songs that are known—because of the circumstances under which they were collected or recorded, or from the testimony of the singers—to have been used to accompany work, or applied to songs whose origins are not certain but have textual reference to a work process.

Work songs, as such, are an integral part of work activity. Singers believe that such songs aid in the execution of their tasks. Singing paces the activity of a single worker, coordinates the motions of a group of workers, diverts the mind from the oppressive tedium of a monotonous task, or cheers flagging spirits. In preindustrial societies, work songs accompany a variety of tasks—agricultural, pastoral, domestic, urban. In different societies at varying times, these have included rope making, grape treading, house building, corn grinding, tree felling, bale toting, weaving, fishing, and street peddling. In the past few decades the vitality of most of these traditions has waned as manual labor—in the field, city streets, and home—has steadily been replaced by mechanized devices whose mechanical screeches or electrical hums leave little room in the acoustic spectrum for vocalization.

In the United States, work songs have been well documented for only a few occupations. The best example in the Anglo-American folk tradition is sea shantying, with cattle-calls a close second. For uncounted generations, soldiers have sung marching songs to help synchronize their steps and rouse their spirits, but there have been no studies of such songs beyond mere collection and publication (generally heavily expurgated). The collection of pastoral and agricultural work songs has been far more successful in outlying parts of the British Isles than in North America, though the bulk of the material was collected early in the twentieth century.

The African American folk tradition in this country is much richer in work songs than is the Anglo-American. Numerous examples of axe songs, riverboat roustabout songs, tie-tamping chants, steel-laying hollers, and shoeshine patters have been preserved in sound recordings—some in artificially recreated circumstances, but others in undisturbed work situations.

Another category of work songs to consider are those in which individuals other than the workers are supposed to be influenced. These include the chants of tobacco auctioneers; the street cries of peddlers, vendors, tinkers, grinders, ragmen, and junk collectors; the sing-song of railroad conductors; and, by extension to contemporary media, the singing commercials of mass media and the voiceless mechanical jingles of outdoor ice cream vendors' trucks.

Some of the work song types, being fairly bound geographically, are discussed throughout this book. I include here are a handful that could be found anywhere in North America. The first is an example of a simple pastoral song:

"Shear 'Um"
Makes no difference how you shear 'um,
Makes no difference how or when;
Makes no difference how you shear 'um,
Just so you shear 'um clean.[20]

Many domestic household chores traditionally can be accompanied by song—whether sung and performed by servants or by the homeowners themselves. Of course, one could just as well hum or whistle some current pop tune, but the ones included here are interesting because their lyrics all concern the task being performed.

In the nineteenth and early twentieth centuries, the city streets were filled with the carts, wagons, and trucks of craftspeople and vendors: scissor-grinders, rag collectors, milkmen, bakery trucks, flower sellers, and so on. Almost the only remaining examples of these dying customs are the ice cream truck and, on the streets of some cities, the small stands selling fast food. Each of these street merchants used to have his or her own distinctive call or song, and the daylight hours in a busy part of town were filled with the mingled sounds of their street cries.

"Spinning Song"	"Come, Butter, Come"
Spin, ladies, spin all day,	Come, butter, come,
Spin, ladies, spin all day	Mistus standin' at the gate,
Sheep shell corn,	A-waitin' for the butter cake
Rain rattles up a horn,	To come, butter, come
Spin, ladies, spin all day,	Come, butter, come, mistus a-waitin',
Spin, ladies, spin all day,	Come, butter, come, mistus a-waitin',
Spin, ladies, spin all day.*	De mis' is a waitin' for the butter cake
	To come, butter, come.**

*"Spinning Song," unidentified informant, collected by Mrs. Richard C. Thompson in Arkansas. Published in Dorothy Scarborough, ed., *On the Trail of Negro Folk-Songs* (1925; repr., Hatboro, PA: Folklore Associates, 1963), p. 215.
**Churning song—"Come Butter, Come," sung by Irene Williams, Rome, MS. Collected by John A. and Ruby T. Lomax, 1940. Recording: Library of Congress, AFS 4011 A3. A very similar text was published in seventeenth-century England. Similar songs have been collected in Georgia, such in Chuck Perdue's "Come Butter Come," *Foxfire* 3:20–24, 65–72.

"Charcoal"

My hands is black, my face is black,
And I sell my coal two bits a sack;
Chah-coal!*

"Flowers"

Yes ma'am I got flowers,
You ask me how I sell 'em,
Yes ma'am ten cents a bunch, three for a quarter,
Yes ma'am who got the money come and buy,
And who ain't got the money stand aside and cry,
Flowers to go and buy.
What you all looking after me so for,
I'm not come to stay;
I just come to let you all know,
This one's the flowers day,
Flowers to go and buy.
I got white lilies, jasmine white,
I got all kinds fresh and fine,
Just off the wine [sic].
Yes ma'am I got flowers,
You ask me how I sell 'em,
Yes ma'am three for a quarter,
All come and buy now,
'Cause I'm here today and tomorrow I'll be gone;
Flowers to go and buy.**

*"Charcoal," from Travis County, TX, recording data not given. Elizabeth Hurley, "Come Buy, Come Buy," in *Folk Travelers: Ballads, Tales and Talk*, ed. Mody C. Boatright, Wilson M. Hudson, and Allen Maxwell (Austin: Publication of the Texas Folklore Society, 1953), p. 134.

**"Flowers," sung by unidentified female street vendor, recorded in Charleston, SC, ca. 1935. Collected by Walter C. Garwick. Recording: Library of Congress, LP album LBC 8, *Folk Music in America*, Vol. 8: *Songs of Labor & Livelihood*, 1978.

Children's Songs, Game Songs, Play Party Songs, and Lullabies

While the oral traditions so far discussed thrive particularly in rural areas, the lore of schoolchildren is indifferent to the cultural distance between rural and urban settings. The persistent association of certain manifestations of oral lore—jokes, rhymes, game songs, parodies—with particular ages or grade levels conjures an image of a house of many rooms, each room housing a particular collection of oral lore, through which children pass in regular succession, one room each year or so. The songs, jokes, and riddles remain in the room for that appropriate age level, left behind by the exiting children to be seized upon by the newly entering ones.

In addition to the songs that originate among the children themselves, which include playground game songs, rhymes, and parodies of popular adult songs, there are the songs and rhymes that adults—parents, nurses, nannies, grandparents, and schoolteachers—sing to children that become part of the children's own repertoire. This "nursery lore" includes nursery rhymes and lullabies. Some of the songs adults sing become the children's possession but in severely distorted or garbled form.

Many songs, often called "nursery songs," found their way into children's lore because adults considered them appropriate to sing to children. Although it used to be parents and nursemaids who transmitted such lore, today it is usually elementary school teachers or children's television characters who keep alive perennial favorites like "London Bridge," "Row, Row, Row Your Boat," "Ring around a Rosie," and "John Jacob Jingleheimer Schmidt." It used to be thought that remnants of ancient rituals and beliefs lurked behind children's games and songs, and many ingenious explanations were produced on that assumption.

One song that may actually contain traces of historic ritual is "London Bridge Is Falling Down." The rhyme, both as a song and as a game, is widespread throughout Europe and Asia, as well as the British Isles and North America. It may be a relic of an old superstition that a bridge or large building will not stand unless a human being is walled into the structure or buried beneath the foundations. The argument is that earth deities (or the Devil) resent such ambitious structures and will repeatedly destroy them unless a sacrificial human is immured in the foundation. This certainly provided an explanation as to why many buildings and bridges did indeed fail soon after construction. The soul of the person entombed would act as guardian, as the usual ending of the game/song suggests:

We will put a man to watch all night . . .
Suppose the man should fall asleep . . .
We will put a pipe into his mouth . . .

Even in the absence of this sequence, there is always the aspect of incarcerating some child in the physical act of locked hands, representing the bridge, as is suggested by the verse, "We'll put him in the keep and lock him up."

"Billy Boy" is an example of an adult song parodied for singing in the nursery. The song is based on one of the most widespread of the Child ballads, "Lord Randall." In the adult version, suspense-filled drama unfolds entirely through dialog between a young man and his mother, gradually revealing that the son has been poisoned by his sweetheart, and concludes with his oral testament (also called a nuncupative testament) in which he leaves his valued possessions to his sister, brother, and parents; but to his "true love" he leaves a rope and a gallows to hang her. "Billy Boy" likewise is built up from dialog between a mother and

> **Nursery Standards from Mid- to Late Nineteenth-Century American Songs**
>
> "Old Dan Tucker" (Dan Emmett, 1843)
> "Oh! Susanna" (Stephen Foster, 1848)
> "Camptown Ladies" (Stephen Foster, 1850)
> "Row Row Row Your Boat" (1852)
> "Pop Goes the Weasel" (1853?)
> "Clementine" (words, 1863; music, 1884)
> "Polly Wolly Doodle" (1880)
> "I've Been Working on the Railroad" (1894)
> "She'll Be Coming Round the Mountain" (music, 1899; words, 1927)

her son, who has visited his sweetheart, but the consequences aren't nearly so startling.

"Lord Randall" was first printed in Scotland in 1792, but a related ballad was known in Italy early in the seventeenth century. "Billy Boy" is just about the same age, having been reported in print in 1791, but it used a tune known over a century earlier.

"Froggie Went a-Courtin'" deserves a medal for being the nursery song of greatest antiquity. This tale of animal miscegenation was published in 1611

The Pickard Family (1930s). *Author's collection.*

under the title, "The Marriage of the Frogge and the Mouse" in Ravenscroft's *Melismata*, but a ballad registered in 1580 titled "A moste Strange Weddinge of the ffrogge and the mowse," is surely related, as is a song mentioned in a 1549 publication, "The frog cam to the myl dur" ("The frog came to the mill door").[21] In the United States it appears in different forms, and at the end of the twentieth century, several illustrated children's books and at least one film were devoted to the celebrated nuptials. The version printed here gets its name from its nonsense internal refrain. (Note that the song has both a chorus and a refrain.)

"Billy Boy"

"Oh, where have you been, Billy Boy, Billy Boy?
Oh, where have you been, charming Billy?"
"I've been to see my wife; she's the joy of my life;
She's a young thing and cannot leave her momma."

"Did she ask you in Billy Boy, Billy Boy,
Did she ask you in, charming Billy?"
"Yes, she asked me in with the dimples in her shin,
She's a young thing and cannot leave her momma."

"Can she bake a cherry pie Billy Boy, Billy Boy,
Can she bake a cherry pie charming Billy?"
"Yes, she can make a cherry pie fast as you can wink your eye,
She's a young thing and cannot leave her momma."

"Can she make a pair of britches Billy Boy, Billy Boy,
Can she make a pair of britches, charming Billy?"
"Yes, she make a pair of britches fast as you can count the stitches
She's a young thing and cannot leave her momma."

"How tall is she, Billy Boy, Billy Boy,
How tall is she, charming Billy?"
"She's as a tall as a pine and as straight as a punkin vine,
She's a young thing and cannot leave her momma."

"How old is she, Billy Boy, Billy Boy,
How old is she, charming Billy?"
"Twice six, twice seven, twice twenty and eleven,
She's a young thing and cannot leave her momma."*

*"Billy Boy," sung by Donnie Stewart and Terry Perkins at the American Folk Song Festival, Kentucky, 1958. Recording: Folkways, FA 2358, *Jean Thomas, the Traipsin' Woman: American Folk Song Festival*, 1960.

"Go Tell Aunt Rhody" is still sung widely by adults to children throughout the United States. The tune is found in Jean-Jacques Rousseau's opera, *Le Devin du Village* (1752) and has long been known as "Rousseau's Dream."[22] The version here is from the repertoire of the Pickard Family, who recorded it in 1930. The parenthetical (3) indicates that the line is sung three times but sometimes without the word in parentheses.

The best-known lullaby is "Rock-a-Bye Baby," first published in *Mother Goose's Melody* in 1765 but set to music, and with the first line that we now know, by Effie I. Crockett (under the pseudonym, Effie Canning) around 1872.

Parodies are most likely to be sung to the tunes of then-current popular songs and may disappear from currency when their models are forgotten. A good tune and clever lyrics, though, can aid longevity. Humorist Alan Sherman's parody, "Hello Muddah, Hello Fadduh! (A Letter from Camp)" (to the tune of Ponchielli's "Dance of the Hours"—already familiar to many because of its use in Disney's *Fantasia*) made #2 on *Billboard*'s pop music charts in 1963 and was probably known to the majority of children in the United States for years afterwards. The Beatles's "Yellow Submarine," though not primarily written as a children's song, certainly achieved that status, and as such was passed along by oral transmission as much as through the mass media. In addition, it spawned some of its own, strictly orally transmitted parodies. Older tunes are still put to work by young parodists. In the 1990s, one could still hear children singing parodies of such old chestnuts as "Battle Hymn of the Republic" (words, 1862):

A page from Gennett Records' catalog of "Old Time Tunes" showing Chubby Parker (1928). *Author's collection.*

> Mine eyes have seen the glory of the burning of the school,
> We have tortured all the teachers we have broken every rule;
> We've barbecued the principal, destroyed the P.T.A.,
> And us kids go marching on.

The following is sung to "Alouette" (1879?):

> Suffocation, its your destination
> Suffocation, its the game we play.

"King Kong Kitchie Kitchie Ki-Me-O"

Frog went a courtin' and he did ride,
King kong kitchie kitchie ki-me-o.
With a sword and a pistol by his side,
King kong kitchie kitchie ki-me-o.

CHORUS:
Ki mo kee mo ki mo kee,
Way down yonder in a holler tree,
An owl and a bat and a bumblebee,
King kong kitchie kitchie ki-me-o.

He rode til he came to Miss Mouse's door,
King kong kitchie kitchie ki-me-o.
And there he knelt upon on the floor.
King kong kitchie kitchie ki-me-o.

He took Miss Mouse upon his knee,
King kong kitchie kitchie ki-me-o.
And he said, "Little mouse, will you marry me?"
King kong kitchie kitchie ki-me-o.

Miss Mouse had sisters three or four,
King kong kitchie kitchie ki-me-o.
And there they came right in the door.
King kong kitchie kitchie ki-me-o.

They grabbed Mr. Frog and began to fight,
King kong kitchie kitchie ki-me-o.
In a holler tree 'twas a terrible night.
King kong kitchie kitchie ki-me-o.

Mr. Frog brought the sisters to the floor,
King kong kitchie kitchie ki-me-o.
With his sword and his pistol he killed all four.
King kong kitchie kitchie ki-me-o.

They went to the parson the very next day,
King kong kitchie kitchie ki-me-o.
And left on their honeymoon right away.
King kong kitchie kitchie ki-me-o.

Now they lived far off in a holler tree,
King kong kitchie kitchie ki-me-o.
And they now have wealth and children three.
King kong kitchie kitchie ki-me-o.*

*"King Kong Kitchie Kitchie Ki-Me-O," sung with banjo accompaniment by Chubby Parker. Recording: Columbia, 78 rpm 15296-D, 1928. Reissue: Yazoo, CD 2051, *The Story the Crow Told Me, Vol. 1*, 2000.

"The Old Grey Goose Is Dead"

Go tell Aunt Rhody (3)
The old gray goose is dead.
(She) died in the haystack (3)
With a toothache in her heel.
('Twas) the one she was saving (3)
To make a feather bed.
(We'll) bury her at daybreak (3)
Just like Aunt Rhody said.
The barnyard is mournin' (3)
And waitin' to be fed.
Aunt Rhody's weepin' (3)
For the old grey goose is dead.

We'll all join the chorus
'Cause the grave is before us
We dug with the shovel
Of old Uncle Ned.
(We'll) eat no more goose head (3)
For the old grey goose is dead.*

*"The Old Grey Goose Is Dead," sung by the Pickard Family, 1930. Recording: Banner, 78 rpm record 0744 and associated labels, 1930. Reissue: Yazoo, CD 2051: *The Story the Crow Told Me, Vol. 1*, 2000. Parentheses around the first words in a line indicate words that are omitted on the repetitions.

To the tune of "Stars and Stripes Forever" (1897):

Be kind to your web-footed friends,
For a duck may be somebody's mother,
They live way down in the swamp,

Where the weather's cold and damp;
You may think that this is the end,
. . . Well it is.

And to "Jingle Bells" (1857):

Jingle bells, Batman smells, Robin laid an egg,
The Batmobile lost its wheel, the Joker broke a leg.

Fiddle and Banjo Songs

Traditional fiddle and banjo tunes can be performed wordlessly; they might
be accompanied by dance calls (if played for a square dance), they might be
associated with a game or a play party song (see the next section), or they might
accumulate random verses mainly to relieve monotony. In the latter cases,
there are few constraints on what verses can be sung other than the necessity of
rhythm and meter, and there can be considerable variation in verses from one
rendition to another, even by the same performer.

All three of the examples shown here are transcribed from 1920s hillbilly
recordings by performers who almost certainly learned them from oral tradition. They are textually very unstable; one finds a wealth of differences among
various renditions. Also, all three have lines that suggest origins on the minstrel
stage in the mid-nineteenth century. The singers of the songs were from Kentucky, north Georgia, and North Carolina, respectively. In the first song, "boil"
is customarily spelled "bile" to represent the usual Appalachian pronunciation—
an archaism from eighteenth-century British pronunciation. The third song
was titled "Possum up a Gum Stump, Coony in the Hollow" on the recording
from which it was transcribed, but is usually known as "Sally Goodin'."

Play Party Songs

Play parties were young adult (primarily of courting age) social dances held
on the western frontier until early in the twentieth century. The music generally
consisted of singing without instrumental accompaniment, because of religious
objections, and in many communities the term "dance" was avoided for similar
reasons. The song texts included some Anglo-American ballad fragments
("Billy Boy," "The Girl I Left behind Me"), fiddle and banjo dance tune lyrics
("Bile Dem Cabbage Down," "Old Joe Clark"), remnants from the minstrel
stage ("Jump Jim Crow," "Little Brown Jug"), rhymes that were often associated
with children's games (e.g., "Go in and out the Window," "Farmer in the Dell,"
"London Bridge"), or local poetry.

One widely known play party song, also used as a children's song in England
as well as throughout the United States, is "Here Come Four Dukes A-Riding."
Boys and girls form separate lines and lock arms, facing each other. During the

Cover from Columbia Records' catalog of "Old Time Tunes" (1929). *Author's collection.*

An ad for Fiddlin' John Carson and Henry Whitter records from *The Talking Machine World* (1924). *Courtesy of the Archie Green and the Southern Folklife Collection, University of North Carolina.*

The Crockett family (*left to right*): Clarence, Alan, Albert, George, Johnny, and Dad (Hollywood, ca. 1930). *Author's collection.*

first stanza, boys advance forward; during the second stanza, girls recede; and so on. After the last stanza, each boy takes the arm of one of the girls and skips away with her.

Religious Songs

In the context of religious songs, the requirement of oral transmission as a criterion for the labels of "traditional" or "folk" is sometimes relaxed. When congregations sing from hymn books, the hymns have a strong component of oral tradition in the styles of the tunes and the performance. Often times, a close association between the hymn tunes and secular song tunes can be heard, the one being borrowed from the other, but borrowing from hymn to secular is more common.

A dichotomy is evident in religious songs: some denominations take simple, folk- or popular-derived musical styles for inspiration, with church members

"Bile Dem Cabbage Down"

Corn blades rustlin' in the
  breeze, punkins on the
  ground,
Squirrels a-chirpin' in the trees,
  bile 'em cabbage down.

CHORUS:
Bile 'em cabbage down, bake
  that hoecake brown,
Only song that I can sing, is bile
  'em cabbage down.

Bobwhite in the meadow,
  buckwheat turnin' brown,
Apple cider in the keg, bile 'em
  cabbage down.

CHORUS.

Sorghum 'lasses in the keg,
  chestnuts roasted brown,
Buttermilk and cornbread, too,
  bile 'em cabbage down.

CHORUS.

Spare ribs in the oven, sweet
  'taters all around,
Brother 'possum fat and fine, bile
  'em cabbage down.

CHORUS.*

"Old Joe Clark"

I went down to Old Joe Clark's
To get me a bottle of wine,
Tied me up to the whipping
  post,
Give me ninety-nine.

Fare ye well, Old Joe Clark,
Goodbye Betsy Brown,
Fare ye well, Old Joe Clark,
I'm gonna leave this town.

I went down to Old Joe Clark's
To get me a bottle of gin;
Tied me to a whippin' post,
Give me hell again.

Massa bought a yeller gal,
Brought her from the South,
Her hair around her head so
  tight,
She couldn't shut her mouth.

Massa had a little mule,
Called him "Peter Brown,"
Every tooth was in his head,
A mile and a half around.**

"Possum up a Gum Stump, Coony in the Hollow" ("Sally Goodin'")

Had a piece of pie, and had a
  piece of puddin'
And I give it all away for to hug
  Sally Goodin'
Night's so dark, and road's so
  muddy,
I hugged Sally Goodin' til I
  couldn't stand studdy.
Possum up a gum stump, coony
  in the hollow,
Pretty gal at our house fast as
  you can holler.
Had a piece of pie, and had a
  piece of puddin'
And I give it all away for to hug
  Sally Goodin'
Can't fool a coon, can't fool a
  possum,
Can't fool a [?] on huckleberry
  blossom.***

*"Bile Dem Cabbage Down," sung by Crockett's Kentucky Mountaineers. Recording: Crown, 78 rpm, 3101, 1931. Reissue: Yazoo 2200: *Kentucky Mountain Music* (7 CD box set), 2003. Repeats of the chorus are not indicated.
**"Old Joe Clark," sung by Fiddlin' John Carson. Recording: Okeh, 78 rpm 45198, 1927. Reissue: Document DOCD 8017, *Fiddlin' John Carson: Complete Recorded Works in Chronological Order, Vol. 4*, 1997.
***Usually titled "Sally Goodin'" but here named "Possum up a Gum Stump, Coony in the Hollow," Charlie Bowman on fiddle with the Hopkins Brothers (vocal by Al Hopkins). Recording: Vocalion, 78 rpm 15377, 1926. Reissue: Document, DOCD 8039, *The Hill Billies/Al Hopkins and His Buckle Busters*, 1999.

doing their own singing, possibly with their own instrumentation. Others aspire to something more elegant, that is, more along the lines of classical music, in which the organizations compose tunes with elaborate melodies, harmonization, and instrumentation that are satisfactorily rendered only by professional or semiprofessional congregational choirs and piano or organ accompaniment. Among more fundamentalist Christian sects—Baptist, Pentecostal, Holiness, Methodist, and so on—once a church member "gets religion," he or she seldom performs secular tunes. More usually, though, singers and musicians keep both

"Here Come Four Dukes A-Riding"

Boys: Here come four dukes a-riding, a-riding, a-riding,
Here come four dukes riding, tis a ma tas a ma tee.

Girls: What are you riding here for here for, here, for,
What are you riding here for here for, tis a ma tas a ma tee.

Boys: We are riding here to get married, married, married,
We are riding here to get married, tis a ma tas a ma tee.

Girls: Please take one of us, sir, us, sir, us, sir,
Why don't you marry us, sir, tis a ma tas a ma tee.

Boys: You are all too black and dirty, dirty, dirty,
You are all too black and dirty, tis a ma tas a ma tee.

Girls: We are just as clean as you are, you are, you are,
We are just as clean as you are, tis a ma tas a ma tee.

Boys: I think then I'll take you miss, you miss, you miss,
I think then I'll take you miss, tis a ma tas a ma tee.*

*Wolford, Leah Jackson, *The Play-Party in Indiana* (Indianapolis: Indiana Historical Commission, 1916), pp. 52–53.

kinds of music in their repertoires and perform whichever kind circumstances warrant.

In colonial America, the most common kinds of religious folk music were hymns, psalms, and anthems. Distinctions between these are not always clear. Psalms utilize texts of the book of *Psalms*, while anthems generally use texts from various books of the Bible. "Anthem" was often used into the twentieth century in African American music as a synonym for what is generally called a "spiritual." Hymns could be based on more liberal renderings of Scriptural texts or could be newly composed texts. Based on available descriptions, singing styles were fairly stilted, sung by the entire congregation and with no great concern for the refinements that characterize modern choral singing. Tunes were rendered slowly with much melismatic decoration (that is, with ornamental notes). Songbooks were often not available (and sometimes congregants were illiterate), so congregations often made use of the "lining out" style from Scotland. In this method, a precentor sings or chants a line of a song, which is then repeated by the congregation.

Attempts to make the singing more congregant friendly began in the early nineteenth century, and most of the elements of religious folk music that still survive—revival songs, shaped note songs, spirituals, and gospel songs—can be traced to that period or soon thereafter. This tendency was apparent in the successive religious revival movements that swept America: the Great Awakening of the first half of the eighteenth century, the camp-meeting movement of the early nineteenth century (also called the Second Awakening), and the gospel song movement associated with late nineteenth-century evangelism.

An early figure on the American religious scene—starting in the 1770s—was the itinerant singing school teacher, who traveled from town to town conducting short sessions that taught the rudiments of music theory, reading, and music notation (see the entry on "shape notes" in the Glossary). A song would be first sung with the solmization, then with the words. The common use of the four-syllable fa-sol-la-fa-sol-la-mi, originating before Shakespeare's time, rather than the now familiar seven-syllables (do-re-mi-fa-sol-la-ti) method gave the name "fasola music" to the genre. Though the source of inspiration was originally religious texts, sentimental and homiletic (morally instructive) ballads and songs can be found in the songbooks as well. It is clearly a style for participation with an audience. Shape-note singing remains a vigorous tradition, primarily but certainly not exclusively in the Southeastern United States where one can still find annual singing conventions that last one or a few days. Regional conventions are also held in California, New York, Massachusetts, Vermont, Kansas, and Illinois, as well as in Florida, Mississippi, Alabama, Kentucky, and the Carolinas. The version printed here of the widely sung "Amazing Grace" is an example from *The Sacred Harp* (1859 edition), which illustrates the fasola notation system.

One important religious movement, the Anglo-American outdoor camp meeting, began in Kentucky in July 1800 and quickly spread through neighboring states. The event started as an opportunity for the traveling evangelical preachers to reach large audiences at a time. Though not anticlerical, the meetings generally took place independent of the organization of the established churches. Free of denominational restrictions, they tended to be very democratic, drawing middle and lower classes, and open to all people, regardless of race or ethnicity.

Music was an important part of the process of repentance and conversion, and because of the logistical complexity of providing books for all participants (sometimes numbering in the thousands), simple music was necessary. Starting with folk hymns (that is to say, hymns using easily sung folk melodies), singers

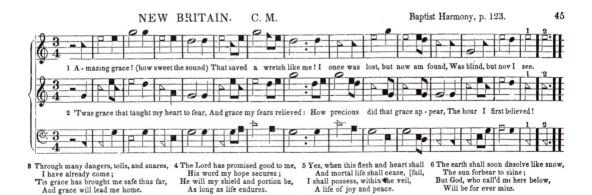

Shape notes: "New Britain" ("Amazing Grace") from *The Sacred Harp* (1859; reprint 1968). *Author's collection.*

"New Britain"

Amazing grace! how sweet the sound,
That saved a wretch like me!
I once was lost, but now am found,
Was blind, but now I see.

'Twas grace that taught my heart to fear,
And grace my fears relieved;
How precious did that grace appear,
The hour I first believed!

Through many dangers, toils, and snares,
I have already come;
'Tis grace has brought me safe thus far,
And grace will lead me home.

The Lord has promised good to me,
His word my hope secures;

He will my shield and portion be,
As long as life endures.

Yes, when this flesh and heart shall fail,
And mortal life shall cease,
I shall possess, within the veil,
A life of joy and peace.

The earth shall soon dissolve like snow,
The sun forbear to shine;
But God, who call'd me here below,
Will be for ever mine.*

*"New Britain," *The Sacred Harp*, 1968. Reprint of 1859 edition, p. 45, where it is credited to the *Baptist Harmony*, p. 123.

streamlined the texts even further, and thus evolved the spiritual, a religious song whose simple tune and text structure facilitated singing by large groups, especially when songbooks were not available or singers were unable to read.

Though initially sung by both white and black singers, the spiritual was particularly favored by African American slaves and their descendents and soon came to be associated primarily with such congregations. Many spirituals dwelt on the issue of slavery and freedom, often couched in texts that referred overtly to the enslaved Israelites in Egypt. Other spirituals sang about crossing Jordan's river and entering Canaan, or the Promised Land; here Canaan was the code word for the North, where slavery had been abolished. Linking early spirituals with a mainly Anglo-American movement, the camp meeting, is not meant to suggest that African and African American contributions to religious song in this period were insignificant. Quite the contrary: African and African American contributions did much to establish the style of the camp meeting music and also to enforce the very idea of music as an important and invigorating form of religious devotion.[23] Nevertheless, establishing the ultimate origins of the spiritual style has occupied many scholars in vigorous debate over the years—a debate that has not been as free of racial bias as scholarly disputation ought to be. Objective writers recognize African elements in American religious singing as early as 1819, and they must have existed even earlier.[24]

At their simplest, spirituals consist of quatrains, either as a verse, sung thrice, followed by a refrain, or as a verse alternating with a refrain. These patterns made for easy group singing; the leader had to sing no more than the first few words of a stanza, and the rest was evident. Alternatively, different members of the group could sing out their own stanzas. The examples reprinted here

"The Ship of Zion"	"Many Thousands Go"
Dis de good ole' ship o' Zion, Dis de good ole' ship o' Zion, Dis de good ole' ship o' Zion, And she's makin' for de Promised Land.	No more peck o' corn for me, No more, no more; No more peck o' corn for me, Many thousand go.
She hab angels for de sailors (3) And she's makin' for de Promised Land.	No more driver's lash for me . . . No more, no more; No more peck o' corn for me, Many thousand go.
And how you know dey's angels? (3) And she's makin' for de Promised Land.	
Good Lord, shall I be de one? (3) And she's makin' for de Promised Land.	No more pint o' salt for me . . . No more, no more; No more peck o' corn for me, Many thousand go.
Dat ship is out a-sailin', sailin' (3) And she's makin' for de Promised Land.	No more hundred lash for me . . . No more, no more; No more peck o' corn for me,
She'll neither reel nor totter, totter, totter (3) And she's makin' for de Promised Land.	Many thousand go.
She's a-sailin' away cold Jordan, Jordan, Jordan (3) And she's makin' for de Promised Land.	No more mistress' call for me . . . No more, no more;
King Jesus is de captain, captain, captain (3) And she's makin' for de Promised Land.*	No more peck o' corn for me, Many thousand go.**

*"The Ship of Zion," from Thomas Wentworth Higginson, "Negro Spirituals," *Atlantic Monthly* 19 (June 1867): 685–694. Reprinted in Jackson, *The Negro and His Folklore in Nineteenth-Century Periodicals*. The parenthetical (3) indicates that the line is sung three times.
**William Francis Allen, Charles Pickard Ware, and Lucy McKim Garrison, "Many Thousands Go," *Slave Songs of the United States* (1867; repr., New York: Oak, 1965), p. 94.

illustrate, respectively, these common patterns. "The Ship of Zion," reprinted from an 1867 publication, illustrates the first pattern. "Many Thousands Go," also printed in 1867, is sometimes known as "No More Auction Block for Me."

Spirituals first came to world-wide attention in the 1870s—often called "Negro Spirituals" at that time—through fund-raising concert tours throughout the United States and Europe by singers from Nashville's African American Fisk University. Other African American college choral groups (such as from the Tuskegee Institute and the Hampton Institute) soon followed suit. But the renditions that the world heard had been heavily Europeanized in style to make them more acceptable to their white audiences. Some of the subsequent argument that spirituals were primarily of European rather than African origin was erroneously based on the touched-up presentations.

After the Civil War, a new evangelical movement arose led by the lay preacher Dwight L. Moody and his colleague, the singer/songwriter Ira Sankey. Moody's program was both secular and religious, and he saw the twin goals of social reform and religious conversion as intertwined. Sankey, a tremendously popular performer who could easily move audiences to tears, had already acquired considerable experience in the secular music business, and he applied his knowledge to this new type of music designed to aid in the conversion/repentance process. Compared with religious music of a century earlier, the new gospel music's text stressed a loving and fatherly deity, inclined to comfort and forgive rather than punish. Song texts spoke fondly of going home to Jesus or of singing with beloved ones in a heavenly choir: "O come, angel band, come and around me stand, / O bear me away on your snowy wings to my immortal home."[25]

Although Moody and his cohorts rejected the more exuberant behavior of the frontier camp meeting, their songs were cheerful and upbeat, both in music and in message. By the end of the nineteenth century, gospel music had begun to displace spirituals. Gospel music is essentially religious song set to secular tunes and styles. Without hearing the words, it is difficult to determine whether the material is secular or not. Early in the twentieth century, black songwriters began to write gospel songs specifically for African American congregations, and soon gospel music was strongly associated with them. As jazz and ragtime developed and became popular, African American gospel music borrowed their styles. Gospel was characterized by much faster tempos, upbeat lyrics, and more overt expressions of emotion. In African American churches, polyrhythms, hand clapping, foot stomping, syncopation, and jazz instrumentation were often an integral part of the service. In rural Anglo-American communities of the Southeastern states, gospel songs continued to find favor through the twentieth century, but without the more exuberant elements of their African American counterparts.

In folk communities in both the North and South, among both Anglo-American and African American singers, the rubric of religious songs can include homiletic and sentimental songs that are not part of the formal church service. An example is "A Conversation with Death," one version of which is still popular through the twentieth century.

Close kin to these moralistic pieces are the many temperance songs from the 1800s. The American temperance movement began early in the nineteenth century, and by 1855, thirteen of the thirty-one states had already passed anti-liquor laws, a number that had swelled to twenty-three out of forty-eight by 1916 when the campaign for a national constitutional prohibition amendment was gathering momentum. In support of this movement, and in the style of the sentimental ballads of the period, appeared a great abundance of tragic songs and ballads about the wretched drunkard and his piteous family, reduced to abject squalor and humiliation because of his weakness. One longtime favorite, still sung in the late twentieth century, was "Licensed to Sell; Or, Little Blossom." It was one of the few such pieces that included a ringing indictment of the liquor seller as the true villain of the tale. The song was written in 1873, one year before the formation of the Women's Christian Temperance Union (WCTU) and a period of great anti-alcohol agitation, and the condemnation of the seller transformed the typical drunkard song from a morality tale to a

"A Conversation with Death"

"Oh, what is this I cannot see,
"With icy hands gets a-hold of me?"
"Oh, I am Death, none can excel,
"I open the doors of Heaven and Hell."

"Oh, Death, Oh, Death, how can it be,
"That I must come and go with thee?
"Oh, Death, Oh Death, how can it be,
"I'm unprepared for eternity."

"Yes, I have come for to get your soul,
"To leave your body and leave it cold;
"To drop the flesh from off your frame,
"The earth and worm both have their claim."

"Oh Death, Oh Death, if this be true,
"Please give me time to reason with you."
"From time to time you heard and saw,
"I'll close your eyes and lock your jaw.

"I'll lock your jaws so you can't talk,
"I'll fix your feet so you can't walk
"I'll close your eyes so you can't see,
"This very hour come and go with me."

"Oh Death, Oh Death, consider my age
"And don't take me in at this stage;
"My wealth now is all at your command
"If you will move your icy hand."

"The old, the young, the rich, the poor,
"Alike with me will have to go;
"No age, no wealth, no silver, no gold,
"Nothing satisfies me but your poor soul."

"Oh Death, Oh Death, please let me see,
"If Christ has turned his back on me;"
"When you were called and asked to bow,
"You wouldn't take heed and it's too late now."

"Oh Death, Oh Death, please give me time,
"To fix my heart and change my mind;"
"Your heart is fixed, your mind is bound,
"I have the shackles to drag you down.

"Too late, too late, to all farewell,
"Your doom is doomed, you're summonsed to Hell;
"As long as God in Heaven shall dwell
"Your soul, your soul shall scream in hell."*

*"A Conversation with Death," sung by Lloyd Chandler. Recorded in Sodom, NC, by John Cohen, 1965. Recording: Rounder, LP 0028: *High Atmosphere*, 1995. Reissue: Rounder, CD 1166-11599-2: *The Art of Old-Time Music*, 2002. Recently published evidence supports Chandler's claim that he himself wrote this version in about 1915.

political message. The cure now is obvious: outlaw alcohol! To that end, the WCTU and later the Anti-Saloon League campaigned tirelessly for the passage of anti-liquor laws in each state. In the 1890s in the Ozarks, on election days when an anti-liquor measure was on the ballot, prim little girls in starched white dresses would sing this song on the courthouse steps hoping to sway undecided voters.[26] Technically, this song fits the criteria of a sentimental ballad as outlined in the previous section.

Hollers

Hollers are (usually) brief, highly idiosyncratic musical expressions utilizing yodels, falsetto, whoops, slides, and other vocal devices. They can be used for communication or self-expression (field hollers), animal herding (cattle calls), or advertisements (street calls). Other terms used are "arhoolie," "whooping," or "loud mouthing." They nearly died out late in the twentieth century, but interest in them was revived by the National Hollerin' Contest held in June

LITTLE BLOSSOM.

O, dear I am so tired and lonesome.
I wish my mother would come.
She told me to close up my blue eyes,
And before I woke up sh'd be home.

She went over to see Grandma;
She lives by the river so bright.
I 'spect my Mother fell in there
And perhaps won't be back tonight.

I think I will go down and meet Daddy;
Perhap's he has stopped at the store.
It is a great pretty store, full of bottles.
Wish he wouldn't go down there any more.

Sometimes he is sick when he comes home
And falls and stumbles up the stairs.
And one night he came into the parlour
And kicked at my poor little chair.

Mother was all pale and frightened,
And hugged me up close to her breast
And called me her poor little Blossom;
And I guess I've forgotten the rest.

But I love him and guess I will go find him.
Perhap's he'll come home with me soon;
Then it will not be dark and lonely
Waiting for Mother to come.

Out into the night went the baby,
Her little heart beating with fright;
Till her tired feet reached the gin palace
All radiant with music and light.

The little hands pushed the door open;
Though her touch was as light as a breeze,
The little feet that entered the portal
Which leads but to ruin and death.

O Daddy, she cried as she reached him;
And her voice rang out sweet and clear:
I thought if I came I would find you,
And I am so glad that I'm here.

The lights are so pretty, dear Daddy,
And I think the music so sweet;

But it is most supper time, dear Daddy,
And Blossom wants something to eat.

A moment the blurred eyes gazed wildly
Down in the face sweet and fair
And as the demon possessed him
He grasped at the back of a chair.

A moment, a second it was over.
The work of the fiend was complete;
Poor little innocent Blossom
Lay quivering and crushed at his feet.

Swift as a light came his reason
Showed him the deed he had done;
With a groan the Devil might pity.
He knelt at the quivering form.

He pressed the pale face to his bosom,
He lifted the fair golden head.
A moment the babies lips quivered,
And poor little Blossom was dead.

Then came the law so majestic
And said this debt with your life you must pay;
That, only a fiend or a mad man
Could murder a child in that way.

But the man who had sold him the poison
That made him a demon of hell;
He must be loved and respected
Because he was licensed to sell.

He may rob you of friends and of money
Send you to prdition and woe,
But as long as he has license
The law must protect him you know.

God pity the women and children
Who are under the curse of rum
And hasten the day when against it
Neither heart, voice or pen shall be dumb.
Select—

Broadsheet from the 1940s: "Little Blossom" (ID: CPM, 002752-Broad). *Courtesy of the Kenneth S. Goldstein Collection, Center for Popular Music, Middle Tennessee State University.*

each year since 1969 in Spivey's Corner, North Carolina. The following field holler was recorded in Mississippi in 1939; the words alone do not give an adequate representation of the song:

"Arwhoolie (Cornfield Holler)"
O-o-o-o-h,
I won't be here long.
O-o-o-o-h,

Oh, dark gonna catch me here,
Dark gonna catch me here.
O-o-o-o-h.[27]

Blues Songs

Blues songs (not to be confused with blues ballads discussed earlier) originated in the Deep South, probably around the 1890s, among African Americans.
Blues is a nonfunctional, leisure-time folk musical entertainment that borrows
some elements of singing style from field hollers and shares structural and
textual ideas with blues ballads.

Blues is an offspring of several African literary traditions incorporating music
not usually associated with dance. Most often, it is performed either by a soloist
accompanying himself or herself with a stringed or other instrument or by a
narrator supported by a participating audience. Recent research suggests the
music of itinerant musicians in the broad savannah hinterland of West Africa
as a possible source for the musical structure of the blues.

The term "blues" has had a succession of meanings since early in the seventeenth century. In the 1820s, a "fit of the blues" meant a "depression of spirits."
In the 1850s "blues" meant "boredom." In the 1880s, it meant unhappiness.
Blues songs tend to be very personal and introspective musical expressions,
rarely as narrative as a ballad; more often they present the singer's feelings
about events in his life. Folk blues do not deal with unique or remote experiences that only the singer could understand or with the experiences of people
unlike the singer and his audience. Thus, in spite of their personal nature, they
serve indirectly as a means of expression for the singer's entire audience. The
blues singer becomes their spokesman, the organizer of their thoughts, opinions,
and fantasies.[28]

Before 1910, folklorists had collected blues and blues-like fragments throughout the South. Sometimes these were in the "classic" blues stanza form of AAA'
(where A' and A rhyme), but more often they were in forms such as AAAA' or,
most simply, AAA. An early example of the latter was the single stanza of "Joe
Turner's Blues," based on Joe Turney, brother of the governor of Tennessee,
who, in the 1890s, used to roundup cheap labor by arresting groups of blacks for
minor offenses.

Dey tell me Joe Turner he done come,
Dey tell me Joe Turner he done come,
Oh, dey tell me Joe Turner he done come.[29]

Memphis bandleader and composer W. C. Handy (1873–1958) is often credited with publishing the first songs with "blues" in the title: "Memphis Blues"
(1912). Published slightly earlier that year was Hart Wand's "Dallas Blues."
However, neither was a blues in the sense that the term is usually used. In his

autobiography, Handy described hearing what sounds very much like blues singers in 1903, and he quoted stanzas such as:

> Boll weevil, where you been so long?
> Boll weevil, where you been so long?
> You stole my cotton, now you want my corn.

and,

> Oh, the Kate's up the river, Stack O'Lee's in the ben',
> Oh, the Kate's up the river, Stack O'Lee's in the ben',
> And I ain't seen ma baby since I can't tell when.[30]

Both of these stanzas occurred frequently in blues songs recorded in the 1920s and later. Handy's first compositions fitting the classic blues definition include "St. Louis Blues" (1914), "Yellow Dog Blues" (1914), "Joe Turner's Blues" (1915), "Hesitating Blues" (1915), and "Beale Street Blues" (1917).

Like the holler, blues singing employs falsetto, raspy voice, slides (portamento), and some vibrato. An important trait is the use of "blue notes," that is, slightly flattened 3rd, 7th, and occasionally 5th notes of the scale that vary between the standard (European) pitch and the flattened note. These pitches may represent survivals from non-Western musical scales common in Africa. Blues are usually accompanied on instrument, most commonly guitar, steel guitar, or piano, or a small band; however, until the 1920s, one also could hear blues accompanied on fiddle or banjo.

As sung by rural singers, the structure of blues songs, although in three-line stanza form, was often ragged and inconsistent—sometimes rhyming, sometimes just assonant, sometimes missing a beat or with an extra beat. As blues gained in popularity, the music was commercialized in the 1910s and 1920s, and a standardized form evolved, in retrospect called "classic" or "city" blues.

The "classic" city blues form is a three-line stanza, generally in twelve measures of music, four measures for each line. The second line is a repeat of the first line, so poetically the stanza form is AAB. Each of the three lines tends to be divided into two parts: the singer's vocal statement, followed by what is effectively a response on the instrument. The musical chordal accompaniment is also fairly consistent. In the key of C, the chords for each measure are first line, C-C-C-C; second line, F-F-C-C; third line, G^7-F-C-C.

Lyric Folk Songs

Non-narrative songs are difficult to treat in a systematic manner. Not having the ballad's constraints of a coherent story nor associated with particular contexts, lyric songs tend toward the subjective, the pensive, the emotional, and the poetical. They are often sung unaccompanied, though fiddle, banjo, dulcimer, or small ensembles are not out of place. Sometimes the lyric song is

"Little Sparrow"

Come all you fair and tender ladies,
Take warning how you court young men;
They are like a star in the cloudy morning,
They will first appear and then they're gone.
They will tell to you some lovely story,
They will prove to you that their love is true;
And away they will go and court some other,
Oh, that is the love they have for you.

I wish I were some little sparrow,
And I had wings and I could fly;
I would fly away to my false lover,
And while he'd talk I would sit and cry.
But I am not a little sparrow,
I have no wings, nor can I fly;

I will sit down here in grief and sorrow,
And pass off trouble until I die.

I wish I had known before I courted,
That love had been such a killing crime;
I would have locked my heart with a key of gold,
And tied it down with a silver line.
Young man, never cast your eyes on beauty,
For beauty is a thing that will decay;
For the prettiest flowers that grow in the garden,
Soon will wither and fade away.*

*"Little Sparrow," collected by Loraine Wyman in *Lonesome Tunes: Folk Songs from the Kentucky Mountains* (New York: H. W. Gray, 1916), pp. 55–57.

composed of the remains of a ballad now forgotten. Other times, it consists of a string of stanzas whose principal attraction for one another is a common rhythm and stanzaic form. Three widely known examples illustrate the variety of lyric songs in American tradition.

"Little Sparrow" (sometimes titled by its first line, "Come All You Fair and Tender Ladies") is an example of folk lyric at its most cohesive; unlike the banjo and fiddle songs of the preceding section, this song was composed as a unified whole. While there is no "story" as the term has been used in this chapter, there is a clearly an implied story, to which this song has an explicit moral. The song was collected in the southern mountains in the 1910s and probably originated there around the turn of the century or shortly before. It is not known in Britain.

"Wagoner's Lad," as sung by Kentucky folk musician Buell Kazee, opens with a mournful condemnation of the fate of American women—protest song at its subtle best. The text lies in the no-man's-land between ballad and lyric song; there are the bones of a story, and the stanzas certainly fit well together in definite sequen-

Buell Kazee in the 1960s. *Author's collection.*

tial fashion. But other versions don't provide any additional lines that flesh out a narrative in the manner of the older ballads. The song is often

"Wagoner's Lad"

The [Oh?] hard is the fortune of all womankind,
They're always controlled, they're always confined;
Controlled by their parents until they are wives,
Then slaves to their husbands the rest of their lives.

I've been a poor girl, my fortune is sad,
I've always been courted by the wagoner's lad;
He courted me daily, by night and by day,
And now he is loaded and going away.

"Your parents don't like me because I am poor,
They say I'm not worthy of entering your door;
I work for my living, my money's my own;
And if they don't like me they can leave me alone."

"Your horses are hungry, go feed them some hay,
Come sit down here by me as long as you stay;"
"My horses ain't hungry, they won't eat your hay,
So fare you well darling, I'll be on the way."

"Your wagon needs greasing, your whip is to mend,
Come sit down by me as long as you can;"
"My wagon is greasy, my whip's in my hand,
So fare you well, darling, no longer to stand."*

*"Wagoner's Lad," sung by Buell Kazee, 1928. Recording: Brunswick, 213. Reissue: Smithsonian Folkways, *Anthology of American Folk Music*, 1997.

Clarence Ashley and Doc Watson on stage in Galax, Virginia (1960). *Photographer, Dan Seeger; courtesy of the Southern Folklife Collection, University of North Carolina.*

combined with "(On Top of) Old Smoky," and they may once have been the same song.

Clarence Ashley's short text of "The Coo Coo Bird" seems to be a meld of two separate songs: "The Coo Coo," which generally consists of verses warning

"Mountain Girl's Lament"

From the top of ole smoke,
All kiver'd with snow,
Thar I lost my true lover:
By a courtin' too slow.
Courtin' is a pleasure;
Partin' is grief;
But an unconscience lover
Is worse than a thief!

A thief will but rob you
And take what you save,
But an unconscience lover
Will bring you to your grave.
Your grave will but hid you
And turn you to dust,
Not one man in a thousand
That a poor gal can trust!*

"The Coo Coo Bird"

Gonna build me log cabin
On a mountain so high;
So I can see Willie
As he goes on by.

Oh, the coo-coo is a pretty bird
She wobbles as she flies;
She never hollers coo-coo
Till the fourth day (of) July.

I've played cards in England,
I've played cards in Spain;
I'll bet you ten dollars
I beat you next game.

Jack o' diamonds, Jack o' diamonds,
I've known you from old;
Now you've robbed my poor pockets
Of my silver and my gold.

I've played cards in England,
I've played cards in Spain;
I'll bet you ten dollars
I beat you this game.

Oh, the coo-coo is a pretty bird
She wobbles as she flies;
She never hollers coo-coo
Till the fourth day (of) July.**

*Robert De Armond, "Mountain Girl's Lament (East Tennessee Mountains)" (Hinds, Hayden & Eldrege, Inc., 1916). The sheet music states, "obtained from natives by Robert De Armond," and "'unconscience lover' is the Mountain term for a lover without a conscience."
**"The Coo Coo Bird," sung by Clarence Ashley, 1929. Recording: Columbia, 15489-D. Reissue: Smithsonian Folkways, *Anthology of American Folk Music*, 1997.

young girls to be wary of untrustworthy lovers (much as does the above version of "Little Sparrow"), and "Jack of Diamonds," about the risks of gambling.

Only the meter and rhythm hold the above stanzas together, although one could speculate that the association of the cuckoo with foolish or irrational behavior (persisting in our own slang today) might provide both themes with an undertone of disapproval. In earlier texts, closer to the British original, occur stanzas like:

The cuckoo is a pretty bird,
She whistles so sweet;
She never sings cuckoo
'Till the Spring of the year.

and,

> The cuckoo is a pretty bird,
> She sings as she flies;
> She brings us sweet tidings
> She tells us no lies.

Ashley's second and final seem to combine these two earlier thoughts. In so doing, the text loses an accurate reflection of the experience of the community's English ancestors, for whom the arrival of that bird signals the beginning of spring.

Bawdy and Erotic Songs

In general, prior to the 1970s published song collections depicted a community of singers and audiences remarkably free from any suggestions of bawdy, erotic, or obscene musical material. Almost all such collections had been scrupulously whitewashed by collectors and publishers to avoid indelicacies that might have offended readers or reviewers. If deleting a stanza or two made the song presentable, that was done, though without any hint of what had taken place. If more extensive doctoring would have been necessary, the song probably never was published. Sometimes the censoring process took place at an earlier stage: some male singers declined to sing bawdy songs for female song collectors or if females were present.[31]

"The Foggy, Foggy Dew" is a good example of how much standards of decorum have changed over the years. It can be printed today with scarcely a murmur in most publications; yet before the 1950s, it was invariably printed or recorded without the third stanza.

In the United States, this ballad has been traced back to about 1900; English versions are not much older. In the 1940s, recordings by folksinger Burl Ives (without the third stanza) did much to enhance its popularity.

"Seven Old Ladies" is in the category of only mildly offensive songs that would be acceptable in publications that tolerate a hint of the naughty. It is a parody of a once familiar nursery rhyme, traced back at least to the 1780s in England, and part of its allure lies in the subversion of the well-known innocent lyrics. The nursery song begins:

> Oh, dear, what can the matter be,
> Oh, dear, what can the matter be,
> Oh, dear, what can the matter be,
> Johnny's so long at the fair.
>
> He promised to buy me a bunch of blue ribbons
> He promised to buy me a bunch of blue ribbons
> He promised to buy me a bunch of blue ribbons
> To tie up my bonny brown hair.

"The Foggy, Foggy Dew"

Now, I am a bachelor, I live by myself,
And I work at the weaver's trade.
The only thing I ever did wrong
Was to woo a fair young maid.
I wooed her in the summer time,
And part of the winter time too;
But the only thing that I ever did wrong
Was to keep her from the foggy, foggy dew.

One night, this maid came to my bed
Where I lay fast asleep.
She laid her head upon my chest
And then began to weep.
She sighed, she cried, she damn near died.
She said, "What shall I do?"
So I took her into bed and I covered up her head
Just to keep her from the foggy, foggy dew.

All through the first part of night,
We did laugh and play.

And through the latter part of the night,
She slept in my arms 'til day.
Then when the sun shone down on our bed,
She cried, "I am undone."
"Hold your tongue, you silly girl,
The foggy dew is gone."

Now I am a bachelor, I live with my son;
I work at the weaver's trade.
And every time I look into his face
He reminds me of the fair young maid.
He reminds me of the summer time,
And part of the winter time too,
And the many, many times I took her in my arms
Just to keep her from the foggy, foggy dew.*

*"The Foggy (Foggy) Dew" (Laws, O 3). As published in Ed Cray, ed. *The Erotic Muse*, 2nd ed. (Urbana, IL: University of Illinois Press, 1992), pp. 61–62.

"Seven Old Ladies"

CHORUS:
Oh, dear, what can the matter be,
Seven old ladies were locked in the lavat'ry,
They were there from Monday till Saturday,
And nobody knew they were there.

The first old lady was 'Lizabeth Porter,
She was the deacon of Dorchester's daughter,
Went there to relieve a slight pressure of water,
And nobody knew she was there.

The second old lady was Abigail Splatter.
She went there 'cause something was definitely the
    matter.
But when she got there, it was only her bladder,
And nobody knew she was there.

The third old lady was Amelia Garpickle,
Her urge was sincere, her reaction was fickle.
She hurdled the door; she'd forgotten her nickel,
And nobody knew she was there.

The fourth old maiden was Hildegard Foyle,
She hadn't been living according to Hoyle.
She was relieved to know it was only a boil,
And nobody knew she was there.

The fifth old lady was Emily Clancy,
She went there when it tickled her fancy,
But when she got there it was ants in her pantsy,
And nobody knew she was there.

The sixth old lady was Elizabeth Bender,
She went there to repair a broken suspender.
It snapped up and ruined her feminine gender,
And nobody knew she was there.

The janitor came in the early morning,
He opened the door without any warning.
The seven old ladies their seats were adorning,
And nobody knew they was there.*

*As published in Ed Cray's *The Erotic Muse*, 2nd ed. (Urbana, IL: University of Illinois Press, 1992), pp. 120–121.

"The Cod Fish Song"

CHORUS:
Singing ti yi yipee, yippy yay, yipee yay,
Singing ti yi yipee, yippy yay.

There was a man who had a little horse.
He saddled it, bridled it, and threw his leg across.
He rode and rode until he came to a brook,
And there sat a fisherman baiting his hook.

"Oh, fisherman, fisherman," said he,
"Have you a codfish for my tea?"
"Oh, yes, oh, yes" said he, "There's two:
One for me and one for you."

Well he took that codfish by the leg bone,
And mounted on his horse and galloped back
    home.
But when he got home he couldn't find a dish,
So into the chamberpot he put the little fish.

All night long he could hear his woman cry,
"There's a devil down below; I can see his
    beady eyes."

Well, in the morning, she sat down to squat,
And the codfish jumped up her you-know-what.

She yelled bloody murder; "Well, well," cried she,
"There's a bloody big something getting up me!"
Well, she hopped and she jumped and she gave a
    roar.
There went the codfish a-skating 'round the floor.

They chased that codfish all around the room.
They hit him with a brush and banged him with a
    broom.
First they hit him on the belly, and they hit him on
    the side.
They hit him on his arse until the poor fellow died.

Well, the moral of the song is easy to define:
None of us has got an eye on our behind.
So better be sure before you squat,
There's nothing swimming in the chamberpot.*

*As published in Ed Cray's *The Erotic Muse*, 2nd ed. (Urbana, IL: University of Illinois Press, 1992), p. 5.

One of the oldest bawdy songs is "The Sea Crab" or, in the version given here, "The Cod Fish Song," a ribald episode that has been traced back to medieval tales. There is no way this song can be scrubbed up for genteel company without totally destroying its character. In fact, it has much of the flavor of one of the risqué stories that Chaucer or Boccaccio so delighted in. This version printed here is sung to the tune of "The Chisholm Trail."

RECOMMENDED RECORDINGS

Recordings listed here are all anthologies. Albums featuring individual artists are listed under the respective artists' names in Biographical Sketches.

Afro-American Blues and Game Songs. Rounder, CD 1513, 1999; originally released as Library of Congress, AFS L4, 1942.

Afro-American Spirituals, Work Songs, and Ballads. Rounder, CD 1510, 1998; originally released as Library of Congress, AFS L3, 1942.

Anglo-American Ballads, Vol. 1. Rounder, CD 1511, 1999; originally released as Library of Congress, 78 rpm album AFS L1, 1942.

Anglo-American Ballads, Vol. 2. Rounder, CD 1516, 1999; originally released as Library of Congress, AFS L7, 1943.

Anthology of American Folk Music. Smithsonian Folkways, 1997, 6 CDs; reissues from 1920s and 1930s.

Ballads and Songs of Tradition from the Folk-Legacy Archives (1956–1964). Folk Legacy, CD-125, 2000.
Been in the Storm So Long: Spirituals, Folk Tales and Children's Games from John's Island, SC. Smithsonian Folkways, CD SF 40031.
Before the Blues, Vols. 1–3: The Early American Black Music Scene. Yazoo, 2015/16/17, 1996.
Close to Home: Old Time Music from Mike Seeger's Collection. Smithsonian Folkways, SF-CD-40097.
Far in the Mountains, Vols. 1 & 2. Musical Traditions, MTCD 321-2, 2002.
Far in the Mountains, Vols. 3 & 4. Musical Traditions, MTCD 323-4.
The Harry Smith Connection. Smithsonian Folkways, SFW 40085.
High Atmosphere. Rounder, CD 0028, 1995; originally issued on LP in 1974.
How Can I Keep from Singing: Early American Religious Music & Song. Yazoo, 2020/21, 1996.
Lomax Collection: Southern Journey: Vols. 1–13. Rounder, CD 1701-13, 1997–1998.
Mountain Music of Kentucky. Smithsonian Folkways, SF CD 40077, 2 CDs.
Negro Blues and Hollers. Rounder, CD 1501, 1997; originally released as Library of Congress, AFS L59, 1962.
Negro Work Songs and Calls. Rounder, CD 1517, 1999; originally released as Library of Congress, AFS L8, 1943.
Ozark Folksongs. Rounder, 1108, 2001.
Sacred Harp Singing. Rounder, CD 1503, 1998; reissue of Library of Congress, AFS L 11, 1943.
A Treasury of Library of Congress Field Recordings. Rounder CD 1500, 1997.
Virginia Traditions: Ballads from British Tradition. Global Village, CD 1002.

The following CDs are reissues from commercial hillbilly and blues 78-rpm recordings of the 1920s and 1930s.

The Cornshucker's Frolic, Vols. 1/2: Downhome Music and Entertainment from the American Countryside: Classic Recordings from the 1920s and '30s. Yazoo, 2045/46, 1999.
Hard Times Come Again No More, Vol. 1/2: Early American Rural Songs of Hard Times and Hardships. Yazoo, 2036/37, 1998.
My Rough and Rowdy Ways, Vols. 1/2: Early American Rural Music, Badman Ballads and Hellraising Songs: Classic Recordings from the 1920s and '30s. Yazoo, 2039/40, 1998.
Old Time Mountain Ballads. County, CD-3504, 1995.
The Rose Grew around the Briar: Early American Rural Love Songs, Vols. 1/2. Yazoo, 2030/31, 1997.
Times Ain't Like They Used to Be: Early American Rural Music, Vols. 1/2. Yazoo, 2028/29, 1997.
Times Ain't Like They Used to Be: Early American Rural Music, Vols. 3/4. Yazoo, 2047/48.

RECOMMENDED VIEWING

The Ballad of Frankie Silver, featuring traditional storyteller Bobby McMillon (video, Davenport Films for the University of North Carolina Curriculum in Folklore).
Chase the Devil: Religious Music of the Appalachians (video, Shanachie, 1208).

NOTES

1. For example:

The farmer in the dell (2),
The farmer in the dell
Hi-ho-the-dario,
The farmer in the dell.

The farmer takes a wife
The farmer takes a wife
Hi-ho-the-dario,
The farmer takes a wife.

The wife takes the child (2) etc
The child takes the nurse (2) etc.

and,

Ninety-nine bottles of beer on the wall,
Ninety-nine bottles of beer;
If one of those bottles should happen to fall,
[or in other versions: Take one down, pass it around,]
Ninety-eight bottles of beer on the wall.

2. For more details, see Evelyn Wells, *The Ballad Tree* (New York: Ronald Press Co., 1953), pp. 206–210.

3. "The Braes O Yarrow" (Child, No. 214, E); from a manuscript of ca. 1801 belonging to James Hogg. Dowy means sad; houms means low ground by riverbank.

4. "Child Waters," published in Francis James Child, *The English and Scottish Popular Ballads*, No. 63, version A, stanza 1.

5. "Lord Lovel" (Child, No. 75). Also published in Josephine McGill, *Folk-Songs of the Kentucky Mountains* (1917), p. 9.

6. "Prince Robert" (Child, No. 87, version B, stanza 10).

7. "Bonny Bee Hom" (Child, No. 92, version C, stanzas 3 and 4).

8. "Child Maurice" (Child, No. 83, version D, stanza 1). Other "milk-white steeds" are found in Child, Nos. 11, 62, 75, and 88.

9. "Willie and Lady Maisry" (Child, No. 70, version B, stanza 11).

10. "Young Johnstone" (Child, No. 88, version B, stanza 5).

11. "Prince Robert" (Child, No. 87, version A, stanza 9).

12. These figures are based on a large number of ballad collections of the twentieth century. The frequencies of recovery range from 437 for "Barbara Allen" to 134 for "Fair Margaret and Sweet William."

13. G. Malcolm Laws Jr., *American Balladry from British Broadsides: A Guide for Students and Collectors of Traditional Song*, vol. 8 (Philadelphia: American Folklore Society, PAFS, 1957).

14. See also the discussion in Chapter 2.

15. G. Malcolm Laws Jr., *Native American Balladry: A Descriptive Study and a Bibliographical Syllabus*, vol. 1, rev. ed. (Philadelphia: American Folklore Society, PAFS, 1964).

16. Seba Smith, "A Corpse Going to a Ball," *The Rover*, no. 15 (December 28, 1843): 2:225. Smith prefaced his text with the headnote, "The incident, from which

the following ballad is woven, was given in the paper three or four years ago as *a fact*. It was stated, that a young lady in the country, while riding some distance to a ball on New Year's evening, actually froze to death." The ballad was the subject of investigation by Phillips Barry (1880–1937); see Helen Hartness Flanders, Elizabeth F. Ballard, George Brown, and Phillips Barry, *The New Green Mountain Songster: Traditional Folk Songs of Vermont* (1939; repr., Hatboro: Folklore Associates, 1966), pp. 111–115.

17. Phillips Barry, ed., *Bull. Folksong Soc. Northeast* 8 (1934): 17–19; text received from Mr. F. L. Tracy of Brewer, ME, in 1934.

18. John Garst, "Chasing John Henry in Alabama and Mississippi," *Tributaries: Journal of the Alabama Folklife Association*, no. 5 (2002): 92–129.

19. Carl Sandburg, *American Songbag* (New York: Harcourt-Brace, 1927), p. 9.

20. "Shear 'Um," text from T. C. Fertic, Kissimmee, FL, and published in Alton C. Morris, ed., *Folksongs of Florida* (1950; repr., New York & Philadelphia: Folklorica, 1981), p. 184.

21. G. L. Kittredge, "Traditional Texts and Tunes," in Albert H. Tolman and Mary O. Eddy, *Journal of American Folk-Lore* 35 (October–December, 1922): 335–432. The publication referred to is Wedderburn, *The Complaynt of Scotland*, 1549.

22. Murl J. Sickbert Jr., "Go Tell Aunt Rhody She's Rousseau's Dream," in *Vistas of American Music: Essays and Compositions in Honor of William K. Kearns*, ed. Susan L. Porter and John Graziano (Warren, MI: Harmonie Park Press, 1999), pp. 125–150.

23. See in particular, Richard Crawford, *America's Musical Life: A History* (New York: W. W. Norton, 2001), p. 124.

24. Dena Epstein, *Sinful Tunes & Spirituals: Black Folk Music to the Civil War* (Urbana, IL: University of Illinois Press, 1977), p. 232.

25. "The Land of Beulah," words by Rev. Jefferson Hascall, music by William B. Bradbury, 1860. Sung in the twentieth century as "Angel Band."

26. Vance Randolph, *Ozark Folk Songs*, vol. 2 (Columbia, MO: State Historical Society of Missouri, 1948), p. 403.

27. "Arwhoolie (Cornfield Holler)," sung by Thomas J. Marshall at Edwards, MS, 1939. Collected by Herbert Halpert. Recording: Library of Congress, LP AAFS L8, *Negro Work Songs and Calls*.

28. David Evans, "Structure and Meaning in the Folk Blues," in *The Study of American Folklore*, rev. ed., ed. Jan H. Brunvand (New York: W. W. Norton, 1986), p. 443.

29. "Joe Turner's Blues," published in Howard W. Odum, "Folk-Song and Folk-Poetry as Found in the Secular Songs of the Southern Negroes—Concluded," *Journal of American Folklore* 24 (October–December, 1911), p. 351. It is not always easy to tell from early descriptions or transcriptions whether a stanza form was AAB or AAAB. For example, Odum wrote ". . . each line is repeated three times; or, if the stanza consists of a rhyming couplet, the first is repeated twice with the second once."

30. W. C. Handy, *Father of the Blues* (New York: Macmillan, 1941), p. 79.

31. An important publication that restores some balance to the printed record is Ed Cray's *The Erotic Muse*, 2nd ed. (Urbana, IL: University of Illinois Press, 1992).

2

Instruments and Musical Aspects

In the preceding chapter, the textual aspects of folk song were considered. The following discussion focuses on aspects of folk music that are not concerned with the words: first, the various instruments commonly encountered in the United States, then some specific musical characteristics.

INSTRUMENTS

All the principal cultural groups that emigrated to the New World brought strong instrumental musical traditions with them. Among most, stringed instruments were prominent. Wind and percussion instruments are found among most groups, except those from the British Isles, although a fragile fife-and-drum tradition still persists among Anglo-Americans in the Northeast.

Fiddle

Most ethnic groups in America have fiddle traditions, but the instrument is particularly prominent among immigrants from the British Isles, Scandinavia, and eastern Europe. In the case of British immigrants, written evidence dates back to colonial days. The familiar vignette of the immigrant debarking on American shores with a bible and a fiddle in a flour sack may be overused, but it has an element of truth. There is also evidence for African and African

Instrument	Date/Origin
Fiddle	Colonial America
	Immigrants from the British Isles, Scandinavia, and eastern Europe
Banjo	Eighteenth century and earlier
	American variant of African instruments
Guitar, Spanish	1810s, in rural communities late in the nineteenth century, rare before 1900
	Probably came from England; possible independent dissemination by immigrants from Mexico; Appalachian musicians credited African American guitarists for their first exposure
Mandolin	Popular by the 1850s
	Italian immigrants; perhaps a separate introduction across the Rio Grande by Hispanic immigrants
Appalachian dulcimer	Until the mid-nineteenth century was found only in the Appalachians
	Central Europe
Hammered dulcimer	Earliest reference is 1717 in Massachusetts; by the early nineteenth century, the instrument was appearing well away from the seaboard colonies
	New World mostly by immigrants from southeastern Europe
Fifes and whistles	Immigrants with Celtic backgrounds
Harmonica	Invented in Germany in the 1820s
Autoharp	Widely popular in the early twentieth century
	Invented in late nineteenth-century Germany; an American variety was patented in 1881
Accordion	Original form was invented in the 1820s
	From German immigrants
Jug, washboard, kazoo, other homemade instruments	In 1900, jug bands gained popularity
	American
Ensemble traditions	Anglo-American and African American

American plantation slaves taking up the fiddle and playing dance tunes (probably British and Anglo-American) for their masters. The African American fiddle tradition has been on the wane since the early twentieth century.

The fiddle of the nineteenth century is physically no different from a classical violin, and until the mid-twentieth century, common performance idiosyncrasies represented survivals of eighteenth-century violin traditions: holding the fiddle against the chest, holding the bow well away from the frog, flattening down the bridge to facilitate playing triple stops (three strings simultaneously), the preference for playing open strings, and the frequent use of nonstandard tuning (scordatura). The traditional fiddler holds the fiddle against the chest, gripping around the fiddle neck with the left hand for support. The classical violinist uses pressure between shoulder and chin to hold up the instrument. This makes it difficult for the fiddler to slide the left hand up and down the neck to stop the strings; consequently, the musician is constrained to playing in first or second position, unable to take full advantage of the strings' length. The advantage, however, is that now the musician can sing. This playing style leads to retuning the instrument to avoid having to play higher up the fiddle neck. Retuning can also facilitate playing double stops that otherwise would require difficult fingering stretches.

Standard devices of the modern classical violinist, such as harmonics, vibrato, pizzicato (plucking the strings), and spiccato (bouncing the bow on the strings), are rarely heard, especially before the late twentieth century. At one time, it was common for a second musician to beat on the fiddle strings (sometimes of a second fiddle) with straws or knitting needles (called "fiddlesticks") for rhythmic backup. In the late twentieth century, fiercely competitive fiddlers participating in contests, particularly in Texas, evolved a highly technical "contest fiddle" style in which many of these rarer devices were used for special effects. Some tunes, such as "Listen

Unidentified mountain fiddler. *From* The Etude Music Magazine, *August 1942.*

to the Mockingbird" or "Orange Blossom Special" in particular, were carefully worked up to allow inclusion of showy pyrotechnics that would dazzle audiences and (sometimes) judges.

British immigrants brought a bulging folio of fiddle music with them, and their descendants kept the tradition vibrant by adapting tunes from nineteenth-century popular music and then by composing new tunes. Fiddle music is basically dance music, and in Canada and the northern United States, the principal types of tunes encountered are distinguished by the kinds of dances (or steps) they were meant to accompany. A major characteristic of a dance is its rhythm (see Glossary). Unlike the big cities, where common dance steps of the twentieth century included the waltz, the foxtrot, and a handful of Latin American dances, in the remoter villages most dancers still favored the dances of the nineteenth century.

Some fiddle tunes are called "airs," which are slow melodies not intended for dancing. Most tunes come in two parts (or "strains"): a "high" (or "fine") part and a "low" (or "coarse") section, so-called because most of the notes of the high part are higher (more toward the right end of the piano keyboard) than those of the low part.

In the South, one finds fewer jigs, schottisches, and quadrilles but will also find what are called breakdowns or hoedowns (faster 2/4 or 4/4 tunes), blues,

A flyer for fiddlers' picnic (1941). The instrument, if real, looks like a viol. *Author's collection.*

and rags. The latter pieces were only occasionally derived from ragtime sheet music popular in the early twentieth century; more generally country rags are

Fiddlin' Bill Henseley, a mountain fiddler in Asheville, North Carolina (1937). *Photographer, Ben Shahn (LC-USF331-006258-M3); from the Farm Security Administration—Office of War Information Photo Collection, Library of Congress Prints and Photographs Division.*

characterized by fast tempo, lots of syncopation, and frequent use of melodies based on a rather specialized chord progression. In general, swing rhythms (alternately long and short notes) and syncopation are more common in the southern states than in the North.

Fiddlers also make use of "blue notes" (deviations from standard pitch) and swing rather than straight rhythms. One also finds (perhaps more often in the South) novelty fiddle songs and imitative pieces, such as "Drunken Hiccups," "Cluck Hen Cackle," or "(Listen to the) Mockingbird." Fiddle tune titles are shamelessly unstable; decidedly different tunes frequently masquerade under the same title or, conversely, a single tune may be known by abundant aliases. The proliferation of tunes is without end: the hybridization of the high part of one tune with the low part of another gives birth to a new tune, and the casual alteration of a few notes (intentionally or not) may give cause for a new title.

Dances of the Nineteenth Century		
Dance Name	Rhythm	Pace
Reel	2/4 or 4/4	Fairly fast
Jig	6/8 or 9/8	Fast
Hornpipe	2/4 or 4/4	Slower than the reel
March	2/4, 4/4, or 6/8	Usually brisk
Quadrille	2/4 or 6/8	Moderate
Waltz	3/4	Usually slow
Schottische	4/4	Slower than the reel

Accompaniment differs considerably between the Northeast and the Southeast. In New England and the Canadian Maritimes, traditional fiddlers are accompanied on piano—something rare in most of the South. In the nineteenth and early twentieth century in the South, banjo accompaniment was most usual, although the combination of fiddle and banjo was often a duet rather than a featured instrument with accompaniment. In the 1920s, the guitar began to supplant the banjo and, in the latter half of the twentieth century, became the accompaniment of choice.

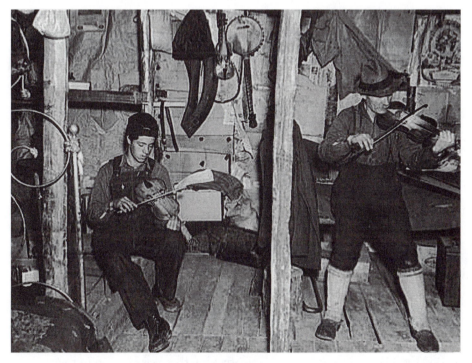

Lon Allen and his son playing their fiddles to the tune of "Arkansas Traveler" near Iron River, Michigan (1937). *Photographer, Russell Lee (LC-USF34-010895-D); from the Farm Security Administration—Office of War Information Photo Collection, Library of Congress Prints and Photographs Division.*

There have always been more fiddlers in the North who could read music than in the South, though everywhere the ability is becoming more common. Over the years, many fiddlers have learned at least some tunes (sometimes with

the help of a music-reading pianist) from a number of influential fiddle tune collections. However, no fiddle tune books include bowings: instructions for when to move the bow up or down. These bowing patterns determine when notes will flow together smoothly (*legato*) and when there will be a more abrupt sound (*staccato*), greatly affecting the overall sound of the music. Without predetermined bowing instructions, there can be considerable differences in the sound of two fiddlers playing the same tune, even when they both learned it from the same printed source.

Mrs. Mary McLean on fiddle at Skyline Farms in Alabama (1937). *Photographer, Ben Shahn (LC-USF33-006296-M2); from the Farm Security Administration–Office of War Information Photo Collection, Library of Congress Prints and Photographs Division.*

Traditional fiddling has experienced some waxing and waning in popularity in different regions, but on the whole the tradition thrives. Contributing to the interest in fiddling for many decades have been the fiddlers' contests and conventions, in which the musicians of a region compete for prizes and public acclaim. A contest in Hanover County, Virginia, is known to have taken place as far back as 1736. In 1913, Atlanta began an annual convention that attracted newspaper coverage and drew spectators from Atlanta's upper crust, as well as farmers from the rural surroundings. In recent years, the number of contestants and the skill level has, if anything, been increasing.

Banjo

The instrument most identified with American folk music has been the banjo, an American variant of several instruments brought from Africa by slaves in the eighteenth century and earlier. Musically aware colonists (such as Thomas Jefferson) wrote down their observations on the strange instrument, which the slaves called something like "banjer," or "banza," by the 1770s.

Though the number of strings was variable, there were generally two or three, and one of the strings was shorter than the other, not extending all the way to the nut at the tuning end. Thus its pitch could not be changed by the fingers of the left hand as with the other strings, a configuration reflecting (or necessitating) its use as a "drone," a steady tone that was not part of the melody, such as the characteristic sound of bagpipes. While early banjos were handmade from gourds and gut strings, by the 1850s, factory-made instruments with standardized parts were available. The modern manufactured instrument, developed in the early twentieth century, has a fretted fingerboard, a drum-like parchment head stretched over a metallic hoop, and steel strings. (Older Appalachian musicians still make and play handmade instruments lacking these innovations.)

In the 1840s, the banjo was a featured instrument in blackface minstrelsy, in which white entertainers parodied and interpreted slave musical culture as they imperfectly understood it. In the southern mountains, whites learned about the instrument either directly from slaves or from minstrel show performers. Since the Civil War, two types of banjo have been used. The tenor, or four-string banjo, lacks the fifth short drone string and is used mostly in jazz and pop music. The five-string, or mountain banjo, has been used by traditional folk musicians. In the early twentieth century, the popularity of the instrument

Samantha Baumgarner with her banjo in North Carolina (ca. 1940). *Courtesy of the Southern Folklife Collection, University of North Carolina.*

led to the invention of many hybrid instruments that had a banjo-like head but the fingerboard and tuning of the other parent: the six-string banjo-guitar, the eight-string banjo-mandolin, the eighteen-string banjo-harp, the short-necked banjorine and banjolin, and the four-string banjo-ukulele.

The banjo became so strongly associated with racist southern white culture that most African Americans abandoned it early in the twentieth century. Likewise, the banjo nearly disappeared from commercial country music in the 1950s because of its association with a rural culture from which many artists were trying to distance themselves. At the same time, thanks largely to North Carolina's Earl Scruggs and his followers, it became a standard fixture in bluegrass music. It also became a featured instrument of the urban folk revival, mainly because of singer and musician Pete Seeger's influence.

The five-string is played either by picking the strings downward with the thumb and upward with the first or first two fingers, much as a classical or parlor guitar is played, or by brushing downward. The former picking styles were most common in North Carolina, at least into the 1930s. The latter style is called "clawhammer," from the way the fingers usually look, or "frailing" style; "frail" is an older form of the verb "flail." This style is widespread in Kentucky and Tennessee. There are other styles—combinations or modifications of these basic ones—but they are less common. Mike Seeger has observed and collected numerous examples of traditional banjo playing and mastered most of them. In his experience, very few traditional players use more than one right-hand technique.

The banjo can be played in various tunings; Seeger believes that most of the fifty or so traditional banjo tunings were developed during the time when both white and black people were playing the banjo in the mountain areas between about 1850 and 1930.[1] If there is a standard tuning—or at least a most common one—it is the G tuning, in which the strings are tuned to the three main notes (do, mi, sol) of a G major chord.[2]

Banjo player Earl Scruggs, one of the first musicians to play with Bill Monroe and his Bluegrass Boys, developed a more complex picking style out of the older two- and three-finger up-picking patterns that he had learned in his youth. His playing style, which was received with great acclaim when he introduced it in 1945, has been highly emulated, and it has become the model for every bluegrass banjo player. Using metal finger and thumb picks, bluegrass banjo playing utilizes characteristic picking patterns that typically surround melody notes (played either with thumb or fingers) with a cluster of drone notes. In the 1960s, other bluegrass banjo players (Bill Keith, in particular) developed picking patterns with successive notes of a run on adjacent strings so that each would continue to sustain (or ring) while the next note was struck, creating a harp-like effect.

Guitar

The Spanish guitar became a popular parlor instrument in the United States in the 1810s. It probably came from England and made its appearance in rural communities late in the nineteenth century, thanks largely to Sears, Roebuck & Company's mail-order catalogs. (The instrument known in colonial America as the guitar was not the now-familiar Spanish guitar but rather the English guitar or "cetra," a smaller, ten-stringed instrument.) The appearance of the guitar in the Southwest in the late 1800s suggests an independent dissemination by Hispanic immigrants from Mexico. Many Appalachian musicians who grew up from 1890 to 1910 credited African American guitarists for their first exposure to the guitar and also asserted that the instrument was rare before the turn of the century.

In addition to their roles as solo instruments or as accompaniment for songs, the fiddle, banjo, and guitar provided the backbone of Anglo-American instrumental ensembles, whose primary function was to provide dance music. Unlike banjos and fiddles, guitars are rarely homemade. The six strings can be struck with a flat-pick (as do jazz guitarists) or plucked with fingers (downwards with thumb and upwards with one to three other fingers) as classical guitarists do, except that often finger-picks are used.

Judging by commercial recordings by Anglo-American musicians in the 1920s (that is, hillbilly musicians), guitar playing then was still primitive, with the instrument being used almost exclusively for simple chordal accompaniment. In folk and country music since the 1930s, a playing style developed and popularized by Maybelle Carter of the Original Carter Family has become ubiquitous. In this method, melody notes are played by picking downward with the thumb (usually wearing a thumb-pick); the other fingers brush the strings up or down to provide a chorded accompaniment. Blues records of the 1920s show that African American musicians were much more competent on the guitar, and a wide range of styles were well developed before that decade ended. These musicians generally used the thumb on the bass strings to provide rhythm while the other fingers picked the melodic notes. In the 1930s, white folk musicians began to use the flat-pick and simultaneously evinced an interest in more complex chordal patterns, both probably borrowed from jazz musicians.

Steel or Hawaiian guitars are set up so that the strings, tuned to an open chord rather than the "standard" tuning, are stopped (that is, fretted) with a hard bar (usually glass or metal) and not pressed against the fingerboard. Sliding the stopper up and down the strings thus produces a sliding pitch that isn't confined to the set notes of the scale. Though usually made of wood, in the 1920s several metal-bodied instruments were introduced. When played in steel-guitar style, these produce particularly distinctive metallic sounds. These instruments are designed to enable the player to produce continuous melodies, much as a violinist does, rather than just strummed chords or plucked separate notes as on a standard guitar.

Mandolin

The mandolin known in American folk music is generally the Neapolitan variety, with four double courses (sets) of strings. The instrument originated in Italy and was doubtless brought here directly by Italian immigrants; it was popular already by the 1850s. The instrument had also made it into the West by the same time, suggesting perhaps a separate introduction across the Rio Grande by Hispanic immigrants.[3] By the late 1890s, it was available through Montgomery Ward's mail-order catalogs, and by the turn of the century, many cities boasted mandolin ensembles or even orchestras, which included not only standard-size mandolins but the larger varieties, such as mandola, mandocello (or mandoloncello), and mandobass (or bass mandolin), in parallel to the viola, cello, and bass viol.

Usually about the size of a violin (twenty-four inches) and tuned similarly, it is played by striking strings with a plectrum (flat-pick). In 1923, the Gibson Company introduced a flat-backed model, which soon mostly replaced the other variety that had a deeply vaulted back. The mandolin's popularity crested in the 1920s, by which time it had also gained currency among both Anglo- and African American traditional musicians. Though there were some jazz mandolinists in the 1920s, for the most part the mandolin was replaced by the banjo and banjo-related instruments, including the banjo-mandolin, an instrument with the strings and tuning of a mandolin but a banjo-like head.

In hillbilly music in the 1930s, guitar-and-mandolin duos were a common instrumental combination, but by 1940, the mandolin had all but disappeared from folk music. Its revival was due to Kentucky mandolinist Bill Monroe, who virtually created the style of music called bluegrass and made his instrument an essential part of the bluegrass stringband. Monroe's virtuosity on the instrument revolutionized the way it was played. Previously, it was used to produce gentle undulating tremolo sounds by rapid and regular up-and-down motions of the right hand. Monroe added syncopations, driving rhythms, and hard percussive sounds that greatly widened the options open to the mandolinist.

Appalachian Dulcimer

The Appalachian dulcimer is a diatonically fretted, plucked zither, typically with three to six strings. The frets are configured for a Mixolydian mode—that

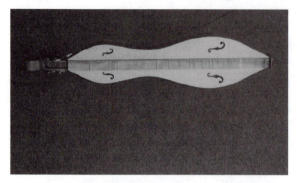

is, a scale with half steps between the third and fourth and between the sixth and seventh notes. The instrument was brought to America from central Europe (it may be descended from the German scheitholt) and, until the folk revival of the mid-nineteenth century, was found only in the Appalachians. Jean Ritchie, who comes from a Kentucky family of folksingers and dulcimer players, observed in her travels in Britain that none of the rural folk had heard of anything resembling the dulcimer, convincing her that it was not of British origin.[4]

Appalachian dulcimer. *Photographer, Verni Greenfield; dulcimer courtesy of Artichoke Music, Portland, Oregon.*

The instruments are usually hour-glass or tear-drop shaped, about thirty- to thirty-six-inches long, and made of wood. A three-string instrument is customarily tuned G-G-C (or sol-sol-do). It used to be customarily played with a turkey or goose quill plucking the strings, one or two of which served to carry the melody and the others, sometimes unfretted, were drone strings.

Hammered Dulcimer

The multi-stringed hammered dulcimer is in essence the same instrument that is called the cimbalom (Hungary), hackbrett (Switzerland), or tsimbal (Jewish eastern Europe), though there are similar instruments elsewhere. It is used to hammer out melodies in much the same way as a xylophone or marimba is played. It was once thought to be of Persian origin, brought to Europe by Arabs. More recent evidence suggests that the instrument originated in medieval Europe. It was brought to the New World mostly by immigrants from southeast Europe (the earliest reference is to Salem,

Hammered dulcimer. *Photographer, Jon Weinberg.*

Massachusetts, in 1717) and played mostly in the home by young women. By the early nineteenth century, the instrument was appearing well away from the seaboard colonies and, until the mid-twentieth century, was most common in (but not exclusive to) Pennsylvania and the upper Midwest. Never very common among traditional musicians, the instrument virtually died out in the early twentieth century only to be resuscitated in later decades by folk revival musicians. In the 1890s, one could purchase a hammered dulcimer from Sears, Roebuck & Company's mail-order catalog, but the selection was modest compared to that of autoharps, mandolins, guitars, and banjos.

The body is made of wood and trapezoid shaped, and it is played with two wooden hammers or strikers. The arrangement of the strings is rather complex. The strings are divided down the middle with two bridges (usually). Modern instruments commonly have seventeen, twenty-three, twenty-nine, or thirty-one sets of strings, with two to four strings per note. The thirty-one-string instrument plays three full octaves, but not every octave contains all the accidentals (sharps and flats). The seventeen-string instrument plays two octaves.

Fifes and Whistles

If portability were the primary criterion for popularity of a folk instrument, fifes would be found everywhere. As it is, there has been little mention of them among traditional musicians for half a century or so. Though once popular, at least in some areas, they have declined considerably from favor. Fifes and whistles would be expected to be found where Celtic (in particular, Irish) traditions thrive. Writing in 1945 about his collecting activities in western Pennsylvania, Samuel Bayard wrote that fifes used to be common in rural communities, as were fife-and-drum ensembles called "martial bands." Like the fiddlers, the fifers occasionally held playing contests. Bayard also encountered small, end-blown pipes or flutes, with a tone resembling that of a soprano recorder, though a trifle shriller. Writing in 1982, he reported that the once common fife-and-drum tradition had all but disappeared:

> Nowadays, aside from a few groups who are carrying on this fifing-and-drumming tradition under somewhat altered circumstances, the bands once found in countless Pennsylvania communities are all gone. Changing times and tastes have worked for their extinction. . . . Once in great demand, the fifers and drummers played on every conceivable occasion of local interest. Memorial Day and Independence Day were outstanding public occasions for the music of these players—when all the bands of a county might assemble at the county seat and parade, then station themselves at various points about town and play all day and far into the night.[5]

Harmonica

The harmonica, also called mouth organ, mouth harp, or French harp, was invented in Germany in the 1820s. Its modest price and portability contributed to its wide acceptance among folk musicians, both Anglo-American and African American. Each instrument is set up for a particular key, with a range of two octaves, in chromatic and diatonic (no accidental notes) varieties. Each hole produces two different tones depending whether air is sucked in or blown out. A favorite device among twentieth-century musicians was to use the harmonica for imitations of trains or foxhounds.

Piano

Though not often thought of as a folk instrument, the piano has functioned in that capacity (usually being played without formal instruction) in African American music (particularly blues, gospel, and jazz) and, to a lesser extent, in the Anglo-American tradition, notably in Virginia. In the Northeastern states and Canadian Maritimes, it is the standard accompaniment to the traditional fiddler. In many rural homes, a small pump-organ (foot pedals provided the air pressure) would have served the same purpose as a piano but at much less expense.

Autoharp

The autoharp, a zither modified to facilitate chords, was invented in the late nineteenth century by C. A. Gütter of Germany. An American variety was patented in 1881 by Charles Zimmermann of Philadelphia to teach his new

musical notation system. His system was soon forgotten, but the instrument became widely popular in Anglo-American tradition in the early twentieth century, available through Sears catalogs.

The instrument has a series of chord bars that lie across the strings; when depressed, each bar damps out certain unwanted strings, thus producing a particular chord when the strings are strummed. Since the chord bars are labeled with the chord name, it is easy to play chord accompaniments. However, some traditional musicians have developed remarkably sophisticated playing styles using finger-picks, including such

Autoharp player (2004). *Photo courtesy of Robert N. Miller.*

devices as picking individual strings and changing bars in mid-stroke. Instruments have been made with various configurations; today's autoharps generally have thirty-six strings and either fifteen or twenty-one chord bars, designed so that the instrument is useful in seven different keys.

Accordion

The accordion, rare among Anglo-American and African American musicians, is a principal instrument in Franco-American and Hispanic American music, as well as among ethnic groups from central Europe (it was from German Americans that Cajuns and others picked up the instrument). Well into the twentieth century, the accordion used was the diatonic button variety (single-note buttons played with the right hand, chord buttons played with the left), which was the instrument's original form when it was invented in the 1820s. The right-hand piano keyboard with its chromatic scale was introduced in the 1850s.

Homemade Instruments

Poverty in many regions has forced inventive musicians to make musical instruments out of common household objects: the jug, the musical saw, the washboard and spoons (as rhythm instruments), the washtub bass as a poor-man's string bass, a comb and tissue paper serving as a kazoo, and the one-string guitar, consisting of a single strand of wire nailed to the outside wall of a house or barn. The first commercially successful jug band (consisting of jug, guitar, and fiddle—its successors also used banjos, washboards, kazoos, and other instruments) took to the streets of Louisville, Kentucky, in 1900, and for the next three decades that city was the center of jug band music. By the 1930s, Memphis had become home to the most successful jug bands, but by the next decade, the genre had all but faded away. Jug band music enjoyed a renaissance in the urban folksong revival of the 1960s.

A "one-man tin-can band" during a blackout in San Francisco (1941). *Photographer, John Collier (LC-USF34-081778-E); from the Farm Security Administration—Office of War Information Photo Collection, Library of Congress Prints and Photographs Division.*

Ensemble Traditions

There are many ensemble traditions among different ethnic communities. Most familiar is the ordinary string band still common in Anglo-American tradition and formerly among African Americans as well. Documentary evidence for two-instrument string bands goes back to colonial days. In 1774, Nicholas Creswell, an eighteenth-century colonial diarist, noted that "a great number of young people met together [in Virginia] with a fiddle and banjo played by two negroes."[6] Documentary and photographic evidence also shows the popularity of ensembles with fiddle(s), banjo(s), and cello in the latter half of the nineteenth century. Since the early 1900s, the mainstay instruments have been guitar, banjo, and fiddle; less commonly used are string bass, mandolin, cello, and/or harmonica.

The string band is primarily for accompanying dancing. However, the blue-grass band is a string band ensemble that developed in the 1940s and is primarily intended for listening rather than dancing. In string bands in the last few decades, the older acoustic guitar has often been replaced by a steel guitar or an electric guitar. Other ensembles deserve mention: fife- (or quills-) and-drum bands among African Americans in Mississippi; fife-and-drum bands among Anglo-Americans in Pennsylvania; African American brass marching bands in Louisiana (one of the forerunners of the jazz tradition) and similar brass band ensembles among Czech Americans in Texas; and tamburitza orchestras in communities of Serbian and Croatian descent.

After the 1920s, the spread of mass media, such as phonograph recordings and radio, exposed the musicians of each distinctive ethnic community to the musical styles of their neighbors, and the exchange of musical instruments, styles, tunes, and ideas flourished.

PERFORMANCE CHARACTERISTICS

For most of its history, American folk music has been transmitted orally from person to person. This does not mean that singers and musicians are illiterate or totally free from printed influences. We have moved a long way from the days of Margaret Laidlaw, one of Sir Walter Scott's ballad informants. In an oft-quoted anecdote, when shown Scott's printed versions of some of the songs she had sung for him, she responded sharply:

> There was never ane o' ma sangs prentit till ye prentit them yoursel' and ye hae spoilt them a' thegither. They were made for singing and no for reading, but ye hae broken the charm now and they'll never be sung mair. And the warst thing o' a', they're nouther right spell'd, nor right setten down.[7]

Certainly since the mid-twentieth century and probably earlier, American singers often learned songs from print and used print to reinforce their memories. Notations in the field collections of the 1920s occasionally mention that the performer sang or recited a song from a manuscript copy. Among some of the field recordings of Vance Randolph in the Ozarks from 1941 to 1942, now and then the rustle of pages in the background can be heard.

One of the advantages of early "instantaneous" recordings—that is, disc recordings made prior to the availability of magnetic tape or modern digital devices—is that one hears exactly what transpired in the recording process. When we hear a modern recording, we have no idea how many different "takes" were made before the performer pulled it all together. Nor can we be sure that what we hear isn't an engineer's artifact made from different pieces of separate takes, easy to do since the advent of magnetic recording tape and easier still with digital capabilities. The recordings of Vance Randolph and John Lomax, on acetate or aluminum disc, betray not only occasional paper rustling but also the singer pausing or stopping, hemming and hawing, muttering to himself, or being prompted by a relative sitting nearby or even by the collector himself. Even traditional singers of considerable skill suffer occasional lapses of memory. Frequently, an unaccompanied singer's pitch or tempo will drop gradually in the course of a song; an instrumentalist may gradually slow down.

Occasional deviations from classical Western scales among both singers and musicians on instruments without frets (fiddle and older, unfretted banjo) can also be heard. Often this reflects the limits of the performer's ability, but just as often, the performer is playing just what she or he wants to play. Thus, some singers consistently sing certain notes sharp or fiddlers fiddle flat.

Nonprofessional singers and musicians play to the limits of their abilities, however those abilities may be criticized by others. During such performances, the performer's intentions are heard as circumscribed by their abilities. When listening to professional musicians and singers from traditional backgrounds, what those communities accept as the aesthetic ideal is heard—and it may not agree with common ideals.

MODES AND SCALES

The modern musical keyboard is constructed so that any of twelve different keys can be sung or played, and they all sound the same—only higher or lower in pitch than one another. Some scales, however, do not sound like one another: for example, major and minor scales. A minor scale sounds different from a major scale because it consists of a different succession of half steps and full steps. It is also possible to play a sequence of eight notes on the piano with a quite different arrangement of half steps and full steps that sound neither major nor minor. These different sequences of notes are called "modes."

Musical modes are what gives a piece of music its recognizable character for most modern listeners (see Glossary). Some songs may sound sad to us because they are in a minor scale (C, D, E♭, F, G, A♭, B♭, C), and if we listen to an old Anglo-American folk tune, we might be aware of a peculiar sound that is neither major nor minor (C, D, E♭, F G, A, B♭, C). Although contemporary Western music, either classical or popular, is almost always written in either a major or a minor key, other musical traditions use other modes. In western European tradition, major and minor scales survived what was once a more extensive range of possibilities available to musicians and singers until the sixteenth century but which were gradually discarded as modern harmony practices evolved.

As with old ballads and fiddle music, old ideas remained in vogue among folk musicians long after being discarded by elite musicians. Two of these now rare modes, in particular, have occurred frequently in British and American folk music: the Dorian and the Mixolydian modes. The other common scales are the modern major scale, also called the Ionian mode, and a fourth mode called Aeolian, which is close to our modern natural minor scale.

It often happens that the notes of a melody do not include all seven notes of the mode. A hexatonic scale has only six of the notes, and a pentatonic scale has but five of them. These are also called gapped scales. The most common pentatonic scales are those that can be played by using only the black keys of the piano. Two of these occur frequently in American folk music: the one starting on D♯ (for example, "I Am a Poor Wayfaring Stranger") and the one starting on F♯ (for example, "Swing Low Sweet Chariot").

Unlike the full scales, tunes in pentatonic scales often do not start and end on the same central note, or tonic note. To modern listeners, this gives them an unfinished feeling, as if the singer should repeat the melody. It should be noted that traditional singers may not share a sense of unfulfillment in such endings. In fact, many aspects of folksong are handled by traditional singers in a manner foreign to outsiders. For example, modern listeners are more likely to be annoyed by extra beats in a measure or lines in a stanza than a traditional singer or instrumentalist would be.

The musical style of American folk music has always been influenced by the style of mainstream popular music, though often with considerable time lag. Well into the twentieth century, Anglo-American folksingers would sing songs and ballads in the older modes or in gapped scales rather than just in major and minor scales that had long since replaced the modes in popular and art music. Of the songs and ballads Cecil Sharp collected in the southern Appalachians from 1916 to 1918 that were published in *English Folk-Songs from the Southern Appalachians*, almost half were in pentatonic scales, and another 14 percent were in Mixolydian or Dorian modes. An unexpectedly small number were in the Ionian or Aeolian modes, remarkable considering that in modern music virtually all compositions are either major or minor. These results are very different from what Sharp collected in Britain, where the most common modes were Ionian. Surprisingly, he found no pentatonic melodies. Musical patterns in the Northeastern United States fall between those of England and those of the southern Appalachians.[8] Gapped scales were a part of African American folk song as well: half the folk songs collected in the late nineteenth century are in pentatonic or hexatonic scales.[9]

Putting these facts together, the following picture emerges: from the early 1900s through mid-century, pentatonic melodies constituted between 40 and 50 percent of American folk tunes in the South but a far smaller share in the North. Later, the composers and singers of newer songs tended to favor the modern major scale. Pentatonic melodies, if ever widespread in England, had died out there by the early 1900s, if not earlier; therefore, either American pentatonics reflects the "survival of the fringe," outliving its English sources, or more likely it represents the musical heritage from Scottish and Scotch-Irish ancestors. Chorded instrumental accompaniment (guitar or piano, in particular) is more suited to melodies in modern major and minor modes; this is one factor contributing to the declining use of other modes.

Although the twentieth century saw a strong movement away from gapped scales and toward the common major scale, there was nevertheless a tendency to avoid chromatic notes (sharps or flats—more accurately called accidental notes—within the major scale). Many nineteenth-century pop tunes by professional songwriters entered oral tradition in the southern United States but with considerable melodic alteration. In many instances the chromatic notes were altered, creating simplified diatonic scales—usually the common major scale.

SINGING STYLE

Older Anglo-American singers (prior to the assimilation of musical characteristics of African American singers and the effects of harmonic instrumental accompaniment, such as guitar, in the early twentieth century) often present a challenge to modern listeners, since they tended to avoid the rounded *bel canto* singing style and accompanying vibrato of trained singers, as well as any blue notes or relaxed swinging that permeate modern popular music. Instead, they commonly sang in a high-pitched, harsh-toned, highly melismatic voice, with many vocal decorations such as passing tones and a metrically uneven presentation reminiscent of speaking tempo (*rubato parlando*). Folk music collector Cecil Sharp noted one idiosyncrasy in the Appalachians that he never observed among English singers, namely, the habit of prolonging certain notes arbitrarily, generally not the strongly accented ones. Taken together these characteristics are often spoken of as "high lonesome style." In the Southeast, some singers favored a peculiar, sharply rising break in the voice at the end of phrases called "feathering"; in the Northeast, it was common for a singer to end a song by speaking, rather than singing, the last several words (called a *declamando* ending). These stylistic traits do not work well if the singer is accompanied on an instrument. The growing reliance on chorded instruments and the harmonic structures that their use required was one practical reason for the disappearance of the older singing traditions and the modal melodies; the influence of popular music was doubtless another.

Traditional singers in most genres avoid other devices commonly employed in art music or pop music, namely, modulation (that is, changing key), variation in dynamics, tempo, or timbre, or emotional display through body language. However, African American blues and gospel singers often use vocal coloration such as falsetto or a gravelly, growling voice, both of which can be used to great emotional effect. Yet to judge the traditional singer's failure to adhere to our modern notions of song presentation is to misinterpret the impact the songs have in their own communities. Ozark folklorist Vance Randolph described one of his experiences that helps to understand the traditional singer's style:

> In order fully to appreciate just how seriously the old songs are taken by the hill folk, one must note the reactions of the audience as well as the behavior of the singer. I have seen tears coursing down many a cheek and have more than once heard sobs and something near to bellowings as the minstrel sang of some more or less pathetic incident, which may have occurred in England

three or four hundred years ago. The old song of "Barbara Allen," which Samuel Pepys enjoyed in 1666, is still a moving tragedy in the Ozark hills.

On one memorable occasion I sat with seven mountain men in a smoky log kitchen, while a very old fellow quavered out the song known as "The Jealous Lover," one verse of which goes something like this:

> Down on her knees before him
> She humbly begged for life,
> But into her snow white bosom
> He pierced the fatal knife!

At this point the old man stopped short with a kind of gasping sob, and then burst out in such a paroxysm of rage that I was startled quite out of my chair. "Oh Gawd!" he shrilled, "the son-of-a-bitch! Dod *rot* such a critter, anyway!" Our host, a hard-faced moonshiner with at least one killing to his credit, muttered some similar sentiment, and there were grunts of sympathetic approval from several other listeners. It would have been a hardy "furriner" indeed who showed the slightest flicker of amusement at that moment.[10]

What makes a good singer? The criteria in a traditional community are (or at least, used to be) very different from those in art music or even in popular music. In art music, such as opera, singers are first of all expected to have beautiful, trained voices and use them in a particular manner of singing. Vibrato, dynamics, brilliance, and tonal clarity, dramatic expression, and some emotional display are all expected. Among traditional singers, most of these characteristics are, at best, irrelevant. In fact, listeners not used to traditional singers often find the singing nasal, piercing, erratic, or otherwise irritating. Pitch is not so flawless as among art or pop music singers; often one hears pitches that are consistent through a song but not consonant with the modern standard scales. Among traditional ballad singers and their own community audiences, most valued are good ballads (which is to say, complete texts), a wide repertoire, and a presentation style that doesn't interfere with the telling of the story. Ozark folksinger Almeda Riddle articulated the importance of story and presentation: "Nearly all the songs I sing have stories to them. I don't care a thing in this world—or hardly a thing—for a song that doesn't tell a story or teach a lesson."[11] And again, "A ballad, or any kind of traditional song (especially one of what I call the classics), you have to put yourself *behind* the song. By that I mean get out of the way of it. *Present* your story, don't *perform* it."[12]

Older secular singing almost always featured a solo voice, unaccompanied or with banjo or fiddle. Since the early twentieth century, guitar or full string band accompaniment has become common, and with it the increasing use of harmonization. In religious music, harmony or polyphony has been customary for much longer. Of course, as with everything else, continuing and increasing exposure to mass media tend to bend traditional aesthetics toward those of the popular genres.

RECOMMENDED RECORDINGS

Recordings listed here are all anthologies. Albums featuring individual artists are listed under the respective artists' names in Respective Biographical Sketches.

American Banjo Three Finger and Scruggs Style. Smithsonian Folkways, CD SF 40037; from Folkways, LP FA 2314.
American Fiddle Tunes [from] the Library of Congress Archive of Folk Culture. Rounder, 1518.
The Art of Traditional Fiddle. Rounder, 1166-11592-2.
Black Banjo Songsters of North Carolina and Virginia. Smithsonian Folkways, SF-CD-40079.
Close to Home: Old Time Music from Mike Seeger's Collection. Smithsonian Folkways, SF-CD-40097.
Lomax Collection: Southern Journey: Vols. 1–13. Rounder, CD 1701-13.
Mountain Music Bluegrass Style. Smithsonian Folkways, CD SF 40038; from Folkways, LP FA 2318.
Mountain Music of Kentucky. Smithsonian Folkways, SF CD-40077, 2 CDs.
The North Carolina Banjo Collection. Rounder, CD 0439/40.

The following CDs are reissues from commercial hillbilly and blues 78-rpm recordings of the 1920s and 1930s.

The Cornshucker's Frolic, Vols. 1/2. Yazoo, 2045/46.
Hard Times Come Again No More, Vol. 1/2: Early American Rural Songs of Hard Times and Hardships. Yazoo, 2036/37.
My Rough and Rowdy Ways, Vols. 1/2. Yazoo, 2039/40.
The Rose Grew around the Briar: Early American Rural Love Songs, Vols. 1/2. Yazoo, 2030/31.
Times Ain't Like They Used to Be: Early American Rural Music, Vols. 1–4. Yazoo, 2028/29 and 2047/48.

NOTES

1. Liner notes to *Southern Banjo Sounds*, p. 6. Recording: Smithsonian Folkways, SFW CD 40107, 1998.

2. More precisely, the strings, starting with the drone, are tuned to g^4 d^3 g^3 b^3 and d^4. The superscripts on the names of the notes indicate the octave, with superscript 1 indicating the lowest octave on the piano and 8, the highest. In general, only in the piano's middle three or four octaves are relevant.

3. Kendall: "Great numbers of the men can strum the mandolin, a species of small guitar," as quoted in *Narr. Santa Fe Exped.* (II) 93 (1844).

4. Jean Ritchie, *The Dulcimer Book* (New York: Oak, 1974), p. 11.

5. Samuel Bayard, *Dance to the Fiddle, March to the Fife: Instrumental Folk Tunes in Pennsylvania* (University Park, PA, & London: Pennsylvania State University Press, 1982), p. 4.

6. Nicholas Creswell, *The Journal of Nicholas Creswell 1774–1777* (New York: Dial Press, 1924).

7. James Hogg, *The Domestic Manners and Private Life of Sir Walter Scott* (Glasgow, 1834), p. 61.

8. Helen Hartness Flanders, *Ancient Ballads Traditionally Sung in New England*, vols. 1–4 (Philadelphia: University of Pennsylvania Press, 1960–1965).

9. Henry Edward Krehbiel, *Afro-American Folksongs: A Study in Racial and National Music* (New York: Ungar, 1962), p. 43. In an analysis of folk songs from half a dozen collections published between 1867 and 1907, Krehbiel found that 63 percent were in the ordinary major scale, 12 percent minor, 21 percent various pentatonic scales, and 30 percent various hexatonic scales (either major lacking the seventh or the fourth or minor lacking the sixth).

10. Vance Randolph, *Ozark Folk-Songs*, vol. 1 (Columbia, MO: Missouri Historical Society, 1946–1950), pp. 34–35.

11. Roger D. Abrahams, ed., *A Singer and Her Songs: Almeda Riddle's Book of Ballads* (Baton Rouge: Louisiana State University Press, 1970), p. 112.

12. Ibid., p. 122.

3
Folk Music of the Northeast

NEW ENGLAND AND THE NORTH ATLANTIC

The nation's first decennial census in 1790 showed that the New England region, including New Hampshire, Massachusetts, Rhode Island, Connecticut, and what were to become the states of Maine and Vermont, was the most ethnically homogeneous in the new nation. Some 77 to 87 percent of each state's population was of English origin. Their ancestors sailed to the New World in the earliest migrations, coming from East Anglia prior to 1640. Most of the remaining immigrants were Scotch-Irish from Northern Ireland. Folk song collectors in the twentieth century found in New England a wealth of older British ballads traceable to the seventeenth and eighteenth centuries; however, the continued contact with England facilitated by the busy seaports meant that ballads originating in England in the nineteenth century also found their way to New England and took root. The American Revolution and the War of 1812 were both fought in or near New England, so that ballads relating to these conflicts remained in oral tradition into the twentieth century.

New England collectors have commented on the high percentage of literacy among traditional singers, a reflection of three centuries of greater attention to schooling and education than elsewhere in the country, starting with the earliest English immigrants. Among eighteenth-century settlers, New Englanders had four to five years of schooling, compared to one to four years in other regions.

As late as 1930, the average number of school attendance days in the Northeast ranged from 135 to 150, in contrast to the 75 to 95 typical of the Southeast.

Many New England singers accumulated their own notebooks of songs and ballads, which seems to have slowed down the rate of text deterioration. Occasionally singers would use these handwritten texts as prompts when they sang into the collector's microphone. Long, carefully preserved ballad texts may suggest the singer was influenced by printed sources.

In the nineteenth century two ethnically distinct communities made their own contributions to the music of the region: the French Canadians, who drifted south when they were expelled from their New World homes in the 1750s; and the Irish immigrants who, in the years following the great Irish potato famine of the 1840s, came in large numbers to the New World, settling mostly in large cities such as Boston and New York. The Irish brought with them the broadside ballad tradition that thrived in England and Ireland in the mid-nineteenth century: songs about sailors and soldiers, merchants and innkeepers that reflected the newly industrialized British Isles. New England ballad tunes often show traces of Irish musical style, in the tunes themselves, in the singing style, and in the language.

For example, one New England characteristic, *declamando*, is a device common among older Irish singers and has recently been deliberately revived by younger Irish singers to create an air of authenticity in their music. In other styles (such as contemporary pop or art music), the end of a song is signaled by the singer slowing the tempo or decreasing the singing volume. These devices are rare among traditional singers, but the *declamando* ending would serve equally well to let the audience know that the song's end had come. In other respects in the presentation of ballads in general, the Northeastern style is remarkably free of such vocal embellishments as passing tones and melisma, traits that are characteristic of the "high lonesome" style of Appalachian singing. In fact, to many modern ears, many Northeastern ballad singers sound drearily flat and monotonous.

Much of this regional distinction between areas north and south of the Mason-Dixon line is a result of the absence of significant African American musical influence in New England, clearly a consequence of the relatively small black population there. The instruments associated with African Americans, in particular banjo but also guitar,[1] are rare in New England, as are the syncopated musical styles evident in such genres as ragtime, blues, and gospel.

Instrumental music in New England also strongly reflects the same two ethnic traditions of the Irish and the French Canadians, with an influence disproportionate to their relative numbers. The instrumental combination one was most likely to find at country dances and other social events until late in the twentieth century was the fiddle with piano accompaniment. Much more than in the South, New England fiddlers often were able to read music. When they couldn't, they could take advantage of their musically literate piano accompanists to help them learn new tunes from the many published songbooks that had been available for over a century.

The music of the North Atlantic states, including New York, Pennsylvania, Delaware, and New Jersey, is similar to that of New England, except that it shows evidence also of the contributions of two European groups whose songs and instrumental music have survived down to our own time. In 1790, for example, only 50 percent of the people of New York and New Jersey were descendants of English settlers, and in Pennsylvania, only 26 percent. Most of the remainder was from Holland (16 percent of New York, 20 percent of New Jersey), Germany (38 percent of Pennsylvania), and Switzerland. Their legacy exists not only in secular songs and instrumental music but also in the religious hymns and spirituals of such central European–derived Protestant sects as the Amish, Mennonites, Moravians, and the Church of the Brethren.

Collectors in the twentieth century found that many of the older Child ballads flourished in New England. Here they are presented in decreasing order of recoveries:[2]

- "Lord Randal"
- "Golden Vanity"
- "The Elfin Knight"
- "The Gypsy Davy"
- "Lady Isabel and the Elf-Knight"
- "Barbara Allen"
- "Lord Bateman"
- "The House Carpenter"
- "The Farmer's Curst Wife"
- "Lord Lovel"
- "Henry Martin"

Apart from a few motifs, such as maritime themes found in "Golden Vanity," "Lord Bateman," "The House Carpenter," and "Henry Martin," the first three of which are rare in the South, it is generally difficult to account for the greater popularity of particular ballads in certain regions. (The plots of these ballads are summarized in the Appendix.)

Of the later imported ballads (broadside ballads), the most frequently found are as follows:

- "Yorkshire Bite"
- "The Bold Soldier"
- "The Butcher Boy"
- "Katie Morey"
- "The Half Hitch"
- "Boston Burglar"

The most frequently reported indigenous ballads are as follows:

- "Springfield Mountain"
- "The Jam on Gerry's Rock"
- "Young Charlotte"

- "Peter Amberley"
- "Jack Haggarty"
- "The Jealous Lover"

When the Northeast was originally settled by Europeans, the first occupations that developed, apart from farming, were determined by the geography: fishing, whaling, and timbering. Northeast folk song collections abound in maritime songs and sea shanties, especially in the neighborhoods of such Massachusetts seaports as New Bedford, Nantucket, Salem, Plymouth, and Boston.

Charles Murphy, a seaman from Nantucket, wrote "A Song on the Nantucket Ladies" in his journal while on the ship *Diana* in 1819. It gives a remarkably detailed view of town life at the time and, in particular, of the young women who "cruised" the streets of Sherbourn—the old name for Nantucket village. Murphy says his ship went around Cape Horn, meaning it was sailed into the Pacific to hunt sperm whales, a voyage that could easily last three years. In that long time one can well imagine how restless the sweethearts left in Nantucket became.

Large sailing and whaling ships required tall, straight timbers for masts, and so Maine woodsmen began to harvest the state's abundant virgin forests. Ballads and songs of lumberjacks were widespread, as expected considering the importance of this occupation in the nineteenth century, especially in Maine, then gradually moving westward as forests were depleted from extensive timber cutting.

One song, "The Lumberman in Town," collected frequently in Maine early in the twentieth century, portrayed the lumberman's life as having a few happy moments but a good deal more of sadness. The experience of the hospitality drying up when the money runs out is certainly not unique to Maine lumbermen. The reference to crowns as a coin is explained by the origin of the song in the Canadian provinces; many Canadians moved down into Maine attracted by the lumbering opportunities there and brought songs from the Maritimes with them. The melancholic mood of self-pity is also more characteristic of Canadian than Maine woods songs.

While whaling and sailing songs, songs of the lumbermen, and textile mill songs all dealt with ongoing daily life in New England, other social and historical events of a more limited duration gave rise to songs, some of which have survived for over two centuries. Massachusetts's woods and vales still echo with the "shot heard 'round the world" that started the American Revolution, and some wonderful songs were composed between military skirmishes. From Martha's Vineyard comes the version printed here of "Gunpowder Tea," a reference to the Boston Tea Party of December 16, 1773, when a band of Boston patriots, disguised as Native Americans, dumped a ship load of tea into the Boston Harbor in angry resentment over the Tea Tax. The song is sung to the tune of the English nursery song "Polly Put the Kettle On." The reference to Saratoga, where British General Burgoyne was humiliatingly defeated by

"A Song on the Nantucket Ladies"

Young damsels all where ever you may be,
I pray attention give to me;
Some braken hints I will lay down
About the girls in Sherbourn town.

When eve comes on they dress up neat,
And go a-cruising through the streets;
To see if they some beaus can find
To suit their fancy and their minds.

Skein laces long and frills so neat
And bunnets worked so complete;
With their painted cheeks and curled hair,
They think to make the young men stare.

Their long silk gowns and sleeves so big
You'd think that they had run the rig;
With their white kid shoes and silken hose
They look like the devil in their clothes.

They get the beaus all for to make
A corset board to make them straight;
They'll bind it to their waist so tight
And through the streets about from morn till night.

Then a few false teeth they're sure to wear
And foretop curls and false hair;
And a false heart that'll ne'er prove true,
We find it's so, it's nothing new.

They go to the factory every day
And work twelve months without their pay;
And then all for to crown the joke
Why Daniel Dusten is broke.

Then Henry Gardner and Peleg West
Then they will do their best,
They say that they do what is right
And pay the girls every Saturday night.

The girls being few with such ideas,
Thinking their master for to please,
For six pense [sic] a day to work they go
And then they cut a dreadful show.

When round Cape Horn their sweethearts go
Then they must have another beau;
To wait two years, they say they can't,
To wait two years, they say they shan't.

And when their beaus they do come back,
Such lamentations they will make;
Saying, "No one has courted me but you dear,
So come along and never fear."

"Oh," says the beaus, "That never do,
I'll never be taken in by you,
If you keep on you'll make me laugh,
You cannot catch old birds with chaff."

But always give the devil his due,
There's some will wait, 'tis very true;
The reason it doth plainly show,
They cannot catch another beau.

This song was made around Cape Horn,
Where most of the young men are gone.
Haul down your flag, cut down your staff,
It is all true, you need not laugh.

Now, to conclude and end my song,
There's women tells me I am rong [sic],
But if by chance they find it's right,
They may sing it from morn till night.*

*Transcribed and published by Gale Huntington in *Songs the Whalemen Sang* (Barre, ME: Barre Publishing, 1965), pp. 165–167. Punctuation has been added, but original spelling is retained. "Braken" is an old-fashioned New England term for torn, flawed; "bunnit" means bonnet.

American troops in October 1777, suggests that the song was not written until a few years after the party in Boston Harbor.

Some folk songs focus on events that were locally important at the time but, at a remove of a couple centuries, seem inconsequential. A good example is "James Bird," a once well-known ballad about the Battle of Lake Erie, which took place on September 10, 1813, during the War of 1812.

"James Bird" was written by a journalist, Charles Miner (1780–1865), who printed it in a newspaper he edited, the Wilkes-Barre, Pennsylvania, *Gleaner* in

"The Lumberman in Town"

When the lumberman comes down,
Every pocket bears a crown,
And he wanders, some pretty gal to find;
If she's not too sly, with her dark and rolling eye,
The lumberman is pleased in his mind,
The lumberman is pleased in his mind.

The landlady comes in,
She is dressed so neat and trim,
She looks just like an evenin' star;
She's ready to wait on him, if she finds him in good
   trim,
Chalk him down for two to one at the bar,
Chalk him down for two to one at the bar.

The lumberman goes on,
Till his earnt money's all spent an' gone,
Then the landlady begins to frown;
With her dark and rolling eye, this will always be
   her cry,
"Lumberman, it is time that you were gone,
Lumberman, it is time that you were gone."

She gives him to understand,
There's a boat to be a-manned,
And away up the river he must go;

Good liquor and a song, it's go hitch your
   horses on,
Bid adieu to the girls of St. Johns,
Bid adieu to the girls of St. Johns.

To the woods he will go,
With his heart so full of woe,
And he wanders from tree after tree;
Till six months have gone and past, he forgets it all
   at last,
"It is time I should have another spree,
"It is time I should have another spree."

When old age does him alarm,
He will settle on a farm,
And he'll find some young girl to be his wife;
But to his sad mistake, she mock love to him will
   make,
And kind death will cut the tender threads of life,
And kind death will cut the tender threads of life.*

*Taken down in 1901 from the singing of Mack Dyer of
East Eddington, Maine, and published in Fannie Hardy
Eckstorm and Mary Winslow Smith, *Minstrelsy of Maine:
Folk-Songs and Ballads of the Woods and the Coast* (Boston
and New York: Houghton Mifflin Co., 1927), pp. 96–97.

"Gunpowder Tea"

Johnny Bull and many more,
Soon they say are coming o'er,
And as soon as they're on shore
They must have tea.

CHORUS:
So Polly, put the kettle on,
Blow the bellows good and strong,
Polly put the kettle on,
We'll give them tea.

They'll want it strong, you need not dread,
Sweetened well with sugar of lead;
Perhaps it will go to their head
And spoil their taste for tea.

As soon as they put foot on shore,
Their cups we'll fill them o'er and o'er,
With such as John Bull drank before,
Nice Saratoga Tea.

So let them come as soon's they can,
They'll find us at our post each man,
Their hides we will completely tan
Before they get their tea.*

*As sung by E. G. Huntington. Recording: *Folksongs from
Martha's Vineyard* (Folkways, LP/Cass FA 2032, 1958).
Learned from the singing of the Tilton brothers of Martha's
Vineyard, Masssachusetts. Sugar of lead means lead ace-
tate, a sweet but poisonous salt, or the phrase may simply
mean, "flavor it with gunshot."

▸ JAMES BIRD.

1. Sons of pleasure listen to me, and ye daughters all give ear,
You a sad and mournful story as was ever told shall hear :
Hull you know his troops surrendered, and defenceless left the West,
Then our forces quick assembled the invader to resist.

2. Among the troops that marched to Erie, were the Kingston Volunteers ;
Captain Thomas them commanded, to protect our west frontiers.
Tender were the scenes of parting; mothers wrung their hands and cried,
Maidens wept in secret ; fathers strove their tears to hide :

3. But there's one among the number tall and graceful in his mein ;
Firm his step, his look undaunted, ne'er a nobler youth was seen ;
One sweet kiss he snatched from Mary, crav'd his mother's prayers once
more,
Press'd his father's hands, and left them for Lake Erie's distant shore.

4. Mary tried to say " farewell James," waved her hand, but nothing
spoke !
Farewell Bird ! may Heaven protect you ! from the rest a parting broke.
Soon they came where noble Perry had assembled all his fleet ;
There the gallant Bird enlisted, hoping soon the foe to meet.

5. Where is Bird?—the battle rages—is he in the strife or no ?
Now the cannons roar tremendous, dare he boldly meet his foe ?
Ah ! behold him ; see with Perry in the self-same ship they fight ;
Though his messmates fall around him, nothing can his soul affright:

6. But behold a ball has struck him, see the crimson current flow.
Leave the deck, exclaimed brave Perry ;—no, cries Bird, I will not go ;

Here on deck I'll take my station, ne'er will Bird his colours fly ;
I'll stand by you, gallant Captain, till we conquer or we die.

7. So he fought, though faint and bleeding, till our stars and stripes arose,
Victory having crown'd our efforts, all triumphant o'er our foes ;
And did Bird receive a pension ? was he to his friends restor'd ?
No, nor ever to his bosom clasp'd the maid his heart ador'd ;—

8. But there came most dismal tidings from Lake Erie's distant shore ;
Better if poor Bird had perish'd midst the battle's awful roar.
Dearest parents, said the letter, this will bring sad news to you ;
Do not mourn your best beloved, though it brings his last adieu !

9. I must suffer for deserting from the brig Niagara—
Read this letter, brothers, sisters, 'tis the last you'll have from me;
Sad and gloomy was the morning Bird was ordered out to die ;
Where's the breast not dead to pity, but for him will heave a sigh ?

10. Though he fought so brave at Erie, freely bled and nobly dar'd,
Let his courage plead for mercy, let his precious life be spar'd.
See him march, and hear his fetters, harsh they clang upon the ear;
Though his steps are firm and manly, for his breast ne'er harboured fear.

11. See he kneels upon his coffin ; sure his death can do no good ;
Spare him—hark ! oh God ! they've shot him ; oh ! his bosom streams
with blood !
Farewell Bird, farewell for ever ; friends and home he'll see no more ;
But his mangled corpse lies buried on Lake Erie's distant shore.

"James Bird," a broadside from the 1840s (ID: CPM, 002729-Broad). *Courtesy of the Kenneth S. Goldstein Collection, Center for Popular Music, Middle Tennessee State University.*

1814. Bird enlisted and fought bravely with Commodore Perry on the *Lawrence* and was wounded. After he recovered, he deserted from guard duty watching over government stores. He was captured, court-martialed, and convicted, and in October 1814, was executed on board the *Niagara*. Miner, a strong Bird partisan, is accurate in his depiction of the events, but he clearly feels that Bird's heroism should have exonerated his infraction. The text is written in a very polished and educated style. It has none of the commonplaces or stylized conventions of other ballads discussed in Chapter 1.

This version, collected in the 1960s, is remarkably close to Miner's original text of 150 years earlier, except for the final stanza, which was added by someone else in the intervening years—possibly a considerable number of years later considering the phrase, "aye, unto this present day." Only around the Great Lakes and New England area did the ballad remain a favorite, but there it could still be heard long after all the participants in the war had departed. That the ballad remained current so widely and so long is a tribute to the durability of oral lore.

As a consequence of where the population was centered and where most of the battles were fought, the ballads from the Revolutionary War and War of 1812 were mainly confined to the Northeastern part of the country. In contrast, Civil War battles took place over a wider geographic region, and so the great

"James Bird"

You sons of freedom listen to me, and you daughters
   too, give ear,
You a sad a mournful story as we ever told shall
   hear;
Hull, you know, his troops surrendered, and
   defenseless left the West,
Our forces quick assembled, the invaders to resist.

There was one amongst the number, tall, graceful
   and serene,
Firm his step, his look undaunted, ne'er a nobler
   youth was seen.
One fond kiss he snatched from Mary, craved his
   mother's prayer once more,
Pressed his father's hand and left them for Lake
   Erie's distant shore.

Soon he came where noble Perry had assembled all
   his fleet.
Here this noble Bird enlisted, expecting soon the
   foe to meet.
Where is Bird when battle rages? Is he in the strife
   or no?
Hark, the cannon's roar tremendous, here we meet
   our furious foe.

But behold! a ball has struck him, see the crimson
   current flow.
"Leave the deck!" exclaimed brave Perry. "No,"
   cried Bird, "I will not go.
Here on deck I took my station, Bird will ne'er his
   colors fly;
I will stand by you, brave Perry, till we conquer or
   we die."

And did Bird receive a pension, or was he to his
   friends restored?
No, nor ever to his bosom clasped the maid his
   heart adored.

But there came most dismal tidings from Lake Erie's
   distant shore;
Better there that brave Bird had perished after the
   battle's awful roar.

"Dearest father, tell my mother when this letter
   reaches you,
Not to mourn, her first beloved oh dearly bids his
   last adieu.
I'm a sufferer for deserting from the brig *Niagary*,
Dearest mother, read this letter, 'tis the last you'll
   hear from me."

Dark and dismal was the morning Bird was ordered
   out to die.
Where's the heart that would not pity or for him
   would heave a sigh?
See him kneel upon his coffin, sure his death can
   do no good.
Spare him! Hark! O God, they've shot him, see his
   bosom stream with blood!

Farewell, Bird, farewell forever! Home nor friends
   you'll see no more,
Now his mangled corpse lies buried on Lake Erie's
   distant shore.
Bird will ever be remembered, aye unto this present
   day.
Oh, what can beset wrong them who engage in war
   or fray?*

*"James Bird" (Laws, A 5). As sung by O. J. Abbott of Hull,
Quebec, Canada. Collected by Edith Fowke. Recording:
Folkways FM 4018: *Songs of the Great Lakes*, 1964.

abundance of Civil War music has left its mark in many parts of the country.
"The *Cumberland*'s Crew" concerns a battle in Chesapeake Bay; nevertheless,
the ballad is remembered primarily in the Northeast and around the Great
Lakes where maritime songs in general thrived the best. The ballad text is written in stanzas of eight lines, which correspond to the double-length melody. In
what used to be a characteristic singing device in the northern states and
Canada, the singer renders the last four words of the song *declamando*.

This ballad describes one of the great naval battles of the Civil War that marked a major change in maritime warfare. On March 8, 1862, off the coast of Newport News, Virginia, the Northern frigate *Cumberland* was engaged by the Confederate *Merrimac*, the first ironclad fighting ship and the secret weapon of the Confederacy. The men in the square rigger watched helplessly as their cannon fire bounced harmlessly off the iron sides of the strange-looking, armor-plated vessel. The *Merrimac* closed in and rammed the *Cumberland* mid-ship, and the stricken vessel quickly sank. Over one hundred sick and wounded, who could not be removed from the ship, perished. The following day the *Merrimac* was in turn defeated by the Yankee ironclad *Monitor*.

Between the War of 1812 and the Civil War, the nation embarked on a program of steady westward expansion. One aspect of the growth was the extensive canal building in the Northeastern states in the early 1800s. Early in the period of westward movement, the rivers offered promise as a principal means of transporting goods and people. Farsighted individuals envisioned canals as manmade extensions of the natural rivers that could greatly facilitate transportation. Today, we recall principally the Erie Canal, which runs west from Albany to Buffalo, but this was just the first of many. Construction on the Erie Canal began in 1817 and was completed in 1825. Many others followed it, and altogether some 3,000 miles of inland waterways had been constructed by the 1840s. Their heyday was cut short in the 1850s with the rapid growth of the railroads, which soon made the canals obsolete. Early opponents to the railroads—who objected to them on various grounds of safety, noise, pollution, and undependability—found natural allies in the canal interests, who saw their own financial investments seriously threatened. The canals

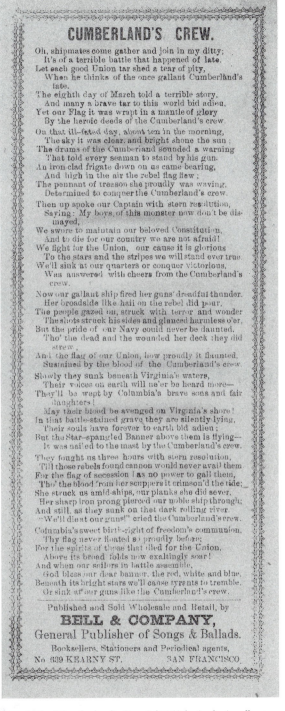

Broadside: "*Cumberland's* Crew" (1860s). *Author's collection.*

"The *Cumberland's* Crew"

Now then, shipmates, come gather and join in my
  ditty,
Of a terrible battle that happened of late;
When each Union tar shed a tear of sad pity,
When he heard of the once gallant *Cumberland*'s
  fate.
On the eighth day of March told a terrible story,
And many brave tars to this world bid adieu;
Our flag it was wrapped in a mantle of glory
By the heroic deeds of the *Cumberland*'s crew.

On the ill-fated day about ten in the morning,
The sky it was clear and bright shone the sun;
The drums of the *Cumberland* sounded a warning
That told every seaman to stand by his gun.
Then an ironclad frigate down on us came bearing,
And high in the air the Rebel flag flew;
The pennant of treason she proudly was wearing,
Determined to conquer the *Cumberland*'s crew.

Then up spoke our captain with stern resolution,
Saying, "Boys, of this monster now don't be
  dismayed;

We've sworn to maintain our beloved Constitution,
And to die for our country, we are not afraid."
Our noble ship fired, our guns dreadfully thundered,
Our shot on the Rebel like hail did we pour;
The people on shore gazed with terror and wonder,
As the shots struck her sides and glanced
  harmlessly o'er.

Now the pride of our Navy can never be daunted,
Though the dead and the wounded our decks they
  did strew;
"We'll die at our quarters or conquer victorious,"
Was answered in cheers by the *Cumberland*'s crew.
We've fought for the Union, our cause it is glorious,
To the Star-Spangled Banner we'll ever be true;
Wherever we are we'll make tyranny tremble,
Or we'll die by our guns like the *Cumberland*'s
  crew.*

*"The *Cumberland*'s Crew" (Laws, A 18). As sung by
Stanley Bâby of Toronto, Onterio, Canada. Collected by
Edith Fowke. Recording: Folkways, LP FM 4018: *Songs of
the Great Lakes*, 1964.

bred a host of songs and ballads, most of which died out in the nineteenth century as the canals themselves became obsolete, but a few, in particular about the Erie, were still well remembered into the twentieth century.

Storms on a canal may seem unlikely today, but they once posed a real hazard. Not as well known as the Erie was the Delaware & Hudson Canal, opened in 1828 and abandoned in 1898. It covered a distance of 108 miles and required as many locks. "The D&H Canal" tells about events during a spring flood of 1878. It was sung to the tune of "Pop Goes the Weasel," a new song in the 1850s.

The most frequently reported ballad of the Northeast (though comparatively uncommon in the Southeast) comes not out of war experience or occupational lore but out of a simple, common domestic tragedy. This is "Springfield Mountain," a tale that describes the death of Timothy Myrick in Connecticut in 1761 and probably the oldest indigenous ballad to survive into the twentieth century. The long and persistent popularity of this ballad must reflect in part the great concern over snakes in rural areas; tales such as this could have served as warnings to young children not to run off alone into the woods.

In the 1830s a comic stage version was published, which soon also entered oral tradition alongside the older serious one, especially in the Southeast. It may puzzle listeners of a later era how the story of a tragic death could have been made into a successful comic song. The language of the latter appears to

"The E-ri-E"

We were forty miles from Albany,
Forget it, I never shall;
What a terrible storm we had one night,
On the E-ri-e canal.

CHORUS:
Oh, the E-ri-e was a-risin', and the gin was a-gettin'
    low;
And I scarcely think we'll get a drink till we get to
    Buffalo,
Till we get to Buffalo.

We were loaded down with barley,
We were chock up full of rye;
The Captain he looked down on me,
With his gol-durn wicked eye.

Two days out from Syracuse,
The vessel struck a shoal;
And we like to all been foundered,
On a chunk of Lackawanna coal.

We hollered to the captain
On the towpath, treadin' dirt;
He jumped on board and stopped the leak
With his old red flannel shirt.

The cook she was a grand old gal,
She wore a ragged dress;
We heisted her upon the pole,
As a signal of distress.

The wind begin to whistle
The waves begin to roll,
We had to reef our royals
On that raging Canal.

When we got to Syracuse,
Off-mule he was dead,
The nigh mule got blind staggers
We cracked him on the head.

The captain, he got married,
The cook, she went to jail;
And I'm the only sea-cook son,
That's left to tell the tale.*

*Pete Seeger, "Erie Canal," *Frontier Ballads* (Folkways, LP
FA 2175, 1954). A towpath is the ground path paralleling
the canal along which mules, pulling the barge by ropes,
were driven; nigh mule and off mule are the mules nearer
to, and further from, the windy side, respectively; blind
staggers is a disease of the brain and spinal cord affecting
horses, mules, and so on; reef means roll up; royals are small
square, usually topmost, sails; the sea cook's son is usually
a son of a gun, which was originally a child born at sea on
voyage long enough that wives were permitted on board.

"The D&H Canal"

Around and 'round the Wurtsburo bend
The big boat chased the squeezer.
Pat Flax's boat had passed them both,
Slicker than the weasel (2).

In Eighteen Seventy-Eight,
The canal was hit by a freshet;
The embankment broke and flooded The Vly,
The damage was terrific (2).

A load of cement went through the break,
Houses and barns were uprooted;
To try and save whatever they could,
To the river the big boat scooted (2).*

*As sung by Harry Siemsen in Sawkill, New York, in 1955.
Published in Norman Cazden, Herbert Haufrecht, and
Norman Studer, *Folk Songs of the Catskills* (Albany, NY:
State University of New York, 1982), p. 624. A "squeezer"
is a canal barge so wide it doesn't leave room for another to
pass. The Vly is a mountain in the Catskills.

"Springfield Mountain"

On Springfield Mountain there did dwell
A handsome youth, was known full well;
Lieutenant Merrill's only son,
A likely youth, near twenty-one.

On Friday morning he did go
Down to the meadows for to mow.
He mowed, he mowed all around the field,
With a poisonous serpent at his heel.

When he received his deathly wound
He laid his scythe down on the ground.
For to return was his intent,
Calling aloud, long as he went.

His calls were heard both far and near
But no friends to him did appear.
They thought he did some workman call;
Alas, poor man, alone did fall.

Day being past, night coming on,
The father went to seek his son,
And there he found his only son
Cold as a stone, dead on the ground.

He took him up and he carried him home,
And on the way did lament and mourn;
Saying, "I heard but did not come,
And now I'm left alone to mourn."

In the month of August, the twenty-first,
When this sad accident was done.
May this a warning be to all,
To be prepared when God shall call.*

*As sung by Josiah S. Kennison in Townshend, Vermont.
Published in Helen H. Flanders and George Brown,
Vermont Folk-Songs and Ballads (1931; repr., Hatboro, PA:
Folklore Associates, 1968), pp. 15–16.

satirize the speech of the rural Yankee, and by trivializing the death, the song was probably intended to make fun of the rustic folk and their agrarian lifestyle in a way no longer considered acceptable. Snakes, after all, tend not to be city dwellers.

While tragedies and disasters, such as the story of "Springfield Mountain," were once the standard fare of folk ballads in the same way that they still fill our newspapers, one also finds an assortment of songs that relate to lifestyle in general rather than specific momentous events. Few natural products are more strongly associated with the Northeast than maple syrup and related products. The delightful "Vermont Sugar-Maker's Song" was attributed to Reverend Perrin B. Fiske, born in Waitsfield, Vermont, in 1837. No tune was given with the text, but it can be sung quite easily to the "Battle Hymn of the Republic." The circumstances of its composition are not known, but one can well imagine that it was written for some local festival or pageant and somehow managed to survive beyond its expected useful lifetime.

The expression "down east" refers to Maine and the Maritime provinces of Canada. A "down-easter" is either a person or a vessel from that region. The term has been used at least since the 1820s. "Away Down East" was a favorite song of the Hutchinson Family, a singing troupe that held concerts throughout New England and the eastern states in the 1840s and 1850s, often supporting such social causes as temperance and abolition. Like the preceding song, this can be sung to the "Battle Hymn of the Republic."

A century or so after the preceding two songs were current, the United States found itself awash in the midst of a social experiment that did not go as well as

"Vermont Sugar-Maker's Song"

When you see the vapor pillars lick the forest and
   the sky,
You may know the days of sugar-making then are
   drawing nigh.
Frosty night and sunny day make the maple pulses
   play
Till congested with their sweetness, they delight to
   bleed away.

CHORUS:
Oh, bubble, bubble, bubble, bubble, bubble goes
   the pan.
Furnish better music for the season if you can;
See the golden billows; watch their ebb and flow;
Sweetest joys indeed we sugar-makers know.

When you see the farmer trudging with his dripping
   buckets home
You may know the days of sugar-making then have
   fairly come;
While the fragrant odors pour through the open
   kitchen door,
How the eager children rally, ever loudly calling
   "more!"

If you say you don't believe it, take a saucer and a
   spoon;
Though you're sourer than a lemon, you'll be
   sweeter very soon,
For the greenest leaves you see on the spreading
   maple tree,
Though they sip and sip all summer will the
   autumn beauties be.

And for home—, or love—, or any kind of sickness,
   'tis the thing.
Take in allopathic doses and repeat it every Spring;
Until everyone you meet, if at home or on the
   street,
Will have half a mind to bite you, you will look so
   very sweet.*

*Contributed by Anna H. Dole of Danville, Vermont.
Published in Helen H. Flanders and George Brown,
Vermont Folk-Songs and Ballads (1931; repr., Hatboro, PA:
Folklore Associates, 1968), pp. 33–34.

its advocates had hoped: this was the attempt to legislate away the consumption of alcoholic beverages by a constitutional amendment. In parts of the southern mountains, moonshiners evaded the restrictions of the Eighteenth Amendment by distilling their own liquors. In Upstate New York the demand for alcohol led to furtive efforts to smuggle the product across the border from Canada, where it was still legal. Enterprising young "rumrunners" brought cases of rum and other alcohol products as far south as New York City, where it found its way into the "speakeasies"—nightclubs that sold illegal liquor to the city's eager customers. One song that arose from this operation was a clever parody of a familiar nursery rhyme, "Sing a Song of Sixpence."

The striking difference between the style (and to some extent, content) of the folk songs of the Northeast and those of the Southeast has been noted several times. Unlike the Southwest (home of western and western swing) and the Southeast (home of hillbilly, bluegrass, and country music), the Northeast did not develop a commercial folk-derived tradition to any great extent. Commercial genres serve to develop and modify their underlying folk traditions, resulting in faster changes than might otherwise have occurred. While some writers have argued for a "country music" tradition in Upstate New York and New England based on the local dance music, its significance is, at best, regional.

"Away Down East"

There's a famous fabled country never seen by
mortal eyes,
Where the punkins are a-growin', and the sun is
said to rise,
Which man doth not inhabit, neither reptile, bird,
nor beast.
But one thing we're assured of, it's away down east!

It is called a land of notions, of apple sauce and
greens,
A paradise of punkin pies, a land of pork and beans.
But where it is who knoweth? neither mortal, man,
nor beast.
But one thing we're assured of, it's away down east!

Once a man in Indiana took his bundle in his hand,
And he went to New York City for to find this
famous land.
But how he stares on learning this curious fact at
least:
He'd nowhere near begun to get away down east!

So he traveled on to Bangor, whereby he soiled his
drabs,
And the first that greets his vision is a pyramid of
slabs.
Oh, sure this must be Egypt, 'tis a pyramid, at least.
And he thought that with a vengeance, he had
found down east.*

*From the singing of Jennie Hardy Linscott, in whose family it was sung for generations. Published by Eloise Hubbard Linscott in *Folk Songs of Old New England* (1939; repr., Hamden, CT: Archon, 1962), pp. 158–160. "The pyramid of slabs" refers to the piles of waste boards near the sawmills, which, with the advent of steam, replaced water as power for the vast lumber operations. "Drabs" was colloquial for clothes made of yellowish-brown homespun.

Nursery Rhyme

Sing a song of sixpence, pocket full of rye,
Four and twenty blackbirds baked in a pie;
When the pie was opened the birds began
to sing;
Wasn't that a dainty dish to set before the king!

Rumrunner's Version

Four and twenty Yankees, feeling mighty dry,
Took a trip to Canada and bought a case of rye.
When the case was opened the Yanks began
to sing:
"To hell with the President! God save the King!"*

*From Allan S. Everest, *Rum across the Border: The Prohibition Era in Northern New York* (Syracuse, NY: Syracuse University Press, 1978), p. 159.

TEXTILE MILLHANDS

A third occupation that developed first in New England was textile milling, but this industry has not left such a rich musical legacy as have whaling and lumbering. The American colonists mostly spun and wove their own textile materials; the few machine-made fabrics they used were imported from Great Britain. After the Revolutionary War, importation became awkward, and the first textile mill in America was established in Pawtucket, Rhode Island, in 1793. (They were called "mills" because they required waterpower to turn the machinery and therefore were always located on rivers, preferably near waterfalls where additional hydropower was available.) Other mills soon sprang up in New England

(Waltham and Lowell, Massachusetts, by the 1820s), and shortly textiles became a major industry of the region. Early mill workers labored under difficult conditions: the average work week in the 1830s and 1840s was seventy-three hours; a sixty-hour work week was usual in the 1870s. Women millhands in the 1850s earned about fifty cents a day; men earned almost twice as much. Young children were similarly exploited. Three-quarters of the typical antebellum workforce consisted of women, most of whom were fifteen to twenty-five years of age and averaged three years of employment in the mill before they returned home, married, or moved to other employment. Beginning in the late 1840s, Irish immigrant workers became an increasingly predominant part of the workforce.

In the 1830s and 1840s, many young women millhands went on strike to protest their working conditions. One of America's oldest textile folk songs is "A Factory Girl," a complaint about the difficult conditions in the mill. One version concerns the Lowell, Massachusetts, mills in particular. The song complains about the difficult conditions in the mill: social hierarchy, the arbitrariness of the supervisor, the tedium, the oppressive surroundings (as contrasted with the "native dell"), and the meager wages. Its author, obviously a mill worker judging by the familiarity with mill terminology, suggests that the only route for escape is to marry a successful husband. The song has not turned up outside of America, and the Irish-influenced refrain (and occasionally the tune) suggest the writer may have been one of the Irish immigrants who frequently became mill workers starting in the 1840s.

Other versions of this complaint are localized elsewhere. A version sung by a woman from Bangor, Maine, in the 1930s (but learned in 1875) was set in Lewiston, a Maine mill town. In 1915, John A. Lomax published a version he had heard in Texas from a woman who said she had learned it in Florida. The song was last sighted in North Carolina in 1961 when folklorist Archie Green heard it sung by former mill workers Dorsey and Nancy Dixon (see Chapter 4).

SEAFARERS AND RIVERMEN

There is no better example of a work song than the nautical shanty. A leader, or shantyman, conveniently perched on the ship or dock within hearing of the hardworking sailors and stevedores, bellows out stanza after stanza to a regular rhythm carefully chosen to abet the task at hand, pausing after each stanza for a hearty refrain or chorus from the workers. Some shanties had brief *staccato* choruses in which the words themselves clued the sailors as to when to pull, hoist, or push, as on the last word of each stanza, "haul," in "Haul on the Bowline" printed here. Shanties are classified according to the type of work they are meant to accompany. Hauling songs, for intermittent operations, include:

- short-drag shanties, for short tasks where only a few strong pulls were needed;
- halyard, or halliard, shanties, also called long-drag shanties, for longer and heavier intermittent tasks, such as hoisting sails;

THE FACTORY GIRL.

When I set out for Manchester,
 Some factory for to find,
I left my native country,
 And all my friends behind.
  CHORUS—Sing ter re a re I re O.

But now I am in Manchester,
 And summoned by the bell,
I think more of the factory girls
 Than of my native dell.

The factory bell begins to ring,
 And we must all obey,
And to our old employment go,
 Or else be turned away.

My overseer has cut my wages down
 To ten-and-six a week,
And before I'll work for that
 My true love's heart I'll seek.

I do not like my overseer,
 I do not mean to stay,
I mean to hire some depot cab
 To carry me away.

No more I'll oil my picker rod,
 No more I'll brush my loom,
No more I'll scour my nasty floor,
 All in the weaving-room.

No more I'll draw the thread
 All through the harness eye,
No more I'll say, " My work goes so,
 O dear me, I shall die."

No more they'll come to me and say,
 "Your ends they are all down,
While I am up in the middle of the room,
 Or acting out the clown."

No more I'll go to my overseer
 To come and fix my loom;
No more I'll go to him and say,
 " May I stay out till noon?"

No more they'll see me read,
 No more they'll see me sew,
No more they'll come to me and say,
 "This work I sha'n't allow."

No more I'll hear the factory bell,
 That calls me from my bed ;
No more I'll wash those dusty drums
 As they roll o'er my head.

The factory life is a harass'd life,
 As I suppose you know,
Do only think in the winter
 How much we undergo.

No longer will I tread the snow
 To get into the mill ;
No longer will I work so hard
 To get one dollar bill.

No more I'll put my bonnet on
 And hasten to the mill,
While other girls are working hard,
 And I am sitting still.

Come all ye pretty factory girls,
 I'll have you understand,
I'm going to leave the factory
 And return to my native land.

By-and-by you'll see me settle down
 With a pretty little man,
Then I will say to the factory girls,
 Come and see me when you can.

"The Factory Girl," a broadside from the 1840s (ID: CPM, 002501-Broad). *Courtesy of the Kenneth S. Goldstein Collection, Center for Popular Music, Middle Tennessee State University.*

"The Lowell Factory Girl"

When I set out for Lowell,
Some factory for to find,
I left my native country,
And all my friends behind.

CHORUS:
Then sing hit-re-i-re-a-re-o
Then sing hit-re-i-re-a.

But now I am in Lowell,
And summon'd by the bell,
I think less of the factory
Than of my native dell.

The factory bell begins to ring,
And we must all obey,
And to our old employment go,
Or else be turned away.

Come all ye weary factory girls,
I'll have you understand,
I'm going to leave the factory
And return to my native land.

No more I'll put my bonnet on
And hasten to the mill,
While all the girls are working hard,
Here I'll be lying still.

No more I'll lay my bobbins up,
No more I'll take them down
No more I'll clean my dirty work
For I'm going out of town.

No more I'll take my piece of soap,
No more I'll go to wash,
No more my overseer shall say,
"Your frames are stopped to doff."

Come all you little doffers
That work in the Spinning room;
Go wash you face and comb your hair,
Prepare to leave the room.

No more I'll oil my picker rods,
No more I'll brush my loom,
No more I'll scour my dirty floor
All in the Weaving room.

No more I'll draw these threads
All through the harness eye;
No more I'll say to my overseer,
Oh! dear me, I shall die.

No more I'll get my overseer
To come and fix my loom,
No more I'll say to my overseer,
Can't I stay out 'till noon?

Then since they've cut my wages down
To nine shillings per week,
If I cannot better wages make,
Some other place I'll seek.

No more he'll find me reading,
No more he'll see me sew,
No more he'll come to me and say,
"Such works I can't allow."

I do not like my overseer,
I do not mean to stay,
I mean to hire a Depot-boy
To carry me away.

The Dress-room girls, they needn't think
Because they higher go,
That they are better than the girls
That work in the rooms below.

The overseers they need not think
Because they higher stand;
That they are better than the girls
That work at their command.

'Tis wonder how the men
Can such machinery make,
A thousand wheels together roll
Without the least mistake.

Now soon you'll see me married
To a handsome little man,
'Tis then I'll say to you factory girls,
Come and see me when you can.*

*John Greenway, "The Lowell Factory Girl," *American Folksongs of Protest* (Philadelphia, PA: University of Pennsylvania Press, 1953), pp. 122–126. Doffers were the workers who removed the empty bobbins and replaced them with full ones. Picker machines untangled the rough cotton and helped to remove impurities. Dressing meant to coat the threads with a starch solution to make it easier to work. The harness was the frame that held the heddles— the vertical wires through which the warp threads are drawn.

- hand-over-hand shanties for hoisting light sails; walk-away shanties, for the easier job of taking up slack in a line; or
- bunt shanties, for stowing a sail on the yard.

Heaving songs, for a continuous task, are:

- windlass or capstan shanties, for catting anchor (i.e., hoisting and securing); or
- pump shanties.[3]

In spite of the elaborate terminology, a comparison of different shanty collections and accounts indicates that certain songs served equally well at different tasks, so that determining the shanty type from the song itself can be difficult. Shanties might have been accompanied by a fiddle or accordion at one time, but in later years, every hand was needed, and shanties were sung without accompaniment.

There is evidence that shanties were sung by British sailors as early as the sixteenth century, and American shanties were derived partly from their British antecedents but with considerable African American infusions owing to the common use of slave and ex-slave labor on ships and docks. Many nineteenth-century shanties and dock songs are descended from the blackface minstrel stage or plantation songs. In spite of the age of shanty singing, the word "shanty" itself seems not to have been used before the mid-1800s and first appeared in print in 1869. It has also been spelled "chantey" or "chanty," on the (mistaken) assumption that the term derived from the French verb *chanter*, to sing.

Notwithstanding the antiquity of the custom, shantying had fallen into disuse during the seventeenth and eighteenth centuries, to be deliberately revived in the early nineteenth century. Most American shanties originated in the period 1820 to 1860, the peak years of American packets (small vessels carrying passengers, goods, and mail on fixed routes, especially on rivers or along coasts) and transatlantic clippers (fast ships designed for speed). The introduction of steam and mechanization diminished the need for manual labor after the Civil War, and shanty singing declined accordingly.

One of the best known shanties, "Haul the Bowline," still makes for a rousing experience when sung by a shantyman and chorus. Possibly this oldest known short haul shanty dates from the days of King Henry VIII, since the "bowline" as a nautical term for ropes has not been used since the early seventeenth century (it now refers to a type of knot). The first couplet usually functions as a refrain in that it is repeated after every other stanza, but it is sung to the same tune.

Not all shanties are so obviously work songs. "Shenandoah," a capstan shanty, is often sung in venues where there isn't a trace of salt spray. "Shenandoah" is a good example of a landlubber's song shanghaied and carried off to serve duty as a work song. Versions from other sources do not preserve the unmistakable evidence of a story line, as does this one. Modern listeners may justly take offense

"Haul the Bowline"

Haul the bowline, the long-tailed bowline,
Haul the bowline, the bowline haul.

Haul the bowline, Kitty, oh, my darling,
Haul the bowline, the bowline haul.

Haul the bowline, we'll haul and haul together,
Haul the bowline, the bowline haul.

Haul the bowline, we'll haul for better weather,
Haul the bowline, the bowline haul.

Haul the bowline, we'll bust, we'll break our
  banner,
*Haul the bowline, the bowline haul.**

*As sung by Richard Maitland at Sailors' Snug Harbor, Staten Island, New York, in 1939. Collected by Alan Lomax. Recording: Library of Congress, LP L26, *American Sea Songs and Shanties*. Born in 1857 and retired at the time of this recording, Richard Maitland had gone to sea when he was only twelve, at which time his lifelong interest in shantying began.

"Shenandoah"

Missouri, she's a mighty river,
Away you rolling river
The redskins' camp lies on its borders
Ah ha, I'm bound away, 'cross the wide Missouri.

The white man loved the Indian maiden
Away you rolling river
With notions his canoe was laden.
Ah ha, I'm bound away, 'cross the wide Missouri.

Oh, Shenandoah, I love your daughter,
Away you rolling river
I'll take her 'cross yon rolling water."
Ah ha, I'm bound away, 'cross the wide Missouri.

The chief disdained the trader's dollars;
Away you rolling river
"My daughter never you shall follow."
Ah ha, I'm bound away, 'cross the wide Missouri.

At last there came a Yankee skipper,
Away you rolling river
He winked his eye, and he tipped his flipper.
Ah ha, I'm bound away, 'cross the wide Missouri.

He sold the chief that fire-water,
Away you rolling river
And 'cross the river he stole his daughter.
Ah ha, I'm bound away, 'cross the wide Missouri.

O, Shenandoah, I long to hear you,
Away you rolling river
Across that wide and rolling river.
*Ah ha, I'm bound away, 'cross the wide Missouri.**

*In W. B. Whall, *Sea Songs and Shanties*, 6th ed. (Glasgow: Brown, Son & Ferguson, 1927), pp. 1–2.

at the negative portrayal of Native Americans, but this is the way the song was sung. Without question, the song's chief charm is its beautiful tune, and for that reason it is continually re-recorded in collections of musical Americana.

Some of the best of the nineteenth-century shantymen were African Americans, but chances are not all of them plied their skills voluntarily. "Mobile Bay" is an example of the African American shantyman's art, probably originating as a work song in the cotton fields of the Deep South. By replacing the word "pump" with "heave," it could be used as an ordinary capstan shanty.

"Mobile Bay" probably moved from the cotton fields to the shantyman's domain via the intermediary, the riverboat. In the nineteenth century, the major

American rivers (including the Mississippi, the Missouri, and the Ohio) were important transportation arteries, and their dock cities bustled with workers loading and unloading rafts and steamboats.

"I'm Goin' Up the Rivuh" was a favorite song that the singer could use to extemporize on the hardships of the life of the deck hand. It was sung along the Mississippi by the African American workers.

In the early 1800s, whalers along the eastern seaboard made their livelihoods hunting the huge mammals for their bone, skin, oil, and flesh. An encounter with one of the leviathans could be fraught with danger when hunter and hunted exchanged roles, as Melville's *Moby Dick* reminded readers. Today's newspapers are filled with stories about whaling, but now the issue is an environmental one: are we hunting these creatures to extinction? That possibility was too remote to be taken seriously two centuries ago. Just as the stampede was the cowboy's dreaded fear, whalers quaked over the prospect of a fatal encounter between the small whaling boat and its prey. "The Greenland Whale" was widely sung through the nineteenth century and even earlier.

The ballad is of English origin and dates back to the beginning of the eighteenth century, if not earlier. One must not place too much trust in the date listed in the first stanza, since other versions diverge widely. In a few versions, the captain declares that the failure to secure the whale is more regrettable than the loss of his crewmen, but while this makes for a good tale of occupational greed and managerial callousness, it was not typical.

Not every ballad about seafarers concerns those who made their livelihoods on the water. Every age has had its civilian maritime disasters; even the great technological achievements of the twentieth century were not sufficient to render it immune. On April 15, 1912, the steamship *Titanic*—only four days out of Southampton, England, bound for the United States on her maiden voyage—struck an iceberg and sank, sending some 1,500 people, more than two-thirds of those aboard, to a watery grave. The *Titanic* has left a deep mark on the culture of America from movies and songs, to poems

---

"Mobile Bay"

SHANTYMAN: Was you ever down in Mobile Bay?

CHORUS: Johnny come tell us and pump away,

SHANTYMAN: A-screwing cotton by the day?

CHORUS: Johnny come tell us and pump away,
Aye, aye, pump away,
Johnny come tell us and pump away.*

*In Johanna Colcord, *Songs of American Sailormen* (New York: Bramhall House, 1938), p. 118. A screw is a press for baling cotton.

"I'm Goin' Up the Rivuh"

I'm goin' up the rivuh, an' I won't stay long;
I'll have plenty money when the boat gits back.

I've packed so many sacks, until it made my shoulder so',
But this heavy load, I can't carry no mo'.

If I don't make but fifteen cents,
Baby, you kin have a dime.
Run here an' git yo' bone, tell what shoulder you want it on.*

*As sung by Uncle Barney Allison. Collected by Mary Wheeler and published in her book, *Steamboatin' Days* (Baton Rouge: Louisiana State University Press, 1944,) p. 32.

"The Greenland Whale"

It was seventeen hundred and eight-four,
On March the seventeenth day;
We weighed our anchor to our bow,
And for Greenland bore away, brave boys,
And for Greenland bore away.

Bold Stevens was our captain's name,
Our ship called the *Lion* so bold;
And our poor souls our anchor away,
To face the storms and cold, brave boys,
To face the storms and cold.

Oh, when we arrived in that cold country,
Our goodly ship to moor;
We wished ourselves safe back again,
With those pretty girls on shore, brave boys,
With those pretty girls on shore.

Our boatswain to the main top stand,
With a spy glass in his hand;
"A whale, a whale, my lads!" he cries,
And she spouts at every span, brave boys,
And she spouts at every span.

The captain walked the quarter-deck,
And a jolly little fellow was he;
"Overhaul, overhaul your davit tackle falls,
And we'll launch our boats all three, brave boys,
And we'll launch our boats all three."

There was harpineery and picaneery,
And boat steerery also;
And twelve jolly tars to tug at the oars,
And a-whaling we all go, brave boys,
And a-whaling we all go.

We struck the whale and down she went,
By the flourish of her tail;
By chance we lost a man overboard,
And we did not get that whale, brave boys,
And we did not get that whale.

When this news to our captain came,
It grieved his heart full sore;
And for the loss of a 'prentice boy,
It was half mast colors all, brave boys,
It was half mast colors all.

It's now cold months is a-coming on,
No longer can we stay here;
For the winds do blow and the whales do go,
And the daylight seldom does appear, brave boys,
And the daylight seldom does appear.*

*From the journal of William Silver, aboard the *Bengal*, which sailed out of Salem in 1832. Transcribed by Gale Huntington in *Songs the Whalemen Sang* (Barre, MA: Barre, 1964), pp. 11–12. Punctuation added. A davit is a crane for lowering boats; harpoonery are harpooners; steerery are steersmen; a tar is a sailor.

and books. The facts in the story—the construction by one of Britain's preeminent shipbuilders, the decision to ignore advice to take precautions against complete loss of buoyancy in the event of a hull penetration, the failure to provide sufficient lifeboat accommodations—have all been told in numerous accounts. The rumor—never substantiated—that those on board who went down with the ship were singing the hymn, "Nearer, My God, to Thee," was reported in newspapers within days of the disaster and captured the imagination of singers and songwriters alike immediately thereafter.

What is worthy of separate examination is the image of the *Titanic* reflected in popular musical traditions of the decades immediately after 1912. This vessel, to which the epithet "unsinkable" clung like drowning men to a raft, was the subject of over a hundred copyrighted popular songs soon after it sank. While few of these endured more than fleeting popularity, in other, folksier genres, the *Titanic*'s story was sung and resung over and over for several decades.

Several other themes, not particularly factual, recur in songs and other lore about the *Titanic*: the overconfidence of the builders, the notion that the rich fared much better in escaping death, and the irresponsibility of the captain himself. In the following version, the penultimate stanza (about Paul) seems totally irrelevant unless one realizes that the song's real purpose is not to recount a specific tragedy but to warn one to place faith in God's hands rather than in the less dependable ones of man.

PENNSYLVANIA DUTCH

German immigration to the New World began in earnest in 1683 following William Penn's establishment of a new colony in 1681. As part of his aggressive promotion of the new colony, in 1682 he published *Some Account of the Province of Pennsylvania*. Translated into German, Dutch, and French and circulated in

---

"The Great *Titanic*"

It was on Monday morning just about one o'clock,
That that great *Titanic* began to reel and rock,
People began to cry, saying, "Lord I'm a-going to die."
It was sad when that great ship went down.

CHORUS:
It was sad when that great ship went down,
It was sad when that great ship went down,
Husbands and wives and little children lost their lives,
It was sad when that great ship went down.

When that ship left England it was making for the shore,
The rich had declared that they would not ride with the poor;
So they sent the poor below, they were the first that had to go,
It was sad when that great ship went down.

While they were building [the *Titanic*] they said what they could do,
They were going to build a ship that the water can't go through,
But God with His mighty power in hand showed the world that it could not stand,
It was sad when that great ship went down.

Those people on the ship were a long ways from home,
With friends all around, they didn't know that the time had come,
Death came riding by, sixteen hundred had to die,
It was sad when that great ship went down.

While Paul was sailing his men around,
God told him that not a man should drown.
If you trust me and obey, I will save you all today.
It was sad when that great ship went down.

You know it must have been awful with those people on the sea,
They say that they were singing, "Nearer, My God, to Thee,"
While some were homeward bound, sixteen hundred had to drown
It was sad when that great ship went down. *

*Collected from singing of African Americans on the streets of Hackleburg, Alabama, in 1915–1916. Published in Newman I. White, *American Negro Folk Songs* (Hatboro, PA: Folklore Associates, 1965), pp. 347–348. In the original printing, the fourth line of the verse is written as part of the chorus, which doesn't make sense musically.

Europe, it aided in the active recruitment of Europeans, Germans in particular, to Pennsylvania.

From provinces along the lower Rhine, Saxony, Bavaria, Alsace, and Switzerland, German-speaking peoples came in increasing numbers in the 1700s, perhaps encouraged by the Germanic heritage of two of the English kings. George I (1714–1727) was always more interested in his German realm than in his inherited English throne, and his son, George II (1727–1760), had similar preferences. The first all-German settlement in America was at Germantown, Pennsylvania, and successive immigrants heavily settled the valleys of southeastern Pennsylvania. They were called "Dutch" because the English settlers misinterpreted the German word "deutsch" ("deitsch" in their dialect), which means "German."

Well into the twentieth century, the Pennsylvania Dutch of the Mahantongo Valley preserved the folklore of their eighteenth-century, German-speaking immigrant ancestors. Their folk songs include lullabies and songs of childhood, courting songs, songs about farm life, drinking songs, and of course, religious songs. Other songs originated in the New World, some as translations or parodies of the American songs they heard their neighbors singing. In contrast to those of the Anglo-Americans of the southern mountains, the repertoire of the Pennsylvania Dutch consists mainly of humorous, light-hearted, or even risqué songs; there are very few sad or tragic songs and ballads. While the texts that are sung are traceable to the region's European ancestors, for the most part the tunes have been borrowed from the neighboring Anglo-American and Celtic

"Sleep, My Baby, Sleep"

Sleep, my baby, sleep!
Your Daddy's tending the sheep;
Your Mommy's taken the cows away,
Won't come home till break of day.
Sleep, my baby, sleep!

Sleep, my baby, sleep!
Your Daddy's tending the sheep;
Your Mommy's tending the little ones,
Baby sleep as long as he wants.
Sleep, my baby, sleep!

Sleep, my baby, sleep!
Your Daddy's tending the sheep;
Your Mommy is cooking schnitz today,
Daddy's keeping the bugs away,
Sleep, my baby, sleep!

Sleep, my baby, sleep!
Your Daddy's tending the sheep;
Your Mommy's gone off on a gossiping flight
And won't be back till late tonight!
Sleep, my baby, sleep!

Sleep, my baby, sleep!
Your Daddy's tending the sheep;
Your Mommy's tending the white cows—
They keep a very manury house!
Sleep, my baby, sleep!*

*As sung by William Brown of Hepler, Pennsylvania, in 1947. Published in Walter E. Boyer, Albert F. Buffington, and Don Yoder, *Songs along the Mahantongo: Pennsylvania Dutch Folksongs* (Hatboro, PA: Folklore Associates, 1964), pp. 31–32. Translation provided by source. *Schnitz* is a piece of sausage.

American traditions. Until the late 1900s, songs were sung without instrumental accompaniment.

The lullaby "Schloof, Bobbeli, Schloof" ("Sleep, My Baby, Sleep"), though it has close relatives in many languages, probably originated in the mountains of Germany. After decades in the United States, it lost some of its pastoral character.

One Pennsylvania Dutch farm song has a hint of a ritual that used to be widespread in colonial and frontier America: bundling. In this courting custom, the young couple would spend the evening or night in the girl's bed as a practical necessity in winter when the rest of the house was freezing and lighting a fire in the parlor fireplace just for the lovebirds seemed wasteful. To ensure moral behavior, the bed was fitted with a vertical board that extended from head to foot. This way, the two could talk and sleep together but with only limited physical contact.

The last example is given in the original German because it is the Pennsylvania Dutch translation of Stephen Foster's "Oh Susanna," published in 1848. The Mahantongo version was written in a young man's manuscript copybook around 1851.

"I've Thrashed All My Oats Fields"

I've thrashed all my oats fields,
My lentils I've sown,
I've swung on the dance-floor
Many a girl of my own.

I've walked along with her
While the winds raged wild—
And slept with her often
And never had a child!*

*As sung by William Brown of Hepler, Pennsylvania, in 1947. Translated and published by Walter E. Boyer, Albert F. Buffington, and Don Yoder in *Songs along the Mahantongo* (Hatboro: Folklore Associates, 1964), p. 115.

"Oh Susanna" in Pennsylvania Dutch
Das Berümte Lied eines Verliebten Negers

Ich kam von Alabama
Mit der Banjo auf dem Knie; Ich geh nach
   Louisiana,
Zu spielen nur für sie,
Geregnet hat's die ganze nacht,
Am Tag, als Ich wegschlich,
Die Sonn' schien heiss, ich fror zu tod,
O weine nicht für mich.
O Susanna, weine nicht für mich!
Ich komm von Alabama her,
Zu spielen nur für dich.*

English Translation
The Renowned Song of a Love-Sick Negro

I come from Alabama
With the banjo on the knee;
I go to Louisiana
To play only for you.
It rained all night
The day I left,
The sun shone so hot I froze to death,
O don't cry for me.
O, Susanna, don't cry for me
I come from Alabama
To play only for you.

*As sung by William Brown of Hepler, Pennsylvania, in 1947. Published in Walter E. Boyer, Albert F. Buffington, and Don Yoder in *Songs along the Mahantongo* (Hatboro: Folklore Associates, 1964), p. 180. Only the first stanza is given; literal translation by the author of this book.

RECOMMENDED RECORDINGS

American Sea Songs and Shanties. Library of Congress Archive of Folk Culture, LP AFC L26/27.

The Boarding Party. *'Tis Our Sailing Time*. Folk-Legacy, CD-97.

Brave Boys. *New England Traditions in Folk Music*. New World Records, CD NW 80239-2.

Brown Lung Cotton Mills Blues. June Appal, LP 006.

Cotton Mills and Fiddles. Flyin' Cloud, LP FC-014; reissues from 1920s and 1930s.

Irish Ballads & Songs of the Sea. Folk Legacy, CD-124.

Joe Glazer. *Textile Voices: Songs and Stories of the Mills*. Collector, LP 1922.

Songs of the Sea. Helen Creighton Folklore Society, CC-SOTS-003, 2 CDs.

Stan Hugill, X Seamen, etc. *Sea Songs: Newport, R.I.: Songs from the Age of Sail*. Folkways, LP and Cass FTS 37312.

NOTES

1. Although the Spanish guitar was introduced in the eastern United States in the early nineteenth century and became very popular, by the time folk song collectors visited New England in the early twentieth century, it was encountered only rarely. That was pretty much true in the Southeast as well; it had become the provenance mainly of African Americans.

2. These rankings are based primarily on an extensive electronic database compiled by English folklorist/librarian Steve Roud. The frequency of recovery ranges from 70 for "Lord Randal" to 26 for "Lord Lovel."

3. Stan Hugill, *Shanties from the Seven Seas* (New York: E. P. Dutton & Co., 1966), p. 26.

4

Folk Music of the Southeast

Beyond the broad generalizations noted in the preceding chapter, the most distinctive features of music of the Southeast that set it apart from music of the Northeast are the prominence of lyric songs, banjo songs, and frolic tunes associated with dances, parties, weddings, corn-shuckings, barn-raisings, and other joyous social occasions. These songs may not be wholly absent in other parts of the country, but they are so typical of the Southeast that they are invariably associated with that region. Sometimes these are performed as instrumental tunes, but most have standard sets of lyrics associated with them. In many of these songs, the evidence points to minstrel shows as one major source and to African American plantation music as possibly another; in both cases beginning in the decades immediately before the Civil War. These include such well-known titles as:

- "Sourwood Mountain"
- "Charming Betsy"
- "Fly around My Pretty Little Miss"
- "Buffalo Gals"
- "Arkansas Traveler"
- "Turkey in the Straw"
- "Old Joe Clark"
- "Going down the Road Feeling Bad"
- "Shady Grove"

- "Bile Dem Cabbage Down"
- "Georgia Buck"
- "Sugar Babe"
- "Ida Red"
- "Cindy"
- "Katy Kline"

UPLAND SOUTH, SOUTHERN APPALACHIANS, AND OZARKS

The upland regions of the South, including the Blue Ridge, the Shenandoah Valley, the Appalachians, the Cumberlands, and the Ozarks, were settled starting in the early eighteenth century, primarily by immigrants from the borderlands of England and Scotland. Some ballads that were exclusively Scottish in the British Isles are found only in the southern Appalachians; and in the case of ballads found in both England and Scotland, it is with the latter that Appalachian versions compare most closely. Similarly, Scottish fiddle tunes and fiddle styles are close kin to those of the uplands, whereas New England provided the soil for transplanted Irish fiddling traditions.

The Appalachians did not draw large numbers of outsiders in the nineteenth century. In 1860, over 90 percent of the populations of Virginia and the Carolinas were native born. Small influxes from outside the region meant few sources for folk music that was not already well established.

The Ozarks were populated mostly by Americans who moved west from the Appalachians. In 1860, for example, only half of all Missourians had been born in that state, while a quarter came from Kentucky, Tennessee, Virginia, Ohio, and North Carolina (in order of decreasing importance). Some immigrant groups resisted integration, and ethnic enclaves persist into the twenty-first century in Missouri: Germans in Harmann and Westphalia; Italians in the Hill district of St. Louis, Belgians in Taos, and Irish in Vienna. In Arkansas the westward migration was even more evident: 51 percent of all Arkansans had come from Tennessee, 14 percent from North Carolina, and another 14 percent from Georgia.

As in New England, the older Child ballads have been found in abundance in the Southeastern states, but the order of popularity (based on number of times collected) is significantly different. In the upland Southeast (primarily the Carolinas, Virginia, Tennessee, and Kentucky), in decreasing frequency, the following ballads were collected:

- "Barbara Allen"
- "The House Carpenter"
- "Lord Randal"
- "Lord Thomas and Fair Ellender"
- "The Maid Freed from the Gallows," or "Hangman"
- "Fair Margaret and Sweet William"
- "The Wife of Usher's Well," or "Lady Gay"

- "The Two Sisters"
- "The Gypsy Davy"
- "Little Musgrave and Lady Barnard," or "Little Matthy Groves"

This list is quite different from that for New England: only four ballads occur in both lists: "Barbara Allen," "The House Carpenter," "Lord Randal," and "The Gypsy Davy."[1]

In the Appalachians of the Carolinas, Tennessee, and Kentucky, there is considerable evidence of African American influence on Anglo-American traditions. The very presence of the banjo itself is some testament to the fact, but the credit is hard to apportion accurately because of the difficulty in separating out the contribution of the minstrel show as an intermediary between African American plantation culture and the Anglo-American borrowers. Other clear shreds of evidence, however, show, for example, that the guitar did not become common in the southern mountains until around 1900 and that the generation of musicians that grew up then almost universally pointed to African American laborers (for example, in railroad construction) as their first introduction to the instrument.

Farther west in the Ozarks, the footprint of the African American is considerably fainter. One of the best regional folksong collections is that of Vance Randolph, whose *Ozark Folk Songs* included over 1,600 texts collected over a period of more than two decades. Judging by this collection, almost the entire body of post-Reconstruction African American folk songs that has elsewhere entered Anglo-American tradition is absent. In particular, the elsewhere ubiquitous African American "John Henry"—the most widespread indigenous American ballad—was not collected in the Ozarks until the 1950s.

The broadside and indigenous ballad lists are very different from what is found in New England. In particular, there is a tendency to favor those ballads that may have been first composed in the typical stilted broadside style, but they have become so streamlined and smoothed out with repeated oral transmission that they approach the story-line simplicity (if not poetic elegance) of the Child ballads. Good examples of this are "Pretty Polly" and "Little Omie Wise." For whatever reasons, the ballads found in the Northeast preserve much more of the original broadside style.

The most often reported broadside ballads are:

- "Pretty Polly"
- "Pretty Little Miss in the Garden"
- "Knoxville Girl"
- "Jack Monroe"
- "The Sailor Boy"
- "Awake, Awake You Drowsy Sleeper"
- "Rich Irish Lady"
- "The Nightingale"
- "The Girl I Left Behind"
- "The Miller's Will"

The most common domestic ballads recorded in the twentieth century include:

- "Little Omie Wise"
- "Little Mohea"
- "The Jealous Lover"
- "John Hardy"
- "Young Charlotte"
- "John Henry"
- "Jesse James"
- "The Arkansas Traveler"
- "Charles Guiteau"

Throughout the Southeast there is in general a difference in style in the common broadside and indigenous ballads compared to what is usually found in the Northeast. Northeast ballads show the characteristic broadside style: flowery or stilted language, come-all-ye beginnings, and a preference for melodies that correspond to a stanza line of seven or eight stresses between rhyme words. Typical examples of the former are "James Bird" and "The *Cumberland*'s Crew" in Chapter 3, and "Loss of the *Persian*," in Chapter 5. In the Southeast, ballad language is simpler and smoother, not so obviously from cheap print. Melodies correspond to a stanza of three or four stresses between rhymes. Typical examples of Southeast style are banjo songs such as "Old Joe Clark," blues ballads such as "John Henry," broadside ballad descendants such as "Pretty Polly" and wholly American compositions such as "Little Omie Wise."

"The Gosport Tragedy" and "Pretty Polly" provide a dramatic example of the differences between northern and southern style. "The Gosport Tragedy" is a Northeastern descendent of a British broadside ballad, "The Cruel Ship's Carpenter." Fortunately, English broadside texts from the mid-eighteenth century have survived, so the evolution of the ballad is easy to follow. The original text is typical of broadside balladry of the eighteenth century: long, detailed, stilted language, supernatural beings, and a moralizing tone. It has been collected in England, but with nothing like the frequency that it has turned up in North America. Carrie Grover, a Maine resident who was born in Nova Scotia, learned a long version from her great-aunt, which is close to the printed original. Texts similar to it have been mainly found in the

Carrie B. Grover on her porch steps in Gorham, Maine (1943). *Courtesy of the Eloise Hubbard Linscott Collection, Archive of Folk Culture, American Folklife Center, Library of Congress.*

Northeastern United States and Canada but occasionally also farther south. In the Southeast, where it is titled "Pretty Polly," this same ballad has changed in a striking manner. The most arresting feature is that the typical four-line ballad stanza has been replaced by the three-line stanzaic structure of a typical blues song.

This southeastern version of "Pretty Polly" has been shortened considerably from the broadside source; in particular, all references to sex and seduction have been removed, as has been the story following the murder, with its supernatural elements. Without the seduction details, the story has no apparent motive, unless the audience is familiar with the background. As a result, the singer of the above version (or his source) felt obliged to add another stanza, accusing Polly of having a shady reputation to justify the murder. The gradual smoothing out of the awkward broadside prose in the course of a century or two is not surprising, although it certainly happened more effectively in the Southeast than in the Northeast. What must have been a single deliberate act of recomposition, however, was the conversion of the four-line stanza (AABB) to the three-line, blues-like stanza (AAB). Whether this happened because of the direct influence of blues songs is not easily decided, but the fact that "Pretty Polly" (or the same stanza form in other songs) does not occur in the Northeastern part of the country makes that a plausible conjecture. Unlike its northern

Ralph Stanley and the Clinch Mountain Boys at the Carter Stanley Memorial Festival in McClure, Virginia (May 24, 1927). (*Left to right*) Ricky Skaggs (hidden), Curly Ray Cline, Keith Whitley, Ralph Stanley (with banjo), Roy Lee Centers, and Jack Cooke (hidden). *Photographer, Carl Fleischhauer.*

The Gosport Tragedy

In Gosport of late, a young damsel did dwell,
For wit and for beauty, few could her excel;
A young man did court her for to be his dear,
And he by his trade was a ship's carpenter.

He said, "Dearest Mary, if you will agree,
And give your consent, dear, for to marry me;
Your love, dear, can cure me of sorrow and care,
Consent then to wed with a ship carpenter."

With blushes as charming as roses in bloom,
She said, "Dearest William, to wed, I'm too young;
For young men are fickle, I see very plain,
If a maid is kind, her they quickly disdain."

"My charming Mary, how can you say so?
Your beauty is the haven to which I would go:
And if I find channel and chance for to steer,
I there will cast anchor and stay with my dear."

It was all in vain that she strove to deny,
For he, by his cunning, soon made her comply;
And by his base deception he did her betray
And in sin's hellish path he did lead her astray.

Now when with young damsel with child she did
    prove
She soon sent the tidings to her faithless love.
He swore by the heavens that he would prove true,
And said, "I will marry no damsel but you."

At length these sad tidings she came for to hear,
His ship is a-sailing, for sea he must steer,
Which pained this poor damsel and wounded her
    heart,
To think with her true love so soon she must part.

She said, "Dearest Willie 'ere you go to sea,
Remember the vows you have made unto me;
If you go and leave me, I never can find rest,
Oh, how can you leave me with sorrow oppressed?"

With tender embraces he to her did say,
"I'll marry my true love 'ere I go to sea;
And if on the morrow, my love, I can ride down,
The ring I can buy our fond union to crown."

With tender embraces they parted that night
And promised to meet the next morning at light;
William said, "Dearest Mary, you must now go
    with me,
Before we are married, our friends for to see."

Pretty Polly

"Oh Polly, pretty Polly, would you take me unkind,
Oh Polly, pretty Polly, would you take me unkind,
Me to set beside you and tell you my mind.

Well, my mind is to marry and never to part,
Well, my mind is to marry and never to part,
First time I saw you it wounded my heart.

Oh Polly, pretty Polly, come and go along with me,
Oh Polly, pretty Polly, come and go along with me,
Before we get married some pleasure to see."

Well, he led her over mountains and valleys
    so deep,
Well, he led her over mountains and valleys
    so deep.
Polly mistrusted and then began to weep.

Sayin' "Willie, little Willie, I'm afraid of
    your ways,"
Sayin' "Willie, little Willie, I'm afraid of
    your ways,
The way you've been rambling, you'll lead me
    astray."

"Well Polly, pretty Polly, your guess is about right
Well Polly, pretty Polly, your guess is about right
I dug on your grave the better part of last night."

Then he led her little farther and what did
    she spy,
Then he led her little farther and what did
    she spy,
A new dug grave with a spade lying by.

Then she knelt down before him a pleading for
    her life,
Then she knelt down before him a pleading for
    her life,
"Let me be a single girl if I can't be your wife."

"Now Polly, pretty Polly, that never can be,
Now Polly, pretty Polly, that never can be,
Your past reputation's been trouble to me."

Then he opened up her bosom as white as any
    snow,
Then he opened up her bosom as white as any
    snow,
He stabbed her to the heart and the blood did
    overflow.

He led her o'er hills and through hollows so deep,
Till at length this fair damsel began for to weep;
"Oh Willie, I fear you have led me astray,
On purpose my innocent life to betray."

He said, "You've guessed right, for no power can
    you save,
For 'twas only last night I was digging your grave."
When poor wretched Mary did hear him say so,
The tears from her eyes like a fountain did flow.

Then down on her knees Mary to him did say,
"Oh take not my life lest my soul you betray.
Oh pity my infant, and spare my poor life;
Let me live full of shame if I can't be your wife."

"Oh there is no time thus disputing to stand,"
And taking his sharp, cruel knife in his hand;
He pierced her fair breast whence the blood it did
    flow,
And into the grave her fair body did throw.

He covered her body and quick hastened home,
And left nothing but the small birds her fate for to
    mourn;
He returned to his ship without any delay
And set sail for Plymouth to plow the salt sea.

One night to the captain this fair maid did appear
And she in her arms held an infant most dear.
"Oh help me, oh help me," she to him did say.
Then to his amazement she vanished away.

The captain then summoned his jovial ship's crew
And said, "My brave fellows, I fear some of you
Have murdered some damsel ere you came away
Whose injured ghost haunts you all on the
    salt sea."

Then poor, frightened Willie he fell on his knees
The blood in his veins seemed with horror to freeze.
It's "Oh cruel monster, and what have I done?
God help me, I fear my poor soul is undone.

Oh poor, injured Mary, your forgiveness I crave,
For soon must I follow you down to the grave."
No one but this poor wretch beheld the sad sight,
And, raving distracted, he died the next night.*

Then he went down to the jailhouse and what did
    he say,
Then he went down to the jailhouse and what did
    he say,
"I killed pretty Polly and tryin' to get a way."**

*Carrie B. Grover, *A Heritage of Songs* (Norwood: Norwood Editions, 1973), pp. 43–45.
**As sung by Ralph Stanley of Virginia. Recording: Rebel, CD 1114, 1991.

115

counterpart, the southern version is never sung unaccompanied, but usually has banjo or guitar accompaniment.

The ballad about the murder of Naomi Wise is a good example of a purely American composition on the same theme as that of "Pretty Polly." The structure of the song is very simple: stanzas consist of rhymed couplets, and the melody repeats with each succeeding stanza.

"Little Omie," originating from a North Carolina murder of 1808, is the most common indigenous ballad in much of the Southeast, but it is not found at all in the Northeast. Why should that be the case, when "Pretty Polly," a ballad from across the Atlantic with no regional American associations, is remembered in both the North and in the South? The answer must lie in the very different degree to which the two ballads provide specific details.

Since colonial days, murders and other crimes of violence were a favorite topic for broadside ballads, as they still are in today's newspapers. When events were similar to preceding ballads, the songwriter could "borrow" an older song, change a few words here and there, and have a timely "new" song about the current event. "Little Omie" is full of specifics that do not permit the ballad to become a template for other murders. "Pretty Polly" is so general that it is easily adapted. This doesn't necessarily mean it will be rewritten to fit other events but rather that, because of its lack of specifics, singers can assume it refers to an event about which they have personal (or hearsay) knowledge.

Murdering a sweetheart, rather than marrying her, is the basis of so many American ballads that foreigners must wonder whether this is our national

"Omie Wise"

I'll tell you all a story about Omie Wise,
How she was deluded by John Lewis's lies.
He told her to meet him at Adams's Spring,
He's bring her some money and some other fine things.

He brought her no money nor no other fine things
But "Get up behind me Omie, to Squire Ellis we'll go."
She got up behind him, so carefully we'll go,
They rode til they came where deep waters did flow.

John Lewis he concluded to tell her his mind;
John Lewis he concluded to leave her behind.
She threw her arms around him, "John spare me my life,
And I'll go distracted and never be your wife."

He threw her arms from 'round him and into the water she plunged,
John Lewis he turned round and rode back to Ellis's home.
He went inquiring for Omie; "But Omie she is not here;
She's gone to some neighbor's house and won't be gone there a-long."

John Lewis was took a prisoner and locked up in the jail,
Was locked up in the jail around and was there to remain a while.
John Lewis he stayed there six months or maybe more,
Until he broke jail, into the army he did go.*

*As sung by G. B. Grayson, recorded in 1927 for Victor Talking Machine Co., 78 rpm Victor, 21625, 1927. Reissue: Smithsonian Folkways, *Anthology of American Folk Music.*

G. B. Grayson (fiddle) and Henry Whitter (ca. 1930). *Courtesy of the Smithsonian Institution.*

pastime. In Kentucky, murdering pregnant sweethearts was only slightly more common than carrying on a bloodletting family vendetta. Eastern Kentucky seems to have been home to more than its share of family feuds, many of which ended up in bloodshed, perhaps another example of Scottish tradition.

Of the many family feuds, "wars," or "troubles" as they were also called, the one between the Hargis and Cockrell clans was one of the most notorious. John B. Marcum was an attorney associated with the Cockrell clan contesting the 1902 election of James Hargis as county judge and Edward Callahan as sheriff. On May 4, 1903, Marcum was shot to death in the doorway of the Breathitt County Court House in Kentucky. Curtis Jett and Thomas White were accused of the murder. Under great pressure, Circuit Judge Redwine, who owed his election to the Hargis faction, granted a change of venue to Morgan County, but because that judge was supposedly also a Hargis man, the commonwealth attorney withdrew the relocation request. At the trial, the jury was hung, reportedly because of the stand of a single juror. The governor ordered a change of venue to Harrison County, outside the mountains, where Jett and White were found guilty and sentenced to life in prison. The events inspired a ballad that has remained in oral tradition ever since. Its unknown author borrowed the common tune of "Jesse James" (see Chapter 5).

In Breathitt County, as well as the rest of eastern Kentucky, eastern Tennessee, and western West Virginia, the coalfields provided not only employ- ment but a way of life for many Appalachian residents. Perhaps also a way of

"J. B. Marcum"

It was on the fourth of May, half past eight o'clock
   that day,
J. B. Marcum then was standing in the door,
Of the courthouse of his town, where Curt Jett was
   waiting round,
Just to get a chance to bring him to the floor.

Thomas White, a friend of Jett, no worse man was
   ever met,
Came a-walking through the court house hall;
And as he was passin' by, he looked Marcum in
   the eye,
Knowing truly that poor Marcum soon would fall.

CHORUS:
Marcum leaves a wife to mourn all her life,
Two little children to be brave;
It was little Curtis Jett, Thomas White and others
   yet,
Were the men who laid poor Marcum in his grave.

P. J. Hewing and his man, Sheriff Edward Callahan,
Was across the street in Harker Brothers Store;
Some believed they knew the plot, hence was
   listening for the shot,
And to see Jett's victim fall there in the door.

White, he walked out on the street, stopped to see
   it all complete,
Expecting soon to hear that fatal shot;
Jett advanced across the hall, and with pistol, lead,
   and ball,
He killed J. B. Marcum on the spot.

They arrested White and Jett, when the courts in
   Jackson met,
Where the prosecution labored with its might;

And when Breathitt's court was o'er, Judge
   Redwine could do no more,
So he left for another court to right.

There the jury disagreed, just one man begin to
   plead,
That he thought both White and Jett should go
   free;
And he held out to the last, and his vote he could
   not cast;
Some believed Judge Jim Hargis paid a fee.

Now they tried these men once more, not in
   Jackson as before,
For they could not get their justice in that town;
Then the courts in Hazard met and condemned
   both White and Jett,
And the verdict of their guilt in it was found.

Now the final trial is past, White and Jett are
   doomed at last,
To the prison house where they will have to stay;
There with men of other crime, have to labor all
   the time,
Until death shall come and take them both away.

Oh their mothers grieve today for the boys so far
   away,
For there's nothing that can sever a mother's love;
She will pray for them each breath, and will cling
   to them till death,
And she longs to meet them in the court above.*

*"J. B. Marcum" (Laws, E 19). As sung by Doc Hopkins in
Los Angeles, 1965. Collected by D. K. Wilgus. Recording:
Birch, LP 1945, *Doc Hopkins*, 1971.

death, because prior to the safety measures instituted following unionization, many miners fell victim to chronic lung disease or sudden mine accidents.

All three states were beset by innumerable mine disasters in the nineteenth and early twentieth centuries, and it is not known from which of them came the song, "Shut Up in the Mine of Coal Creek." Two disasters are good candidates: a methane explosion at the Fraterville mine at Coal Creek, Tennessee, in 1902, which killed 184 miners; and a later tragedy in the Cross Mountain mine in 1911, when 84 miners died. At Fraterville many trapped miners wrote farewell letters to their wives and children as they slowly suffocated underground.

The perspective of this particular song, written from the vantage point of the trapped miners themselves, is unusual among ballads about mine disasters and makes a particularly powerful impact. The ballad is written in 3/4 time and is a good example of how that rhythm can be very effective for narrative songs.

The singer of this ballad, Green Bailey, was born in Kentucky in 1900. He learned the ballad in around 1920 from a coalminer who had come west to Clark County, a region without any coalmines.

While songs of death and tragedy occupy a major part of this chapter, they are by no means the totality of American folk song. Other aspects of life, in particular courtship and marriage, have always been a favorite topic for songs and ballads. Courting songs can be serious, sad, silly, or spiteful. One type makes fun of members of the opposite sex, as if they were the furthest thing from the singer's mind. Presumably, the listeners knew better.

"The Arkansas Boys" is a localization of a song formerly familiar in many parts of the country, for example, from Wyoming:

> Come all you pretty girls and listen to my
> noise,
> I'll tell you not to marry the Cheyenne boys,
> For if you do a portion it will be;
> Cold butter milk and johnny cake is all you'll
> see (2).[2]

Doc Hopkins (ca. 1965). *Photographer, Henry Gilbert.*

These songs are all based on a minstrel stage song, "Free Nigger,"[3] published in 1841 as sung by R. W. Pelham, which began

> Come all you Virginia Gals and listen to my noise,
> Neber do you wed wid de Carolina boys,
> For if dat you do your portion it will be
> Corn cake and harmony [hominy ?] and Jango lango tea.

Such lyrics are easily adapted to one's own region and afford a quick means of putting together songs that can be used either to affirm regional solidarity or to fan the flames of mock conflict between adolescent boys and girls.

In 1864 a song making fun of Idaho and its residents (see Chapter 6) was sufficiently popular that it was used as the basis for a similar song about Arkansas

"Shut Up in the Mine of Coal Creek"

Shut up in the mine of Coal Creek,
We know that we must die;
But if we trust in Jesus,
To heaven our souls shall fly.

Our lamps are burning dimly,
Our food is almost gone;
Death's grasp is sure but awful,
Till we will be carried home.

Goodbye dear wives and children,
May you be treated kind;
For now our time has come to die,
Shut up in the Coal Creek mine.

Eleven of us were prisoned,
And two dear ones have died;
Nine more are left to suffer,
And die in the Coal Creek mines.

Farewell, dear wives and mothers,
You're left behind to mourn;
But if you follow Jesus,
We'll meet in heavenly home.

Dear friends, you should take warning,
And listen to what we say;
You're now in the world of sunlight,
So there you'd better stay.

Shut up in the mine of Coal Creek,
We know that we must die;
But if we trust in Jesus,
To heaven our souls shall fly.

Goodbye, dear wives and children,
May you be treated kind;
For now our time has come to die,
Shut up in the Coal Creek mine.*

*As sung by Green Bailey of Kentucky in 1929. Reissue: Rounder, LP 1026.

titled "Eureka!" the name of an Arkansas town. At first it sounds like this is a delightful place, but by the song's end the listener is not so sure.

Banjo and fiddle music are essential parts of the traditions of the Appalachians and surrounding regions. As noted previously, fiddle music was based on the traditions brought from the British Isles and therefore has roots in the eighteenth century and earlier. The banjo seems to have become established in the

"The Arkansas Boys"

Come all you Missouri gals an' listen to my noise,
Mind how you marry them Arkansas boys;
For if you do your portion it will be,
Cold johnny cake an' venison is all you will see.

They will lead you out in them blackjack hills,
There so much against your will;
Leave you there for to perish on the place,
For that's the way of the Arkansas race.

Sandstone chimney an' a batten door,
Clapboard roof an' a puncheon floor;
Some gets a little an' some gets none,
An' that's the way of the Arkansas run.

When they go to meetin' the clothes they wear
Is a old brown coat all tore an' bare,
A old white had without no crown,
An' old blue duckins [?] the whole year around.*

*As sung by Ed Stephens of Jane, Missouri, in 1928. Published by Vance Randolph in *Ozark Folksongs*, vol. 3 (Columbia, MO: State Historical Society of Missouri, 1980), pp. 12–13.

southern mountains shortly before the Civil War, and its musical roots are not much deeper. In the case of the older fiddle tradition, there are still evident distinctive regional styles that reflect a combination of the backgrounds of the transatlantic immigrants and also the influences of particular fiddlers. In several regions one or two exceptional fiddlers were so influential that their styles pervaded an entire region, to the extent that it is uncertain what existed before them.

In Kentucky, three distinct fiddle styles have been documented. One, characteristic of the northeast part of the state, has its background in New England and England, shows little ornamentation or syncopation, and relies on major or minor scales. A second, found in the southeastern part of the state, is derived from Scotch-Irish music and exhibits more ornamentation, syncopation, and pentatonic scales. A third style, localized in the bluegrass region of the south central part of the state, shows the most African American influence, with greater syncopation. Two influential fiddlers of the area were Dock [sic] Phil Roberts (b. 1897) and Leonard Rutherford (b. ca. 1900), both of whom made many commercial recordings in the 1920s.[4]

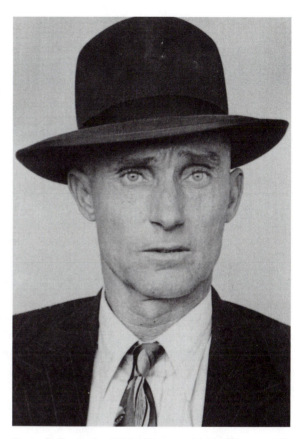

Green Bailey in the 1920s. *Courtesy of Archie Green and the Southern Folklife Collection, University of North Carolina.*

Other regions with distinctive older fiddle styles are central West Virginia, southwestern Virginia, and Grayson and Carroll counties, Virginia. The Grayson County style, centering around Galax, Virginia, seems to trace back to a nineteenth-century fiddler named Greenberry Leonard. No recordings by Leonard exist, but there are some by fiddlers of the next generation who learned from him or from his disciples. Characteristic tunes of the region include "Susannah Gal," or "Fly around My Pretty Little Miss," "Ducks on the Millpond," and "Old Dad," elsewhere known as "Wild Horse" or "Stony Point."

Banjo styles tend to be even more diverse than those of the fiddle. Perhaps this is due to the fact that fiddlers always had the classical violin as a stylistic guidepost, while banjoists had neither a "proper" instrument nor means of playing it to guide them. As a result, the banjo was homemade according to a variety of designs, tuned in even more ways, and played with a bewildering diversity of styles. The main playing styles are determined by whether the right hand plays notes by plucking in an upward motion, strumming in a downward

---

"Eureka!"

There is a stream, they say,
Where crystal waters flow,
Will cure any man whether sick or well,
If he will only go.

CHORUS:
We're coming, Arkansas,
We're coming, Arkansas,
Our four-horse team will soon be seen
In the hills of Arkansas.

To Eureka Springs we are bound
To go and try our luck;
But the chicken-hearted people had better stay
    home
And try a sick man's pluck.

I tell you the roads are rough,
If you don't believe it just go;

There are hills and hollows, rocks and stumps
On the way to Arkansas.

I tell you the Springs are tough,
And you will find them so;
The ways of the people so wicked and rough,
Then away from the Springs we'll go.

CHORUS:
We're leaving Arkansas,
We're leaving Arkansas,
Our four-horse team will no more be seen
In the hills of Arkansas.*

*As sung by Maggie Morgan of Springdale, Arkansas, in 1942. Published by Vance Randolph in *Ozark Folksongs*, vol. 3 (Columbia, MO: State Historical Society of Missouri, 1980), pp. 14–16.

---

motion, or with a combination of these. Within these methods, there are subtler differences determined by which fingers play melody and which play drones or rhythm, whether the right thumb is confined to the fifth or drone string or drops down to other strings, and whether the left hand is used to hammer-on or pull-off to sound additional notes. Some regional consistencies are around (North Carolina players favored up-picking styles; Kentuckians specialize in drop-thumb playing), but to a great extent style is determined by individual preferences.

Among the lyrics frequently associated with banjo or fiddle tunes are "Ida Red," "Sourwood Mountain," "Cindy," and "Crawdad." All are widely known, but the texts are remarkably variable; the same singer will not necessarily sing the same verses twice in a row. Some versions of "Cindy," for example, have no stanzas in common with the text given below. There is no deep recurrent theme to these three songs, except for the fact that all of them, to some extent, are very rural in their imagery. These are not the vignettes that are a part of city life, by any means. "Crawdad," in particular, a widely known lyric, could not be more rural in its focus on the old fishing hole and the adventure to fish for crawdads, the common term mostly west of

"Ida Red"

Ida Red, Ida Red,
I'm plum fool about Ida Red.
Ida Red, Ida Blue,
I got stuck on Ida, too.
Ida Red, Ida Brown,
Ida Red, she lives in town.
Down the road an' 'cross the creek
Can't get a letter but once a week.
Down the road, down the road,
My little Ida lives down the road.*

*Most of these stanzas are from Robert W. Gordon, "Folk-Songs of America, XI: Fiddle Songs," *New York Times Magazine*, November 27, 1927.

the Appalachians, for crayfish. The song evokes images of humid, sunny summer afternoons in the country and local Huck Finns and Tom Sawyers, poles over shoulders and terriers nipping at their heels, traipsing down the road to the woods without a care in the world.

THE DEEP SOUTH

In some regions, the earliest settlers were Spanish and French; for example, in Mississippi, Biloxi was established in 1699, Natchez in 1716. Outside of southern Louisiana, however, these cultures were soon supplanted by the numerically superior immigrants from the British Isles, with English and Scotch-Irish heritage. On the eve of the Civil War, 55 percent of white Mississippians were born within the state; most of the others came from Alabama (11 percent), South Carolina (8 percent), Tennessee (6 percent), Georgia (5 percent), and North Carolina (5 percent), indicating a regular westward and southward movement. Considering that most Alabamians came from

> **"Sourwood Mountain"**
>
> Chickens crowing on Sourwood Mountain,
> Hey ho diddle dum dee-ay,
> Get your guns and we'll go a-hunting,
> Hey ho diddle dum dee-ay.
> My true love lives in Letcher,
> She won't come and I won't fetch her.
> My true love's a blue-eyed daisy,
> If I don't get her I'll go crazy.
> Big dog bark and little one bit you,
> Big girls court and little ones slight you.
> My true love lives up the river,
> A few more jumps and I'll be with her.
> My true love lives in the hollow,
> She won't come and I won't follow.*
>
> *As sung by James Taylor Adams from Big Laurel, Virginia. Published by E. Henry Mellinger in *Folk-Songs from the Southern Highlands* (New York: J. J. Augustin, 1938), p. 400.

these other states, the conclusion is that most white Mississippians came from the Appalachians and other southern uplands, which means a heavy British-derived and, in particular, Scotch-Irish influence. The Irish (as distinct from Scotch-Irish) contribution at the same time was very small.

> **"Cindy"**
>
> You ought to see my Cindy,
> She lives away down south;
> She's so sweet the honey bees
> Swarm around her mouth.
>
> CHORUS:
> Get along home, Cindy, get along home,
> Get along home, home, Cindy
> I'm going to leave you now.
>
> When she saw me coming,
> She puckered up and cried;
> When I went to leave her,
> She fainted away and died.
>
> I wish I was an apple,
> A-hangin' on a tree,
> Every time that Cindy passed,
> She'd take a bite of me.
>
> Cindy in the summer time,
> Cindy in the fall,
> If she can't be Cindy all the time,
> She won't be Cindy at all.*
>
> *Selected stanzas from "Cindy," in Bradley Kincaid's *Favorite Old-Time Songs and Mountain Ballads, Book 2* (n.p., 1929), p. 23.

"Crawdad Song"

You get a line and I'll get a pole, honey,
You get a line and I'll get a pole, honey,
You get a line and I'll get a pole,
We'll go down to the crawdad hole
Honey, baby, mine.

Set on the bank till my feet got cold, honey,
Set on the bank till my feet got cold, honey,
Set on the bank till my feet got cold,
It's a sight to see the crawdads jump in that hole,
Honey, baby, mine.

Yonder come a man with a sack on his back, honey,
Yonder come a man with a sack on his back, honey,
Yonder come a man with a sack on his back,
He's got more crawdads than he can pack,
Honey, baby, mine.

Now, he fell down and he busted that sack, honey,
Now, he fell down and he busted that sack, honey,
Now, he fell down and he busted that sack,
It's a sight to see the crawdads back to back,
Honey, baby, mine.

Now, what did the hen duck say to the drake, honey,
Now, what did the hen duck say to the drake,
   honey,
Now, what did the hen duck say to the drake,
Well, there ain't no crawdads in that lake,
Honey, baby, mine.*

*As sung by Clint Howard and Doc Watson (both from North Carolina) in 1962. Recording: Smithsonian/Folkways, CD SF 40029/30, *Doc Watson and Clarence Ashley: The Original Folkways Recordings: 1960–1962*.

By far, the most common Child ballad found in the Deep South, including Florida, Georgia, Alabama, Mississippi, Louisiana, is "Barbara Allen." Other common ballads are similar to those of the upland South, but the numbers are much lower. Broadside ballads have been reported too infrequently to draw any reliable generalizations. The most common domestic ballads are blues ballads from the African American tradition:

- "John Henry"
- "Boll Weavil"
- "Stagolee"
- "Frankie"

The hot, flat plains of the coastal tidewater regions of Virginia, the Carolinas, and the Deep South proved suitable to growing cotton and tobacco, and large plantations devoted to those crops were established. These geographically expansive enterprises required extensive manual labor, which provided partial justification in some minds for the introduction and persistence of slave labor from earliest days until it was outlawed. The slave population grew from 698,000 in 1790 to 3.95 million in 1860. After its acquisition from the Spanish, Florida attracted enterprising settlers from the tidewater sections of Carolinas and Virginia in search of new lands for cotton plantations.

African slaves brought their own musical culture with them to the New World, and their African American descendants went on to make contributions to American music to an extent that completely belied their marginal social status. Although certain elements of society struggled to maintain the

The cover from Bradley Kincaid's second song folio (1929). *Author's collection.*

separation of the "races," the social fences and gates were easily breached by music. Some plantation owners considered musically skilled slaves both economic and social assets: they could help keep the other slaves happy and improve their work ethic, and they could also provide the white masters with music when needed.

The history of American popular music since the Civil War is the story of successive infusions of musical ideas from African American and other marginalized cultural groups. From minstrel shows to jazz to today, white Anglo-Saxon Protestant America danced time and again to the creations of the fertile musical genius of "those other groups." The folk music traditions, to the extent that they were free of commercial influences, could maintain significant distinctions, but even so cross-cultural exchanges occurred. In general, the characteristics of southern white folk music that are distinctive from those of the northern regions are attributable to the influences of African Americans and, to a lesser extent, Hispanic and Franco-Americans.

"Little Sally Walker"

Little Sally Walker sitting in a saucer,
Rise, Sally, rise; wipe your weeping eyes.
Put your hand on your hip,
And let your backbone slip.

Oh, shake it to the east, oh, shake it to the west,
Oh, shake it to the one that you love the best.

Your mama says so, your papa says so.
That's the way you do it, and you'll never catch a
   beau.
The milk in the pitcher, the butter in the bowl,
You can't catch a sweetheart to save your soul.*

*"Little Sally Walker," as sung, with hand clapping, by
Nettie Mae and Aleneda Turner, 1971, near Senatobia,
Mississippi. Collected by Cheryl Thurber. Recording:
Library of Congress, LP AFS L67, 1978. Reissue: Rounder,
1515-2, *Afro-American Folk Music from Tate and Panole
Counties, Mississippi*, 2000.

**"This Little Light of Mine," as sung by Ada Turner,
1970, near Senatobia, Mississippi. Collected by David
Evans. Recording: Library of Congress, LP AFS L67, 1978.
Reissue: Rounder, 1515-2, *Afro-American Folk Music from
Tate and Panole Counties, Mississippi*, 2000.

"This Little Light of Mine"

This little light of mine, I'm gonna let it shine,
This little light of mine, I'm gonna let it shine,
This little light of mine, I'm gonna let it shine,
Let it shine, shine, shine, let it shine.

Everywhere I go, I'm gonna let it shine,
Everywhere I go, I'm gonna let it shine,
Everywhere I go, I'm gonna let it shine,
Let it shine, shine, shine, Lord, let it shine.

God give it to me, I'm gonna let it shine,
God give it to me, I'm gonna let it shine,
God give it to me, I'm gonna let it shine,
Shine, shine, shine, Lord, let it shine.

All in my home, I'm gonna let it shine,
All in my home, I'm gonna let it shine,
All in my home, I'm gonna let it shine,
Let it shine, shine, shine, Lord let it shine.

God said, "Don't hide your light," I'm gonna let it
   shine,
"Don't hide your light," I'm gonna let it shine,
"Don't hide your light," I'm gonna let it shine,
Let it shine, shine, shine, Lord, let it shine.**

Many songs in the repertoires of children show no color boundaries. "Little Sally Walker" and "This Little Light of Mine," though recorded from African Americans, are sung by Anglo-Americans in the region as well. The first is a clapping song and comes from an old English children's game; the second is known primarily as a spiritual.

The latter's verse structure, AAAB, with extensive repetitions and only slight changes from stanza to stanza, made it ideal for singing by congregations without any books; the leader had only to sing the first line of a stanza and the rest of the congregation knew exactly what followed. The song recalls a passage from the *New Testament* in Matthew 5:16: "Likewise, let your light shine before men, that they may see your fine works and give glory to your Father who is in the heavens." Folklorist David Evans, who collected "This Little Light of Mine," noted that, like other songs in the community, it served as both a spiritual and as a work song; the singer used it to accompany her butter churning because it suited the rhythm of the task perfectly. This illustrates a point made elsewhere in this book: the categorizations that outsiders such as folklorists and anthropologists establish for folk songs are not necessarily distinctions that make sense within the community where the songs originate.

The pine forests of the Southeastern states gave rise to an important turpentine manufacturing industry. Turpentine mill camps sprang up where the wood was chemically processed to produce the turpentine, and there the workers developed a musical culture of their own, generally a blend of Anglo-American and African American elements. A type of holler evolved that soon spread into other occupational areas. Several blues songs, recorded in the 1920s and 1930s originated in the turpentine camps.

Hudson Whittaker, the singer of the "Turpentine Blues," was born in Georgia in 1900 and grew up in Tampa, Florida. Possibly the lyrics, recorded in the depths of the Great Depression, reflected some of his own work experiences in Florida turpentine camps.

SEA ISLANDS

Off the coast of South Carolina, Georgia, and Florida is a chain of low-lying, sandy islands that were settled and claimed by Spain in 1568. By the end of the seventeenth century, they were part of the English colony of Carolina. In the eighteenth century, they were private estates awarded to various individuals. After the American Revolution, parts of the lands were integrated into the

---

"Turpentine Blues"

Turpentine's all right, providin' that wages are good,
Turpentine's all right, providin' that wages are good;
But I can make more money now at somewhere choppin' cord-wood.

Turpentine business ain't like it used to be,
Turpentine business ain't like it used to be;
I can't make enough money now to even get on a spree.

I ain't gonna work no more, I tell you the reason why,
I ain't gonna work no more, I tell you the reason why;
Because everybody wants to sell and nobody want to buy.

You can work in the field, you can work at the sawmill too,
You can work in the field, you can work at the sawmill too;
But you can't make no money at nothin' you do.

So, lordy, please tell me, what we turpentine people are gonna do,
So, lordy, please tell me, what we turpentine people are gonna do;
We may work one week, but we got to lay off for a month or two.

Turpentine is just like dice, to shoot you are bound to lose,
Turpentine is just like dice, to shoot you are bound to lose;
That's the reason why I've got those turpentine blues.*

*Recorded by Tampa Red [Hudson Whittaker] in 1932. Recording: 78 rpm Vocalion, 1699. Transcribed by R. R. MacLeod in *Document Blues—2* (Edinburgh: PAT Publications, 1995), p. 380.

respective American states. Eventually, Spain ceded the lands still under its control to the United States with the rest of Florida in 1821.

Plantations on the islands cultivated rice and cotton. After the Civil War, abandoned plantations were confiscated, and the land was given to freed slaves. The Carolina islands still are home to a largely African American population that has retained many old African-derived customs and folk-ways. The local language dialect is called gullah, and it has been shown to retain many old Africanisms that have long since disappeared elsewhere in the New World. The music of the region, as late as the 1930s, was found also to have retained many elements of African music. Among the types of songs that have been found there are various kinds of maritime work songs.

One boating song that was revived with success in the urban folk song re-vival of the 1960s was "Michael, Row the Boat Ashore." The source for this piece was a collection of folk songs made in the 1860s, mainly in the Georgia Sea Islands. Some of the many verses are reproduced here.

An old African song style to survive was the ring shout, or ring dance: a circle dance in which dancers move counter-clockwise in a circle, singing or chanting in call-and-response fashion. Sometimes these were carried out in a religious context, after prayer meeting and church service. In a secular context, the same type of activity can become a children's play game.

The warning refrain, "plumb de line," in the sample shown here means something like "you have to stay on the straight and narrow path." Possibly there is a suggestion of mari-time origin: one plumbs the line to make sure the water is deep enough for the boat.

"Michael, Row the Boat Ashore"

Michael, row de boat ashore, hallelujah,
Michael, row de boat ashore, hallelujah.
Michael boat a gospel boat, hallelujah,
Michael boat a gospel boat, hallelujah.

I wonder where my mudder den [there],
I wonder where my mudder den.
Michael boat a music boat,
Michael boat a music boat.

Brudder, lend a helpin' hand,
Brudder, lend a helpin' hand.
Sister, help for trim dat boat,
Sister, help for trim dat boat.

Gabriel, blow de trumpet horn,
Gabriel, blow de trumpet horn.
Jordan stream is wide and deep,
Jordan stream is wide and deep.*

*As printed in William Francis Allen, Charles Pickard Ware, and Lucy McKim Garrison, *Slave Songs of the United States* (1867; repr., New York: Dover, 1995).

AFRICAN AMERICAN INFLUENCES

Slavery was a part of American life almost from the moment the first Europeans set foot on New World soil. The first slaves debarked at Jamestown, Virginia, in 1619, a scant dozen years after the colony was established. This is not the place to dwell on the complex and shameful relationship; the point is that African American music is as old as Anglo-American or Franco-American or other types of folk music. Part of the slave trade took advantage of inter-tribal raids and dynastic rivalry in West Africa that led to the selling into slavery of kings, priests, and other tribal leaders. As a result, the slaves who were shipped off to the New World were not necessarily the weak and help-less outcasts of society; some of the Africans were the best educated and most talented. The result was that some of the best musical carriers were shipped across the Atlantic; whether their privileged status made them any more likely to survive the harrow-ing voyage on the overcrowded slave ships is another question. Nevertheless, slave traders soon learned that music and song lifted spirits, thereby increasing survival rates and, there-fore, profitability.

> ### "Plumb de Line"
>
> Members, *plumb de line.*
> Members, *plumb de line.*
> O, members, *plumb de line.*
> Wan't t' go t' Heaven got a *plumb de line.*
> You got t' sing right, *plumb de line.*
> You got t' sing right, *plumb de line.*
> Wan't t' go t' Heaven got a *plumb de line.*
> O sister, *plumb de line.*
> O sister, *plumb de line.*
> O sister, *plumb de line.*
> Wan't t' go t' Heaven got a *plumb de line.*
> You got t' shout right, *plumb de line.*
> You got t' shout right, *plumb de line.**
>
> *As collected and published by Lydia Parrish in *Slave Songs of the Georgia Sea Islands* (1942; repr., Hatboro, PA: Folklore Associates, 1965), p. 67.

Attitudes in different American colonies towards the slaves diverged widely. In the Latin/Catholic colonies, the planters tended to be relatively permissive of the survival of the West African traditions. Portuguese, Spanish, and French planters dominated their slaves' lives outwardly but weren't overly con-cerned about what they did in their (very lim-ited) spare time as long as it didn't interfere with their duties.

On the other hand, the British/Protestant colonial slave owners, trying to justify slavery on the grounds that it might convert a heathen into a Christian, tried to impose their own religious prac-tices on the Africans. As a result, Protestantism superimposed on African music led to revival music, ring dances and ring shouts, and spirituals. In the Latin colonies, secular music more often thrived: march music, satirical love songs, and complex polyrhythmic instrumental music, leading eventually to jazz in its various forms.[5]

As stated previously, one of the reasons European and West African music were able to blend so easily is that they had many similarities. Both used the diatonic scale and both employed a certain amount of harmony, a musical fea-ture rare in other parts of the pre-Industrial world. Some musicologists have identified the sources of these similarities in Arabic/Islamic influences in both Africa and Europe in the pre-Columbian centuries.

For the most part, our earliest documentation of the music of Africans and African Americans is of the African-cum-Protestant religious music called anthems or spirituals, the work songs (boating, cane cutting, tree felling, and so on), and the semi-religious dance music (ring dances and ring shouts). Ring dances were permitted by religious Protestant masters, who rejected dancing as sinful, because of a quirk: dancing was defined as a movement that involved crossing the feet. The African ring dances, however, involved a shuffling movement that never crossed the feet; hence, to the British, it didn't count as dancing.

Black musicians playing accordion and washboard in front of a store near New Iberia, Louisiana (1938). *Photographer, Russell Lee (LC-USF33-011902-M2); from the Farm Security Administration—Office of War Information Photo Collection, Library of Congress Prints and Photographs Division.*

The children's clapping ring game is perhaps the secular equivalent of the religious ring shouts that were once widespread in the African American communities and have clear African antecedents. The performance tempo of these games usually increases until it builds up to a frenzied pace, a characteristic that the written text alone cannot show. In "I'm Going Up North—Satisfied," one child sings the first phrase; the group replies, "Satisfied."

Folklorist Harold Courlander noted the social allusions in the text, which make fun of those folks who go north to better themselves but find no improvement in their situation. Many children's songs and games show this kind of trickling down of an attitude that must have been from their elders.

The ring shout "Move, Members, Move Daniel" was recorded in a secular context, but it straddles the line between spiritual and secular song.

John A. Lomax and his son Alan Lomax traveled through the South in the 1930s under the auspices of the Library of Congress, hauling recording equipment to collect the folk music of America. They found some wonderful singers in the prisons and work farms of the South. Back in the nineteenth and early twentieth centuries, it was common for the prisons to lease out groups of convicts whenever work gangs were required for grading roads, clearing forests, breaking rocks, and other strenuous tasks. If money was exchanged in these arrangements, it generally went to the prison officials rather than to the workers, who were invariably African Americans. After the end of World War II,

"I'm Going Up North—Satisfied"

I'm goin' up North—*Satisfied!*
An' I would tell you—*Satisfied!*
Lord I am—*Satisfied!*
Some peoples up there—*Satisfied!*
Goin' to bring you back—*Satisfied!*
Ain't nothin' up there—*Satisfied!*
What you can do—*Satisfied!*
Mamma cooked a cow—*Satisfied!*
Have to get all the girls—*Satisfied!*
Their bellies full—*Satisfied!*
I'm goin' up North—*Satisfied!*
And I would tell you—*Satisfied!*
Lord I am—*Satisfied!*
Mamma cooked a bull—*Satisfied!*

Their bellies full—*Satisfied!*
I'm goin' up North—*Satisfied!*
And I would tell you—*Satisfied!*
Lord I am—*Satisfied!*
Some peoples up there—*Satisfied!*
Goin' bring you back—*Satisfied!*
Mamma cooked a chicken—*Satisfied!*
Have to get all the girls—*Satisfied!*
Their bellies full—*Satisfied!**

*As sung by a group of children of East York School, East York, Alabama, 1950. Collected by Harold Courlander. Recording: Folkways, LP FE 4417, *Negro Folk Music of Alabama*, 1956; Folkways, LP FA 2691, *Music Down Home: An Introduction to Negro Folk Music, USA*, 1965.

better and smaller tape recording machines became available, and Alan Lomax returned to the South to revisit and better record the singers who had so impressed him and his father in the previous decade. Although the singers had changed, many of their work songs had not.

In "Rosie," the vocal accompanies and is punctuated by the swinging of axes. The singing takes the form of call and response, with one singer leading and the rest of the men acting as chorus. The text, which is very fluid, starts with some bitter commentary about the singer's current situation, which he might have avoided (he says) had he left Mississippi (in other words, gone north). Then

"Move, Members, Move Daniel"

Move, members, move, Daniel! (3)
Move, members, move, Daniel! there;
Move till I get home, Daniel! (4)

Got on my little John shoes!
Got on my little John Shoes, Daniel! (3)
Shoes gonna rock-a me home, Daniel! (4)

Move, members, move!
Move, members, move, Daniel! (3)
Who want to buy this land, Daniel? (3)
Who want to buy this land?
Who want to buy this land, Daniel?

Move, members, move, Daniel!
Move, members, move, Daniel! there

Move till I get home, Daniel! (2)
Move till I get there, Daniel! (2)
Move till I get home, Daniel! (4)

Got on my little John shoes!
Got on my little John Shoes, Daniel!
Shoes gonna rock-a me home, Daniel! (6)*

*As sung by Rosie Hibler and family in Marian, Mississippi, about 1950. Collected by Harold Courlander. Recording: Folkways, LP FE 4417, *Negro Folk Music of Alabama*, 1956; Folkways, LP FA 2691, *Music Down Home: An Introduction to Negro Folk Music, USA*, 1965. Numbers in parentheses indicate how many times the line is sung.

the lyrics turn to women, with overt sexual references that are to be expected from young men who have been deprived of the company of women for months or maybe years.

Religious songs have always constituted a major share of the music of American folk communities, and African Americans are no exception. What distinguishes a folk community from the mainstream culture is that these religious songs are as likely to be heard outside the building of worship as within.

Many African American gospel spirituals took Biblical themes and worked them into a story song. The Samson and Delilah story was recorded in the 1920s by several gospel artists. It is easy to see the underlying social message in this favorite Biblical story. Samson, the world's strongest man, beset by treachery, ultimately triumphs over his human and animal adversaries; likewise, the oppressed African American hoped to triumph over persecutors and yearned for the physical strength and, later, the political strength to do so.

COAL MINERS

America's coal mining culture is divided into regions determined by geology: the anthracite (hard coal) mines, located mostly in eastern Pennsylvania, and the bituminous (soft coal) mines, scattered over some twenty-two states but most prominently in western Pennsylvania, Ohio, Illinois, Indiana, Virginia, West Virginia, Kentucky, Tennessee, and Alabama. Over the years, annual bituminous coal production has exceeded that of anthracite by a factor of up to

"Rosie"

Ain't but one thing I done wrong (3)
Stayed in Mississippi just a day too long.
A day too long, Lordy, day too long,
In Mississippi, a day too long.

Well Lord, Rosie, O Lord, gal! (4)

I'm in the pen, mama, got a hundred year, (3)
Tree fall on me, I don't bit mo' care.
I don't bit mo' care, baby, bit mo' care,
Tree fall on me, I don't bit mo' care.

Well, 'Berta in Meridian but she got my mind, (3)
I'm on Lambert, tryin' to do my time.
Do my time, baby, do my time,
I'm on Lambert, tryin' to do my time.

Lord, Rosie, O Lord, gal!
Lord, Rosie, O Lord, gal!

Oh, 'Berta, oh Lord, gal,
Won't do nothin' but to starch and iron, (3)
Starch and iron, baby, starch and iron,
Won't do nothin' but to starch and iron.

Lord, Rosie, O Lord, gal
Lord, Rosie, O Lord, gal

Ain't been to Georgia, but I've been told, (3)
Georgia women got a sweet jelly roll.
Sweet jelly roll, baby, sweet jelly roll,
Georgia women got a sweet jelly roll.

Lord, Rosie, O Lord, gal!
Lord, Rosie, O Lord, gal!*

*As sung by a gang of African American workers at Parchman, Mississippi, prison farm, 1947. Collected by Alan Lomax. Recording: Rounder, CD 1715, *Prison Songs*. Numbers in parentheses indicate how many times the line is sung.

"If I Had My Way"

CHORUS:

If I had my way,
If I had my way,
If I had my way,
I would tear this old building down.

Well, Delilah she was walking, she was fine and
fair,
She had good looks, God knows, and coal black
hair;

Delilah, she came on Samson's mind,
When the first he saw the woman [that looked so
fine?]

Delilah she sat down on Samson's knee,
"If you tell me where your strength lie, if you
please."

She spoke so kind, God knows, she talked so fair,
Samson says "Delilah, you cut off my hair,

You can shave my head, [clean as my hand?]
My strength done left me [just like any man?]."

CHORUS.

Well, you read about Samson, in the verse,
He was the strongest man that had ever lived on
earth.

So one day while Samson was a-walking along,
He looked on the ground and saw an old jawbone.

He stretched out his arm, God knows, it broke like
thread
[Great God almighty, the lion was dead?].

CHORUS.*

*By Reverend Gary Davis, recorded in 1958 in concert.
Recording: Folkways, FN 2512, *Hootenanny at Carnegie
Hall*. Reissue: Smithsonian Folkways, *Folk-Song America:
A 20th-Century Revival*. (The lines in brackets are difficult
to understand and are conjectured from other recordings.)

ten. The earliest recorded commercial mine in the United States dates to 1750,
near Richmond, Virginia; Pennsylvania's first coalmine was opened in 1760.
Such beginnings were small in scale, and the modern mining industry can be
said to have begun in about 1840. In the 1880s, coal overtook wood as the
principal source of fuel in the United States, and from the same time on, the
industry has been dominated by large corporations. Around 1910 coal's percentage share of total U.S. energy production peaked and has declined steadily
ever since.

The anthracite workforce had a large Celtic component: Irish immigrants
were the largest constituency, with the Welsh in second place. The ballads and
songs of this region show a heavy Irish influence, as in the incipit broadside
ballad style and a penchant for Irish or Irish-derived melodies. While it's not
easy to describe in general what an "Irish or Irish-derived melody" sounds like,
there are a few common patterns. One is a common melodic structure where
the first and fourth line of the stanza are sung to nearly the same tune, as are the
second and third. A characteristic stanza ending (in the key of C) is C-C-C or
C-B-C, with the middle note much shorter than the other two.

The more sprawling bituminous region had its share of Irish and Welsh, but
also Scotch-Irish, African American, and the other population groups that

settled in various parts of the Appalachians. In 1880 to 1920, a great influx of Slavic and Italian workers occurred. Many of them were put to work in the mines before they had acquired even a passing command of the English language and as a result became safety hazards to others as well as to themselves.

In the bituminous regions, the company-owned mine village, where most miners lived, was called the coal camp; in the anthracite region it was called a mine patch. It used to be compulsory for the miners to live there, which gave the owners an extraordinary degree of control over the miners, to the extent that they were required to attend the local (that is, in the coal camp) church, to send their children to the local school, and to participate in all local social events. Often they were paid in scrip—a form of token money that could be used for commodity transactions—rather than actual dollars. Since only the company store (in the coal camp) accepted the scrip, the miners were forced to shop there, giving the mine owners a virtual monopoly over all their purchases. Corporate owners enforced a system, the "yellow-dog contract," of giving employment to workers only on condition that they promised not to join the union (and, in many cases, to forswear constitutionally guaranteed rights). Even to leave the premises of the coal camp temporarily, one needed a written pass from a superintendent. The mine camps were rigidly segregated according to social station and ethnicity.

Mine owners, for the most part, were unconscionably indifferent to the working conditions of their miners, resisting any changes in working conditions that might make life safer for their workers at the expense of profits. Because of inadequate safety precautions, mine explosions and cave-ins were a constant danger. Explosions were a result of either of two combustibles: the mostly methane gas that is often liberated in the mining process (called firedamp), and secondly, the fine coal dust that is also generated. The coal dust was the source of another threat even when it didn't explode: black lung disease, or pneumoconiosis. Cave-ins resulted from inadequate attention to shoring up newly excavated mine tunnels. In the mine camps, not only adult men worked in the mines, but young boys would be put to work as well. A family could have several members employed in the mines and could easily lose all of them in a disaster.

As miners and their families constantly faced the threat of such tragedies, superstitions thrived. Dream portents were not taken lightly, as illustrated by "Don't Go Down in the Mine" (also called "Dream of the Miner's Child"), a ballad that is still sung in the Southeast.

Once out in the sunlight, the miners were still not assured of safety. Coal was taken out of the mines in hopper cars on a rail line, the operation of which could pose additional dangers. In the days before hydraulic brakes and couplers, brakemen had to set the old link-and-pin couplers manually, and if a "brakie" wasn't sufficiently spry and alert, an arm or leg could easily be crushed as the cars clashed together. George Korson, a journalist with a lifelong interest in mining folklore, collected "The Dying Mine Brakeman" from West Virginia miner-composer Orville Jenks, who claimed to have written the ballad in 1915.

"Don't Go Down in the Mine"

A miner was leaving his home for his work
When he heard his little child scream,
He went to his bedside, his little face white,
Oh, daddy, I've had such a dream.
I dreamt that I saw the mine all on fire,
And men struggled hard for their lives;
The scene it then changed and the top of the mine
Was surrounded by sweethearts and wives."

CHORUS:
"Don't go down in the mine, Dad,
Dreams very often come true;
Daddy, you know it would break my heart
If anything happened to you.
Just go and tell my dream to your mates,
And as true as the stars that shine,
Something is going to happen today,
Dear daddy, don't go down in the mine."

The miner, a man with a heart good and kind,
Stood by the side of his son.

He said, "It's my living, I can't stay away,
For duty, my lad, must be done."
The little one looked up and faintly he said,
"Oh, please stay today with me, Dad."
But as the brave miner went forth to his work
He heard this appeal from his lad.

Whilst waiting his turn with his mates to descend
He could not banish his fears.
He returned home again to his wife and his child—
Those words seemed to ring through his ears.
And ere the day ended the mine was on fire,
When a score of brave men lost their lives.
He thanked God above for the dream his child had,
As once more the little one cries.*

*In *UMWJ*, Feb. 9, 1911. Reprinted by George Korson, *Coal Dust on the Fiddle* (1943; repr., Hatboro, PA: Folklore Associates, 1965), pp. 213–214.

Subsequently, it spread through the Appalachians and was rewritten to fit other incidents. Most of the text could easily be adapted to an accident on any railroad. Jenks's reference to the "weighboss"—the man who weighs the mined coal and credits the miners with their due amounts—localizes it to the minefields.

The hardships of mine life were not successfully challenged until the miners attempted to unionize, a goal not achieved without great loss of lives owing to the mine owners' bitter resistance. While there are a few mining songs and ballads that date back to the 1840s, the bloody conflicts of unionization efforts of the 1920s and 1930s provided an abundance of material for the songwriters and singers of the period—not only the ballads descriptive of the hardships of life, such as characterized the other occupations surveyed here, but also militant protest songs speaking out stridently against the workers' hardships and demanding better conditions. "A Miner's Prayer" was recorded in Pennsylvania in 1940; though it is not widely known, it expresses emotions that were common in the mining communities before unionization helped improve working conditions, and accurately records the families' plight.

When labor union representatives began serious efforts to establish unions among the mineworkers in the 1930s, the mine camps themselves often became the scenes of pitched battles between the miners and the hired thugs of the owners, between strikers and strikebreakers. The spirits of the downtrodden miners and their families were often uplifted with the help of proud and militant

"The Dying Mine Brakeman"

See that brave and trembling motorman,
Said his age was twenty-one;
See him stepping from his motor,
Crying, "Lord, what have I done?"

"Have I killed my brave young coupler,
Is it right that he is dying?
Well, I tried to stop the motor,
But I could not stop in time."

See the car wheels running o'er him,
See them bend his weary head;
See his sister standing o'er him,
Crying "Brother, are you dead?"

"Yes, sister, I am dying,
Soon I'll reach a better shore;
Soon I'll gain a home in heaven,
Where this coupling will be no more.

Tell my brother in the heading—
These few words I'll send to him;
Never, never venture coupling,
If he does, his life will end.

Tell my father—he's a weighboss,
All he weighs to weigh it fair,
They will have true scales up yonder,
At that meeting in the air.

Tell my mother I've gone to glory,
Not to grieve for me no more;
Just to meet me over yonder,
On that bright and golden shore."*

*As sung by Orville J. Jenks of Welch, West Virginia, in 1940. Collected by George Korson. Recording: LC AFS L60, *Songs and Ballads of the Bituminous Miners*, 1965.

union songs, though even the mere singing of such lyrics placed the singers in physical danger. The songwriters typically took tunes that the miners already knew well, such as spirituals. West Virginia miners in 1931 wrote "We Shall Not Be Moved" from the gospel hymn, "I Shall Not Be Moved," which began,

"A Miner's Prayer"

I keep listening for the whistles in the morning,
But the mines are still; no noise is in the air.
And the children wake up crying in the morning,
For the cupboards are so empty and so bare.

And their little feet are oh, so cold they stumble,
And we have to pin the rags upon their backs.
And our home is broken down and very humble,
While the wintry wind comes pouring through each
    crack.

CHORUS:
Oh, it's hard to hear the hungry children crying
While I have two hands that want to do their share,
Oh, you rich men in the city, won't you have a
    little pity,
And just listen to a miner's prayer?

Down beneath the frozen ground the coal is laying,
Only waiting till we seek it from its bed,
While above the earth with aching heart we're
    praying,
While each wife and mother waits with bowed
    down head.

Oh, we only ask enough to clothe and feed them,
And to hear the hungry children sing and play.
Oh, if we could give these things to those who need
    them,
I know that would be a miner's happy day.*

*Recorded on May 1940 in Pittsburgh, Pennsylvania, by George Korson; sung by Mrs. Ralph B. Thompson of Tarentum, Pennsylvania. Published in George Korson, *Coal Dust on the Fiddle* (1943; repr., Hatboro, PA: Folklore Associates, 1965), pp. 76–77.

I shall not, I shall not be moved,
I shall not, I shall not be moved,
Just like a tree that's planted by the waters,
I shall not be moved.

The original spiritual took its inspiration from Jeremiah 17:7–8, "Blessed is he who trusts in the Lord . . . he shall be like a tree planted by waters. . . ." Not only was the union song set to a familiar and easily sung tune, but the verse structure made it possible for everyone to join in after the leader sang out the first few words of a stanza. Furthermore, other participants could easily add their own stanzas. Using a tune with religious associations also unconsciously helped establish the righteousness of the union cause in the singers' minds.

TEXTILE WORKERS

By the last quarter of the 1800s, cheap labor and plentiful water power had made the Southern states' textile mills competitive with the older New England mills discussed in the preceding chapter. Mills were established in the Piedmont region of the Southeast (from Virginia to Georgia and Alabama), and by 1900, one-quarter of all cotton spindles, or milling machines, were located in the South. In 1961, while collecting folk songs from former mill workers Dorsey and Nancy Dixon in North Carolina, folklorist Archie Green heard them sing fragments of "A Factory Girl," which Nancy had learned in 1899 when she first went to work in the mills.

Gastonia, North Carolina, developed into an important mill city in the early 1900s and was the site of violent labor union strikes in 1929 that resulted in the murder of one of the strike leaders. In spite of such strife, one musically skilled mill worker, Dave McCarn, wrote and recorded a couple of songs of generalized protest against working conditions that didn't touch upon specific union issues.

Protest songs complain about some aspect of social conditions; students write and sing them as readily as miners and "lintheads" (as textile workers are sometimes called). Usually a song that expresses discontent in a humorous manner is more effective at making its point than one that is militantly confrontational. Protest songs generally do no more than protest; they offer no solutions. When a song does suggest remedies, it enters the ranks of political songlore.

"We Shall Not Be Moved"

We shall not, we shall not be moved,

John L. Lewis is our leader, we shall not be moved,
. . . .
Mitch is our district president, we shall not be moved,
. . . .
You can tell de henchmen, we shall not be moved,
. . . .
Run an' tell de super'tendent, we shall not be moved,
We shall not, we shall not be moved,
Jus' like a tree dat's planted by de water,
We shall not be moved.*

*Recorded in Columbus, Ohio, on February 1, 1940, by George Korson from the singing of Charles Langford of Alabama and published in his *Coal Dust on the Fiddle* (1943; repr., Hatboro, PA: Folklore Associates, 1965), p. 315.

Dorsey Dixon and Nancy Dixon in Rockingham, North Carolina (1962). *Photographer, Gene Earle; courtesy of the Southern Folklife Collection, University of North Carolina.*

"A Factory Girl"

Yonder stands that spinning room boss,
He looks so fair and stout,
I hope he'll marry a factory girl
Before this year goes out.

CHORUS:
Pity me all day, pity me I pray,
Pity me, my darling, and take me far away.

I'll bid you factory girls farewell,
Come see me if you can;
For I'm a-gonna quit this factory work
And marry a nice young man.

No more I'll hear that whistle blow,
The sound of it I hate;
No more I'll hear that boss man say,
"Young girl, you are too late."

No more I'll hear this roaring,
This roaring over my head,
While you poor girls are hard at work
And I'll be home in bed.*

*As sung by Mike Seeger. Recording: Folkways, LP FH 5273, *Tipple, Loom and Rail.* Put together from the versions of Dorsey Dixon and Nancy Dixon, issued on Hightone, CD HMG 2502, *Babies in the Mill.* See also the version of this song in Chapter 3.

"Cotton Mill Colic"

When you buy clothes on easy terms,
The collectors treat you like measly worms;
One dollar down and then, Lord knows,
If you don't make a payment they'll take your
    clothes.

When you go to bed, you can't sleep,
You owe so much at the end of a week;
No use to colic, they're all that way,
Picking at your door till they get your pay.

I'm gonna starve, everybody will,
'Cause you can't make a living at a cotton mill.
When you go to work, you work like the devil;
At the end of the week, you're not on the
    level.

Payday comes, you pay your rent,
When you get through, you've not got a cent
To buy fatback meat, pinto beans,
Now and then you get turnip greens.

No use to colic, we're all that way,
Can't get the money to move away.
I'm gonna starve, everybody will,
'Cause you can't make a living at a cotton mill.

Twelve dollars a week is all we get,
How in the heck can we live on that?
I got a wife and fourteen kids,
We all have to sleep on two bedsteads.

Patches on my britches, holes in my hat,
Ain't had a shave since my wife got fat.
No use to colic, everyday at noon,
The kids get to crying in a different tune.

I'm gonna starve, everybody will,
'Cause you can't make a living at a cotton mill.
They run a few days and then they stand,
Just to keep down the working man.

We can't make it, we never will,
As long as we stay at a lousy mill.
The poor gettin' poorer, the rich a-gettin' rich,
If I don't starve, I'm a son of a gun.

No use to colic, no use to rave,
We'll never rest till we're in our grave.
I'm gonna starve, everybody will,
'Cause you can't make a living at a cotton mill.*

*As sung by its composer, Dave McCarn of Gastonia, North Carolina, in 1930 for RCA Victor. Reissue: Yazoo, CD 2037, *Hard Times Come Again No More, Vol. 2*, 1998.

Both "A Factory Girl" and Dave McCarn's recording a century later express dissatisfaction with mill life, though McCarn's is more pointed about the reasons for complaint. The factory girl's only hope for salvation lies in marriage; McCarn's fellow workers had no such option. His litany concerns the financial aspects: the insufficient pay, the inequity between the workers' and the bosses' rewards, the inability to pay the bills, and the dim prospect of ever escaping from the cycle. "The Factory Girl" was distributed on a printed broadside; McCarn recorded his song on a 78-rpm hillbilly recording—the twentieth-century functional equivalent of the penny broadside.

FRANCO-AMERICANS: FRENCH CANADIAN, CAJUN, AND CREOLE

An important non–English-speaking group in the New World was the French, who first established colonies in what they called Acadie, or Acadia, in 1604 to 1605 on both sides of what is now the U.S. border with Canada. Conflicts between the British and the French settlers in the region continued on and off for a century and a half, until the conclusion of the French and Indian Wars in 1763 put all the lands under British rule. In the 1750s, when the Acadians refused to take the oath of allegiance demanded by the British, they were ordered to leave their villages. In a decade, more than eight thousand were deported, half of whom died at sea. Nevertheless, the French cultural influence was firmly established, and French language folk songs and French-influenced instrumental music remain a part of the regional lore.

Eventually, many of the exiles took haven in southern Louisiana, which was then still under French rule. Two related but distinct cultures still thrive there today: the "Cajun" (from the word "Acadian"), and Creole, which represents the hybridization of the Franco-American with the local African American population. The music of the latter group is called Zydeco. In the nineteenth century, the Cajuns developed an ensemble utilizing primarily fiddle, accordion, and guitar; percussion instruments, especially the once common triangle, lost popularity in the twentieth century. Cajun music interchanged considerably with mainstream country music starting in the 1930s and 1940s, thanks to the radio and records.

Other Franco-American communities persist along the Mississippi in what was originally New France, where the French were the earliest white settlers. Place names such as Lafayette, Mississippi, St. Louis and Ste. Genevieve, Missouri, St. Croix and La Crosse, Wisconsin, La Salle and Marquette, Michigan, and Joliet and Champaign, Illinois, are all reminders of the French presence.

RAGTIME AND JAZZ

As the dance craze of the early 1900s captured the nation's fancy, instrumental and dance music began to supplant the sentimental ballads and songs of the Victorian era. The term "ragtime" carries two different connotations. In the narrow sense, it designates the formal creations of classically oriented composers, such as Scott Joplin, James Scott, and Joseph Lamb; more broadly, it encompasses an earlier body of syncopated or ragtime music that existed on a folk level, which professional composers drew upon and formalized. A few formal rags entered the traditional fiddler's repertoire and were recorded frequently in the 1920s and later: "Maple Leaf Rag," "Dill Pickles," "Black and White Rag," and "St. Louis Tickle," were the best known. More pervasive was the influence from the older African American folk ragtime tradition on later raggy (that is, syncopated) pieces that one still hears played at fiddle contests, such as "Beaumont Rag," "East Tennessee Blues," or "Ragtime Annie." Though ragtime was primarily an instrumental style, there were songs written with ragtime elements (most notably in the syncopation and the chord progressions) that also entered folk tradition, such as "At a Georgia Camp Meeting" and "Alexander's Ragtime Band."

While its folk roots are older, jazz as a style with major exposure and impact emerged in the 1910s, especially in New Orleans but soon also northward along the Mississippi River, to some extent displacing ragtime as the dominant music of interest. The ethnic origins of jazz music have been disputed from time to time but the majority view is that African Americans played a major (if not exclusive) role in the early years. Many hillbilly musicians of the 1920s who had grown up with traditional folk music—notably the younger ones—were fascinated by jazz and incorporated it into their recorded repertoires. Jazz favorites ("Farewell Blues," "House of David Blues," "Take Me to the Land of Jazz," "Tiger Rag," and "12th St. Rag") found their way into the repertoires of noncommercial fiddlers. In the Southwest, this association was even stronger, with western swing pioneers such as Milton Brown and Bob Wills regularly listening to, and borrowing from, jazz and blues hits of the day.

HILLBILLY MUSIC, COUNTRY MUSIC, AND BLUEGRASS

Prior to about 1920, if a traditional singer or musician wanted to earn a living though music, there weren't many options. He (they were rarely women) could become a street singer, perhaps peddling broadsides or small songbooks of his own compositions and singing them in hopes of a few pennies. A number of blind musicians, both black and white, took this route, as there may have been little else they could do. In a booklet he sold, blind Dick Burnett of Kentucky included his composition "Farewell Song," which has enjoyed a recent revival under the title "I Am a Man of Constant Sorrow," partly because of its appearance in the film *Oh Brother, Where Art Thou.* A musician might perform at public events, especially dances and fiddle contests, and make a modest living. Most musicians had to be content with letting music be their avocation while they earned their living at something else—such as farming, manual labor, or handicrafts.

Two new media, the radio and the phonograph, changed all that in the early 1920s. Between 1922 and 1924, a few traditional musicians and phonograph company representatives grasped the potential of recordings (the phonograph had actually been around since 1877) and approached each other to arrange trial recordings. At first, the music was marketed under different designations: old-time music, old familiar tunes, or hillbilly music. The latter term became the most widespread until the mid-1940s, notwithstanding its negative connotations to many Southerners. In the parallel universe of African American music, the designations "race music" or "music of the race," and then "blues and gospel," were employed. To control advertising and distribution, each genre (classical, popular, hillbilly, blues, and ethnic) was issued in its own distinct numerical series. From the companies' perspective, selling phonograph recordings by rural traditional artists might induce more people to buy records and phonographs. From the artists' perspective, it was a possible avenue to fame and fortune.

Although the imagined avenue to fame and fortune turned out to be a cul-de-sac for most, soon the industry of recording traditional folk musicians and marketing their recordings in the areas from whence they came had grown significantly. Within a few years, there were artists—Vernon Dalhart, Jimmie Rodgers, the Carter Family—whose appeal transcended regions, and a national market emerged. As this took place, artists with limited appeal, or whose styles were too archaic or localized, had to change or else drop out of the business. In the first years, from 1922 to 1930, approximately 7,000 different songs and tunes were issued, a substantial proportion of which were traditional. Once artists exhausted the traditional repertoire of their youth, if they wanted their careers to continue, they had to find new material. Most took to composing their own songs or working with songwriters who could provide suitable material. A few who did not feel at home with newer songs chose to visit friends and neighbors to learn songs from them; or, if they were simultaneously radio performers, would solicit songs from listeners. In effect, people like Virginian A. P. Carter of the Carter Family and Kentuckian Bradley Kincaid became folk song collectors themselves, but as community members rather than as academic outsiders.

While hillbilly music (later country music) was the folk-derived commercial genre of the Southeastern part of the country, distinctive music styles developed in the Southwest. Western music, which emerged in the 1930s, deemphasized instrumentation and substituted carefully arranged elaborate vocal harmonies. Following the songwriting lead of Tim Spencer and Bob Nolan of the Sons of the Pioneers, western music's themes dealt less with family, farm, and femininity than with the range, cattle, cowboys, and horses. Also in the 1930s, western swing developed, an offshoot of the old-time string band as it existed in Texas and Oklahoma but with heavy infusions from jazz, big band swing, and blues. The second part of the name country western refers to these idioms. Western and western swing music are not so relevant to the study of folk music as country music, because there was never as much of a traditional component to the music, and as far as can be told at present, much less western music is entering oral tradition than country music.

Simultaneously, radio became a medium for the traditional musician. In its first few years, radio was strictly local and rather homespun. Local performers from fiddlers to classical pianists to jazz ensembles to pop singers trouped into the studios for a fifteen- or thirty-minute slot. Another opportunity opened for hillbilly musicians when some stations inaugurated "barn dance" programs: variety shows deliberately aimed at the rural audience and featuring old-time fiddlers, string bands, and old favorite ballads and songs. Successful performers on radio built up a voluminous correspondence with listeners, who submitted or requested favorite songs over the airwaves. Some performers began to gather favorite songs into booklets or folios and advertise them over the air.

All of these media—phonograph records, radio programs, song folios—continued the process of eroding the regional character of folk music by effectively increasing the territory that a performer's music could reach. So, although in the first few years hillbilly and race records were another type of field recording, documenting the older folk tradition, by the 1930s they had become a repository of new songs written in the style of older folk songs but increasingly influenced by the popular music of the day.

Some of these newly composed hillbilly and blues songs endured sufficiently to enter folk tradition alongside the older material that was still being sung. By the 1940s and 1950s, folk song collectors were finding folksingers and musicians whose repertoires now included material from hillbilly or blues recordings of the 1920s and 1930s: songs such as "The Death of Floyd Collins" (recorded by Vernon Dalhart), "Wildwood Flower" (Carter Family), "Muleskinner Blues" (Jimmie Rodgers), and "You Are My Sunshine" (Jimmie Davis).

One very successful singer/songwriter was Reverend Andy Jenkins of Georgia. Though he also made some recordings, his main importance was as a composer. In 1925, the country was galvanized when the news spread that a young spelunker, Floyd Collins, had become trapped in an unexplored cave on his family's property in Kentucky, not far from Mammoth Caves. This was the first broadcast of on-the-site radio news coverage. Collins was trapped in the cave on January 30th, and rescue

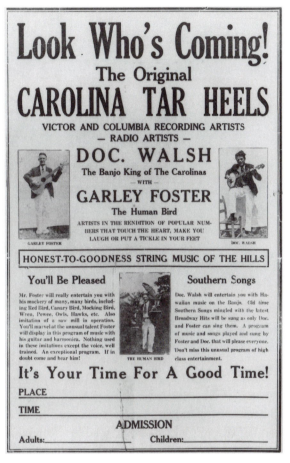

Poster for an appearance of the Carolina Tar Heels (ca. 1930). *Author's collection.*

efforts continued for two weeks until it was determined that he was dead. Jenkins hastily wrote a ballad, "The Death of Floyd Collins," which was recorded a number of times starting in April 1925. The version by Vernon Dalhart was one of the best selling hillbilly records of the 1920s and subsequently has been collected from oral tradition numerous times. The version printed here, from Virginia by way of Michigan, is very close to the original text. The verses about Collins's dream are Jenkins's invention, but very much in the tradition of such tragedy ballads (as is the stern warning in the last stanza), comparable in particular to "Don't Go Down the Mine."

It is difficult to make generalizations about hillbilly styles of the 1920s because of the diversity. Some regions seem to have their own characteristic trademarks: bands from north Georgia, western North Carolina, the Galax,

"Floyd Collins"

O come all ye good people, and listen while I tell,
The fate of Floyd Collins a lad we all know well;
His face was fair and handsome, his heart was true
and brave;
His body now lies sleeping in a lonely sandstone
cave.

"O mother, don't you worry, dear father, don't
be sad;
I'll tell you all my troubles in an awful dream
I had.
I dreamed I was a prisoner; my life I could not
save.
I cried, 'O must I perish within this sandstone
cave?' "

The rescue party labored; they worked both night
and day,
To move the mighty barriers that stood within
the way.
"To rescue Floyd Collins," this was their battle cry,
"We'll never, no, we'll never let Floyd Collins die!"

But on that fatal morning, the sun rose in the skies;
The workers still were busy, "We'll save him by
and by."
But O how sad the ending; his life could not be
saved;
His body then was sleeping in a lonely sandstone
cave.

Young people, O take warning from Floyd Collins'
fate,
And get right with your Maker before it is too late;
It may not be a sandstone cave in which we find
our tomb,
But at the bar of judgment we too will meet our
doom.*

*(Laws, GA 20). Concord Depot, Virginia, 1931. Published
in Emelyn Elizabeth Gardner and Geraldine Jencks
Chickering, *Ballads and Songs of Southern Michigan* (1939;
repr., Hatboro, PA: Folklore Associates, 1967), p. 308.

Virginia, area, and eastern Kentucky often had their own consistent styles. But the decade was one of great transformations. The advent of the phonograph record meant one could hear a fiddler three states away as easily as one next door. Kentucky fiddler "Snake" Chapman (b. 1919) once said that in his youth "if you lived thirty miles from a fiddler, you didn't know about him."[6] Consequently, almost as fast as new and unusual styles could be recorded, they disappeared—or, at least, lost their distinctiveness. Through the 1930s, the numerous regional styles gradually disappeared from the records to be replaced by a few broader styles.

Recording activity in the early 1940s was minimal—both because of the war and also because of some industry disputes. After World War II, when recording recommenced, the music had changed significantly. True, the name "hillbilly" had by now given way to "country and western," later to become just "country" music. More importantly from the perspective of this study, the traditional component of the music had greatly diminished. By the 1940s, most of the recordings consisted of newly composed material. One persistent connection with older music was in the arena of religious songs. Country and blues performers who grew up in the South prior to the 1950s or so all had prior experience with church music, and many sang in their local church choirs. When they became professionals, they maintained their closeness with religious music and often included it in public performances or recordings. These genres are different from pop music, whose artists rarely step across the line separating sacred from secular music.

As mainstream country music in the 1940s moved away from its folk roots, its place was taken by a new idiom: bluegrass music. Bluegrass was essentially the creation of a single individual: Bill Monroe of Kentucky (1911–1996). Kentucky is the bluegrass state, hence the name. In 1945 and 1946, Monroe put together a string band (mandolin, fiddle, banjo, guitar, and string bass—there was also an accordion for a short while) that stressed instrumental virtuosity to a degree not seen in most country music. For a short while, Monroe and His Bluegrass Boys played songs that were similar to the country music of the day, but before long they gave more attention to older string band music representative of hillbilly groups of the late 1920s and 1930s. Soon it seemed as if bluegrass was old-time string band music but at a faster tempo, with greater instrumental technique, with more blues influence, and with the New Orleans jazz custom of rotating solos (or "breaks") among the various instruments—in particular, mandolin, banjo, and fiddle. Increased tempo, as well as the complex instrumental performances, made bluegrass primarily a listening music—unlike older string band music or country music, both of which were well suited for dancing. Earlier string bands invariably took an ensemble approach to the music, never giving a single instrument a solo break. Within a few years, other bands began to emulate the sounds of the Bluegrass Boys, but it was a decade or more before the music slipped out of the southern mountains and into the northern cities.

It was to be expected that bluegrass music found fans among northern college students who had just experienced the beginnings of the folk revival, but interestingly, the style also found many enthusiasts among southern mountain folk who considered Nashville-based country music too modern. As the bluegrass bands imitating Bill Monroe proliferated, musicians explored ways to expand the bluegrass envelope. The original instrumental lineup of all acoustic mandolin, fiddle, banjo, guitar, and string bass was gradually extended to allow entry for drums, keyboards, and electrified instruments. The guitar developed from strictly a rhythm back-up to a lead instrument. Bands composed their own new songs, or looked outside the standard bluegrass repertoire to rock, pop, jazz, blues, and other genres to find new combinations.

In recent decades, young southern musicians interested in preserving and relearning the traditional music of their region have occasionally turned to the 78-rpm recordings of popular hillbilly bands of the 1920s, but increasingly they have looked to bluegrass music for inspiration. The style is thus becoming a part of the traditional music of the Southeast.

RECOMMENDED RECORDINGS

Afro-American Blues and Game Songs. Rounder, CD 1513. (Reissue of Library of Congress, LP AFS L4)

Afro-American Folk Music from Tate and Panola Counties, Miss. Rounder, CD 1515. (Reissue of Library of Congress, LP AFS L67)

Afro-American Spirituals, Work Songs, and Ballads. Rounder, CD 1510. (Reissue of Library of Congress, LP AFS L3)

Alabama Stringbands (1924–1937). Document, DOCD-8032. (Reissues from commercial 78 rpm recordings of the 1920s and 1930s) *Mississippi String Bands, Vols. 1/2.* County, CO-CD-3513/4. (Reissues from commercial 78-rpm recordings of the 1920s and 1930s)

American Banjo Three Finger and Scruggs Style. Smithsonian Folkways, CD SF 40037; from Folkways, LP FA 2314.

American Roots Collection. Smithsonian Folkways, SF CD 40062.

Anthology of American Folk Music (Edited by Harry Smith). Smithsonian Folkways, 3 CDs. (Reissues from commercial 78-rpm recordings of the 1920s and 1930s)

Appalachia—The Old Traditions: Blue Ridge Mtn Music from Virginia & North Carolina, Vols. 1/2. Home-Made Music (UK), LP 001/002.

Ballads & Songs of the Blue Ridge Mountains: Persistence & Change. Folkways/Asch, LP AH 3831.

Been in the Storm So Long: Spirituals, Folk Tales and Children's Games from John's Island, South Carolina. Smithsonian/Folkways, CD SF 40031.

Before the Blues, Vols. 1/2: The Early American Black Music Scene. Yazoo, 2015/16. (Reissues from commercial 78-rpm recordings of the 1920s and 1930s)

Black Banjo Songsters of North Carolina and Virginia. Smithsonian Folkways, CD SF 40079.

Classic Ragtime: Roots and Offshoots (1907–1939). RCA, CD 09026-63206-2.

Close to Home: Old Time Music from Mike Seeger's Collection. Smithsonian Folkways, SF-CD-40097.

Coal Mining Women. Rounder, CD 4025.

Deep River of Song: Alabama. Rounder, CD 1829.

Deep River of Song: Big Brazos. Rounder, CD 1826.

Deep River of Song: Black Appalachia. Rounder, CD 1823.

Deep River of Song: Black Texicans. Rounder, CD 1821.

Deep River of Song: Georgia. Rounder, CD 1828.

Deep River of Song: Mississippi—Saints & Sinners. Rounder, CD 1824.

Deep River of Song: South Carolina. Rounder, CD 1831.

Deep River of Song: Virginia and the Piedmont. Rounder, CD 1827.

Doc Watson and Clarence Ashley. *The Original Folkways Recordings: 1960–1962.* Smithsonian/Folkways, CD SF 40029/30.

Dorsey, Nancy, and Howard Dixon. *Babies in the Mill.* Hightone, HMG 2502.

Echoes of the Ozarks, Vol. 1/2. County, CD-3506/7. (Reissues from commercial 78-rpm recordings of the 1920s and 1930s)

Far in the Mountains, Vol. 1/2. Musical Traditions (UK), MTCD 321-2. (Appalachian field recordings made by Mike Yates, 1979–1983)

Far in the Mountains, Vol. 3/4. Musical Traditions (UK), MTCD 323-4. (Appalachian field recordings made by Mike Yates, 1979–1983)

Great Big Yam Potatoes: Anglo-American Fiddle Music from Mississippi. Mississippi Dept. of Archives & History, H-102.

Harry Smith's Anthology of American Folk Music, Vol. 4. Revenant, RVN 211. (Reissues from commercial 78-rpm recordings of the 1920s and 1930s)

Hazel Dickens, Phyllis Boyens, and others. *They'll Never Keep Us Down: Women's Coal Mining Songs*. Rounder, LP 4012.

High Atmosphere: Ballads & Banjo Tunes from Virginia & North Carolina. Rounder, CD 0028.

I'm Old But I'm Awfully Tough: Traditional Music of the Ozark Region. Missouri Friends of the Folk Arts, LP 1001.

Kentucky Mountain Music. Yazoo, 2200; 7 CDs. (Reissues from 78-rpm commercial recordings of 1920s and 1930s)

The Land Where the Blues Began (Alan Lomax Collection). Rounder, CD 1861.

Lomax Collection. *Southern Journey, Vols. 1–13*. Rounder, CD 1701-13.

Mike Seeger. *Tipple, Loom & Rail: Songs of the Industrialization of the South*. Folkways, LP/Cass FH 5273.

Mississippi String Bands, Vol. 1 (1928–1935). Document, DOCD-8009. (Reissues from commercial 78-rpm recordings of the 1920s and 1930s)

Mississippi String Bands, Vol. 2 (1928–1930). Document, DOCD-8028. (Reissues from commercial 78-rpm recordings of the 1920s and 1930s)

Mountain Music Bluegrass Style. Smithsonian Folkways, CD SF 40038; from Folkways, LP FA 2318.

Music Down Home: An Introduction to Negro Folk Music, USA. Folkways, LP/Cass FA 2691; 2 LP/cass box.

Music from the South, Vols. 1–10. Folkways, LP/Cass FA 2650-59.

Negro Blues and Hollers. Rounder, CD 1501. (Reissue of Library of Congress, LP AAFS L59)

Negro Folk Music of Alabama, Vols. 1–6. Folkways, LPs/cass FE 4417/18, 4471-74.

Negro Religious Songs and Services. Rounder, CD 1514. (Reissue)

Negro Work Songs and Calls. Rounder, CD 1517. (Reissue of Library of Congress, LP AAFS L8)

Nimrod Workman, Sara Gunning, and others. *Come All You Coal Miners*. Rounder, LP 4005.

Ozark Folksongs (from the Vance Randolph Collection). Rounder, CD 1108; 1941–1942 recordings.

Prison Songs Vol. 1: Murderous Home. Rounder, CD 1714.

Prison Songs Vol. 2: Don'tcha Hear Poor Mother Calling? Rounder, CD 1715.

Ragtime, Vol. 1 (1897–1919). Jazz Archives, CD 120.

Seedtime on the Cumberland, Vol. 3. June Appal, JA0074CD.

Somewhere in Arkansas: Early Commercial Country Music Recordings from Arkansas: 1928–1932. Center for Arkansas and Regional Studies, 3 CDs. (Reissues from commercial 78-rpm recordings of the 1920s and 1930s)

Songs and Ballads of the Anthracite Miners. Library of Congress Archive of Folksong, LP AAFS L16.

Songs and Ballads of the Bituminous Miners. Rounder, CD 1522; formerly Library of Congress Archive of Folksong, LP AAFS L60.

Sounds of the South. Atlantic, 7-82496-2, 4 CDs.

There Is No Eye: Music for Photographs. Smithsonian Folkways, SF CD 40091.

Traditional Fiddle Music of the Ozarks, Vols. 1–3. Rounder, CD 0435/7.

Will Slayden. *African-American Banjo Songs from West Tennessee*. Tennessee Folklore Society, TFS 123; 1952 recordings.

RECOMMENDED VIEWING

Appalachian Journey: From the Original Ballad of Tom Dooley to the Origins of Bluegrass.
Featuring Tommy Jarrell, Stanley and Ray Hicks, Bob and Laurence Eller, A. Mae,
Hinton, the Thomas Brothers, Frank Profitt Jr., and Raymond Fairchild (video,
Vestapol, 13079).

Legends of Old Time Music. Featuring Tommy Jarrell, Clarence Ashley, Roscoe Holcomb,
Doc Watson, Sam McGee, Pete Steele, Jean Ritchie, Corbett Grigsby, Walker
Family, Edna Ritchie, Clint Howard, Fred Price, Marion Sumner, Martin Young
(dvd and video, Vestapol, 13026).

Shady Grove: Old Time Music from North Carolina, Kentucky & Virginia. Featuring Kilby
Snow, Dock Boggs, Tommy Jarrell, Roscoe Holcomb (dvd and video, Vestapol,
13071).

Traditional Music Classics. Featuring Doc Watson, Roscoe Holcomb, Buell Kazee, Kilby
Snow (dvd and video, Yazoo, 516).

NOTES

1. These rankings are based primarily on the extensive electronic database compiled by English folklorist/librarian Steve Roud. The frequency of recovery ranges from
370 for "Barbara Allen" to 151 for "Two Sisters." Ballad collecting in the Appalachians
has been much more intensive than in New England, so the statistics are considerably
more reliable.

2. Louise Pound, *American Ballads and Songs* (New York: Charles Scribner's Songs,
1922), p. 175.

3. R. W. Pelham, "Free Nigger" (1841). The word "nigger" is so racially offensive
these days that respectful people leave it out of their speech and writings entirely. In
the nineteenth century, the word was commonly used by both Anglo-Americans and
African Americans, but on the lips of the former it was generally disparaging at best
and maliciously degrading at worst. Nevertheless, such words (and also the quaint
representation of slave speech as in the preceding example) were once common, and,
unacceptable as they are today, they are reprinted here as a historical record of what
once was the norm.

4. These styles have been studied and characterized by Jeff Todd Titon in *Old-Time
Kentucky Fiddle Tunes* (Lexington: University Press of Kentucky, 2001).

5. This discussion borrows from Marshall Stearns, *The Story of Jazz* (New York:
Oxford University Press, 1956), especially Ch. 2.

6. Liner notes to Rounder, CD 0418, *Walnut Gap* (1999), p. 3.

5

Folk Music of the Midwest and Great Lakes Region

Broadly speaking, the styles of music from the Midwest and Far West are basically extensions of those from the Northeast or the Southeast, depending on the backgrounds of the migrants. Regional distinctions exist primarily in the content that reflects local folkways.

THE GREAT LAKES REGION

Unlike New England, the regions further west (including parts such as Ohio, Michigan, Wisconsin, Minnesota, Illinois, and Indiana) were settled by a varied range of immigrants: Americans who were gradually moving west as well as Europeans new to the continent. Immigrations in the nineteenth century brought people of Germanic, Scandinavian, and Celtic backgrounds to these regions. Between 1845 and 1854, 2.2 million Irish and Germans immigrated, equivalent to 10 percent of the U.S. population of 1850. In the last half of the nineteenth century, Scandinavian immigrants topped the list of new arrivals.

Wisconsin's demographics are representative of the region. In 1860 only 32 percent of all Wisconsin residents had been born in that state; 16 percent had been born in New York, 16 percent in Germany, and 10 percent in the British Isles including Ireland. Later in the century large numbers came from eastern

Kentucky. All these groups brought musical lore with them, some in English, but much in German, Dutch, and other tongues.

Michigan's first big foreign population influx was from Germany in the 1830s. By the time of the Civil War, large numbers of Dutch and Irish had also settled there. From 1860 to 1890, attracted by the growing lumber industry, Swedes, Norwegians, Finns, Italians, and Canadians streamed in. Southern Michigan had a large non–English-speaking population, including significant numbers of Poles, Czechs, Greeks, Armenians, Belgians, Germans, Dutchmen, and Swedes. Only the Polish tradition has been canvassed sufficiently to result in a published collection.[1] Among the Anglo-American population of the Lower Peninsula, the songlore is consistent with migrations from New England, the Mid-Atlantic states, and Canada.

Lumber camps provided an important venue for the preservation and dissemination of old ballads and songs in the last decades of the nineteenth century. The most frequently found older Child ballads were:

- "Barbara Allen"
- "The House Carpenter"
- "Lord Randal"
- "Lord Lovel"
- "Lord Thomas and Fair Ellender"
- "Lady Isabel and the Elf Knight"

The broadside ballads reported most often were:

- "The Butcher Boy"
- "Awake, Awake You Drowsy Sleeper"
- "The Sailor Boy"
- "The Girl I Left Behind"
- "Knoxville Girl"
- "Mary of the Wild Moor"
- "Boston Burglar"
- "Jack Monroe"

The leading indigenous ballads, including four that relate specifically to lumbering, were:

- "The Jealous Lover"
- "Jack Haggarty"
- "Young Charlotte"
- "The Little Mohea"
- "The Jam on Gerry's Rocks"
- "The Little Brown Bulls"
- "Springfield Mountain"
- "Fuller and Warren"
- "Charles Guiteau"

- "Canaday-I-O"
- "Paul Jones"

States such as Wisconsin and Michigan developed a vigorous lumber industry, and the Great Lakes region produced an abundance of songs and ballads about the maritime life on the lakes that spawned its own lore. In the 1800s the lakes were constantly traversed by sailing schooners carrying freight from one port to another. Better living conditions, higher wages, and milder discipline lured many Atlantic seamen to the Great Lakes. One song celebrating those virtues is "It's Me for the Inland Lakes," collected in 1933.

Notwithstanding the cheery optimism of this song, storms on the Great Lakes could produce waves as treacherous as any out on the open ocean, and many gale-battered schooners sank to a watery grave during a storm. Some accidents unaccountably occurred during the best conditions.

One popular Great Lakes sailing disaster ballad, "Loss of the *Persian*," recounted a collision between the *Persian* and the schooner *E. B. Allen* in 1868 while the former was returning to Oswego, New York, with a load of wheat from Chicago.

The ballad's author was Irish-born Patrick Fennell, who immigrated to the United States in 1849 and settled in Oswego, New York. It's possible that he knew the first mate, Sullivan, also from Oswego, personally. His ballad is written more as a eulogy to the crewmen than to chronicle the details of the accident, which are not part of the text.

Roughly one hundred miles west of Oswego, standing at the western end of the Erie Canal and the eastern end of Lake Erie, is Buffalo, a railroad terminus as well as shipping port. Its Canal Street was described as "the hands-down

---

"It's Me for the Inland Lakes"

If ever I follow the ships again
To gather my spuds and cakes,
I'll not be working a deep-sea hack,
It's me for the inland lakes.

You get a berth that's really a berth,
An' the jaw that the skipper takes—
No end I swear—it's a wonderful life,
It's me for the inland lakes.

The runs are short, the vessels good,
An' real men are the mates;

They're men and they can handle a ship,
It's me for the inland lakes.

Late gales may blow an' seas run high,
An' the lees feel of country Jakes;
But quarters are warm and the grub is great,
It's me for the inland lakes.

Two dollars a day they often pay,
Much better than ocean crates;
An' when the season's done, all winter you bum,
It's me for the inland lakes.*

*Sung by Captain Walkingthaw of Port Colborne, Ontario, Canada, 1933. Published in Ivan H. Walton and Joe Grimm, *Windjammers: Songs of the Great Lakes Sailors* (Detroit: Wayne State University Press, 2002), p. 86. "Lee" is the side of the ship away from the wind; "jake" means a rube, or country bumpkin.

"Loss of the *Persian*"

Oh, sad and dismal is the tale I now relate to you,
'Tis of the schooner, *Persian*, her officers and crew.
They sank beneath the dark blue waves, to rise in
life no more;
Where winds and desolation sweep Lake Huron's
rock-bound shore.

They left Chicago on their lee, their songs they did
resound;
Their hearts were filled with joy and glee for
homeward they were bound;
How little they thought the sword of Death would
meet them on their way;
Down in the deep they all do sleep far from their
friends away.

Her captain he is now no more, he lost his precious
life.
He now lies on Lake Huron's shore far from his
home and wife.
That barren coast now hides from view his manly
lifeless form,
Though he with heart so brave and true had
weathered many a storm.

No mother's hand were there to press his cold
distracted frame,
No loving wife was there to kiss his cold lips warm
again.
No brother nor no sister nigh, no little ones to
mourn,
Down in the deep he now does sleep far from his
friends and home.

Oh, Daniel Sullivan was the mate's name, a man as
bold and brave
As ever was compelled by rate to fill a sailor's grave.
Oh Dan, your many friends will mourn, your hand
they'll clasp no more,

For now you sleep down in the deep, lost on Lake
Huron's shore.

Oh Dan, your many friends do mourn, for fate has
on you frowned.
They look in vain for your return back to Oswego
town.
They'll miss that glad look of your eye, your hand
they'll clasp no more,
For now you sleep beneath the deep by Lake
Huron's rockbound shore.

The sailors' names I did not know excepting one or
two,
Down in the deep they all do sleep; they were a
luckless crew.
Not one of them escaped to land to tell these
mysteries o'er,
But each one found a watery grave by Lake Huron's
rockbound shore.

The mystery of their fate is sealed. Did they collide
some way?
But this will never be revealed until the Judgment
Day.
When the angels they shall take their stand upon
those waters blue
And summon forth by Heaven's command the
schooner *Persian*'s crew.

Oh, it's all around the Presqu'ile buoys the lake
gulls flit and skim,
They all join in the chorus of the *Persian*'s funeral
hymn.
They skip along the water's edge and then aloft
they soar,
In memory of the *Persian*'s crew lost on Lake
Huron's shore.*

*Sung by Stanley Bâby of Toronto, Ontario, Canada. Collected by Edith Fowke. Recording: Folkways, FM 4018, *Songs of the Great Lakes*, 1964. For more information on the ballad, see Norm Cohen, "'The *Persian*'s Crew'—The Ballad, Its Author, and the Incident," *New York Folklore Quarterly* (December 1969): 289–296.

loudest, drinkingest, carousingest, bare-knuckle fightingest, wildest street for lakeshore amusement on perhaps the whole of the Great Lakes."[2] The incident described in "The Buffalo Whore" has been associated with other cities as well, most commonly Winnipeg, Ontario, Canada, and although its original venue is not known, it has unquestionably become a song of the Great Lakes.

Patrick Fennell's song about the *Persian* is remembered in the specific region that was home to the men involved, the incident, and the author himself. Songs like "The Buffalo Whore" are sung more widely but become regionalized by simple textual changes such as the introduction of the names of local places and people.

In addition to songs about the local houses of ill repute, every region of the country has its own jail-lore. One common song type is a catalog of complaints about all the things wrong with the local jail. The characters in these songs and ballads are usually not hardened criminals but merely those unfortunates who were caught for some lesser offense, such as drunkenness, disturbing the peace, or petty larceny. That way, the listener can sympathize in good conscience with their complaints. "Fond du Lac Jail" is a Wisconsin contribution to this genre. The town so remembered is at the southern end of Lake Winnebago, about thirty-five miles west of Lake Michigan.

Other localizations of "Fond du Lac Jail" abound. For example, Virginia folksinger Dock Boggs made up his own variant based on events in his home county:

It's a piece of cold meat,
And cold corn bread;
It's so cold it's heavy lead,
It's hard times in the Wise county jail,
It's hard times I know.[3]

> **"The Buffalo Whore"**
>
> My first trip down old Lake Erie,
> With some sailors to explore;
> Then I met Rosy O'Flannagan,
> Best of all the Buffalo whores.
>
> She says, "Boy, I think I know you,
> Let me sit upon your knee;
> How'd you like to do some lovin'?
> A dollar and a half will be my fee."
>
> Some were singing, some were dancing,
> Some were drunk upon the floor;
> But I was over in a corner
> A-making love to the Buffalo whore.
>
> She was slick as oil on water,
> I didn't know what she was about;
> 'Til I missed my watch and wallet,
> Then I popped her on the snout.
>
> Out came the whores and sons-of-bitches,
> They came at me by the score;
> You'd have laughed to split your britches
> To see me flying out that door!*
>
> *As sung by Norman "Beachie" MacIvor of Goderich, Ontario, Canada, in 1934. Published in Ivan H. Walton and Joe Grimm, *Windjammers: Songs of the Great Lakes Sailors* (Detroit: Wayne State University Press, 2002), p. 115.

Wisconsin had, in addition to its share of seafaring, mining, and lumbering, another industry that was highly localized, cranberry harvesting. When the two glacial lakes of Oshkosh and Wisconsin in the central part of the state retreated, they left behind expansive lake-bed swamps and bogs that became fertile ground for growing and marketing cranberries. One song survives from this industry, where once Poles, Bohemians, and Irishmen, among others, gathered to harvest the berries and spend their evenings in music and dance.

When an event takes place that moves folksingers and writers to compose a ballad or song about it, the choices are to take an older song and adapt it to the new circumstances or, alternatively, to begin afresh and write a completely new piece. A grisly murder near Greencastle, Indiana, inspired both. In February 1896, twenty-three-year-old Pearl Bryan was murdered by her lover, dental student Scott Jackson, and Jackson's roommate, Alonzo Walling. Pearl had become pregnant; the two men attempted an abortion, failed, dispatched Pearl, decapitated her (to prevent identification), and abandoned her headless corpse in a farmer's field not far from Fort Thomas, just over the Kentucky state line. Pearl's head was never found—a bizarre detail that was preserved in many of the ballads as well as in local lore: in the Cincinnati area three-quarters of a century later, dressmakers' headless dummies were still called "Pearl Bryans." At least half a dozen ballads were written about the event, in which stanzas gradually shifted as authors borrowed from one another. One ballad was based on an older, widespread murdered girl ballad, "The Jealous Lover," and simply inserted the names of Bryan and Jackson into an existing text without any attempt to tailor it to the unusual circumstances of the actual event. The other ballads are more interesting from an historical viewpoint because of the details that they preserve. One example, which circulated on a broadside, is reprinted here as "The Ballad of Pearl Bryan and Her Sad Death in the Kentucky Hills at Fort Thomas." Apart from historically accurate details, this text is striking because of the apparently irrelevant inclusion of a standard bit of "friendship verse" normally found in autograph albums. The insertion of this quatrain makes sense if the ballad is viewed as the ballad writer's farewell to

---

"Fond du Lac Jail"

In the morning you receive a dry loaf of bread
That's hard as a stone and heavy as lead.
It's thrown from the ceiling down into your cell,
Like coming from Heaven popped down into Hell.

CHORUS:
Oh, there's hard times in Fond du Lac jail,
There's hard times, I say.

Your bed it is made of old rotten rugs,
Get up in the morning all covered with bugs.
And the bugs they will swear that unless you get bail
You're bound to go lousy in Fond du Lac jail.*

*As sung by Charles Robinson of Marion, Wisconsin, in 1941. Collected by Helene Stratman-Thomas. Published in Harry B. Peters, *Folk Songs Out of Wisconsin* (Madison: State Historical Society of Wisconsin, 1977), p. 184. The song has five more verses that are not printed here.

"The Cranberry Song"

You ask me to sing, so I'll sing you a song;
I'll tell how, in the marshes, they all get along,
Bohemians and Irish and Yankees and Dutch.
It's down in the shanties you'll find the whole clutch.

Did you ever go to the cranberry bogs?
There some of the houses are hewed out of logs.
The walls are of boards; they're sawed out of pine
That grow in this country called cranberry mine.

It's now then to Mather their tickets to buy,
And to all their people they'll bid them goodbye.

For fun and for frolic they plan to resign
For three or four weeks in the cranberry kline.

The hay is all cut and the wheat is all stacked,
Cranberries are ripe so their clothes they will pack;
And away to the marshes, away they will go
And dance to the music of fiddle and bow.

All day in the marshes their rakes they will pull,
And feel the most gayest when boxes are full;
In the evening they'll dance 'til they're all tired out,
And wish the cranberries would never play out.*

*As sung by Frances Perry of Black River Falls, Wisconsin, in the 1940s. Collected by Helene Stratman-Thomas. Published in Harry B. Peters, *Folk Songs Out of Wisconsin* (Madison: State Historical Society of Wisconsin, 1977), p. 45.

poor Pearl, the writing of which stirred old memories of exchanging farewells in albums or high school annuals.

THE MIDWEST

As the lands east of the Mississippi filled with swelling numbers of pioneer settlers, the hardier ones—those who felt crowded if they could see the smoke from their neighbor's chimney—packed their wagons to find more space farther west. Before long, "farther west" meant the flat, grassy plains of what became Iowa, Kansas, Nebraska, and the Dakotas.

"The Ballad of Pearl Bryan and Her Sad Death in the Kentucky Hills at Fort Thomas"

It was one winter evening,
The sorrowful tale was told;
Scott Jackson said to Walling,
"Let's take Pearl for a stroll";
Oh, soon the cab was ordered,
To go out for a stroll,
And if you will only listen
The half has never been told.

Pearl went to Cincinnati,
She'd never been there before;
She said to Sweetheart Jackson,
"I'll never see Mama no more."
She said to Sweetheart Jackson,
"Why do you want to take my life?
You know I've always loved you,
And would have been your wife."

Little did Pearl think
When she left her home that day,
That the little grip she carried
Would hide her head away.
There's room for your name in my album,
There's room for your love in my heart;
There's room for us both in Heaven
Where true lovers never part.

Oh, then some bloodhounds were ordered,
They found no trail, they said;
"Here lies a woman's body,
But we can't find no head."
They telephoned for miles around,
At last an answer came;

It was from Pearl Bryan's sister:
It must be Pearl that's slain.

In came Pearl Bryan's sister,
Falling on her knees;
A-pleading to Scott Jackson,
For sister's head—oh, please!
But Jackson was so stubborn,
A naughty word he said:
"When you meet Pearl in Heaven
You'll find her missing head."

In came Walling's mother,
A-pleading for her son,
A-saying to the jury,
"It's the first crime they ever done;
Oh, send him not to prison,
'Twould break my poor old heart;
My son's my darling one,
How from him can I part?"

The jury soon decided,
And from their seat they sprung;
For the crime the boys committed
They both now must be hung;
On January the thirty-first,
This awful crime was done;
Scott Jackson and Alonzo Walling,
Together they were hung.

Oh, boys and girls, take warning,
Before it is too late;
The worst crime ever committed
In old Kentucky state.*

*Printed in the Louisville *Courier-Journal*, June 29, 1953, from a broadside sent to a columnist from Mrs. Verna Jeffers of Whitley City, Kentucky. Published in Anne Cohen, *Poor Pearl, Poor Girl! The Murdered-Girl Stereotype in Ballad and Newspaper* (Austin and London: University of Texas Press for the American Folklore Society, 1973), pp. 65–67.

Iowa was legally opened to white settlers in 1833, the first of whom came from eastern and southern states. In the 1840s immigrants arrived from Ireland, Scotland, Germany, and Scandinavia. In the last third of the nineteenth century, Nebraska to the west was settled by two groups of American-born pioneers. The larger number came from New England, New York, and Pennsylvania via the states of the old Northwest Territory. Fewer came from farther south: Virginia and the Carolinas, as well as Kentucky, southern Illinois, Indiana, and Missouri. It was the latter group that, though numerically fewer, was more significant to the history of the tales, songs, and folkways brought to the territory. The largest group of non-English-speaking immigrants was from Germany. In neighboring Kansas, the story was much the same: Americans came from states to the east and northeast; foreigners came from Britain and Germany. In the Dakota Territory, the earliest white settlers included Norwegians, Canadians, and Germans. By 1890, foreign-born people constituted about 43 percent of the population, a higher percentage than in any other state.

An immensely popular song of 1871 was Will S. Hays's "Little Old Log Cabin," a sentimental reminiscence of the old rural homestead and the singer's longing for parents and friends who once occupied it. Hays's song inspired many parodies in the decade following its publication: "Little Old Caboose behind the Train," "My Little New Log Cabin in the Hills," and "Little Old Sod Shanty on My Claim," the latter published at least as early as 1884 in an Ashland, Kansas, newspaper, the *Clark County Clipper*.

A homesteader in the land development area of Pennington County, South Dakota (1936). *Photographer, Arthur Rothstein (LC-USF34-004512-D); from the Farm Security Administration—Office of War Information Photo Collection, Library of Congress Prints and Photographs Division.*

After President Lincoln signed the Homestead Act of 1862, any citizen over twenty-one was allowed to file a claim on 160 acres in certain designated areas of public land. If certain minimal improvements were made and the land was lived on for five years, it became the pioneer's property. Using cubes of sod as substitute bricks, a sod house was a quick and inexpensive way to build the required homestead in which the claimant could live in minimal comfort. "Little Old Sod Shanty on My Claim" was one Midwestern poet's response to trying to establish his frontier homestead.

"Little Old Sod Shanty on My Claim" was probably written by a Kansas or Nebraska man. On the same subject is "The Lane County Bachelor," definitely a Kansas song. It is sung to the fiddle tune, "Irish Washerwoman."

"Little Old Sod Shanty on My Claim"

I am lookin' rather seedy now, while holdin' down
  my claim,
And my victuals are not always served the best;
And the mice play shyly 'round me as I nestle down
  to rest
In the little old sod shanty on my claim.

CHORUS:
Where the hinges are of leather and the windows
  have no glass,
And the board roof lets the howling blizzard in;
And I hear the hungry coyote as he slinks up
  through the grass,
'Round the little old sod shanty on my claim.

When I left my eastern home a bachelor so gay,
To try and win my way to wealth and fame,
I never thought I'd come down to burnin' drifted
  hay,
In the little old sod shanty on my claim.

CHORUS:
For I rather like the novelty of living in this way,
Though my bill of fare is always rather tame;
And I'm happy as a clam on the land of Uncle Sam,
In the little old sod shanty on my claim.

My clothes are plastered o'er with mud, I'm looking
  like a fright,
And everything is scattered 'round the room

Still I wouldn't give the freedom that I have out in
  the west,
For the comfort of the eastern man's own home.

CHORUS:
Still I wish that some kind-hearted girl would pity
  on me take,
And relieve me from the mess that I am in;
Oh the angel, how I'd bless her if this her home
  she'd make,
In the little old sod shanty on my claim.

We would make our fortunes on the prairies of the
  west,
Just as happy as two lovers we'd remain;
We'd forget the trials and troubles we endured at
  the first,
In the little old sod shanty on my claim.

CHORUS:
Where the hinges are of leather and the windows
  have no glass,
And the board roof lets the howling blizzard in;
And I hear the hungry coyote as he slinks up
  through the grass,
'Round the little old sod shanty on my claim.*

*As sung by John White, under the pseudonym of Whitey
Johns, in 1929 for the American Record Corp.

There must have been many pioneers who set out to go farther west with high hopes of finding, if not their fortunes, at least a comfortable piece of land on which to farm. Many, however, arrived only to lose heart and return east. Lots of clever songs poked fun at those who decided that after all, in spite of its unpleasantness, what they had left was better than what they found. In the late 1800s, Kansas, Nebraska, and Dakota Territory all inspired songs expressing similar sentiments of discouragement, such as "Comin' Back to Kansas," "The Dreary Black Hills," and "Dakota Land."

After the Civil War many veterans moved westward and tried to make a new life for themselves on the plains. Tattered old blue or grey army jackets behind a horse or mule and plow were a familiar sight. Some ex-soldiers and ex-guerillas were unable to adjust to civilian life and consequently turned to crime. One of them was Jesse James (1847–1882): he grew up in turbulent times, marked by border warfare, the Civil War (he joined Quantrill's raiders, the most murderous of guerillas), and postbellum violence. He committed his

"The Lane County Bachelor"

Frank Baker's my name and a bachelor I am,
I'm keeping old batch on an elegant plan.
You'll find me out west in the county of Lane,
I'm starving to death on a government claim.

My house it is built of the natural soil,
The walls are erected according to Hoyle.
The roof has no pitch but is level and plain,
And I always get wet when it happens to rain.

CHORUS:
Hurrah for Lane County, the land of the free,
The home of the grasshopper, bed bug and flea.
I'll sing loud its praises and tell of its fame,
While starving to death on a government claim.

My clothes they are ragged, my language is rough,
My bread is case-hardened both solid and tough.
The dough is scattered all over the room,
And the floor it gets scared at the sight of a broom.

My dishes are scattered all over the bed,
They are covered with sorghum and Government
   bread.
Still I have a good time and live at my ease
On common sop-sorghum, old bacon, and grease.

CHORUS:
Then come to Lane County, here is a home for you
   all,
Where the winds never cease and the rains never
   fall,
And the sun never sets but will always remain
Till it burns you all up on a Government claim.
Till it burns you all up on a Government claim.

How happy I feel when I crawl into bed,
And a rattlesnake rattles a tune at my head.
And the gay little centipede, void of all fear,
Crawls over my neck and down into my ear.

And the little bed bugs so cheerful and bright,
They keep me a-laughing two-thirds of the night.
And the gay little flea with sharp tacks in his toes,
Plays "Why don't you catch me" all over my nose.

CHORUS:
Hurrah for Lane County, hurrah for the west,
Where farmers and laborers are ever at rest.
For there's nothing to do but to sweetly remain
And starve like a man on a Government claim.

How happy am I on my government claim,
For I've nothing to lose nor I've nothing to gain.
I've nothing to eat and I've nothing to war,
And nothing from nothing is honest and fair.

Oh, it is here I am solid and here I will stay,
For my money is all gone and I can't get away.
There is nothing that makes a man hard and
   profane,
Like starving to death on a Government claim.

CHORUS:
Hurrah for Lane County, where blizzards arise,
Where the winds never cease and the flea never
   dies.
Come join in the chorus and sing of its fame,
You poor hungry hoboes that's starved on the
   claim.

No, don't get discouraged, you poor hungry men,
For we are all here as free as a pig in a pen.
Just stick to your homestead and battle the fleas
And look to your Maker to send you a breeze.

Now all you claim holders I hope you will stay
And chew your hardtack till you are toothless and
   grey.
But as for myself I'll no longer remain
And starve like a dog on a Government claim.*

*As given to the Forsyth Library, Ft. Hays, Kansas State College, by Mr. and Mrs. Ed Kepner, Dighton, Kansas, in April 1933. Published in Henry H. Malone, "Folksongs and Ballads," in *Kansas Folklore*, ed. Henry H. Malone, S. J. Sackett, and William E. Koch (Lincoln, NE: University of Nebraska Press, 1961), pp. 148–149.

first bank robbery in 1866 and was implicated in ten others. He engineered his first train robbery in 1873 near Adair, Iowa; he was involved in six more by 1881. While James was still alive, there began a gradual transformation of his image in the public's mind to that of a latter day Robin Hood, a characterization that owed less to fact than to wishful thinking. Most of the noble deeds

"Comin' Back to Kansas"

They are comin' back to Kansas,
They are crossin' on the bridge,
You can see their mover wagons
On the top of every ridge.

On the highways and the
   turnpikes
You can see their wagons come,
For they're comin' back to
   Kansas
And they're comin' on the run.

Who's a comin' back to Kansas?
Why, the migratory crowd
That left the state some months
   ago
With curses long and loud,

And they swore by the eternal
They would never more return
To this Kansas land infernal
Where the hot winds blast and
   burn.

Where the rivers run in riot
When you want it to be dry,
Where the sun so fiercely
   scorches
When you want a cloudy sky.

So they loaded up the children
And they whistled for the dog,
Tied a cow behind the wagon,
To the butcher sold the hog.

Hitched the ponies to the
   schooner,
Turned her prow toward the
   east,
Left this beastly state of Kansas
For a land of fat and feast.

Did they find it? No, they didn't,
Though they roamed the
   country o'er,
From the lakes up in the
   northland
To the far off ocean shore.

And they found that other
   sections

"The Dreary Black Hills"

Now friends if you'll listen to a
   horrible tale,
It's getting quite dreary and its
   getting quite stale;
I gave up my trade selling Ayers'
   Patent Pills;
To go and hunt gold in the
   dreary Black Hills.

CHORUS:
Stay away, I say, stay away if you
   can,
Far from that city they call
   Cheyenne;
Where the blue waters roll and
   Comanche Bill
Will take off your scalp, boys, in
   those dreary Black Hills.

Now, friends, if you'll listen to a
   story untold,
Don't go to the Black Hills
   a-digging for gold;
For the railroad speculators their
   pockets will fill,
While taking you a round trip to
   the dreary Black Hills.

I went to the Black Hills, no
   gold could I find,
I thought of the free land I'd left
   far behind;
Through rain, snow, and hail,
   boys, froze up to the gills,
They call me the orphan of the
   dreary Black Hills.

The round house at Cheyenne is
   filled every night,
With loafers and beggars of
   every kind of sight;
On their backs there's no
   clothes, boys, in their pockets
   no bills,
And they'll take off your scalp in
   those dreary Black Hills.**

"Dakota Land"

We've reached the land of desert
   sweet,
Where nothing grows for man to
   eat;
The wind it blows with feverish
   heat,
Across the plains so hard to
   beat.

CHORUS:
Oh! Dakota land, sweet Dakota
   land,
As on thy fiery soil I stand,
I look across the plains
And wonder why it never rains
Till Gabriel blows his trumpet
   sound
And says the rain's just gone
   around.

We have no wheat, we have no
   oats,
We have no corn to feed our
   shoats;
Our chickens are so very poor,
They beg for crumbs outside the
   door.

Our horses are of bronco race,
Starvation stares them in the
   face;
We do not live, we only stay,
We are too poor to get away.***

continued

Had their tales of woe to sing,
So they're humpin' now for
    Kansas
At the breakin' forth of spring.*

*As sung by Clara Ballard of Butler County, Kansas, in 1958. Collected by Joan O'Bryant. Published in Joan O'Bryant, "Folksongs and Ballads, Part II," in, *Kansas Folkore*, ed. S. J. Sackett and William E. Koch (Lincoln, NE: University of Nebraska, 1961), pp. 180–181.
**From Louise Pound, *Folk-Song of Nebraska and the Central West: A Syllabus*, vol. 9 (Lincoln, NE: Nebraska Academy of Sciences, 1915), pp. 22–23.
***From Louise Pound, F*olk-Song of Nebraska and the Central West: A Syllabus*, vol. 9 (Lincoln, NE: Nebraska Academy of Sciences, 1915), p. 28. A shoat is a young, weaned pig.

attributed to James—such as leaving a $1,000 bill at the table of a poor widow who fed him—have no factual basis.

On April 3, 1882, James was living in St. Joseph, Missouri, under the assumed name of Thomas Howard when he was shot in the back by his cousin, Robert Ford. It was a pleasant Sunday morning; James was standing on a chair to adjust a picture of Andrew Jackson hanging askew on the wall. With his back to Ford, he presented a perfect target. Ford and his brother Charlie had joined the James gang some months earlier, planning to betray him for the sizable reward on his head. Ford's cowardly act failed to win him the hero status he was hoping for; he was killed some time later in a barroom brawl after living the life of a social outcast.

Several ballads were written about James, some probably very soon after the assassination. The one reprinted here, a version of the most widespread one, is America's best-known outlaw ballad. Its authorship has been attributed to Billy Ga(r)shade, a Missouri printer who knew the James brothers, but that is by no means certain. The ballad has spread far beyond the Missouri area where the events described took place.

On the frontier, the institution of the play party provided entertainment for the entire community—or even countryside. These were party games that appealed mainly to the young adults of marriageable age, but older and younger folks occasionally participated as well. One very widely known game was "Skip to My Lou," reported from Idaho, Iowa, Nebraska, and Indiana, as well as further east in the Ozarks and Appalachians. Participants stand around in a circle, boys to the left of their partners. One boy skips around and takes the arm of another girl and skips on with her; her partner then skips after them to catch them before they return to the girl's original position. If he does, he gets his partner back. If he can't overtake her, he must skip around the circle and repeat the cycle. In east Tennessee, "lou" was another word for "sweetheart."

While the young adults amused themselves in play parties, enterprising school teachers sat up nights trying to fashion songs and poems to help their young

"Jesse James"

All the cowboys out west stopped a while and held
 their breath,
When the news of Jesse's death did arrive;
For they knew there was no man with the law in his
 hand,
That could take Jesse James when alive.

Down on Blue River bank, where Jesse said to
 Frank,
"Let's feed our horses here and make our bed;
If you'll stand by my side like you promised once
 you'll do,
I'll fight a thousand men until I'm dead."

CHORUS:
Oh, there's no more desperadoes in our land,
There's no more desperadoes in our land;
When Jesse turned his head, Bob Ford shot him
 dead,
There's no more desperadoes in our land.

Jesse James had a friend and through kindness took
 him in,

Never dreaming that his cousin was a spy;
Well, he ate of Jesse's bread and he slept in Jesse's
 bed.
One morning he shot him on the sly.

Jesse was in his room, a-standing in the chair,
Dusting a picture by the door;
When Bob Ford's pistol ball brought him a-tumblin'
 from the wall,
And Jesse lay a-dyin' on the floor.

Jesse James was a man, kind of heart and quick of
 hand,
He would never turn the needy from his door;
All the folks throughout the land read about Jesse
 and his band;
He robbed the rich and gave to the poor.

Jesse leaves a wife to mourn all her life,
Two little children to be brave;
Oh, that dirty little coward that shot Captain
 Howard
Has laid Jesse James in his grave.*

*"Jesse James" (Laws, E 1). As sung by Doc Hopkins in Los Angeles, 1965. Collected by D. K. Wilgus. Recording: Birch,
LP 1945, *Doc Hopkins*, 1971.

students learn the alphabet, multiplication tables, capitals of states, or names of
counties. Drummed into resistant but impressionable young heads, these ditties
were remembered far longer than the children would like to admit. Few of these
interested any folk song collectors enough to be included in published collections. The two from Iowa reprinted here are representative of the genre. "County
Song" was learned in the 1880s (only the first part is quoted). "Was It Right?" is
an example of using songs to teach young students good manners and morals.

LOGGERS

In America, logging began in the most northeastern corner, in Maine, where the
maritime industry had created a need for sturdy beams for ship masts and spars. By
the 1840s, good timber from Maine's virgin forests having been exhaustively har-
vested, the loggers slung their axes over their shoulders and pushed westward. From
Maine they moved into New Hampshire, Vermont, New York, and Pennsylvania,
then further west, reaching Michigan and Minnesota. The heydey of Maine
logging ended in around 1860, but by the 1850s New York's timber industry had
already surpassed New England's. The first Maine woodsmen were of English stock.

By the 1830s there were considerable numbers of Irish, and by the 1850s, the Scandinavians, French Canadians, and Slavs were becoming prominent there.

In Michigan large-scale logging began in the 1830s. By the 1880s those forests had yielded their harvests, and construction of transcontinental railroads made the Pacific Northwest's softwood forests in Oregon and Washington enticing. Also, the 1914 completion of the Panama Canal allowed timber to be shipped conveniently to the industrial East. Musically speaking, the "golden age" of lumbering was in the period from 1870 to 1900.

The loggers' emotional equivalent of a stampede was a logjam: natural forces, whether animate or inanimate, suddenly violently out of man's control, unleashed unimaginable terror. Thousands of logs piled helter-skelter in a jumble that stretched from shore to shore and could tower ten stories high. "The Jam on Gerry's Rocks" was for decades the best known of the logjam ballads, widely sung in the Northeast and also in the Great Lakes region on both sides of the U.S.–Canadian border.

This favorite lumbermen's song was the subject of years of investigation by folklorists in the early decades of the twentieth century, but no factual basis for the story was ever found. An important element of the story—one that may be lost on today's audiences—was the belief that working on the Lord's day is a sin sure to lead to some misfortune. In an interesting juxtaposition of Christian and pre-Christian elements, the last stanza records the burial of the two lovers beneath a hemlock tree, which ballad audiences a century ago would have recognized as a symbol of death.

"Skip to My Lou"

The cat's in the buttermilk, skip-to-my-lou,
The cat's in the buttermilk, skip-to-my-lou,
The cat's in the buttermilk, skip-to-my-lou,
Skip to my lou, my darling.

I'll get another one, skip-to-my-lou, (3)
Skip to my lou, my darling.

Little red wagon painted blue, (3)
Skip to my lou, my darling.

Flies in the biscuit, two by two, (3)
Skip to my lou, my darling.

If I can't get her back another one'll do, (3)
Skip to my lou, my darling.

Hurry up slow poke, do, oh, do, (3)
Skip to my lou, my darling.

Gone again, what shall I do? (3)
Skip to my lou, my darling.

I'll get another one sweeter than you, (3)
Skip to my lou, my darling.*

*Selected stanzas from Leah Jackson Wolford, *The Play-Party in Indiana* (Indianapolis: Indiana Historical Commission, 1916), pp. 88–89. The (3) indicates that the first line of each stanza is sung three times.

Although death was a predominant theme among the occupational songs of early Americans, there was room for lighter-hearted subjects. "The Lumberjack's Alphabet" catalogued some of the facets of the workers' lives, both the good and the bad, but talk of death and tragedy was avoided.

Other occupations had their own equivalent alphabet songs. For example, sailors sang:

A is the anchor and that you all know,
B is the bowsprit that's over the bow,
C is the capstan with which we heave 'round,
And D are the decks where our sailors are found.[4]

"County Song"

Our home is in Iowa westward toward the setting
    sun,
Just between two mighty rivers where the flowing
    waters run;
It has towns, it has cities, it has many noble
    streams,
It has ninety-nine counties. Will you join and sing
    their names?

Lyons, Osceola, Dickinson, where the Spirit Lake
    we see;
Howard, Winneshiek, and Allamakee so fine
Makes eleven northern counties on the Minnesota
    line.
Clayton, Dubuque, Jackson, Clinton, together with
    Scott and Muscatine,
Lee, Louisa, and Des Moines on the Eastern line are
    seen.*

"Was It Right?"

If you girls and boys will listen,
I will tell you in my song,
Of a sad thing that I noticed
As to school I came along.
'Twas a fight, 'twas a fight, 'twas a fight!

'Twas between two little children
Who had fallen out in play;
And alas they beat each other
In a rude and angry way.
Was it right? Was it right?

All their little books so pretty
Lay upon the dusty ground;
They were torn and soiled and tumbled
As their owner pushed around,
In such a plight, in such a plight, in such a plight!

That they never will be decent
To be used in school again,
But the boys had both forgotten
All about their lessons then.
Was it right? Was it right?

Then along the street came singing
Such a merry little lad,
But his voice soon ceased its singing
And his happy face was sad
At the sight, at the sight, at the sight;

And he parted them so gently,
And he begged them so to cease,
That they turned their arms together
And all went to school in peace—
That was right. That was right.**

*Contributed by Marie Schlapkohl of Dysart, Iowa, as sung by her father in the 1880s. Published in Earl J. Stout, *Folklore from Iowa* (New York: G. E. Stechert and Co. for the American Folk-Lore Society, 1936), pp. 127–128.
**Contributed by Ernestine Morrett of Corydon, Iowa. Her grandmother wrote the song down in 1884 or 1885. Published in Earl J. Stout, *Folklore from Iowa* (New York: G. E. Stechert and Co. for the American Folk-Lore Society, 1936), p. 131.

In Canada during World War II, airmen sang:

A is for those Air Force boys, with hearts so brave and true,
B is for the battlefield, we're bound to win it, too;
C is for our country, lads, in hope 'twill always stand,
D is for the duty that we pledge unto her land.[5]

Such songs depend on a commonality of language, tools, and activities and
help to build feelings of solidarity within the folk community. The texts are
easily updated as the specifics change with time.

"The Jam on Gerry's Rocks"

Come all of you bold shantyboys, list while I relate,
Concerning a young river lad and his untimely fate;
Concerning a young shantyboy, most manly, true
  and brave,
'Twas on the jam of Gerry's Rock that he met his
  watery grave.

'Twas on a Sunday morning as you will quickly
  hear,
Our logs were piled up mountain-high, we could
  not keep them clear;
Our foreman said, "Turn out, brave boys, your
  hearts devoid no fear,
We'll break the jam on Gerry's Rock and for
  Reganstown we'll steer."

Some of them were willing while others they were
  not,
To work a jam on Sunday, they did not think they
  ought;
But six of our Canadian boys did volunteer to go,
To break the jam on Gerry's Rock with their
  foreman, young Monroe.

They had not rolled off many logs when they heard
  his clear voice say,
"I'd have you boys be on your guard, for the jam
  will soon give way."
These words were scarcely spoken and the mess did
  break and go;
It carried off those six brave youths and their
  foreman, young Monroe.

When the rest of our bold shantyboys the sad news
  came to hear,
In search of their dead comrades to the river they
  did steer;
Some of their mangled bodies a-floating down did
  go;
There crushed and bleeding near the bank lies the
  form of young Monroe.

They took him from his watery grave, brushed back
  his raven hair.

There was one fair form among them whose sad
  cries rose through the air;
One fair girl among them, a maid from Saginaw
  town,
Whose moans and cries rose through the skies for
  her true love who'd gone down.

Fair Clara was a noble girl, the riverman's true
  friend,
She and her widowed mother dear lived at the
  river's end.
The wages of her own true love the boys to her did
  pay,
And for the shanty they rigged up a generous purse
  next day.

They buried him in sorrow deep, it was on the first
  of May.
Now come, you tender shantyboys, it's for your
  comrade, pray;
Engraved upon a hemlock tree that by the grave did
  grow,
Was the name and date of the sad, sad fate of that
  river lad, Monroe.

Fair Clara did not long survive, her heart broke in
  the grief,
And scarcely two months afterward there came to
  her relief;
When the time had passed away and she was called
  to go,
Her last request was granted her: to be laid by
  young Monroe.

Come all of you bold shantyboys, I would have you
  come and see,
The two green mounds by the riverside where grows
  a hemlock tree;
The shantyboys cleared out the wood and there the
  loves laid low,
The handsome Clara Vernon and her true love,
  Jack Monroe.*

*Sung by Jim Kirkpatrick of Sault Sainte Marie, Michigan, in 1948. Collected by Harry B. Welliver. Recording: Library of Congress, LP AFS L56, *Songs of the Michigan Lumberjacks*, 1960.

"The Lumberjack's Alphabet"

A is for axe which we swing to and fro,
B is for boys that handles them so;
C is for canthooks, the logs we make spin,
D is for danger that we're always in.

CHORUS:
And so merry, so merry, so merry are we,
We are the boys when we're out on a spree;
Sing hi-derry, col-derry, hi-derry-dum,
Give the lumberjacks whiskey and nothing goes
   wrong.

E is for echo which through the woods ring; and
F is for foreman that pushes our gang;
G is for grindingstone, the axes we ground,
H is for handle that turns them around.

I is for ink which our letters we've wrote, and
J is for jacket we wore for a coat;

K is for kindling, the fires we'd light,
L is for lice that bothers by night.

M is for money, which everyone owes,
N is for needle that patches our clothes;
O is for oxen the road we swing through, and
P is for Peerless, which everyone chews.

Q is for quiet, when we are asleep,
R is for rabbits which everyone eats;
S is for sleigh so stout and strong, and
T is for teams that tote them along.

U is for use which we put ourselves to,
V is for valley, we tramp it right through;
W is for women when we're down to the Spring,
And triple-X beer is the best beer to drink.*

*Sung by Gus Schaffer of Greenland, Michigan, in 1938.
Collected by Alan Lomax. Recording: Library of Congress,
LP AFS L56, *Songs of the Michigan Lumberjacks*, 1960.

RECOMMENDED RECORDINGS

Anglo-American Ballads, Vol. 1. Rounder, CD 1511; reissue of LC AFS L1.
Anglo-American Ballads, Vol. 2. Rounder, CD 1516; reissue of LC AFS L7.
Ellen Stekert. *Songs of a New York Lumberjack*. Folkways, LP FA 2354.
Fine Times at Our House: Indiana Ballads, Fiddle Tunes, Songs. Folkways, LP FS 3809.
Loman D. Cansler. *Folksongs of the Midwest*. Folkways, LP FH 5330.
Songs of the Great Lakes. Folkways, LP FE 4018; from Canadian singers.
Songs of the Michigan Lumberjacks. Library of Congress Archive of Folk Culture, LP
   AAFS L56.
Wolf River Songs. Folkways, LP FE 4001; from Wisconsin.

NOTES

1. See Harriet M. Pawlowska, *Merrily We Sing: 105 Polish Folksongs* (Detroit: Wayne State University Press, 1961).

2. Ivan H. Walton and Joe Grimm, *Windjammers: Songs of the Great Lakes Sailor* (Detroit: Wayne State University Press, 2002), p. 114.

3. Written and distributed on a 1929 broadside by Moran Dock Boggs. Recording: Folkways, LP/Cass FA 2392, *Dock Boggs, Vol. 2*, 1965.

4. As sung by Captain Leighton Robinson, 1951. Recording: LC AFS L 26, *American Sea Songs and Shanties*.

5. MacEdward Leach, *Folk Ballads and Songs of the Lower Labrador Coast* (Ottawa, ON: National Museum of Canada, 1965), pp. 197–198.

6

Folk Music of the Far West

The musical style of the Northwest is very similar to the style of the Midwest that, in turn, reflects the traditions of the Northeast or the Southeast, depending on which migrant groups settled a particular area. The regional distinctions that exist are evident primarily in the content of the songs and ballads that reflect local folkways, rather than in their styles. From the late nineteenth through the twentieth centuries, the instruments most commonly encountered were the guitar and fiddle, with the banjo running a distant third.

THE NORTHWEST

Although exploration of the Northwest began with the trail-blazing adventures of Lewis and Clark in the first decade of the nineteenth century, it wasn't until the 1880s and 1890s that the European American population burgeoned. The first pioneers were lured by the prospect of furs: the Northwest's abundant forests were home to many animals whose pelts were prized in the East and Europe. Fur trappers went to work in what was to become Oregon in 1828, although after a decade or two, the trade began to wane as the animal population was quickly depleted.

Gold was discovered in the 1850s in Idaho, Montana, and eastern Oregon, but it was a series of promising placer gold strikes (gold in gravel and sand

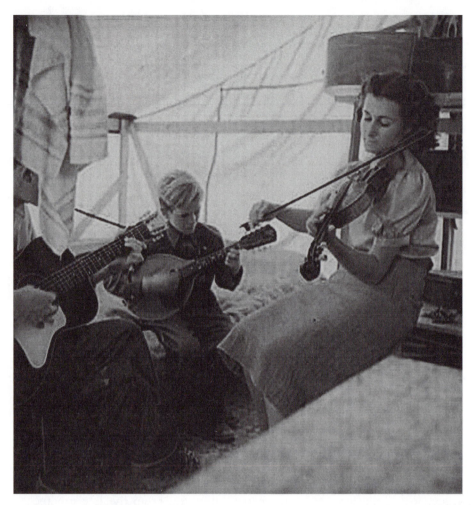

A migrant family from Arkansas playing hillbilly songs in California (1939). *Photographer, Dorothea Lange (LC-USF34-019320-E); from the Farm Security Administration—Office of War Information Photo Collection, Library of Congress Prints and Photographs Division.*

deposits) in the 1860s that brought in a raging torrent of eager prospectors, doubtless hoping for a repeat performance of California's fortune-making gold panning of the preceding decade. Montana's gold rush was in full swing in 1862. Idaho's gold rush peaked in about 1884 in the Coeur d'Alene region. Gold mining fever was soon boosted by the lure of another precious metal, silver, discovered in Montana in 1875 near Butte. Industrial metals, such as copper, lead, tungsten, and zinc, were found, especially in western Montana. Mining for all these metals is called hard-rock mining, as distinguished from the more widespread mining of coal. Irish, Cornish, and Welsh miners were lured in the 1870s and later to the mines in Montana. The Cornish were traditionally hard-rock men, while the Irish and Welsh favored the coalmines like those found in their native countries.

Another great enterprise of the Northwest was timber, today a major source of revenue in Washington and Oregon. As the Northeast was stripped of its old growth forests in the late 1800s, loggers lumbered west to the virgin timber of the Pacific coastal states. Cattle raising also proved profitable in Montana and Idaho in the 1860s and 1870s, but the industry was badly hurt in the mid-1880s by a series of severe winters and poor grazing conditions, exacerbated by the increasing sheep industry. When sheep graze, they nibble the vegetation so close to the ground that it becomes useless for cattle grazing; as a result, traditionally there is great animosity between shepherds and ranchers. In 1886, 60 percent of all Montana's cattle died because of these combined conditions.

All of these occupations gave rise to ballads and songs, many of which recycled the tunes of then-popular pieces or traditional songs from further east and south and put new, appropriate words to them. The practice of singing in the hard-rock mines was common before the turn of the century. Many of the Cornish and Welsh miners brought songs with them from Great Britain, though they also were fond of the Methodist hymns of America. During the Christmas season the streets, hotels, and theaters of Butte were filled with the carol singing of these transplanted choristers. The custom of singing in the mines died out around 1900, partly because of the increasing mechanization of the mining process that made it impossible to hear fellow miners and join them in song. Although the extent of song collecting in the Far West has been too little to make quantitative statements about the most popular songs and ballads, in general collectors have encountered far fewer of the older ballads than are found in the Northeast and Southeast.

In 1946–1948, folklorist Wayland Hand collected a number of songs from the hard-rock miners that originated either late in the 1800s or early in the 1900s. One song honored the Cornish miners, who were called "Cousin Jacks." Their womenfolk were called "Cousin Jennies."

"Cousin Jack"

You ask me for a song, folks,
And I'll try to please you all;
Don't blame me if I do not suit,
For nature has its call.

CHORUS:
But for singing and for mining,
They have somehow got the knack;
It's a second nature to that class
Of lads called "Cousin Jacks."

You'll find them on the mountain top,
You'll find them on the plains;
You'll find those boys where'er you go,

And you'll find their mining claims.

They come from distant Tombstone
And Virginia on the hill;
You ne'er can beat a Cousin Jack
For hammering on the drill.

Amongst you other Irishman,
Do justice if you can;
For there's none that can compete
With the good old Cornishman.*

*Reported by Duncan Emrich in "Mining Songs," *Southern Folklore Quarterly* 6 (1942): 103–106.

The Cousin Jacks worked side-by-side with other British immigrants, as well as Americans who had come West from various parts of the country. "The Big Diamond Mine," another Montana song, mentions several of the different ethnic groups who worked there. Though the song takes a poke at supervisor Ed Kane, he was apparently well liked by his workers.

"The Big Diamond Mine"

There was hoboes from Kerry, and hoboes from
  Cork,
Some from New Jersey, and more from New York.
Well, they come from the near, and the near and
  the far;
They're the Sons of Old Erin that pushes the car.

And the big-bellied Dutchman from over the
  Rhine,
Come a rustling a job in the Big Di'mond Mine.
Well, I got me a job on the first day of May,
Four and six bits they said was the pay.

Well, I worked four shifts and I dragged me time;
To hell with you, Ed Kane, and your Big Diamond
  Mine.

There were tinkers and tailors, shoemakers and
  slobs,
And all kinds of pickers to put waste in the gob.
There was raisemen from Bisbee and timbermen
  from Butte,
And all kinds of muckers to put the rock in the
  chute.*

*As sung by John Dell Duffy, who learned the song in about 1921. Collected by Wayland Hand et al. Published in Wayland D. Hand, Charles Cutts, Robert C. Wylder, and Betty Wylder, "Songs of the Butte Miners," *Western Folklore* 9 (January 1950): 23. "Gob" means the worked-out chambers and tunnels into which waste rock is dumped; "pickers" are muckers who hand pick the waste rock; "raisemen" are miners who operate the raisers that connect the horizontal mine shafts on different levels; "rustling" means hunting for a job.

When a folk song parodies a pop hit, it usually can be dated to within a few years after the pop song was published. "When I Was a Miner, a Hard-Rock Miner" was sung to the tune of "When You Wore a Tulip," one of the big hits of 1914, so it must have been written soon afterward. The additional reference to making moonshine suggests a date soon after Prohibition passed. The song comments on what was a common experience: all the local tradespeople were especially friendly to miners as long as they were gainfully employed and had money to spend. When the supply of money dried up, so did the hospitality.

In the hard-rock mines, a "mucker" was a worker who shoveled waste rock into cars for removal. His wages were typically fifty cents a day less than that of the miner; consequently, in the song "Says the Miner to the Mucker," he responds to the miner's request for a chaw of

---

"When I Was a Miner, a Hard-Rock Miner"

When I was a miner, a hard-rock miner,
Down in a deep, deep mine.
The hashers all caressed me,
The chambermaids blessed me;
My contract drift was paying fine.

But I soon grew weary,
My eyes got getting bleary;
My lungs they wheezed most of the time.
So to dodge the undertaker,
I turned a moonshine maker,
And gave up the deep, dark mine.*

*Reported by Wayland D. Hand, Charles Cutts, Robert C. Wylder, and Betty Wylder in "Songs of the Butte Miners," *Western Folklore* 9 (1950): 1–49.

tobacco with angry resentment but reveals, in the third stanza, that he'd still rather be a miner. "The Miner Boy" is also from Montana, but it has the opening phrases of a good number of nineteenth-century Irish and English broadside ballads and probably originated in the Old World.

"Says the Miner to the Mucker"

Says the miner to the mucker,
"Will you give me a chew?"
Says the mucker to the miner,
"I'm damned if I do!"

Save up your money,
Save up your rocks,
And you'll always have a chew
In your old tobacco box.

Says the mucker to the miner,
"If I give you a chew,
Will you make me a miner
Just the same as you?"

Says the miner to the mucker,
"You would never do,
You can't be a miner
Till you can drink, swear, and chew!"*

"The Miner Boy"

One morning as I rambled,
Through the fields I took my way,
In hopes of seeing my miner boy
And for a while to stay,
In hopes of seeing my miner boy,
My love, my life, my joy,
My heart was depressed, I could find no rest
For the thoughts of my miner boy.

Said the mother to the daughter,
"I'll confine you to your room,
You never shall marry a miner boy,
It would certainly be your doom;
For the way they have of living,
And of toiling on through life,
Daughter, dear, now do you hear,
You can't be a miner's wife."

Said the daughter to the mother,
"Why are you so unkind?
I never shall marry no other one,
He's the one that suits my mind,
With his trousers made of corduroy
And jacket of true blue,
I'd rather marry my miner boy
Than live at home with you."

So fill the glasses to the brim,
Let the toast go merrily round,
Drink to the health of the miner boy
That works down in the ground.
When his work is over,
He comes whistling home with joy,
Happy is the girl
That marries the miner boy.**

*Collected by Duncan Emrich—the first two stanzas from "Deacon" Blake, who learned it in the 1890s, and the last two stanzas from "Dinger" Williams. Published in Duncan Emrich, "Songs of the Western Miners," *California Folklore Quarterly* 1 (July 1942): 229. Muck is rock broken in blasting; a mucker is a miner who shovels waste rock into cars for removal from the workings.

**Collected by Duncan Emrich from Mrs. Walter Mosch of Central City, Colorado, who learned it from her mother in the Joplin country in the 1890s. Published in Duncan Emrich, "Songs of the Western Miners," *California Folklore Quarterly* 1 (July 1942): 223–224.

Late in 1860, not long after the California gold rush, the yellow metal was discovered in Nez Perce tribal country of the Idaho territory, and another rush was on. It lasted only a few years, but it lured nearly 20,000 more white settlers. Popular songwriter Frank French wrote a song, "We're Coming, Idaho," about the excitement, and it was published in 1863. The enthusiastic lyrics proclaim the gold seekers' confidence that once they're in Idaho, there will be gold nuggets lying around for the picking, and they'll know poverty no more. The text given here is very close to French's original and can be compared also to the song "Eureka!" in Chapter 4, which is based on French's song.

When Idaho gold was discovered again in 1884 near Coeur d'Alene, another population boom followed. During the 1880s settlers came mainly from the South and Southwest; later, they came from the Midwest. By 1900 logging was becoming an important industry. "Fifty Thousand Lumberjacks" was collected in northern Idaho in 1917 and details some of the unsavory work conditions of the day.

In 1846, the boundary between the United States and Canada, long the subject of contentious dispute, was established at its present latitude. Nevertheless, with good forests on both sides of the new border, the Northwest logging industry paid no attention to the arbitrary line of demarcation. Philip J. Thomas collected "The Grand Hotel" about a hotel in Vancouver, British Columbia, where the loggers used to stay. Though collected in 1975, it refers to events of three-quarters of a century earlier. The tune for this song is very Irish.

The growth of mining, lumber, and cattle ranching in the Northwest created the need for a rail link with the rest of the country. In 1881 the Oregon Short Line (OSL) was chartered to connect the Union Pacific (UP), which owned controlling interest in the OSL, with the Oregon Railway & Navigation Company of the far Northwest. This would give the UP another route to the

---

"We're Coming, Idaho"

They say there is a land,
Where crystal waters flow,
O'er bed of quartz and purest gold,
Way out in Idaho.

CHORUS:
O! wait, Idaho!
We're coming, Idaho;
Our four hoss team
Will soon be seen
Way out in Idaho.

We're bound to cross the plains,
And up the mountains go,
We're bound to see our fortunes there,
Way out in Idaho.

We'll need no pick or spade,
No shovel, pan, or hoe,
The largest chunks are top of ground,
Way out in Idaho.

We'll see hard times no more,
And want we'll never know,
When once we've filled our sacks with gold,
Way out in Idaho.*

*In Rosalie Sorrels, *Way Out in Idaho* (Lewiston, ID: Confluence Press, 1991), p. 30. Found in a manuscript book of the late 1800s.

"Fifty Thousand Lumberjacks"

Fifty thousand lumberjacks
Goin' out to work,
Fifty thousand honest men
That never loaf or shirk,

Fifty thousand lumberjacks
They sweat and swear and strain,
Get nothin' but a cussin'
From the pushes and the brains.

Fifty thousand lumberjacks
Goin' in to eat
Fifty thousand plates of slum
Made from tainted meat,

Fifty thousand lumberjacks
All settin' up a yell
To kill the bellyrobbers
An' damn their souls to hell.

Fifty thousand lumberjacks
Sleepin' in pole bunks,
Fifty thousand odors
From dirty socks to skunks,

Fifty thousand lumberjacks
Who snore and moan and groan
While fifty million graybacks
Are pickin' at their bones.

Fifty thousand lumberjacks
Fifty thousand packs,
Fifty thousand dirty rolls
Upon their dirty backs,

Fifty thousand lumberjacks
Strike and strike like men,
For fifty years we packed our rolls,
But never will again.*

*Collected by William Alderson from Professor Harold Barto, who learned it in the logging camps of northern Idaho in 1917. Published in William Alderson, "Notes and Queries," *California Folklore Quarterly* 1 (October 1942): 375–376.

"The Grand Hotel"

There's a place in Vancouver you all know so well,
It's a place where they keep rot-gut whiskey to sell.
They also keep boarders, they keep them like hell,
And the name of that place is the Grand Hotel.

In the Grand Hotel when the loggers come in,
It's amusing to see the proprietor grin.
He knows they've got money, he'll soon have it all;
"Come on boys, have a drink!" you will hear
    Tommy call.

Oh, the bartender laughs as the money rolls in;
They drink beer and whiskey, champagne, rum and
    gin,

Till they all get so boozy they can't drink no more,
And the loggers lay scattered all over the floor.

In the morning, the loggers wake up from their bed
Their money's all gone and, oh Lord, what a head!
They rush for the bar and call for a drink,
And Tommy gets busy a-slinging the ink:

"Four bits for your bed, though you slept on the
    floor,
And the breakfast you missed that will be four bits
    more;
And a four-dollar meal ticket, good at the bar,
And a pass back to camp on the old *Cassiar*."*

*Collected by Philip J. Thomas from Bennett King Lesley in Vancouver, 1975. Published in Thomas's *Songs of the Pacific Northwest* (Saanichton, BC: Hancock House, 1979), p. 123. The Grand Hotel's proprietor was Thomas J. Roberts, who came to Vancouver from New Brunswick in 1888 and opened the Grand Hotel a few years later. Four bits was fifty cents; "slinging the ink" meant adding up the bill; the S.S. *Cassiar* was a steamship that took the loggers back to camp.

West Coast to supplement the primary one, the link with the Southern Pacific at Ogden, Utah. Several spur lines were constructed from 1882 to 1884. All but one of these lines were standard railroad gauge (4 feet 8 inches between the rails); one section, from Pocatello, Idaho, through Silver Bow County, Montana, was a "narrow gauge" track. This would pinpoint the origin of "Way Out in Idaho," both in time (1882–1884) and place. The song is very similar to "Buffalo Skinners" and "Canaday-I-O," discussed later in this chapter.

During the Great Depression, a major land reclamation project in the Northwest was undertaken involving the construction of several dams on the mighty Columbia River. A result of this project would be inexpensive electric power for rural homes and undeveloped areas in and around the Columbia basin. In 1937 the Bonneville Power Administration (BPA) was created as an agency

---

"Way Out in Idaho"

Come all you jolly railroad men and I'll sing you if I can
Of the trials and tribulations of a godless railroad man,
Who started out from Denver, his fortunes to make grow,
And struck the Oregon Short Line way out in Idaho.

CHORUS:
Way out in Idaho, way out in Idaho,
A-workin' on the narrow gauge, way out in Idaho.

I was roaming around in Denver, one luckless rainy day,
When Kilpatrick's man-catcher stepped up to me and did say,
"I'll lay you down five dollars as quickly as I can,
And you'll hurry up and catch the train, she's starting for Cheyenne."

He laid me down five dollars, like many another man,
And I started for the depot, was happy as a clam.
When I got to Pocatello, my troubles began to grow,
A-wading through the sagebrush in frost and rain and snow.

When I got to American Falls, it was there I met Fat Jack,
They said he kept a hotel in a dirty canvas shack;
Said he, "You are a stranger and perhaps your funds are low,
Well, yonder stands my hotel tent, the best in Idaho."

I followed my conductor into his hotel tent,
And for one square and hearty meal I paid him my last cent.
Jack's a jolly fellow, and you'll always find him so,
A-working on the narrow gauge way out in Idaho.

They put me to work next morning with a cranky cuss called Bill,
And they gave me a ten-pound hammer to strike upon a drill.
They said if I didn't like it I could take my shirt and go,
And they'd keep my blankets for my board way out in Idaho.

Oh, it filled my heart with pity as I walked along the track,
To see so many old bummers with their turkeys on their backs.
They said the work was heavy and the grub they couldn't go,
Around Kilpatrick's dirty tables way out in Idaho.

But now I'm well and happy, down in the harvest camp,
And there I will continue 'til I make a few more stamps.
I'll go down in New Mexico and I'll marry the girl I know,
And I'll buy me a horse and buggy and go back to Idaho.*

*As sung by Blaine Stubblefield in 1938 at the Library of Congress in Washington, D.C. Recording: Rounder, CD 1508, *Railroad Songs and Ballads*.

within the Bureau of the Interior to manage the new dams, the largest of which was the Grand Coulee Dam. In 1941, after almost a decade, work on the Grand Coulee was nearing completion. The BPA hired a young troubadour, Woody Guthrie, to come to the Northwest for a month and write a batch of songs for use in a public information film about the new dams and how they would improve the region. Guthrie and his wife piled their belongings into a rickety car and drove from Los Angeles to Portland, Oregon, where Guthrie wrote twenty-six songs in about as many days. Some of these songs have been practically forgotten, but a few were destined to enter oral tradition and remain popular for many years. Perhaps the best-known of these songs is "Roll On, Columbia, Roll On," written to a tune similar to Huddie Ledbetter's "Irene Goodnight." Widely sung, not only in the Northwest, "Roll On" has a good chance of entering oral tradition.

Railroaders

Railroads not only changed the American way of life, they were also directly responsible for the pace and direction of westward expansion. They were the nation's preeminent mover of freight and people, a principal employer, a major financial institution, and the prime mail carrier. Trains were responsible for the creation of our now-familiar time zones that were adopted on October 18, 1893, and went into effect a month later. Entire towns sprang up because of the needs created by the rails and by the westward lure of extravagant railroad advertisements. Handbills posted as far away as Europe enticed the economically disadvantaged to come to America's wide open West, where prosperity and comfort, they claimed, could be plucked like fruits from the trees.

The first American railroad to offer public transportation was the Baltimore & Ohio, regularly operating almost fourteen miles of track in Maryland by 1830. Early travel by rail was hardly a pleasurable excursion. Starts and stops were crude maneuvers, jerking passengers violently from their seats. Locomotive fuel was from pitch-pine wood, producing a dense black cloud of choking smoke billowing back over the passengers who sat in open coaches. Sparks as large as thumbnails hurtled from the smokestack, compelling passengers to flail wildly extinguishing the little tongues of fire constantly erupting on their clothing. Umbrellas or parasols were sometimes thrown up for protection, but they were quickly burnt down to the frame and rendered useless. To non-passengers, railroads were not merely a temporary annoyance but a continual terror, panicking horses, frightening small children, showering bystanders with soot and cinders, and often setting farm fields ablaze from wayward sparks.

Nevertheless, rail growth after 1830 was steady and spectacular. For nearly a century track mileage, number of employees, number of passengers carried, and volume of freight shipped grew apace. In 1930 a peak was reached of 303,000 miles of track in use; then a steady decline occurred thereafter to 132,000 in 1998. From 1830 passenger traffic grew steadily until 1920, during which year each American traveled an average of 445 miles by train. After 1920 the volume of traffic declined, but freight traffic continued to increase. As the railroads grew, a steadily larger fraction of the population worked for them. In 1920 one out of twenty-eight people between the ages of twenty and sixty-five worked for the railroads, a number that had shrunk to about one in 900 by 1998.

With the passage of each decade, public attitudes toward the railroads shifted. By the 1830s, once the initial mistrust of the noisy, dirty, uncomfortable giants was allayed, the public attitude was generally approving. During the 1840s and 1850s, as the novelty wore off in some areas, enthusiasm began to cool. As they proliferated, railroads resorted to pricing practices that aroused considerable public opposition, which reached its peak in the 1870s and 1880s.

Hostility in this era was due to other factors as well: supervisors behaved as if the railroads were above governmental regulation; employees were often arrogant in their dealings with the clientele; Western farmers were antagonized by exorbitant freight rates. In those days, railroads were financial institutions like the banks, buying and selling property, lending money, and holding mortgages. In these arenas, railroads aroused animosity for their heartless treatment of small debtors, and the public complained of blatant favoritism shown to men of influence. Railroads became a faceless enemy, and the common citizen secretly admired those brazen outlaws, like Jesse James and Cole Younger, who dared challenge them. Public feelings remained predominantly negative until after World War I when railroads had tried to improve their image by acts of patriotism.

Each of these changing attitudes toward the railroads engendered its own type of songs, both popular and folk. The focus here is songs reflecting views and experiences of the railroaders, themselves, rather than the public. One prime example from the nineteenth century, "Jerry Go 'Il That Car," was probably written by a railroader, and it certainly was sung by railroaders ("Il" represents the Irish pronunciation of "oil"). This wonderful contribution of the Irish workers to railroad songlore originated out West along the Santa Fe route in around 1881. Irish characteristics are evident in the tune, the incipit, the language, and the workers' names; furthermore, there is some documentary evidence that it was written by an Irish American who was known only as Riley the Bum. From its point of origin in the Southwest, the song rapidly spread eastward and northward; it was collected in western Canada, Winnipeg, Missouri, and Nebraska. The singer of this version, Harry "Haywire Mac" McClintock, railroaded, hoboed, and herded sheep out West (among many other occupations) before he became a minor star of radio and recordings, and he could have learned the song then.

In the early years, trains in both directions used the same track, obliged to pass one another at specified points where there was a short passing track available. The railroader's biggest fear was of a train wreck, and over the years about ten times as many railroadmen died in train wrecks as did passengers. Most of the songs and poems written about wrecks were from the railroaders'

"Jerry Go 'Il That Car"

Come all ye railroad section men and listen to my
  song,
It is of Larry O'Sullivan, who now is dead and gone;
For twenty years a section boss, he never hired a
  tar,
And it's "j'int ahead and center back, and Jerry go
  and 'il that car."

For twenty years a section boss, he worked upon the
  track,
And be it to his credit he never had a wreck;
For he kept every j'int right up to the p'int with a
  tap of the tamp and bar,
And while the boys were shimmin' up the ties, it's
  "Jerry, would you 'il that car."

And every Sunday morning unto the gang he'd say,
"Me boys, prepare ye be aware, the old lady goes to
  church today;
Now I want every man to pump the best he can,
  for the distance it is far,
And we have to get in ahead of Number Ten, so
  Jerry, go and 'il that car."

'Twas in November in the wintertime and the
  ground all covered with snow,

"Come put the handcar on the track and over the
  section go."
With his big soldier coat buttoned up to his throat,
  all weathers he would dare,
And it's "Paddy Mack, will you walk the track, and
  Jerry, go and 'il the car."

God rest ye, Larry O'Sullivan, to me you were kind
  and good;
Ye always made the section men go out and chop
  me wood;
And fetch me water from the well and chop me
  kindlin' fine,
And any man that wouldn't lend a hand, 'twas
  "Larry, give him his time."

"Give my respects to the road-master," poor Larry
  he did say,
"And leave me up that I may see the old handcar
  before I die.
Then lay the spike maul on me chest, the gauge
  and the old plow-bar,
And while the boys will be fillin' up the grave, oh
  Jerry, would you 'il that car."*

*As sung by Harry "Mac" McClintock (Laws, H 30). Recording: Victor Talking Machine Co., 1928. Reissue: Rounder, 1009, *Hallelujah! I'm a Bum*. A section man is a track worker; a hand car is a flat, four-wheeled truck propelled by a two-handled pump used to carry section crews back and forth to work; jerry means section worker; shimmin' means aligning; a tar is a fireman; j'int (i.e., joint) means a length of rail, usually thirty-three- to thirty-nine-feet long; j'int ahead means move on to the next track section; center back means align with respect to the preceding track; a spike maul is a heavy hammer for driving spikes; a plow-bar is another aligning tool.

perspective; it was never the number of people killed in a wreck that determined whether a song was written about it or whether that song survived. The
most popular wreck ballad certainly did not have the most fatalities: "Wreck of
the (Old) 97."

Although this song was developed in the Southeast, it is illustrative of
the lyrics that flourished as the trains crossed the Great Plains. Number 97
was a fast mail train on the Southern Railway that ran from Washington,
D.C., to Atlanta, Georgia, between December of 1902 and January of 1907.
On September 27, 1903, because of various delays, 97 reached Monroe,
Virginia, 165 miles south of Washington, about an hour late. At that station,
the crew was changed; the new engineer was Joseph A. Broady, who had
been with the Southern for only a month and was unfamiliar with Old 97's
route. Outside of Danville, Virginia, the tracks crossed Stillhouse Trestle, a

wooden bridge spanning Stillhouse Creek. The trestle was preceded by a dangerous combination of curve and descending grade. Broady, trying to make up lost time, approached the trestle too fast and lost control of the train; the locomotive and the five wooden cars behind it flew off the rails and hurtled into the ravine below. Nine people were killed and seven others injured.

Seventeen-year-old Fred Jackson Lewey, who lived in Danville, was one of the first on the scene of the accident. A week or so later he began writing a song about it. Other locals added verses to it, and the song gained some local currency. Several commercial hillbilly recordings after 1923 served to spread the ballad around the country, making it one of the best-known traditional train wreck ballads of all time.[1]

"Wreck of the 97"

Steve Broady kissed his loving wife,
By the rising of the sun;
And he said to his children, "May God bless you,
For your dad must now go on his run."

'Twas the twenty-second day of that November,
And the clouds were hanging low,
He took Old 97 out of Washington Station
Like an arrow shot from a bow.

I was standing on the mountain that cold and frosty morning,
And I watched curling smoke below;
It was streaming from Old 97's smokestack
Way down on that Southern road.

97 was the fastest mail train
Ever run the Southern line;
But when she reached into Richmond, Virginia,
She was twenty-seven minutes behind.

He received his orders at the Richmond station,
Saying, "Steve, you're far behind;
Now this isn't 38, but it's Old 97,
You must put her into Spencer on time."

When he read his orders, he said to his fireman,
"Do not obey the whistle or the bell;
And we'll put Old 97 into Spencer on time,
Or we'll sink her in the bottom pits of hell."

He saw the brakeman signal and threw back his throttle,
Although his air was bad;
And the signalman said when he passed Franklin Junction
You could not see the man in the cab.

Steve looked at his watch and said to his fireman,
"Just throw in a little more coal,
And when we reach those Cumberland Mountains,
You can watch Old 97 roll."

He went over the grade making ninety miles-an-hour,
And his whistle broke into a scream;
He was found when dead with his hand on the throttle,
And was scalded to death by steam.

When the news went in o'er the telegraph wires,
This is what the Western said:
That brave, brave man that was driving 97
Is now laying in North Danville, dead.

The people waited at the depot,
Till the setting of the sun;
It was hours and hours the dispatch was waiting
For the fastest train ever run.*

*As sung by the Arizona Wranglers of Hollywood, California, in 1929. Recording: Rounder, CD 1143, *Train 45: Railroad Songs of the Early 1900s*.

THE SOUTHWEST AND FAR WEST

Folk song collections from the Southwest differ from those found east of the Mississippi due to the much greater number of ballads about pioneers, Mormons, and other Western themes. There are, to be sure, older imported and domestic ballads, but overall their proportion seems to be a lot smaller. In Oklahoma, for example, the majority of the singers of the older ballads came from the Ozarks or further to the Southeast; however, quite a significant fraction were born in Scotland. Utah's population, on the other hand, is more varied, reflecting the immigration of converts to the Church of Jesus Christ of Latter-Day Saints from many states as well as from Great Britain. Thus, both immigration and internal migration have contributed to the Southwest's folk song stock. Early observers commented on the use of the mandolin, the banjo, and the fiddle, but through the twentieth century fiddle and guitar have been the most common instruments.

The total number of ballads collected is much smaller than in other regions, so it is harder to draw up a list of "most popular" ballads, but based on the available evidence, two favorites are "Barbara Allen" and "Lord Randal," as in most of the other regions of the country. "Lord Ransom" is a Utah-based version of the latter.

The broader picture, then, reveals a British folk song heritage that survived not only in New England and the southern mountains, but also in all regions of the country well into the twentieth century. Looking in more detail, though, the relative frequencies of occurrence of different particular ballads vary considerably from region to region.

Lord Ransom

"O where have you been, Lord Ransom, my son?
O where have you been, my own darling one?"
"I have been a–courting, mother; make my bed soon,
For I'm sick to my heart and want to lie down."

"O what did she give you, Lord Ransom, my son?
O what did she give you, my own darling one?"
"Fried fish and salt butter, mother; make my bed soon,
For I'm sick to my heart and want to lie down."

"What do you will to pretty Polly, Lord Ransom, my son?
What do you will to pretty Polly, my own darling one?"

"Hell fire and damnation, mother; make my bed soon,
For I'm sick to my heart and want to lie down."

"What do you will your mother, Lord Ransom, my son?
What do you will your mother, my own darling one?"
"I will my milch cows, mother; make my bed soon,
For I'm sick to my heart and fain would lie down."*

*As sung by Salley A. Hubbard of Salt Lake City in 1947. Collected and published by Lester A. Hubbard in *Ballads and Songs from Utah* (Salt Lake City: University of Utah Press, 1961), p. 6. In older Scottish versions, he has been fed "eels boiled in eel's broth," and the stanza damning his false sweetheart comes more dramatically at the end.

In addition to their role in bringing older songs and ballads westward, the Mormons inspired a body of new songs reflecting their own particular lifestyles and the attitudes of "gentiles" (the Mormon term for non-Mormons) toward them. Such songs often touched upon Mormon religious and social views (such as polygamy), but the political conflicts with the outside communities also provided important topics. "Tittery-irie-aye" contains historical references to the Mormons' expulsion from Nauvoo, Illinois, in 1846 and the halt of those fleeing west at Council Bluffs, Iowa. It also describes with some accuracy early domestic folk architecture in Salt Lake City. Thus it would seem to be a song from within the Mormon community; on the other hand, the descriptions of Mormon social practices are not entirely sympathetic. Note the Irish influence in the text in the "come all ye" incipit and in the characteristically Irish nonsense phrase of the refrain.

A hint of the Irish can also be found in two songs associated with Texas. One was said to be very popular among the Irish American soldiers who fought in

---

"Tittery-irie-aye"

Come all my good people and listen to my song,
Although it's not so very good, it's not so very long.
And sing tittery-irie-aye, sing tittery-irie-o.

Now concerning this strange people, I'm now
　a-going to sing,
For the way they have been treated, I think it is a
　sin.
And sing tittery-irie-aye, sing tittery-irie-o.

They've been driven from their homes and away
　from Nauvoo,
For to seek another home in the wilderness anew.
And sing tittery-irie-aye, sing tittery-irie-o.

Oh, they stopped among the Indians, but they don't
　deem to stay,
And they'll soon be a-packing up and jogging on
　their way.
And sing tittery-irie-aye, sing tittery-irie-o.

They made a halt at Council Bluffs, but there don't
　mean to stay,
Some feed the cattle rushes, and some per-airie hay.
And sing tittery-irie-aye, sing tittery-irie-o.

Oh, of logs we build our houses, of dirt we have for
　floors,
Of sod we build our chimneys, and shakes we have
　for doors.
And sing tittery-irie-aye, sing tittery-irie-o.

There is another item, to mention it I must.
Concerning spiritual women that make a hell of a
　fuss.
And sing tittery-irie-aye, sing tittery-irie-o.

Some men have got a dozen wives, and others have
　a score,
And the man that's got but one wife's a-looking out
　for more.
And sing tittery-irie-aye, sing tittery-irie-o.

Now, young man, don't get discouraged, get
　married if you can,
But take care don't get a woman that belongs to
　another man.
And sing tittery-irie-aye, sing tittery-irie-o.

Now concerning this strange people, I've nothing
　more to say,
Until we all get settled in some future day.
And sing tittery-irie-aye, sing tittery-irie-o.*

*Sung by Joseph H. Watkins at Brigham City, Utah, 1946. Collected by Austin E. Fife. Recording: Library of Congress, AAFS L30, *Songs of the Mormons and Songs of the West*, 1952. Reissue: Rounder, CD 1520, *Songs of the Mormons and Songs of the West*, 2002.

the Southwest in the U.S.–Mexican War of 1846–1848. Variously titled "Green Grow the Lilacs" or "Green Grows the Laurel," the song tells of two lovers who part. Subsequently one (sometimes the man, sometimes the woman) writes the other that a new love has taken the old one's place. The song undeniably comes from Britain and is well known throughout the United States, including the Southwest, and was used by playwright Lynn Riggs as the title of his play, *Green Grow the Lilacs*, which was the basis for the Rodgers and Hammerstein musical, *Oklahoma*.

The plants and colors vary in different versions. In some Irish texts, the last line of the first stanza is "and change the green laurels for the orange and blue," from which some infer a political message: blue represents the English, orange is the color of the Irish Protestants, and green is the color of the Irish Catholics. In America these subtleties are lost. The rose and thyme in the third stanza used to represent love and strength, respectively.

Also showing signs of Irish American authorship is "Texas Rangers." Though its author has never been identified, the plain language suggests a nonprofessional hand. While some versions of "Texas Rangers" are localized to events of the Civil War, it was probably composed in the 1830s. The ballad captures in simple but effective verse the dreadful fears of the young soldiers facing their first battle. On the 1890s broadside, under the title is the statement, "This song was sent to us by Nelson Forsyth (Showman), Groesbeck, Limestone Co., Texas." This illustrates graphically how a resourceful publisher, exploiting the cheap print medium, did much to preserve the folk song tradition. The text of the broadside seems to have scrambled some stanzas, in particular, the last two couplets:

My old mother in tears to me did say,
To you they are all strangers, with me you'd better stay

"Green Grow the Lilacs"

Green grow the lilacs, all sparkling with dew,
I'm lonely, my darling, since parting from you,
And by the next meeting I hope to prove true,
And change the green lilacs to the red, white, and
 blue.

Once I had a sweetheart, but now I have none,
Since he has gone and left me, I care not for one,

Since he has gone and left me, contented I'll be,
For he loves another much better, you see.

I wrote him a letter with roses entwined,
He wrote me an answer all bound up in thyme,
He wrote me an answer all bound up in thyme,
Saying, "You write to your sweetheart and I'll write
 to mine."*

*Sung by Neal Nixon of Tulsa, Oklahoma. Published in Ethel Moore and Chauncy O. Moore, *Ballads and Songs of the Southwest* (Norman, OK: University of Oklahoma, 1964), p. 201. A common bit of folk etymology attributes the origin of the Mexican term "gringo" to the fact that American soldiers were always singing the song beginning with "Green grow the lilacs (laurel)." More careful etymology shows it is a corruption of the Spanish word, *Griego*, "Greek," a term for any foreigner (such as Shakespeare's use in "Julius Caesar": "It's Greek to me").

But I thought she was old and childish, the best she did not know;
My mind was bent on ranging and with them I was bound to go.

These couplets probably should occur much earlier in the ballad, perhaps after the opening couplets:

Come all you Texas Rangers, wherever you may be,
I'll tell you a story that happened unto me.
My name it's nothing extra, to you I will not tell;
I am a jolly ranger, although I wish you well.

Another song from Texas has acquired an interesting legendary history, the truth of which is still undecided. The song is "The Yellow Rose of Texas," written in 1836 and said to refer to Emily West, who helped Texas General Sam Houston defeat the Mexican General Santa Anna at the Battle of San Jacinto, the decisive battle for the Texas Republic's independence. In the following text, from a 1930 recording by cowboy singer Gene Autry, the singer replaces the word "darky" by the word "fellow" in an effort to remove any offensive terminology. That the hero and heroine are African American is still apparent from the phrase, "she's the sweetest rose of color" and the reference to playing the banjo, which was almost exclusively an African American instrument in the 1830s.

The war with Mexico had scarcely been concluded when the cry of "Eureka!" from Sutter's Mill in California's Central Valley in 1848 proclaimed to the world that gold had been discovered, and a westward rush of fortune seekers across the continent was on. Among those who sought their fortunes were a large number of Missourians from Pike County.

General Zebulon Pike discovered a mountain peak in Colorado that has immortalized his name. The general was also the source of the name of Pike County on Missouri's eastern border as well as counties in other states. Many of Missouri's Pike County inhabitants went West in the 1850s, drawn by the lure of gold, and Pike County is mentioned in numerous Western songs and ballads. In most, these pioneers are treated scornfully or, at best, humorously. Quite possibly the poor impression they made on their new Western neighbors contributed to the nickname for a Missourian from Pike County—"piker," which meant a poor sport, cheapskate, or small-time gambler.

The ballad "Joe Bowers" is a Western adaptation of "The Girl I Left Behind," discussed in some detail in Chapter 1. The author of "Joe Bowers" is not known for certain, but a likely candidate is John A. Stone, also called "Old Put," the author of several songsters of the 1850s and credited with over fifty songs from the gold rush days. Stone crossed the plains from Pike County to California in 1849 to 1850 and toured the mining camps with a small group of singers. He died in 1864, so the ballad must have been composed in that period. It has been recovered not only from singers out West, but also in outlying states like Michigan, West Virginia, Minnesota, and Pennsylvania.

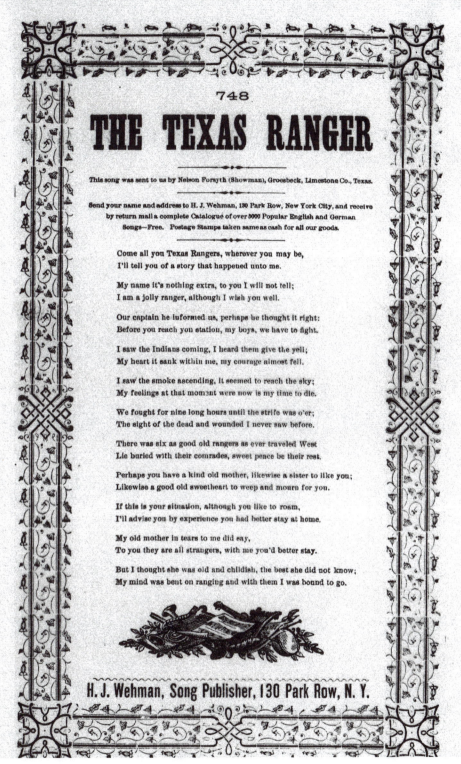

748

THE TEXAS RANGER

This song was sent to us by Nelson Forsyth (Showman), Groesbeck, Limestone Co., Texas.

Send your name and address to H. J. Wehman, 130 Park Row, New York City, and receive
by return mail a complete Catalogue of over 5000 Popular English and German
Songs—Free. Postage Stamps taken same as cash for all our goods.

Come all you Texas Rangers, wherever you may be,
I'll tell you of a story that happened unto me.

My name it's nothing extra, to you I will not tell;
I am a jolly ranger, although I wish you well.

Our captain he informed us, perhaps he thought it right:
Before you reach yon station, my boys, we have to fight.

I saw the Indians coming, I heard them give the yell;
My heart it sank within me, my courage almost fell.

I saw the smoke ascending, it seemed to reach the sky;
My feelings at that moment were now is my time to die.

We fought for nine long hours until the strife was o'er;
The sight of the dead and wounded I never saw before.

There was six as good old rangers as ever traveled West
Lie buried with their comrades, sweet peace be their rest.

Perhaps you have a kind old mother, likewise a sister to like you;
Likewise a good old sweetheart to weep and mourn for you.

If this is your situation, although you like to roam,
I'll advise you by experience you had better stay at home.

My old mother in tears to me did say,
To you they are all strangers, with me you'd better stay.

But I thought she was old and childish, the best she did not know;
My mind was bent on ranging and with them I was bound to go.

H. J. Wehman, Song Publisher, 130 Park Row, N. Y.

A broadside for "The Texas Ranger" (ca. 1880s) (ID: CPM, 002501-Broad). *Courtesy of the Kenneth S. Goldstein Collection, Center for Popular Music, Middle Tennessee State University.*

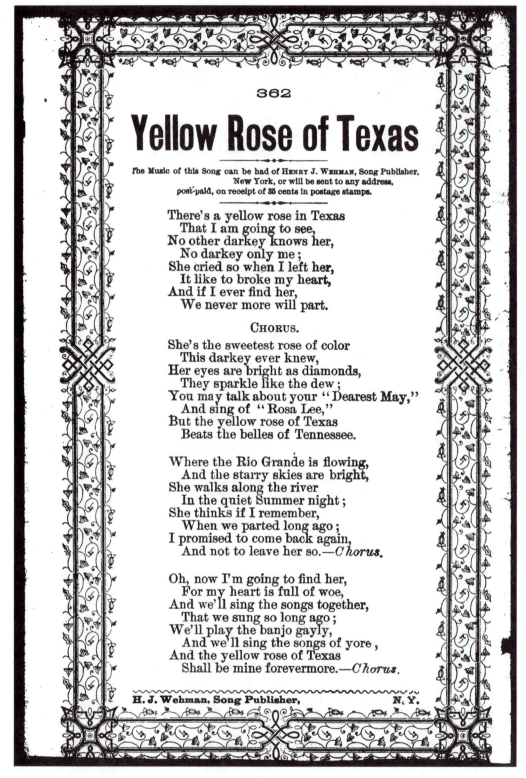

"Yellow Rose of Texas," a broadside from the 1880s (ID: CPM, 002214-Broad). *Courtesy of the Kenneth S. Goldstein Collection, Center for Popular Music, Middle Tennessee State University.*

"The Yellow Rose of Texas"

There's a yellow rose in Texas, I'm goin' there to see,
No other fella knows her, nobody else but me,
She cried so when I left her, it like to broke her heart,
And if we ever meet again we never more will part.

CHORUS:
She's the sweetest rose of color this fellow ever knew,
Her eyes are bright as diamonds, they sparkle like the dew;
You may talk of all [about] your dearest maids and sing of Rosalie,
But the Yellow Rose of Texas beats the belles of Tennessee.

Where the Rio Grande is flowing, the stars are shining bright,
We walked along the river on a quiet summer night;
She says, "If you remember, we parted long ago,"
I promised to come back again and not to leave her so.

I'm a-goin' back to find her, for my heart is full of woe,
We'll sing a song together we sang so long ago;
I'll pick the banjo gaily, and sing the songs of yore,
And the Yellow Rose of Texas will be mine forever more.*

*As sung by Gene Autry, recorded in 1930.

John Stone was definitely responsible for another lighthearted gold rush ballad that has enjoyed popularity for a century and a half: "Sweet Betsy from Pike." It was first published by Stone in his *Put's Golden Songster* (San Francisco, 1858). The original printing bore instructions that it was to be sung to the tune of "Villikins and His Dinah," a popular stage parody written in 1853 of an older serious ballad, "William and Dinah." That tune, in 3/4 time, is very easily sung and has since been used as the vehicle for many songs (including some political election songs). As in the case of "Joe Bowers," identifying Betsy and her lover/husband Ike as from Pike County probably immediately set up the audience for a story of some lower-class folk; in much the same way, "okie" and "arkie" came to have pejorative connotations a century later. Long forgotten is the fact that for frontiersmen of the period, "Betsy" would have had an additional connotation: it was invariably the name they gave to their rifles.

The songs the gold seekers sang as they departed Eastern and Midwestern towns and cities were invariably optimistic; they were practically counting the gold nuggets before they even crossed the Mississippi. Not everyone's expectations were met, but they started out with high hopes.

The chorus of "Ho for California!" also called "Banks of the Sacramento," is sung to the chorus of Stephen C. Foster's "Camptown Races." The respective verse tunes to this California song also are related. This song was written for members of a band of overland emigrants who left Massachusetts in the spring of 1849. The song proved so popular that it was even translated into Finnish. Also, with slight changes, the song went to sea and did service as a capstan shanty:

A bully ship and a bully crew,
Doo da, Doo da!

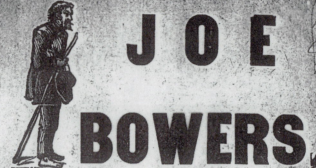

JOE BOWERS,

Words and Music by Will S. Hays.

My name is Joe Bowers, I have got a brother Ike,
I came from old Missouri, all the way from Pike,
I'll tell you why I left thar, and how I came to roam,
And leave my poor old mammy, so far away from home.

I used to court a gal there, her name was Sally Black;
I axed her if she'd marry me, she said it was a whack;
Says she to me; Joe Bowers, before we hitch for life
You ought to get a little home to keep your little wife.

Oh! Sally, dearest sally, Oh! Sally, for your sake,
I'll go to California and try to raise a stake;
Says she to me, Joe Bowers, you are the man to win,
Here's a kiss to bind the bargain, and she hove a dozen in.

When I got in that country, I hadn't "nary red,"
I had such wolfish feelings, I wished myself most dead;
But the thoughts of my dear Sally soon made them feelings git
And whispered hopes to Bowers, I wish I had 'em yit.

At length I went to mining, put in my biggest licks,
Went down upon the boulders just like a thousand bricks,
I worked both late and early, in rain, in sun, in snow.
I was working for my Sally, 'twas all the same to Joe.

At length I got a letter from my dear brother Ike,
It came from old Missouri, all the way from Pike,
It brought to me the darndest news, that ever you did hear,
My heart is almost bustin,' so pray excuse this tear.

It said that Sal was false to me, her love, for me had fled,
She got married to a butcher, the butcher's hair was red
And more than that the letter said, it's enough to make me swear,
That Sally had a baby, the baby had red hair.

Now I've told you all I can about this sad affair,
'Bout Sally marrying a butcher, that butcher had red hair,
But whether 'twas a boy or gal child, the letter never said,
It only said that the baby's hair was inclined to be red.

W. J. SCHMIDT, 1231 Myrtle Avenue, Baltimore Md

WORLD OF RIDDLES No 17
Sold Everywhere   One cent.

A "Joe Bowers" broadside (ca. 1860s) (ID: CPM, 001358-Broad). *Courtesy of the Kenneth S. Goldstein Collection, Center for Popular Music, Middle Tennessee State University.*

A bully mate and a captain, too,
Doo da, doo da, day.
Then blow, ye winds, Hi-oh,
For Californy O!
There's plenty of gold, so I've been told
On the banks of the Sacramento.

The earliest accounts of travelers to the Western plains invariably express astonishment at the immense herds of wild buffalo (more properly, bison) that roamed the range. Early frontiersmen saw in those clouds of thundering hooves an abundant supply of food and clothing, and they proceeded to decimate the herds as fast as they could reload their rifles. "The Buffalo Skinners" seems to be an adaptation of a lumberjack ballad, "Canaday-I-O," believed to have been composed in about 1853 by a Maine lumberman, Ephraim Braley. Braley's first and last two stanzas are shown here for comparison.

The date in the first stanza of "Buffalo Skinners" is historically accurate: in 1873 professional buffalo hunters from Dodge City, Kansas, first entered the northern part of the Texas panhandle, where Jacksboro is. Based on other textual relationships, it appears likely that a Maine woodsman went out West to seek employment in the 1870s and adapted the Down East song, written some two decades earlier and already widespread in oral tradition in New England, to events that he encountered in the West.[2]

Unlike some other ballads and songs that romanticized life on the frontier, whether in the Northeastern woods or the Western plains, these related songs share a cynical and bitter view of the hardships of employ-

Cover of *Put's* (John A. Stone) *Golden Songster* (1858). *Author's collection.*

ment, made worse by the dishonest enticements of the men who signed them up. The logger's ballad simply tells that those con men "found their match, I know"; in "Buffalo Skinners," Crego's fate is far worse and is, in the ethics of the time and place, justified. In the 1870s and perhaps later, several cowboy adaptations were also written based on "Buffalo Skinners," including "The Hills of Mexico" and "The Crooked Trail to Holbrook."

Perhaps the best-known ballad about a cowboy's death is "Streets of Laredo," which, like "Bury Me Not on the Lone Prairie" (quoted below in Cowboys section), was based on earlier songs about death and dying. "Streets of Laredo" was written in 1876 by Francis Henry Maynard, a cowhand, trader, and buffalo hunter, under the title "The Cowboy's Lament," using as a model a nineteenth-century, Anglo-American broadside ballad, "The Dying Girl's Lament." That ballad in turn

---

"Sweet Betsy from Pike"

Oh, don't you remember sweet Betsy from Pike?
She crossed the White Mountains with her lover, Ike,
With two yoke of cattle, an old yaller dog,
A tall shanghai rooster an' a old spotted hog.

CHORUS:
Sing too-ra-lay, too-ra-lay, too-ra-lay lay (4).
One evening plumb early they camped on the Platte,
'Twas near by the road on a green shady flat,
When Betsy got tired an' lay down to repose
While Ike stood an' looked at his Pike county rose.

They traveled an' traveled till Betsy give out,
An' down on the ground she was rollin' about,
Then Ike he looked at her with lots of surprise,
Sayin', "Git up from there, you'll git sand in your eyes."

The wagon it fell with a mighty loud crash,
An' rolled out some bundles of all sorts of trash,
A little kid's fixin's all wrapped up with care,
You needn't to laugh, for it's all on the square.*

*"Sweet Betsy from Pike" (Laws, B 9). Sung by May Kennedy McCord, Springfield, Missouri, 1938. Published in Vance Randolph, *Ozark Folksongs*, vol. 2 (Columbia, MO: State Historical Society of Missouri, 1980), pp. 209–210.

"Ho for California!"

We've formed our band, and are well-manned,
To journey afar to the promised land,
Where the golden ore is rich in store,
On the banks of the Sacramento shore.

CHORUS:
Then ho! Brothers ho!
To California go;
There's plenty of gold in the world we're told,
On the banks of the Sacramento.
Heigh O, and away we go,
Digging up the gold in Francisco.

O! don't you cry, nor heave a sigh,
For we'll all come back again, bye-and-bye;
Don't breathe a fear, nor shed a tear,
But patiently wait for about two year.

As the gold is thar, most any whar,
And they dig it out with an iron bar;

And where 'tis thick, with a spade or pick,
They can take out lumps as heavy as brick.

As we explore that distant shore,
We'll fill our pockets with the shining ore;
And how 'twill sound, as the word goes round,
Of our picking up gold by the dozen pound.

O! the land we'll save, for the bold and brave
Have determined there never shall breathe a slave;
Let the foes recoil, for the sons of toil
Shall make California God's Free Soil.

CHORUS:
Then, ho! Brothers, ho!
To California go;
No slave shall toil on God's Free Soil,
On the banks of the Sacramento.
Heigh O, and away we go,
Chanting our songs of Freedom O.*

*In Robert W. Gordon, "Songs of the Pioneers," *The New York Times Magazine*, January 15, 1928. Reprinted in his *Folk-Songs of America* (New York: National Service Bureau, 1938), pp. 95–96. Typographical errors have been corrected.

"The Buffalo Skinners"

It happened in Jacksboro in the year of 'seventy-
three,
A man by the name of Crego came stepping up to
me;
Saying, "How do you do, young fellow, and how
would you like to go
And spend one summer pleasantly on the range of
the buffalo?"

It's me being out of employment, boys, this to
Crego he did say,
"This going out on the buffalo range depends upon
the pay;
But if you will pay good wages, give transportation,
too,
I think that I will go with you to the range of the
buffalo."

The season being over, old Crego he did say,
The crowd had been extravagant, was in debt to
him that day.
We coaxed him and we begged him, and still it was
no go;
We left old Crego's bones to bleach on the range of
the buffalo.

Oh, it's now we've crossed Pease River, boys, and
homeward we are bound,
No more in that hell-fired country shall ever we be
found;
Go home to our wives and sweethearts, tell others
not to go,
For God's forsaken the buffalo range and the
damned old buffalo.*

"Canaday- I-O"

Come all ye jolly lumbermen, and listen to my song,
But do not get discouraged, the length it is not long;
Concerning of some lumbermen, who did agree to
go
To spend one pleasant winter up in Canada I O.

It happened late one season in the fall of fifty-three,
A preacher of the gospel one morning came to me;
Said he, "My jolly fellow, how would you like to go
To spend one pleasant winter up in Canada I O?"
line of periods for missing stanza

. . . .

Our hearts were made of iron and our souls were
cased with steel,
The hardships of that winter could never make us
yield;
Fields, Phillips and Norcross [the foremen] they
wound their match, I know,
Among the boys that went from Maine to Canada
I O.

But now our lumbering is over and we are returning
home,
To greet our wives and sweethearts and never more
to roam;
To greet our friends and neighbors; we'll tell them
not to go,
To that forsaken goddamn place called Canada
I O.**

*"The Buffalo Skinners" (Laws, B 10). As sung by John
A. Lomax of Dallas, Texas, at Washington, D.C., 1941.
Recording: Library of Congress, LP AAFS L28, *Cowboy
Songs, Ballads, and Cattle Calls from Texas.*
**Sent from Anne V. Marston to Fannie Hardy Eckstorm
and Mary Winslow Smyth, who published it in *Minstrelsy
of Maine* (Boston and New York: Houghton Mifflin
Company, 1927), pp. 22–23.

was based on an Anglo-Irish ballad perhaps written in the late eighteenth century, "The Unfortunate Rake," which tells the sad fate of a soldier who has contracted a fatal venereal disease (probably syphilis) and with his dying words gives instructions for a military funeral.

Salts of white mercury is another name for calomel, or mercury chloride, the treatment for syphilis at the time, and the clue to the soldier's affliction. In warm weather, corpses decompose quickly and without deodorants quickly become offensive, hence the reference to laurel sprigs. In the Western ballad, the details

"Streets of Laredo"

As I walked out in the streets of Laredo,
As I walked out in Laredo one day,
I spied a poor cowboy wrapped up in white linen,
Wrapped up in white linen as cold as the clay.

Oh, beat the drums slowly, and play the fife lowly,
Play the dead march as you carry me along,
Take me to the green valley, there lay the sod o'er
  me,
For I'm a young cowboy, and I know I've done
  wrong.

Let sixteen gamblers come handle my coffin,
Let sixteen cowboys come sing me a song,
Take me to the green valley, there lay the sod o'er
  me,
For I'm a poor cowboy, and I know I've done
  wrong.

It was once in the saddle I used to go dashing,
It was once in the saddle I used to go gay,
First to the dram house, and then to the card house,
Got shot in the breast, and I'm dying today.

Get six jolly cowboys to carry my coffin,
Get six pretty maidens to bear up my pall.
Put bunches of roses all over my coffin,
Put roses to deaden the sods as they fall.

Oh, bury me beside my knife and my six-shooter,
My spurs on my heel, my rifle by my side,
And over my coffin put a bottle of brandy,
That's the cowboy's drink, and carry me along.

We beat the drums slowly, and played the fife lowly,
And bitterly wept as we bore him along,
For we all loved our comrade so brave, young, and
  handsome,
We all loved our comrade, although he'd done
  wrong.*

"The Unfortunate Rake"

As I was a-walking down by St. James's Hospital,
I was a-walking down by there one day;
What should I spy but one of my comrades,
All wrapped up in flannel though warm was the
  day.

I asked him what ailed him, I asked him what failed
  him,
I asked him the cause of all his complaint;
"It's all on account of some handsome young
  woman,
'Tis she that has caused me to weep and lament.

And had she but told me before she disordered me,
Had she but told me of it in time,
I might have got pills and salts of white mercury,
But now I'm cut down in the height of my prime.

Get six young soldiers to carry my coffin,
Six young girls to sing me a song;
And each of them carry a bunch of green laurel,
So they don't smell me as they bear me along.

Don't muffle your drums and play your fifes merrily,
Play a quick march as you carry me along;
And fire your bright muskets all over my coffin,
Saying: 'There goes an unfortunate lad to his
  home.'"**

*"Streets of Laredo" (Laws, B 1). As sung by Johnny Prude for John A. Lomax at Fort Davis, Texas, 1942. Recording: Library of Congress, LP AAFS L28, *Cowboy Songs, Ballads, and Cattle Calls from Texas.*
**As sung by A. L. Lloyd. Recording: Folkways, FS 3805, *The Unfortunate Rake: A Study in the Evolution of a Ballad*, 1960.

of the rake's descent are not nearly so graphic as in the earlier one; we are merely told of his descent from drink to gambling and ultimately to death in a card table shooting. The more specific details of any sexual sins that he presumably committed, are absent. The laurel sprigs have become, in some versions, sweet smelling

"The Lineman's Hymn"

As I walked out in the streets of old Burley,
As I walked out in Burley one day,
I spied a young lineman all wrapped in white linen,
All wrapped in white linen and cold as the clay.

"I see by your scare-strap that you are a lineman,"
These words he did say, as I boldly walked by;
"Come sit down beside me, and hear my sad story,
I fell off the pole and I know I must die.

'Twas once up the poles I used to go dashing,
Once up the poles I used to go gay;
First up the sixties, and then up the nineties,
But I fell off an eighteen, and I'm dying today.

Oh, ring the phone softly, and climb the pole
   slowly,
Check your D-rings when you go aloft;
Keep your hooks sharpened, and grease up your
   scare-strap,
I'm telling you, buddy, that ground ain't so soft.

Get me six drunken linemen to carry my coffin,
Six splicers' helpers to mud-in my grave;
Take me to Kline, the Great White Father,
And let him mourn over his gallant young slave."*

"The Ballad of Bloody Thursday"

As I went walking one day down in Frisco,
As I went talking in Frisco one day;
I spied a longshoreman all dressed in white linen,
Dressed in white linen and cold as the clay.

I see by your outfit that you are a worker,
These words he did say as I slowly walked by;
Sit down beside me and hear my sad story,
For I'm shot in the breast and I know I must die.

. . . .

Don't beat the drums slowly, don't play the pipes
   lowly,
Don't play the dead march as they carry me along;
There's wrongs that need righting, so keep right on
   fighting,
And lift your proud voices in proud union songs.

Fight on together, you organized workers,
Fight on together, there's nothing to fear;
Remember the martyrs of this bloody Thursday,
Let nothing divide you, and victory is near.**

*As sung by Rosalie Sorrels, whose husband, a former linesman, learned it in 1953 in Burley, Idaho. Recording: Folkways, FH 5343, *Folk Songs and Ballads of Idaho and Utah*; and Folkways, FS 3805, *The Unfortunate Rake: A Study in the Evolution of a Ballad*, 1960. A scare-strap is the leather belt linemen use to secure themselves to the pole; hooks are spurs on the lineman's shoes; mud-in means refilling a hole, as after a wooden pole has been set in the ground; Great White Father is a sarcastic reference to Harry Kline, a legendary tough boss in Burley at the time.

**As sung by John Greenway. These and other related ballads are the subject of a fascinating LP album, Folkways, FS 3805, *The Unfortunate Rake*, 1960, edited by Kenneth S. Goldstein. Goldstein's primary source was Kenneth Lodewick's article, "'The Unfortunate Rake' and His Descendents," *Western Folklore* 14 (1955): 98–109.

roses, but without knowing the ballad's history, it's hard to understand why they are being used to "deaden the sods."

"Laredo" and its ancestors have proven a remarkably fertile family, giving rise to a host of parodies. For example, from Burley, Idaho, came the telephone lineman's song, "The Lineman's Hymn," collected in 1953. A longshoreman's strike in San Francisco in 1934 prompted another adaptation, the first and last two verses of which are reprinted here.

And in Vietnam in the 1960s an anonymous version began:

As I was escorting a Spectre one evening
And we were in orbit 'round Delta One-One,
A non-Christian gomer who didn't speak English
Was shooting at us with a Communist gun.[3]

Unlike some clusters of ballads, which evolve by the gradual accumulation of small changes, these ballads are whole new compositions that depend for their impact on the listener's familiarity with the source ballad that has been carefully rewritten to reflect the new circumstances, without obliterating the pattern of the old.

War turns the adversary into a figure of hatred and contempt, as these songs illustrate. Xenophobia is not confined, however, to scenes of war on foreign soil. Few immigrant groups to America have escaped the prejudice, hostility, or ridicule of the mainstream population. The plight of African Americans in the South is the best-known example; the Irish, even though they were white-skinned and spoke English, were subjected to humiliating abuse in the mid-1800s, as the once-ubiquitous notice, "No Irish need apply," appended to employment advertisements attests. In the Far West, Asian immigrants, particularly the Chinese who provided cheap labor on the Western railroads, were the objects of unconcealed, often bitter, discrimination. One song, "Sing Ha-Ha, Come from China," from the late 1800s displays an unusual mixture of dislike and sympathy for the foreigners.

In the twentieth century, the steady flow of migration northward from Mexico and Central America wrought great changes in California's social structure, changes that have not taken place without a good deal of hostility, rancor, and racism. An early inducement to immigration was the need for cheap labor in California's fertile San Joaquin and Central valleys. In 1942, when the Hispanic population was just a fraction of what it became a half century later, the ditty "A Monterey County Song" was reported to be a great favorite at Salinas Valley barbecues and other gatherings. It captures the

"Sing Ha-Ha, Come from China"

My name Sing-Ha-Ha, come from China,
Keep a little wash shop way down street.
No like-a 'Melican man, too much chin-chin,
No pay wash bill, him a dead beat.

Me got an Irish girl, she well nice-ee
Me make her some day my wife.
We have a nice time, go back China,
Eat plenty much good rats and mice.

My name Sing-Ha-Ha, come from China,
Run away soon, no come back.
Me catch-a Irish girl on-a 'Melican man's lap
Kissee her—smack, smack, smack.

Got a little house in Bottle Alley,
Two little rooms top side high;

We get married, drink much gin-gin,
She get tight and hit my eye.

P'liceman come along—take me up—lock me up a shop,
Put me in a room and make me stay;
Judge send me up for a very long time-ee,
My pretty Irish girl she run away.

Oh! My name Sing-Ha-Ha, come from China,
Me like-a Irish girl, she like-a me.
Me from-a Hong Kong, 'Melican man come along,
Steal an Irish girl from a poor Chinee. *

*Reported by J. W. Green, whose mother used to sing the song in the 1880s, in *Western Folklore* 6 (July 1947): 278.

Spanish American musicians at a fiesta in Taos, New Mexico (1940). *Photographer, Russell Lee (LC-USF33-012870-M4); from the Farm Security Administration—Office of War Information Photo Collection, Library of Congress Prints and Photographs Division.*

Hispanic folklore between pure Mexican and complete Anglicization. Although not much to it, it highlights the immigrants' migratory life and the racism encountered. "Por qué" means "why," while "porque" means "because." "Andale, muchacho" means "get going, kid." The first part of the song is chanted to the tune of the chorus of "La Paloma," a popular Spanish song.

COWBOYS

Although the mythical figure of the cowboy remained a powerful icon in American literature, film, music, and art throughout most of the twentieth century, the heyday of the real western range cowboy lasted only three decades, from the end of the Civil War until the mid-1890s. It was during this era that the two primary characteristics of ranching arose and eventually faded away: the roundup and the long trail drive.

According to the popular myth perpetuated in Western novels and Hollywood movies for most of the twentieth century, the cowboys were all

---

"A Monterey County Song"

All: From Monterey to Castroville,
From Castroville to Watsonville,
From Watsonville to Sotoville,
From Sotoville to Natividad,
From Natividad to Soledad,
From Soledad to Jolon.

Questioner: And didn't you know
That the court would convict you for that?

Answerer: Por qué, for what?

Questioner: Porque for that!

All: Andale, muchacho.*

*In Parker, Paul, "Notes and Queries," *California Folklore Quarterly* 1 (October 1942): 378.

Anglo-Saxon males; in reality, there were quite a few African American ex-slaves and Mexicans. The language of the latter group greatly enriched the "lingo" (a word derived from the Spanish lengua meaning "tongue" or "language") of the cowboy and was reflected in the lyrics of the cowboy songs. Most of the white cowboys were probably Southerners, but Midwesterners were also represented, as were a number of Englishmen. Roundups and trail driving were strenuous work, and only hardy young men were fit to carry it out. Older men might become cooks; younger boys were the "wranglers" who tended the horses.

In 1867 the completion of the transcontinental railroad established the pattern for marketing beef. By the mid-1880s several factors conspired to weaken the cattle industry as it had been known: cattle prices dropped from $35 to $10 a head in a period of a few years; severe winters from 1884 to 1886 devastated the cattle herds and their caretakers; and the invention of barbed wire and the subsequent fencing off of the plains meant that open ranging and the long drive were no longer possible.

Most of the widely popular ballads about the cowboy were written during the halcyon days of the long drives. But the end of that era did not mean that cowboys were no longer employed in cattle rearing nor that no more cowboy poems, songs, and ballads were to be written. Long evenings around the campfire without urban amusements not only were conducive to the writing of many a cowboy verse but also provided a natural (not to say, captive) audience for its performance. Cowboy poetry was published in abundance in Western newspapers of the 1880s and 1890s, some originally written with music in mind (". . . to the tune of . . .") and others readily set to familiar tunes. Such pieces were not necessarily the crude products of semiliterate scribblers but often works of great sophistication, many betraying the author's familiarity with the works of Shakespeare or Shelley. In fact, Shakespeare was so popular on the frontier that numerous towns and other places were named after him or his characters. The literary poetry tradition lives on vigorously even today, as a visit to the annual Cowboy Poetry Gathering at Elko, Nevada, shows.

One of the most widely known and beloved songs about the unsettled plains, particularly after Franklin Roosevelt proclaimed it his favorite song, is "Home on the Range." Its newfound fame in 1934, following the president's endorsement, prompted a complicated legal suit over its authorship, and lawyers were engaged to undertake lengthy investigations. The conclusion of their sleuthing was that the song had been written in about 1873 by Dr. Brewster Higley and first published in the Kirwin, Kansas, Chief in 1874. Higley's original title, first verse and chorus are reprinted here. The song remained obscure except very locally; until its publication in John Lomax's influential book, Cowboy Songs and Other Frontier Ballads (1910), disseminated it much more widely.

Many songs were associated with the "night watch": while most of the cowboys slept, a few had night-guard duty. They would circle the dozing herd in opposite directions, watching for signs of restlessness or any other disturbances. On watch, they usually sang, hummed, chanted, or whistled; it seemed to soothe

the cattle and probably helped to keep the night watchmen awake. In an 1873 Kansas City newspaper, this custom was described as such: "Each 'cow boy' as he rides around the herd, sings or shouts a sort of lullaby, old Methodist hymns being the most popular, although good, old-fashioned negro minstrel songs have been found equally effective in soothing the breast of the wild Texas steer."[4] To take advantage of the soothing effects of song, some drovers hired singers to accompany the long drives. In 1882 one cattle-buying firm hired an entire band of Negro minstrels to sing to the cattle at night during the drive from eastern Oregon to the Midwest markets.[5]

In spite of the careful precautions to prevent it, occasionally a herd was suddenly spooked by something and pandemonium ensued. "When the Work's All Done This Fall" is a suspenseful fictitious ballad built around that constant dread of every cowboy—fatal injury in a stampede. This song, originally titled "After the Roundup" by D. J. O'Malley, was published in 1893 in *Stock Growers' Journal* of Miles City, Montana. O'Malley intended it to be sung to the tune of one of the big hits of 1892, "After the Ball" by Charles K. Harris, but by the 1920s it had become associated with a different tune.

Dominick John O'Malley (1867–1943) was born in New York City and moved to the Wyoming Territory in 1876 with his mother and stepfather. Early in his career as a cowboy he began writing verses, and his first publication appeared in 1889. The text given here is quite different from O'Malley's original; in particular, the final stanza is another writer's addition, firmly affixed to the poem by the time John A. Lomax published it in *Cowboy Songs and Other Frontier Ballads* in 1910. Like many cowboy songs, this one has traveled widely around the country and been collected hundreds of times in dozens of states.

O'Malley incorporated a familiar traditional element in his song, namely, the oral last will and testament of the dying hero. His text deftly outlines the character of life on the range: the longing for home and mother, the spirit of camaraderie and mutual affection, and finally the need to brush aside sentiment in the face of the urgent tasks at hand. Unlike many occupational songs, O'Malley's used no in-group slang, a fact that may have contributed to its wide popularity.

The range cowboy spent many of his waking hours in the saddle, so the ability to ride well was a necessity and a source of pride. Sometimes, an experienced cowboy grew overconfident in his abilities; his *compadres* then took it upon themselves to take him down a peg, as illustrated in "The Strawberry Roan."

"Western Home"

Oh! Give me a home where the Buffalo roam,
Where the Deer and the Antelope play;
Where never is heard a discouraging word,
And the sky is not clouded all day.

Chorus:
A home! A home!
Where the Deer and the Antelope play,
Where seldom is heard a discouraging word,
And the sky is not clouded all day.*

*From the *Kirwin Chief* (Kansas), February 26, 1876, reprinted in Kirke Mechem, "Home on the Range," *The Kansas Historical Quarterly* 17 (November 1949), pp. 11–40.

The author of this tune was California-born Curley W. Fletcher (1892–1954), who first published the yarn in 1915 in the *Arizona Record* under the title "The Outlaw Bronco." It achieved widespread popularity, inspiring numerous parodies and sequels, some not printable in family magazines.

Cowboy poets created their own special brand of nondenominational religious songs in which familiar Western imagery was put to metaphorical use. "Roll on Little Dogies," a well-known favorite, was first published in 1895 by Will Croft Barnes in his short story, "The Stampede on the Turkey Track Range." Barnes had heard fragments of the song back in 1886 or 1887 out on the range, and he eventually made his own additions and smoothed it out into a song. It was sung by the central character of his story to the tune of "My Bonnie Lies over the Ocean."

The theology behind the poem is not profound, but the use of everyday cowboy language would have made it instantly understandable to the herders out on the range and doubtless just as effective as a more formal sermon in a conventional church. As good folk songs have a habit of doing, this one "got away" from Barnes: his role in its composition was forgotten and was soon being claimed by other writers, many of whom wrote new stanzas. It helps a song to enter oral tradition when its language and style are so easily assimilated that anyone feels he could have written (or rewritten) it, and under such circumstances it becomes a song that seems not to have a proper author.

In the springtime cattle were rounded up and driven along trails to the nearest railroad station. For Texas cattlemen this meant a two- to six-month trail drive covering eight hundred miles, pushing herds from 500 to 1500 head to cow towns such as Abilene, Ellsworth, Newton, Wichita, and Dodge City, all in Kansas. From the boarding station on the railroad, the cattle were taken to slaughter houses in Kansas City or Chicago, and meat from there sent to local markets and ultimately to the nation's dining tables, where a large steak was an expected dish at wealthier Americans' breakfasts, not to mention lunch and dinner. The roundup process, which took thirty to thirty-five days, began in west Texas in mid-May, in South Texas earlier, and in the Northwest later.

Carl T. Sprague (1920s). *Courtesy of the Southern Folklife Collection, University of North Carolina.*

"When the Work's All Done This Fall"

A group of jolly cowboys discussing plans at ease,
Says one, "I'll tell you something boys, if you will listen, please.
I'm an old cow puncher and here I'm dressed in rags,
I used to be a tough one and take on great big jags.

But I have a home, boys, a good one, you all know,
Although I have not seen it since long, long ago.
But I'm going back to Dixie once more to see them all;
Yes, I'm going back to see my mother when the work's all done this fall.

When I left home, boys, my mother for me cried,
She begged me not to leave her, for me she would have died.
My mother's heart is breaking, breaking for me, that's all,
And with God's help I'll see her when the work's all done this fall."

That very night this cowboy went out to stand his guard;
The night was dark and cloudy and storming very hard.
The cattle all got frightened and rushed in wild stampede;
The cowboy tried to head them while riding at full speed.

While riding in the darkness so loudly did he shout,
Trying his best to head them and turn the herd about;
His saddle horse did stumble and upon him did fall;
The boy won't see his mother when the work's all done this fall.

"Boys, send my mother my wages, the wages I have earned,
For I'm afraid, boys, my last steer I have turned.
I'm going to a new range, I hear the Master's call,
And I'll not see my mother when the work's all done this fall.

George, you may have my saddle; Bill, you may have my bed;
Jack, you may have my pistol, after I am dead.
But think of me kindly as you look upon them all,
For I'll not see my mother when the work's all done this fall."

Poor Charlie was buried at sunrise, no tombstone at his head,
Nothing but a little slab, and this is what it said:
"Charlie died at daybreak, he died from a fall,
And he'll not see his mother when the work's all done this fall."*

*"When the Work's All Done This Fall" (Laws, B 3). As recorded by Carl T. Sprague, 1925, for Victor Talking Machine Co. (Victor, 19747). Reissue: RCA Victor, LPV-522, *Authentic Cowboys and Their Western Songs*, 1965.

Of all the trails that the cowboys followed between Texas and the stations on the railroad, the Chisholm Trail was the most famous. Its southern terminus was at Brownsville, the southern tip of Texas, and it extended due north through Oklahoma and on to Abilene, Kansas, where it met the Kansas-Pacific Railroad. Its northern endpoint was selected in 1867 by Illinois stockman Joseph G. McCoy, and part of it followed along a wagon trail earlier laid out by Jesse Chisholm, an Oklahoma pioneer of Cherokee and Scottish ancestry.

The origins of the song on the trail are shrouded in the dust of the Texas plains, but there are hundreds—if not thousands—of verses, possibly one for each of the legions of cowboys who drove ten million cattle to the rail stations in less than three decades. Taken collectively, these verses memorialize the hardships of the long cattle drives, during which the harried cowboys were subjected to a passel of indignities ranging from irascible cattle to inclement

"The Strawberry Roan"

Well, I'm laying round town just a-spending my
time,
Out of a job, not makin' a dime;
When up stepped a feller, and said, "I suppose,
You're a bronco buster by the look of your
clothes."

Well, he guesses me right, "And a good one," I'll claim,
"Do you happen to have any bad ones to tame?"
He said he had one that's a good one to buck
At throwin' good riders he's had lots of luck.

He says this old pony ain't never been rode,
And the guy that gets on him, he's sure to get
throwed;
Well, I gets all excited and I ask what he pays,
To ride this old pony for a couple of days.

Well, he offers a ten spot, I said, "I's your man,
Oh, the bronc never lived that I cannot stand;
No the bronc never tried, no he never drew a
breath,
That I cannot ride till he starves plumb to death."

Well, he says, "Get your saddle, I'll give you a
chance,"
So we got in the buck-board and went to the ranch;
I waited till morning and right after chuck
I went out to see if that pony could buck.

Down in the horse corral standing alone,
Was this old caballo of a Strawberry Roan;
He had little pin ears that tucked at the tip,
And a forty-four brand upon his left hip.

He was spavined all round and he had pigeon toes,
Little pig eyes and a big Roman nose;
Yew-necked and old with a long lower jaw,
I could tell at a glance he was a regular outlaw.

Well, I buckles on my spurs and was feelin' plum fine,
Pulled down my hat and curled up my twine;
When I threw the loop on him well I knew then,
That before I had rode him I'd sure earn my ten.

I got the blind on him with a terrible fight,
Next come the saddle and I cinched 'er down tight;
Then I stepped on him and I pulled up the blind,
I'm a settin' in the middle to watch him unwind.

Well he bowed his old neck, and I'll say he
unwound,
He seemed to quit livin' down there on the ground;
He went up to the east and come down to the west,
Me settin' on him a-doin' my best.

He sure was a frog walkin', I heaved a big sigh,
He only lacked wings for to be on the fly,
He turned his old belly right up to the sun,
For he sure was a sun-fishin', son of a gun.

He was the worst bronco I've seen on the range,
He could turn on a nickel and make you some
change;
While he was buckin' he squalled like a [colt?]
I tell you that outlaw, he sure got my goat.

I tell all you people that outlaw could step,
And I was still on him a building my rep,
He come down on all fours and he turned up his
side,
But I stuck on his back like a bee in the hive.

And I'll bet all my money there's no hoss alive,
That I cannot ride when he makes his high dive.*

*"The Strawberry Roan" (Laws, B 18). As sung by Rex
Kelly, 1932. Recording: Paramount, 569; Broadway, 8331.
Reissue: JEMF, LP 103, *Paramount Old Time Tunes*. A
bronco buster is a cowboy who breaks in wild horses; *caballo*
means horse in Spanish; yew-necked is Fletcher's spelling
of ewe-necked: a horse with a long, thin, neck like that of
a ewe; spavined means decrepit, broken-down; sun-fishin'
are the movements of a horse when he twists his body into
a crescent, alternately to one side and the other; and frog-
walkin' is using straight, easy hops.

weather to dishonest foremen. Other range songs do not treat the catalog of
hardships so lightheartedly. Most versions that have been printed have been
cleaned up somewhat, on the assumption that genteel readers cannot abide the
unexpurgated lingo of the genuine article.

"Roll on Little Dogies"

Last night as I lay on the prairie,
And looked at the stars in the sky,
I wondered if ever a cowboy
Would drift to that sweet bye-and-bye.
The road to that bright mystic region
Is a dim narrow trail, so they say.
But the broad one that leads to perdition
Is posted and blazed all the way.

CHORUS:
Roll on, roll on,
Roll on, little dogies, roll on, roll on.
Roll on, roll on,
Roll on, little dogies, roll on, roll on.

They tell me there'll be a big roundup,
And the cowboys like dogies will stand.
To be marked by the Riders of Judgment
Who are posted and know every brand.
I know there's many a stray cowboy
Who'll be lost in that great final sale.
When he might have gone on to green
   pastures
Had he known of the dim, narrow trail.

I wonder if ever a cowboy
Stood ready for that judgment day,
He could say to the Boss of the Riders:
"I'm ready, come drive me away."
For they, like the cows that are loco,
Stampede at the sight of a hand,
And are dragged with a rope to the roundup
To get marked by some crooked man's brand.

They tell me of another big owner
Who's nigh overstocked so they say,
Who always makes room for a sinner,
Who drifts from the straight narrow way.
They say He will never forget you,
That He knows every action and look.
For safety, you better be branded,
Have your name in that Great Tally Book.*

*Sung by Carl T. Sprague, 1972. Recording: Folk Variety, FV 12001, *The First Popular Singing Cowboy*, West Germany, 1972. A dogie is a scrubby calf that has not wintered well and is anemic from the scant food of the cold months; loco means crazy in Spanish.

The death of a co-worker is always a tragic event. Those gathered around their dying comrade are overwhelmed with conflicting feelings: grief and sadness for the victim, compassion for the bereaved loved ones too far away to attend, and fear and anxiety over who will be the next to die. This is a painful moment; but there is still a job to be done, and when last rites have been uttered and the body hastily interred in a simple prairie grave, the mourners will have to resume the work at hand. Some of these emotions are expressed in the cowboy classic, "Bury Me Not on the Lone Prairie." It is a reworking of "The Ocean Burial," a poem written by Reverend Edwin H. Chapin and published in 1837, set to music by George N. Allen. Its first, fourth, and penultimate stanzas are the closest to the cowboy version.

The poet responsible for the Western recomposition is unknown. Jack Thorp, who published the first book of traditional cowboy songs in 1908, first heard the song in 1886 and asserted his belief that it had been composed by H. Clemons of South Dakota as "The Dying Cowboy" in 1872. Other collectors, however, have disputed this claim. In any case, it seems to have first appeared in the 1870s and was widespread by the 1880s.

Like the nautical original on which the cowboy poem was based, there is no hint of what caused the cowboy's death—whether killed in a stampede, done

The cover of Harry K. McClintock's 1932 song folio. *Author's collection.*

"The Old Chisholm Trail"

Now, come along boys, and listen to my tale,
And I'll tell you of my troubles on the Chisholm
   Trail.

CHORUS:
Come-a ti-yi yippee, yippee yay, yippee yay,
Come-a ti-yi yippee, yippee yay.

I started up the trail October twenty-third,
Left old Texas with the 2-U herd.

Oh, a ten-dollar horse and a forty-dollar saddle,
I'm a-gonna punchin' them longhorn cattle.

Woke up one mornin' on the Chisholm trail,
With a rope in my hand and a cow by the tail.

Old Ben Bolt was a mighty good boss,
But he'd go to see the gals on a soreback hoss.

Well I'm up in the mornin' before daylight,
An' before I sleep the moon shines bright.

It's cloudy in the west and a-lookin' like rain,
And my derned old slicker's in the wagon again.

Well, I crippled my hoss but I don't know how,
Ropin' at the horns of a 2-U cow.

No chaps, no slicker and its pourin' down rain,
And I swear by gosh I'll never night herd again.

Last night on guard and the leader broke the ranks,
Hit my hoss down the shoulders and I scored him in
   the flanks.

With my foot in the stirrup and my hand on the
   horn,
I'm the best derned cowboy that ever was born.

I'm on the best horse and I'm goin' on a run
I'm the quickest shootin' cowboy that ever pull a
   gun.

Well, we rounded them up, and we brought 'em on
   the cars,
And that was the last of the old two-bars.

Then I went to the boss for to draw my roll,
He had it figured nine dollars in the hole.

So I sold old Bolly and I hung up my saddle,
And I bid farewell to the longhorn cattle!*

*As sung by Harry "Haywire Mac" McClintock, 1928, for
Victor Talking Machine Co., Victor, 21421.

in by Indians, or shot in a saloon brawl. The core of the song is the idea of the desolate loneliness of the plains and the sobering thought of spending eternity there. Like other cowboy songs, this one spoke of the deep fears of every cowhand.

The early cowboy was totally dependent on his steed for his means of locomotion on the ranch. Without mechanized transport and with distances too long to cover by foot, the horse was his indispensable companion. "Goodbye Old Paint" was a favorite cowboy song in early Western movies, and it reflects the cowboy's love for his horse. The language slips so easily from horse references to lady references that one wonders whether the cowboy mixed them up in his own mind.

Jess Morris (1878–1953), the Texas fiddler/singer who gave this song to collector John A. Lomax—and from there to the world—learned it when just a boy of seven from Charley Willis, an ex-slave working on Morris's father's ranch.

Cowboy songs were not without their moments of satire and outright hilarity. While uppity cowboys whose self-esteem exceeded merit were happily cut

"Bury Me Not on the Lone Prairie"

"Oh, bury me not on the lone prairie."
These words come low and mournfully,
From the pallid lips of a youth who lay
On his dying bed at the close of day.

"Oh, bury me not on the lone prairie.
Where the kyotes [sic] howl and the wind blows
    free.
In a narrow grave just six by three,
Oh, bury me not on the lone prairie."

"It matters not, I've oft been told,
Where the body lies then the heart grows cold.
Yet grant, oh grant this wish to me,
And bury me not on the lone prairie."

"I had always hoped to be laid when I died
In the old churchyard on the green hillside.
By my father's grave, there let mine be,
And bury me not on the lone prairie."

"Oh, bury me not"—and his words failed there.
But we paid no heed to his dying prayer.
In a narrow grave just six by three,
We buried him there on the lone prairie.

We buried him there on the lone prairie.
Where the wild rose blooms and the wind blows
    free.
And the buffalo roams o'er the grassy sea,
By his lowly grave on the lone prairie.*

"The Ocean Burial"

"Oh, bury me not in the deep, deep, sea!"
These words came low and mournfully
From the pallid lips of a youth who lay
On his cabin couch at the close of day

. . . .

"It matters not, I have oft been told,

Where the body may lie, when the heart grows
    cold;
But grant, oh, grant this boon to me,
Oh, bury me not in the deep, deep sea!"

. . . .

"Oh, bury me not—" and his voice failed there,
But they gave no heed to his dying prayer;
They have lowered him slow o'er the vessel's side,
And above him has closed the dark, cold tide.

*"Bury Me Not on the Lone Prairie" (Laws, B 2). From *Cowboy Songs as Sung by Charles Marshall, the "Singing Cowboy" in Death Valley Days* (Wilmington, CA, 1934).

down a notch or two in songs, a better subject for humor was the awkwardness of the cowboy when face to face with the fairer sex. "The Cowboy's Dance Song" was written by James Barton Adams, who was born in 1843 in Ohio and worked as a cowboy in New Mexico before becoming a journalist in Denver. He published it in a book of poetry, *Breezy Western Verse*, in Denver in 1889.

There is no specifically Western slang in Adams's poem, but he does a wonderful job of creating the illusion of it and of contrasting the shy and awkward cowboys, further embarrassed by their stiff church-meeting clothes, with the amused and casual manners of the fancily dressed and thoroughly at ease young ladies.

"Goodbye Old Paint"

Farewell, fair ladies, I'm a-leaving Cheyenne,
Farewell, fair ladies, I'm a-leaving Cheyenne,
Goodbye, my little dony, my pony won't stand.

Old Paint, old Paint, I'm a-leaving Cheyenne,
Goodbye old Paint, I'm a-leaving Cheyenne,
Old Paint's a good pony, and she paces when she can.

In the middle of the ocean there grows a green tree,
But I'll never prove false to the girl that loves me.

Oh, we spread down the blanket on the green
  grassy ground,
And the horses and cattle were a-grazing all 'round.

Oh, the last time I saw her, it was late in the fall,
She was riding old Paint, and a-leading old Ball.

Old Paint had a colt down on the Rio Grande,
And the colt couldn't pace, and they named it
  Cheyenne.

For my feet's in my stirrups, and my bridle's in my
  hand,
Goodbye, my little dony, my pony won't stand.

Fare well, fair ladies, I'm a-leaving Cheyenne,
Fare well, fair ladies, I'm a-leaving Cheyenne,
Goodbye, my little dony, my pony won't stand.*

*As sung by Jess Morris for John A. Lomax at Dalhart, Texas, 1942. Reissue: Library of Congress, LP AAFS L28, *Cowboy Songs, Ballads, and Cattle Calls from Texas*. Dony, meaning sweetheart, comes from the Spanish word *doña*, but probably via British slang rather than directly from Mexico.

AMERICAN INDIAN MUSIC

Owing to the many similarities between African and European musical forms, it was easy for these two musical traditions to intermingle and influence one another in the New World. On the other hand, the music of America's indigenous peoples is sufficiently different that hybridization has been slow. In recent decades there have been developments in the Southwestern states that show cross fertilization between Native American, Hispanic American, and other population groups.[6]

HISPANICS

Although fragments of Hispanic American culture can be traced back to the first generations of colonists who came to Florida from eighteenth-century Spain, in California, and points in between, the more important Spanish-language contributions to contemporary American music are from immigrants who came in the twentieth century from Cuba, Puerto Rico, Mexico, and Central and South America.

Glenn Ohrlin (ca. 1965). *Courtesy of the Southern Folklife Collection, University of North Carolina.*

"The Cowboy's Dance Song"

Well you can't expect a cowboy to agitate his
  shanks
In the etiquettish fashion in aristocratic ranks,
He's always been accustomed to shake a heel and
  toe
In the rattlin' ranchers' dances where much
  etiquette don't go.

You can bet I set 'em laughin' in a stoney sort of way,
A givin' of their squinters an excited sort of play,
When I happened into Denver and was asked to
  take a prance
In the smooth and easy measures of a high-toned
  dance.

When I got amongst the ladies in their frocks of
  fleecy white,
And the dudes togged out in wrappings simply out
  of sight,
Tell you what, I was embarrassed and somehow I
  couldn't keep
From feeling like a burro in a flock of pretty sheep.

Every step I took was awkward and I blushed a
  flamin' red,
Like the principal decorations on a turkey gobbler's
  head.
The ladies said 'twas seldom that they ever got a
  chance
To see an old-time puncher at a high-toned dance.

I cut me out a heifer from that flock of pretty girls,
I yanked her to the center to dance in dreamy
  whirls.
She laid her head upon my bosom in a lovin' sort of
  way
We drifted into heaven as the band begin to play.

I could feel my neck a burnin' from her nose's
  breathin' heat
As she dosey-doed around me, half the time upon
  my feet.

And she gazed up in my blinkers with a soul-
  dissolvin' glance
Quite conducive to the pleasures of a high-toned
  dance.

Every nerve just got to tinglin' to that music of
  delight,
I hugged that little sage hen uncomfortably tight;
But she never made a beller, the glances of her eyes
Seemed to thank me for the pleasures of a genuine
  surprise.

She cuddled up against me in a lovin' sort of way,
I hugged her all the tighter for her trustifyin' play,
Tell you what, the joys of heaven ain't a cussed
  circumstance
To the huggamania pleasures of a high-toned
  dance.

When they struck that old cotillion on the music
  bill of fare,
Every bit of devil in me seemed to fetch out on a
  tear;
I let out a cowboy war whoop and I started in to rag
Till the rafters started shaking and the floor begin
  to sag.

Then my partner she got sea sick, and she staggered
  for a seat,
I balanced to the next one but she dodged me slick
  and neat.
Tell you what, I took the creases from their go-to-
  meeting pants
When I put the cowboy trimmings on that high-
  toned dance.*

*Sung by Glenn Ohrlin as "The High Toned Dance."
Recording: Rounder, 1166-11599-2, *The Art of Old-Time
Mountain Music*, 2002.

RECOMMENDED RECORDINGS

Back in the Saddle Again:…Cowboy Songs. New World, 80314-2, 2 CDs.
Carl T. Sprague. *Cowtrails, Longhorns, and Tight Saddles.* Bear Family, BCD 15979AH;
  reissue of 1925–1929 recordings.

Cattle Call—Early Cowboy Music and Its Roots. Rounder, CD 1101.

Classic Cowboy Songs. Bear Family, BCD 15456.

Cowboy Songs, Ballads, and Cattle Calls. Rounder, CD 1512; reissue of Library of Congress, LP AFS L 28.

Cowboy Songs on Folkways. Smithsonian Folkways, CD SF 40043.

Don't Fence Me In—Western Music's Early Golden Era. Rounder, CD 1102.

Glenn Ohrlin. *A Cowboy's Life.* Rounder, 0420.

The New Beehive Songster, Vol. 1. Okehdokee (University of Utah Press), LP OK 75003.

The New Beehive Songster, Vol. 2. Okehdokee, LP OK 76004.

Railroad Songs and Ballads. Rounder, CD 1508; reissue of Library of Congress, LP AFS L 61.

Songs of the Mormons & Songs of the West. Rounder, CD 1520; reissue of Library of Congress, LP AFS L 30.

Stanley G. Triggs. *Bunkhouse and Forecastle Songs of the Northwest.* Folkways, LP/Cass FG 3569.

Train 45: Railroad Songs of the Early 1900's. Rounder, CD 1143.

When I Was a Cowboy, Vols. 1/2. Yazoo, CDs 2022/23; reissues from the 1920s–1930s.

NOTES

1. For more details about the accident, the ballad's early history, and the litigation regarding its disputed authorship, see Norm Cohen, *Long Steel Rail: The Railroad in American Folksong,* 2nd ed. (Urbana: University of Illinois Press, 2000), pp. 197–226.

2. Fannie Hardy Eckstorm, in "Canaday-I-O," *Bull. Folk-Song Soc. Northeast* 6 (1933): 10–13, explores the relationships among these ballads.

3. Joseph F. Tuso, *Singing the Vietnam Blues: Songs of the Air Force in Southeast Asia* (College Station, TX: Texas A&M University Press, 1990), pp. 80–81. A spectre is a turboprop fighter plane; gomer means Viet Cong or North Vietnamese soldier; Delta One-One is a geographical chart position.

4. "On the Cattle Trail," Kansas City *Daily Journal of Commerce,* June 19, 1873, in Jim Bob Tinsley, *He Was Singin' This Song* (Orlando: University Presses of Florida, 1981), p. 17.

5. Ibid.

6. American Indian music will be treated more fully in another volume of this series.

7

Urban Centers and Folk Music

The study of American folk music would be greatly simplified if it were isolated from other kinds of music; however, since the first colonists arrived in the seventeenth century, this has not been the case. The European immigrants came from societies with vibrant musical traditions in the concert hall, on the stage, and in church. Even as the pioneers pushed westward, while the ties that bound them to the Old World were stretched thin, they never broke.

After the American Revolution as the new American nation gradually acquired a sense of its own cultural as well as political identity, various popular media arose, flourished, and faded, but each one facilitated a two-way interchange with the noncommercial folk traditions. Blackface minstrelsy, cheap print, ragtime, jazz, Tin Pan Alley, blues, hillbilly music—all of these were, in their day, important commercial entertainment media that either contributed to or borrowed from traditional folk music. This chapter deals with the commercial and noncommercial music associated with urban centers scattered around the country and the folk music that emanated from them.

FOLK-DERIVED COMMERCIAL MUSIC

A consistent pattern more or less repeats itself in the history of almost all folk-derived commercial music: hillbilly, blues, jazz, gospel, soul, rock and roll, salsa, rap, hip hop. Initially, a strong regional, traditional music style attracts the recording industry's attention, generally because of the success of recordings or performances of a few dynamic performers. The industry can see great commercial potential and tries to capitalize on what appears to be a new and exciting musical style but which may actually be quite old in a particular region. In the process of commercializing the music, control of its content slips away from the musicians themselves and into the hands of the producers, promoters, managers, engineers, and lawyers. As the genre gains national attention and recording sales and concert attendance grow, the music moves further away from its folk roots, until the connection is apparent only to those who have watched the steady transformation.

As this happens, the folk-derived genre becomes less "folk" and more "derived." Sometimes the transformation is so complete that little of the traditional components remains. Inevitably, some nonprofessional or semi-professional traditional musicians will find some interesting ideas in the commercial material and will incorporate it into their own music. Thus, the circle will be completed as it moves from folk to commercial back to folk music. The completed circle will not be broken into the traditional and the commercial parts; the transitions are often very smooth and gradual, and different observers will put the imaginary dividing line at different points along the arc.

Blackface Minstrelsy

Colonial Americans viewed African slaves with fear and fascination: they looked different, they spoke unintelligible languages, they moved differently. Were they a different species altogether? Many slave owners tried to foist that perception on an uncertain public so that they could justify subhuman treatment. Some slave holders acknowledged that their African property might be human but of such a primitive sort that they needed to be taken in hand like children and sanitized, civilized, and Christianized. As time passed, some slaves revealed tremendous musical abilities: they sang, danced, played their own instruments, and—if given a chance—played their masters' instruments. Some slavery apologists took these as demonstrations of the slaves' happiness: they wouldn't sing and dance if they didn't like their lot in life. It didn't cross their minds that music could be a substitute for happiness rather than a manifestation of it. By the 1820s and 1830s, astute musicians began to turn a scrutinizing eye to these exotic Africans, watching their dances, memorizing their tunes—in short, seeing commercial potential. In about 1828 in Cincinnati, actor Thomas D. "Daddy" Rice witnessed a crippled slave boy, who worked in the stables of a Mr. Crow, singing and dancing in a strange way that completely mesmerized him. The lad performed a little dance routine that he accompanied with lyrics that included a phrase something like, "every time you turn around you jump, Jim Crow." Watching carefully, Rice memorized the patter and later, outfitted in similarly shabby clothing and face blacked up with burnt cork, performed impersonations on stage. This tradition became so widespread that it lent its name to the punitive segregation measures, official and unofficial, that plagued the South long after emancipation. These statutes and customs of the South came to be known as Jim Crow laws.

In 1843 a quartet of young entertainers, mostly Northerners, applied the burnt cork and assembled a show in New York. They were Billy Whitlock, banjo; Dan Emmett, fiddle; Dick Pelham, tambourine; and Frank Brower, bones (a rhythm instrument, like castanets). Within a month, now calling themselves The Virginia Minstrels, they were performing regularly to enthusiastic audiences in Boston and elsewhere. Soon other quartets sprang into existence with similar shows: the African Melodists, the Congo Minstrels, the Christy Minstrels, Bryant's Minstrels, and others. Picking up on the names of many of the troupes, the new medium was called minstrelsy.

Minstrelsy's debt to African American music was enormous. It was through the minstrel stage that many Northern European–Americans first were exposed to the banjo and its music. In the South some whites learned directly from blacks rather than from traveling blackface troupes. The minstrels learned many songs and instrumental tunes from African Americans (slaves and free men) and incorporated them into their stage shows. Like the banjo itself, this music was then picked up by whites and soon became a part of their folk music. As a result, many banjo and fiddle tunes in the South and southern mountains ("Cindy," "Jimmy Crack Corn," and "Rock the Cradle Lucy," for example) have African American origins. Other songs written for the minstrel stage by white composers may also have had some African American influences:

- "Oh Susanna" (Stephen Foster)
- "Camptown Races" (Stephen Foster)
- "Jordan Is a Hard Road to Travel" (E. P. Christy)
- "Old Dan Tucker" (Daniel D. Emmett)
- "Jimmy Crack Corn," or "De Blue Tail Fly" (Daniel D. Emmett)
- "Jawbone" (Daniel D. Emmett)
- "Dixie" (possibly Daniel D. Emmett, but strongly contested)
- "Carve Dat Possum" (Sam DeVere)

Others of unknown authorship include:

- "Shortenin' Bread"
- "Hot Corn, Cold Corn"
- "It Ain't Gonna Rain No More"
- "Shinbone Alley"

A version of "Shinbone Alley" was published in 1833, though its origins may be still older.

Old Miss Tuck and my aunt Sallie
Both lived down in shinbone alley.

No sign on the gate, no number on the door;
Folks around here are gittin' mighty poor.[1]

In 1945, Bob Wills and his Texas Playboys recorded a version of this as "Stay a Little Longer." The appearance of these lyrics in a Texas western swing band in the 1940s is evidence that the song had been in oral tradition for over a century:

You ought to see my blue-eyed Sally
She lives way down on shinbone alley,
The number on the gate, the number on the door,
And the next house over is the grocery store.

Also of uncertain origin is one of minstrelsy's earliest and most popular pieces, "Old Zip Coon." (Coon was a slang term, often pejorative, for an African American.) The man described in the lyrics (and illustrated on the cover of the sheet music) was an urban dandy—fancy clothing, boastful, self-important—whose crude speech revealed his ignorance. Actor and singer George Washington Dixon popularized the song, but his source is not known. The tune of the song was later borrowed for "Turkey in the Straw," which remained current in Southern Anglo-American tradition through the twentieth century. The version of "Old Zip Coon" included here, collected around 1915, retains two stanzas of the earliest sheet music version of 1834.

As a social institution, blackface minstrelsy was complex. It is generally reviled as a deliberately degrading caricature of African Americans whom the Anglo-Americans could not accept as equals and had no interest in portraying accurately. It has also been argued, however, that the entertainers copied African Americans out of genuine admiration, using the medium to heap social

---

"Old Zip Coon"

I went down to Sandy Hook t'other afternoon
I went down to Sandy Hook t'other afternoon
I went down to Sandy Hook t'other afternoon
And the first man I met there was old Zip Coon

CHORUS:
Old Zip Coon is a very learned scholar
Old Zip Coon is a very learned scholar
Old Zip Coon is a very learned scholar
He plays upon de banjo "Cooney in de holler."
Old Sukey Blue-skin fell in love with me,
She 'vite me to her house to take a cup o' tea.
What do you think Old Suke had for supper:
Chicken foot, sparrow-grass, apple sass and butter.

Did you ever see the wild goose sail upon the ocean?
The wild goose motion is a very pretty motion.

And when the wild goose winks he beckons to de
    swallow;
Den de wild goose holler goggle, goggle, goller.

Oh, my old Mistis, she is mad with me
Because I wouldn't go with her and live in
    Tennessee.
Master built a barn there and put in all de fodder,
This thing and that thing and one thing another.*

*Sung by Amy Henderson of Burke County, North Carolina, ca. 1915. Published in Henry M. Belden and Arthur Palmer Hudson, eds., *The Frank C. Brown Collection of North Carolina Folklore*, Vol. 3: *Folk Songs* (Durham, NC: Duke University Press, 1952), p. 504.

A. W. AUNER, SONG PUBLISHER & PRINTER,
Tenth and Race Sts., Philadelphia, Pa.

OLD ZIP COON.

I went down to Sandy Hook, toder arternoon;
I went down to Sandy Hook, toder arternoon;
I went down to Sandy Hook, toder arternoon,
And de first man I met dere was old Zip Coon.

CHORUS.

Old Zip Coon is a very larned scholar,

Old Zip Coon is a very larned scholar,

Old Zip Coon is a very larned scholar,

He plays upon the banjo "Cooney in de Hollor."

Old Sukey Blueskin fell in lub wid me,
She vite me to her house to take a cup a tea:
What do you think old Suke had for de supper?
Chicken-foot, sparrow-grass and apple-sauce butter.
Old Zip Coon, &c.

Did you ever see de wild-goose sail upon de ocean?
O de wild-goose motion is a very pretty motion;
And when de wild-goose winks he beckons to the swallor,
And den de wild-goose hollor, goggle, goggle, gollor.
Old Zip Coon, &c.

O my old mistress is very mad wid me,
Because I wouldn't go wid her and live in Tennessee,
Massa build a barn dere an put in all de fodder,
Dere was dis ting and dat ting and one ting oder.
Old Zip Coon, &c.

"Old Zip Coon," a broadside from the 1850s (ID: CPM, 000491-Broad, Auner). *Courtesy of the Kenneth S. Goldstein Collection, Center for Popular Music, Middle Tennessee State University.*

criticism on white America from behind the safety of the mask of burnt cork, and that they supported abolition and racial equality. The dust has yet to settle on this disagreement, but if there were any benefits to come from minstrelsy, in either fame or fortune, African Americans received none of it. In any case, blackface minstrelsy was the first important commercial entertainment medium in the United States to have demonstrable influence on folk culture in both form and content, in areas musical and non-musical.

The minstrel show developed a three-part format, the influence of which lasted into the twentieth century. The first part featured the entire company seated in a semicircle. The Interlocutor (the straight man) was placed in the center; at the end were the two comics, Tambo and Bones. The routine included serious and comic songs, jokes, dances, and often a "stump speech": a mock-serious rambling performance that poked fun at current political or social topics or at particular types of public characters, deliberately misusing language in the manner of a self-important ignoramus (usually using an African American dialect). The second part was called the "olio" and included a variety of acts, music, juggling, dance, and comic speeches. The third part was a one-act play, usually a comedy.

In addition to these banjo songs and similar pieces, there was room in the format for serious sentimental numbers, such as the music of Stephen C. Foster. Sometimes the song lyrics were written in pseudo–African American dialect, but the melodies were virtually all European American. Many of these pieces, created for the minstrel stage, long outlived that form of presentation: Stephen Foster's "My Old Kentucky Home" (1853) and "Old Black Joe" (1860),

---

"Darling Nelly Gray"

There's a low green valley on the old Kentucky
  shore
Where I've whiled many happy hours away,
A-sitting and a-singing by the little cottage door,
Where once lived my darling Nelly Gray.

CHORUS:
Oh, my poor Nelly Gray, they have taken you
  away,
And I'll never see my darling any more;
I'm a-sitting by the river and I'm weeping all the
  day,
For you've gone from the old Kentucky shore.

When the moon had climbed the mountain, and
  the stars were shining, too,
Then I'd take my darling Nelly Gray,

And we'd float down the river in my little red canoe,
While my banjo so sweetly I would play.

My eyes are getting blinded, and I cannot see my
  way,
Hark! There's somebody knocking at the door,
Oh, I hear the angels calling, and I see my Nelly Gray,
Farewell to the old Kentucky shore.

Oh, my darling Nelly Gray, up in heaven there,
  they say,
That they'll never take you from me any more;
I'm a-coming—coming—coming, as the angels
  clear the way,
Farewell to the old Kentucky shore.*

*In Michael C. Dean, *The Flying Cloud* (1922; repr., Norwood, PA: Norwood Editions, 1973), p. 73.

B. R. Hanby's "Darling Nelly Gray" (1856), and others all entered oral tradition. Hanby's song is set in Kentucky, a slave state; the additional clue of the banjo reveals that the narrator and his Nelly are slaves and that she had been sold to another owner.

After the Civil War (and occasionally even before it) African American minstrelsy troupes began to compete with their European American counterparts for attention on the stage. Ironically, the practice of blacking one's face with burnt cork to emulate—if not caricature—the facial features of African American slaves, once a defining hallmark of the minstrel stage, was so well established that African American minstrel entertainers after Reconstruction were obliged to use burnt cork, also. The custom continued into the 1920s: for example, Al Jolson in the film *The Jazz Singer*. In more rural settings, blackface survived in traveling musical troupes such as tent shows and medicine shows that persisted in the South into the 1950s. During the Civil Rights era of the 1960s, heightened sensitivities to the insulting images of blackface comedy brought down the final curtain on the few surviving shows that featured burnt-cork routines.

Cheap Print of the Nineteenth Century

While well-heeled music patrons could always purchase expensively printed sheet music for popular and classical favorites, at the same time, cheaper media available to less prosperous individuals provided at least the words, if not the music, to popular and favorite songs of the day. The two principal types of cheap print in America from the late eighteenth century into the early twentieth were broadsides and songsters, both of which rarely included the music.

An enormous number of traditional songs were distributed on broadsides in nineteenth-century America. Some songs were already traditional at the time they were printed; others entered oral tradition as a result of their increased availability. Through the nineteenth century most of the songsters were printed in New York, Philadelphia, Boston, or Baltimore. Two very important Boston publishers in the first half of the nineteenth century were Nathaniel Coverly and Leonard Deming, both of whom issued hundreds of ballad and song texts whose relation to oral tradition needs to be further explored. Either they were the sources for traditional texts, or they were taken from tradition sources (or possibly both).

Until the 1830s or so, most American songsters consisted of popular songs (many from Britain) and poems. The style of popular song, by today's standards, was excessively flowery and ornate. Hardly any songs from this period—except perhaps a few by Thomas Moore and Robert Burns—are still remembered. In the 1830s and 1840s, some songsters' repertoires were broadened to include older traditional ballads and songs. Two important examples were *The Forget-Me-Not Songster: Containing a Choice Collection of Old Ballad Songs, as Sung by Our Grandmothers* and *The American Songster, a Collection of Songs, as Sung in*

The frontispiece and title page of *The Forget-Me-Not Songster* (1850s). *Author's collection.*

the Iron Days of '76. Both were 256 pages, covered in simulated leather, about 2½ by 4 inches, and cost twenty-five cents (about $3.00 today). In this period the songsters were distributed primarily in New England and the Northeast, and their contents reflected Northern rather than Southern folk song repertoires. *The Forget-Me-Not* sold well in excess of 150,000 copies—an impressive figure considering that the national population was less than 20 million. The widespread popularity of the ballad "Barbara Allen" was largely due to its distribution on broadsides and in songsters. A version printed in *The Forget-Me-Not Songster* contains a stanza (the fourth in the text reprinted here) not found in earlier sources; therefore, versions collected from American traditional singers containing that stanza were almost certainly learned from the songster.

Once the most popular of all the British ballads in America, "Barbara Allen" tells the quintessential unrequited love story in a few brief scenes: Sir James declares his love for Barbara Allen, but somehow slights her in the tavern. Other versions have a stanza (after the thirteenth) that may explain his behavior:

"Oh, yes, I remember in yonder town,
In yonder town a-drinking,
I gave a health to the ladies all 'round
But my heart to Barbara Allen."[2]

"Barbara Allen"

In fell about the Martinmas day,
When the green leaves were falling,
Sir James the Graham in the west country
Fell in love with Barbara Allen.

She was a fair and comely maid,
And a maid nigh to his dwelling,
Which made him to admire the more,
The beauty of Barbara Allen.

"O what's thy name my bonny maid.
Or where has thou thy dwelling?"
She answer'd him most modestly,
"My name is Barbara Allen."

"O see you not yon seven ships,
So bonny as they are sailing,
I'll make you mistress of them all
My bonny Barbara Allen."

But it fell out upon a day,
At the wine as they were drinking,
They toasted their glasses around about
And slighted Barbara Allen.

O she has taken't to ill out
That she'd no more look on him,
And for all the letters he could send,
Still swore she'd never have him.

"O if I had a man, a man,
A man within my dwelling,
That will write a letter with my blood
And carry't to Barbara Allen.

Desire her to come here with speed,
For I am at the dying!
And speak one word to her true love,
For I'll die for Barbara Allen."

His man is off with all his speed,
To the place where she is dwelling.
"Here's a letter from my master dear,
Gin ye be Barbara Allen."

O when she looked the letter upon,
With a loud laughter gi'd she,
But e'er she read the letter through
The tear blinded her eye.

O hooly, hooly, rose she up,
And slowly gaed she to him,
And slightly drew the curtains by,
"Young man, I think you'er dying."

"O I am sick, and very sick,
And my heart is at the breaking,
One kiss or two of thy sweet mouth
Would keep me from the dying."

"O mind you not, young man," said she,
"When you sat in the tavern,
Then you made the health go round,
And slighted Barbara Allen."

And slowly, slowly, rose she up,
And slowly, slowly left him,
And sighing said she could not stay,
Since death of life had reft him.

She had not gone a mile from the town,
Till she heard the dead bell knelling,
And every knell that dead bell gave,
Was woe to Barbara Allen.

Now when the virgin heard the same,
Sure she was greatly troubled.
When in the coffin his corpse she view'd
Her sorrows all were doubled.

"What! hast thou died for me," she cried,
"Let all true lovers shun me,
Too late I may this sadly say,
That death has quite undone me.

O mother, mother make my bed,
O make it soft and narrow,
Since my love died for me to-day,
I'll die for him, to-morrow."*

*(Child, 84). From *The Forget-Me-Not Songster* (New York: Nafis & Cornish, n.d. [ca. 1848]), pp. 142–144. Quotation marks have been added, and typographic errors, corrected. Hooly, hooly means cautiously, gently; gaed ("go'ed") means went.

The offended Barbara refuses to answer his letter. Dejected James falls fatally ill and begs Barbara to come. Her treatment of him is unrelentingly cold, until she spies his coffin and realizes he actually did die for her and must therefore truly have loved her. She quickly takes sick herself and dies. While such behavior may seem extreme today, it might help to remember that the heroes and heroines of the old ballads were probably fifteen or sixteen years old (like Romeo and Juliet in Shakespeare's play), governed by the impetuous passions of adolescence. Scottish dialect indicates where the British source of this text came from, but it has never been found there.

After the Civil War, the common songsters were larger in size (4 by 6 inches) but with fewer pages (thirty-two to sixty-four), using cheap newsprint paper and with flimsy paper covers, so they fell apart quickly. They carried mostly new songs of the day rather than older favorites. In this era, they became a source for traditional songs, as many singers learned texts from them and kept them in oral tradition. "The Poor Tramp Has to Live" is an example of a song whose only known source is some songsters and broadsides from the 1880s. It entered oral tradition and was frequently recorded or collected in the early 1900s.

The song is long on sympathy and short on explanation. Somehow the man was betrayed by his wife, but the circumstances are not revealed. Did she

---

"The Tramp"

How many men there are who ride in fortune's car
And who bar and bolt their door against the poor
Just because they've lots of gold their hearts are
   turned icy cold,
They ought to be condemned for that I'm sure.
In regard to that poor race who tramp from place to
   place,
There are many who are men from top to toe;
Altho' they're forced to beg, they're not all a
   dreadful plague,
If you study it I'm sure you'll find it so.

CHORUS:
So if you meet a tramp who bears misfortune's
   stamp,
God forbid a kick or frown that you might give;
Render him a welcome grip, wish him luck upon his
   trip,
Remember that the poor tramp has to live.

Once I knew a tramp who misfortune called a scamp,
They let loose their dog for fear that he might steal;
And as he turned away, I saw him kneel down and
   pray,

I'm sure that God above heard his appeal.
How little do we know as he tramps through rain
   and snow,
But once he was as happy as a king;
Until misfortune's cruel dart came and pierced his
   noble heart,
And robbed him of his name and everything.

Once I heard a tramp related, a sad story of his fate,
And why he was an outcast, shunned by all;
Once he led a happy life, he loved him home and
   wife,
But alas! like Eve that woman had to fall.
When she grew weak and pale, I've no need to tell
   the tale,
It turned his manly brow to sad distress;
He left his home and child, and never since has
   smiled,
Sadly now he tramps from place to place.*

*As printed in Edward J. Abraham, *When the Moonbeams Gently Fall Songster* (New York, n.d. [ca. 1882]), p. 54. Typographic errors have been corrected.

commit adultery, or did drugs render her weak and pale? In any case, the song's moral is outspoken: the shameful status of society's lowliest may be due to circumstances beyond their control, for which they should not be blamed.

Tin Pan Alley and Vaudeville

In the late 1880s the sheet music publishing business became centralized on New York's 28th Street, near Union Square. Because of the constant din from song pluggers demonstrating their wares to publishers on poorly tuned pianos, the neighborhood was dubbed "Tin Pan Alley." Out of this cluster of publishers came most of America's popular music for over four decades. Since a major product of this activity during the 1880s and 1890s was the sentimental ballad, it has been customary to use the terms "Tin Pan Alley music" and "sentimental songs" interchangeably, although the overlap is not complete.

In the same period the nature of blackface minstrelsy began to change under the competitive pressure of African American minstrel performers. White performers gradually eliminated the raucous and offensive elements, striving for a wholesome presentation acceptable to the whole family. In this manner Variety emerged. As its name suggests, it was a form of stage entertainment featuring a continuous succession of various stage acts. It was renamed in 1871 with the French term "Vaudeville," which refers to a region famous for satirical songs. In England, the equivalent medium was called "music hall."

Some producers acquired chains of theaters in different cities, and performers would make the circuit from one theater to another. After the introduction of film, these theaters offered a combination of live entertainment interspersed with film showings. In the 1920s Vaudeville shows in larger Southern cities occasionally included hillbilly acts on the bill, thus increasing the opportunity for popular and folk repertoires to borrow from one another.

Among the sentimental songs and ballads published in sheet music between the end of the Civil War and the 1890s are many that entered oral tradition and found their way into folk song collections in the 1920s and later. Among the most frequently encountered by folk song collectors were as follows:

- "When You and I Were Young, Maggie" (written by Johnson and Butterfield, 1866)
- "Little Rosewood Casket" (Goullaud and White, 1870)
- "Little Old Log Cabin in the Lane" (Hays, 1871)
- "Silver Threads among the Gold" (Rexford and Danks, 1873)
- "In the Baggage Coach Ahead" (Davis, 1896)
- "The Letter Edged in Black" (Nevada, 1897)
- "Lightning Express" (Helf and Moran, 1898)
- "Down by the Old Mill Stream" (Taylor, 1910)

Many of these actually predate "Tin Pan Alley," but they came from the same urbane professional songwriting tradition.

"When You and I Were Young, Maggie"

I wandered today to the hill, Maggie,
To watch the scene below,
The creek and the old rusty mill, Maggie,
Where we sat in the long, long ago.
The green grass is gone from the hill, Maggie,
Where first the daisies sprung;
The old rusty mill is still, Maggie,
Since you and I were young.

CHORUS:
And now we are aged and gray, Maggie,
The trials of life nearly done,
Let us sing of the days gone away, Maggie,
When you and I were young.

They say I am feeble with age, Maggie;
My steps are less sprightly than then.
My face is a well-written page, Maggie,
But time alone was the pen.
They say we are aged and gray, Maggie,
As spray by the white breakers flung,
But to me you're as fair as you were, Maggie,
When you and I were young.*

*As sung by Grandad Abernethy. Published in
Francis Edward Abernethy, *Singin' Texas* (Dallas,
TX: E-Heart Press, 1983), pp. 133–134.

The words to "When You and I Were Young, Maggie" were written by a Canadian schoolmaster, George W. Johnson. Maggie was his sweetheart, and they used to meet at a mill on the creek. In 1865 they married, but Maggie died soon after. The touching sentiments and the beautifully crafted lines, supported by a simple, singable melody, kept this antique a favorite for well over a century.

Also important in this period were novelty songs, in particular the "coon songs," which were compositions in pseudo-African American dialect. Most of these portrayed the African American in a deprecatory light, though a few (for example, "Golden Slippers," written by African American James Bland in 1879 and almost gospel-like) were fairly neutral. The following fragment was collected from African Americans in Alabama in 1915 or 1916:

Oh, dem golden slippers
Oh, dem golden slippers
Dem's de slippers I'se a-gwine to wear,
Because dey looks so neat.
Oh, dem golden slippers
Oh, dem golden slippers
Dem's de slippers I'se a-gwine to wear,
When I walk on the golden street.[3]

Blues

The early history of blues recordings roughly parallels that of hillbilly music. The earlier traditional repertoire of spirituals and secular folk songs more quickly gave way, however, to blues and gospel, which tended to be original compositions by the artists performing them but still relied heavily on older songs, tunes, and language. Three fairly distinct blues styles were being recorded by 1924. City blues, also called "Harlem blues" or "classic (12-bar) blues," was mostly sung by women with small jazz band or piano accompaniment. Much more individualized were the country blues, sung mostly by male singers accompanying themselves on guitar or piano. Although they first appeared on record a few years earlier, the city blues represented a much more commercial, smoothed-out sound than the rougher country blues. The country blues singers generally wrote their own material, borrowing heavily from the traditional language of blues music; the city blues were often written by professional African American songwriters who were not necessarily performers themselves. Slightly earlier than both were the orchestral recordings of the pop blues by such writers as W. C. Handy, who created a formal style of blues out of a folk tradition, much as Scott Joplin did with ragtime.

Big sellers by major country blues artists such as Papa Charlie Jackson, Blind Lemon Jefferson, Blind Blake, Charley Patton, and others were learned by the next generations of African American blues musicians. It seems logical to expect that, because a new artist could keep referring to the recordings, successive interpreters would not stray far from the original, but the tradition doesn't work that way. Musicians may take inspiration from an earlier recording, but they soon develop their own particular interpretations so that there is almost as much variation as one would find in the absence of a "permanent" record.

Abundant evidence shows that in the 1920s, in spite of the record companies' marketing strategies that aimed at placing each kind of music within its own community, Southern whites still found and listened to the records of black musicians such as Blind Lemon Jefferson ("Match Box Blues"), the Mississippi Sheiks ("Corrine Corrina" and "Sitting on Top of the World"), Leroy Carr ("How Long Blues"), and others, and learned from them. The best evidence for that process is in the hillbilly recordings (called "white blues") reinterpreting African American blues recordings. While white blues is based on black tradition, in general the interpretations seem to be more smoothed out, less ragged, and generally less exciting than the originals. In this way, commercial blues records served as a medium by which traditional African American music entered Anglo-American Southeastern oral tradition.

Several of W. C. Handy's compositions also became hillbilly and/or early western swing standards, which means they were becoming part of the repertoires of traditional string bands as well. These include "The Hesitating Blues," "Beale Street Blues," "St. Louis Blues," and "Basin Street Blues."

URBAN FOLK MUSIC

While the most productive song collecting has been done in rural areas or remote villages, large cities are not devoid of folk songs. Migration from farm to city is responsible for some folk songs becoming established in urban surroundings. The differences in social life, in the way urban dwellers entertain themselves, and in common day-to-day concerns, however, often serve to weaken, or at least modify, tradition's hold on oral culture in the cities.

Labor Songs

One type of folk song often associated with city life is labor union and protest songs. Some examples have already been given in previous chapters. Woody Guthrie wrote and performed a number of union songs in the 1940s; his "Union Maid," written in Oklahoma City in 1940 to the tune of the very popular song "Redwing," became an instant favorite among workers all over the country. Shortly before Guthrie was born, an immigrant balladeer wrote a parody of another American pop song, "Casey Jones."

The union song was written by Joe Hill (or Joe Hillstrom), supposedly for a 1910 or 1911 Southern Pacific Railroad strike; the details have not been verified. That would put it a year or two after the Vaudeville song "Casey Jones" was published, at the peak of its popularity. Hill, a Swedish-born migratory

---

"Casey Jones, the Union Scab"

The workers on the S.P. line to strike sent out a call,
But Casey Jones, the engineer, he wouldn't strike at all;
His boiler it was leaking, and its drivers on the bum,
And his engine and its bearings, they were all out of plumb.

CHORUS:
Casey Jones, kept his junk pile running,
Casey Jones, was working double time;
Casey Jones, got a wooden medal,
For being good and faithful on the S.P. line.
The workers said to Casey, "Won't you help us win this strike?"
But Casey, said, "Let me alone, you'd better take a hike."
Then Casey's wheezy engine ran right off the worn-out track,
And Casey hit the river with an awful crack.

Casey Jones, hit the river bottom;
Casey Jones, broke his bloomin' spine;
Casey Jones, was an angelino,
He took a trip to heaven on the S.P. line.

When Casey got up to heaven to the Pearly Gate,
He said, "I'm Casey Jones, the guy that pulled the S.P. freight."
"You're just the man," said Peter, "Our musicians went on strike,
You can get a job a-scabbing any time you like."

Casey Jones, got a job in heaven,
Casey Jones, was doing might fine;
Casey Jones, went scabbing on the angels,
Just like he did to workers on the S.P. line.

The angels got together, and they said it wasn't fair,
For Casey Jones to go around a-scabbing everywhere;
The Angels' Union Number 23, they sure was there,
And they promptly fired Casey down the golden stair.

Casey Jones, went to hell a-flying,
"Casey Jones," the Devil, said, "Oh fine!
Casey Jones, get busy shoveling sulfur—
That's what you get for scabbing on the S. P. line."*

*In John Greenway, *American Folksongs of Protest* (New York: Perpetua Books, 1960), p. 186.

worker and labor organizer, composed a number of long-remembered union songs. He was executed in Salt Lake City in 1919 for a robbery murder on evidence that was circumstantial at best.

Children's Songs

Union and labor songs are written for specific political purposes and to forge bonds of worker solidarity. The songs that children sing and make up have no political agendas, but they do help forge bonds of friendship.

American children's songs used to be passed from generation to generation on neighborhood streets, in schoolyards, and at summer camps. Nowadays it is more likely children will learn these songs from television programs or organized song sessions in elementary school classrooms. A sheet music version of "Bill Grogan's Goat" was published in 1904 under the title of "The Tale of a Shirt," but some form of the song probably was in circulation as early as the mid-1800s.

Many young children's games involve playing at being adults. Today this happens with the aid of elaborate toys, such as miniature stoves and refrigerators, supermarkets and airports, fire stations and police stations. A century ago children made do with crude substitute objects fashioned from sticks and wire, or, more likely, with imaginary objects. "Mulberry Bush" and its many variants can be traced back to an English ring dance, with appropriate acting out motions, at least as old as the 1840s. The first line of each stanza forms the theme for each, as seen in the first two stanzas reprinted here.

> **"Bill Grogan's Goat"**
>
> Bill Grogan's goat was feeling fine,
> Ate three red shirts right off the line.
> His master came and beat his back,
> And tied him to a railroad track.
>
> The whistle blew, the train drew nigh,
> Bill Grogan's goat knew he must die.
> He gave three bleats of mortal pain,
> Coughed up the shirts and flagged the train.
>
> The engineer looked out to see,
> What in the world this thing could be.
> And when he saw 'twas but a goat,
> He drew his knife and slit its throat.
>
> When Billy got to heaven, Saint Peter said,
> "My darling Bill, where is your head?"
> "I do not know and cannot tell,
> For all I know, it may be in...
> Way down yonder in the cornfield!"*
>
> *In Norm Cohen, *Long Steel Rail*, 2nd ed. (Urbana, IL: University of Illinois Press, 2001), p. 291.

The same simple melody is used for another children's game/song:

Here we go gathering nuts in May, nuts in May, nuts in May;
Here we go gathering nuts in May, on a cold and frosty morning.

"The Green Grass Grew All Around" is a familiar example of a cumulative song: each verse repeats the preceding one but adds a line or phrase, a process that can be continued not quite indefinitely but long enough for most young singers. Parallel versions are also sung in French, Flemish, and German.

"Here We Go Round the Mulberry Bush"

Here we go round the mulberry bush,
The mulberry bush, the mulberry bush.
Here we go round the mulberry bush,
So early in the morning.

This is the way we wash our clothes,
Wash our clothes, wash our clothes.
This is the way we wash our clothes,
All of a Monday morning.

This is the way we iron our clothes,
. . . .
All of a Tuesday morning

This is the way we scrub our clothes
. . . .
All of a Wednesday morning.

This is the way we mend our clothes,
. . . .
All of a Thursday morning.

This is the way we sweep the house,
. . . .
All of a Friday morning.

This is the way we bake our bread,
. . . .
All of a Saturday morning.

This is the way we go to church,
. . . .
All of a Sunday morning.*

*Slightly modified from text in William Wells Newell, *Games and Songs of American Children*, 2nd ed. (New York/London: Harper & Brothers, 1903), p. 86.

"The Green Grass Grew All Around"

There was a tree stood in the ground,
The prettiest tree you ever did see;
The tree in the wood, and the wood in the ground,
And the green grass growing all round, round,
    round,
And the green grass growing all round.

And on this tree there was a limb,
The prettiest limb you ever did see;
The limb on the tree, and the tree in the wood,
The tree in the wood, and the wood in the ground
And the green grass growing all round, round,
    round,
And the green grass growing all round.

And on this limb there was a bough,
The prettiest bough you ever did see;

The bough on the limb, and the limb on the tree,
. . . .
And on this bough there was a twig,
The prettiest twig you ever did see;
The twig on the bough, and the bough on the limb,
. . . .
Down on the feather, feather on the wing,
Wing on the bird, bird in the eggs
Eggs in the nest, nest on the twig,
Twig on the bough, bough on the limb
. . . .*

*In William Wells Newell, *Games and Songs of American Children*, 2nd ed. (New York/London: Harper & Brothers, 1903), pp. 111–112.

Songs of Military Servicemen

History books recount the major features of a war: the causes, the big battles, the political decisions, and the social consequences. In the world of folk song, history is probed at a different level. Folk songs preserve those events that are of more immediate interest in a community; ones in which "favorite sons" are involved, regardless of the larger consequences. Even if the event is a major

---

"The Faded Coat of Blue"

My brave lad sleeps in his faded coat of blue,
In a lone and silent grave lies a heart that beat so
   true;
He fell faint and hungry among the Spaniards
   brave,
And they laid him sad and lonely within his
   nameless grave.

He cried, "Give me water, and just one little crumb,
And my mother, she will bless you in the many
   years that come;
Go and tell my dear sister, so gentle and so true,
That I'll meet her up in heaven in my faded coat of
   blue."

CHORUS:
No more the bugle calls a weary one,
Rest, lonely spirit, in thy grave unknown,

I'll know you and find you among the good and
   true,
When the robe of white is given for the faded coat
   of blue.

Long, long years have vanished and though he
   comes no more,
Yet my anxious heart will start with each footfall at
   my door;
I gaze at the hilltop where he waved a last adieu,
But no gallant lad I see in his faded coat of blue.*

*As sung by David Miller in 1929. Recording: Paramount
Records, 3159.

---

one, folk songs focus on details of local interest that may not be significant in the history book sense. Some other folk songs describe, in general terms, army life. Some are not even specific to a particular conflict.

"The Faded Coat of Blue" was originally a popular song written by a professional songwriter and published in sheet music in 1865. In the mid-nineteenth century, popular songs (for example, those of Stephen C. Foster) tended to sound much more like art songs than they do now.

"The Faded Coat of Blue" was written by J. H. McNaughton and originally subtitled "The Nameless Grave." The color of the faded coat identifies it as a Northern rather than Confederate song, though the lyrics don't dwell on partisan politics. Like many Civil War songs, it was dusted off and rehabilitated for the brief Spanish-American War in 1898, which explains the third line, ". . . among the Spaniards brave" in this rendition, but originally read ". . . among the famished brave." The reference to "nameless grave" evokes the theme of the tomb of the unknown soldier and suggests that the fear of anonymity, or loss of identity, was almost as strong as the fear of loss of life.

Major wars devastate civilization and nature alike, not to mention the toll on the emotional stability of the participants. Even at the front, soldiers seek relief from the stress and fear with moments of levity, so every war has produced its share of jocular songs. "Goober Peas" was such a contribution from the Civil War. "Goober" is a Southern term, derived from an African word for peanut. As the war wore on and Southern troops were reduced to increasingly meager rations, many a weary Confederate had to make do with meals consisting of little more than a handful of moldy peanuts. When it

[72]

THE FADED COAT OF BLUE.

My brave lad, he sleeps in his faded coat of blue :
In his lonely grave, unknown, lies the heart that beat so true ;
He sank, faint and hungry, among the famished brave,
And they laid him, sad and lonely, within his nameless grave.

CHORUS.

No more the bugle calls the weary one :
Rest, noble spirit, in thy grave unknown ,
I shall find you and know you among the good and true,
Where a robe of white is given for the faded coat of blue.

He cried : "Give me water and just one little crumb,
And my mother, she will bless you through all the years to come;
Oh ! tell my sweet sister, so gentle, good and true,
That I'll meet her up in Heaven in my faded coat of blue ! "

No more the bugle calls, &c.

"Oh ! he said, my dear comrades, you cannot take me home,
But you'll mark my grave for mother; she will find it if she comes,
I fear she will not know me among the good and true,
When a robe of white is given for the faded coat of blue."

No more the bugle calls, &c.

No dear one was by him to close his sweet blue eyes,
And no gentle one was nigh him to give him sweet replies.
No stone marks the sod o'er my lad so brave and true,
In his lonely grave he sleeps, in his faded coat of blue.

No more the bugle calls, &c.

Henry J. Wehman, Song Publisher, 50 Chatham St. (Up-Stairs), New York.

A broadside for "The Faded Coat of Blue" (1860s) (ID: CPM, 001776-Broad). *Courtesy of the Kenneth S. Goldstein Collection, Center for Popular Music, Middle Tennessee State University.*

"Goober Peas"

Sitting by the roadside on a summer day,
Chatting with my mess mates, passin' time away,
Laying in the shadow underneath the trees,
Goodness, how delicious, eatin' goober peas!

CHORUS:
Peas, peas, peas, peas,
Eating goober peas,
Goodness how delicious,
Eating goober peas.

Just before the battle the General hears a row,
He says, "The Yanks are coming, hear their rifles now."
He turns around in wonder, and what do you think he sees?
The Tennessee Militia—eatin' goober peas!*

*As sung by the Wear Family on Rural Rhythm 123, *Country and Blue Grass with the Great Wear Family*, 1960s.

---

was published in 1866, the sheet music was credited pseudonymously to "A. Pindar" and "P. Nutt." "Pindar" (or pinder) derives from a Congolese word for peanut. The irony of borrowing from the language of the African American while fighting to keep him in chains probably escaped Johnny Reb.

World War I and World War II provided material for a great number of patriotic songs by professional songwriters. The creative efforts of lesser-known talents were also used, usually written to the melodies of current popular standards or old favorites, or sometimes recycling earlier folk songs. "I Don't Want No More Army (Life)" consists of unrelated couplets that can be extended indefinitely, allowing for everyone in the company to contribute at least one stanza.

"I Don't Want No More Army"

The officers live on top of the hill
We live down in the slop and swill—*cho*

CHORUS:
I don't want no more army,
Lordy, how I want to go home!

They showed me the mule that I could ride;
They didn't show the shovel on the other side—*cho*

We've got a kitchen on four wheels,
Just a-warming beans for our meals—*cho*

I've learned a little, more or less;
Now I know why they call it mess—*cho*

The meat was rotten, and the spuds were bum;
They mixed it all together and they called it slum—*cho*

We had a major and his name was Tack;
He rode a horse and we carried a pack—*cho*

The lieutenants, they all work and sweat;
The captain sits around like a vi-o-let—*cho*

We loaded up the wagon and then,
We had to take it all off again—*cho*

The officers, they don't work a bit;
I don't see how they get away with it—*cho*

We do work for the lieutenant, and then,
The captain makes us do it all over again—*cho**

*Contributed by Lieutenant William W. Webster, who learned it in the Army of Occupation in Germany in the 1980s. Published in Edward Arthur Dolph, *"Sound Off!": Soldier Song from Yankee Doodle to Parley Voo* (New York: Cosmopolitan Book Corp., 1929), pp. 10–11.

"Dashing through the Sky"

Dashing through the sky,
In a Foxtrot 105,
Through the flak we fly,
Trying to stay alive;
The SAMs destroy our calm,
The MiGs come up to play;
What fun it is to strafe and bomb
The D. R. V. today!

CHORUS:
CBUs, Mark 82s, 750s, too,
Daddy Vulcan strikes again,
Our Christmas gift to you!

Head up, Ho Chi Minh;
The Fives are on their way!

Your luck it has gave out,
There's gonna be hell to pay!
Today it is our turn
To make you gawk and stare;
What fun it is to watch things burn
And blow up everywhere!!!*

*In Joseph F. Tuso, *Singing the Vietnam Blues: Songs of the Air Force in Southeast Asia* (College Station, TX: Texas A&M University Press, 1990), pp. 71–72. A Foxtrot 105 is another name for the F-105 fighter plane; fives are also F-105s; SAM stands for surface-to-air missile; a MiG is a Soviet-built fighter plane; D.R.V. is the abbreviation for Democratic Republic of Vietnam; a CBU is a cluster bomb unit; a Mark 82 is 500-lbs. iron bomb; a 750 is a 750-lbs. iron bomb; and a Vulcan is a high-speed airborne cannon.

The songlore of the Korean War has not been well documented, but the Vietnam War has several collections of songs. Many of the young men in that war had grown up listening to music of the urban folk song revival; consequently, they used traditional songs as well as old standards when they penned their own compositions about wartime life. "Dashing through the Sky" uses the melody of "Jingle Bells."

Immigrant Groups

It is difficult to cover systematically the folk music of the many immigrant groups that have brought their own lore to the United States in their own languages. The music falls into several categories: folk songs from native lands and in native languages, popular songs from native lands and in native languages, and songs written in America about the expectations or experiences of moving to a new country. In the context of a book about American folk music, the latter category is the most relevant. By and large, the songs, regardless of the place of origin of the singers, repeatedly reflect similar themes: hardships of life in the old country, the hope of a better life in America, and finally, the realization that life in the New World is not necessarily better than the old for a multitude of reasons—persecution and prejudice, language, religion and culture barriers, and difficulties in finding employment.

A few texts are offered here to illustrate some of these issues. They come, respectively, from Finnish American, Norwegian American, Greek American, Jewish American, and Danish American traditions.

"Song of a Wanderer to America"

America is the place I'm bound,
And it's there the boys will roam.
We will be searching the open world,
Just looking for a new home.

When we left from the Finnish shores
There were drinks in every hand.
And we could hear all the loud hurrahs
From our dear fatherland.
. . . .
After the trip of ten long days,
Our sorrows turned to cheer
When that famous America
We realized was so near.

There you don't bow down to a master,
You are not bound to priests,
Instead, as among equal men,
You can do just as you please.*

"America Song"

Farewell, you mother Norway, I'm traveling far
    from you.
You did your best to bring me up, but it would
    never do.
I never had enough food, the times were always
    rough,
But educated people, they always had enough.

I travel 'cross the ocean unto an unknown land.
There life it will be better, as I do understand.
If we work hard once we get there, we're sure to
    earn our pay,
So thanks to you, Columbus, for showing us the
    way.
. . . .
If ever it should happen, when many years have
    passed,
That I could cross the ocean, and come back home
    at last,
I'd go back to the village, the place that gave me
    birth—
For I cannot forget my home on Norway's sacred
    earth.**

*Words copyrighted by Jerry Silverman, published in *Mel Bay's Immigrant Songbook* (Pacific, MO: Mel Bay Publications, 1992), pp. 110–111. Selected stanzas only.
**Words copyrighted by Jerry Silverman, published in *Mel Bay's Immigrant Songbook* (Pacific, MO: Mel Bay Publications, 1992), pp. 252–253. Selected stanzas only.

"The Immigrant's Heartbreak"

I leave, sweet, I leave, sweet mother of mine,
Ah, I leave, sweet mother of mine, don't sigh
    painfully;
And poor, and poor heart of mine,
Ah, poor heart of mine, don't break.

I will go, I will go to America,
Ah, I will go to America soon to get rich;
Those tears of yours, those tears of yours, mother of
    mine,

Ah, those tears of yours, mother of mine, wipe
    them away.

Of what benefit, of what benefit is America,
Ah, of what benefit is America and all her wealth;
After I have withered, after I have withered,
Ah, after I have withered the leaves of my mother's
    heart?*

*As sung by Menas Vardoulis, a Greek American worker in Pittsburgh's steel mills, in 1920. Published in Theodore C. Grame, *America's Ethnic Music* (Tarpon Springs, PA: Cultural Maintenance Associates, 1976), pp. 57–58.

"A Mother's Letter"

My child, my comfort, you are riding away;
Be a good son.
I am asking with tears and with fear,
Your faithful, loving mother.

You are going, my child, my only child,
Over far oceans;
Come there fresh and healthy,
And don't forget your mother.
Yes, go in good health and arrive there with
  happiness.
And every week, send a letter,
To refresh your mother's heart.

A letter to mother, don't delay this;
Write soon, beloved child, give her consolation.
Your mother will read your letter and she will be
  comforted.
Ease her pain, her bitter heart; renew her spirit.*

"We Will Love the Soil"

We will love the soil where we build and swell,
Hold in esteem the common tongue,
One day we will fight under the starry flag,
But Danes we'll remain and live as a people.

If in chorus fools cry on America's soil
That we may not remain what at birth we became,
Let them cry! Surely we know better than they,
Almighty God in hearts this inscribed.

While our voices still ring in speech and in song,
We'll preserve our language as the dearest treasure,
It shall fill our homes, it shall carry us forth,
In our churches and schools where our goals
  are set.

Hear us, Danes, who dwell on America's soil:
Don't give up your true selves! Our strength may
  be small,
But we have enough might amid other peoples;
If only our hearts beat together in love.**

*Written in 1907 by Solomon Shmulowitz and widely popular in the Yiddish American communities in the following decades.
**By F. N. Grundtvig and published in *Sangbog for det danske Folk i America*, 2nd ed. (Cedar Falls, IA, 1891). Reprinted and translated in Rochell Wright and Robert L. Wright, *Danish Emigrant Ballads and Songs* (Carbondale and Edwardsville, IL: Southern Illinois University Press, 1983), pp. 237–238.

THE FOLK REVIVAL

In the middle of the twentieth century, sophisticated, culture-conscious, urban musicians "discovered" traditional American folk music and sought to present it, by means of concerts and recordings, to audiences of social backgrounds similar to their own. This presentation of traditional music taken from folk society and offered, sometimes modified, to and by individuals outside that society has been called the "urban folk music revival" or "folk song revival." Though it had roots much earlier, with stage presentations by Burl Ives, Richard Dyer-Bennet, Carl Sandburg, and others, it grew exponentially in the 1950s and 1960s with the enormous success of performers like the Weavers, Harry Belafonte, the Kingston Trio, Bob Dylan, Peter, Paul and Mary, Joan Baez, and a host of others. An important component of this revival was political—a continuation of efforts dating back to the 1930s to use folk songs and folk tunes for labor unionization and other liberal advocacy movements.

The Beginning of the Folk Revival

The beginning of the folk revival in America can probably be traced to the work of John A. Lomax. Born in Bosque County, Texas, in 1867, he became fascinated by cowboy songs early on and began writing them down when still a small boy. He carried a manuscript of texts with him to the University of Texas in 1895, whereupon showing it to his Shakespeare professor, he was embarrassed to hear it denounced as "tawdry, cheap, and unworthy." Feeling humiliated by that assessment, Lomax made a bonfire that night and burned up "every scrap of my cowboy songs." Lomax graduated and went on to Harvard, where in 1906, he took a course in American Literature from Barrett Wendell. Wendell warned his students that the same tired, old essays on Emerson, Hawthorne, and Poe bored him. "You fellows come from every section of the country. Tell us something interesting about your regional literary productions." When Lomax offered to write about the songs of the cowboy, telling Wendell that "the cowboys themselves had made up songs describing the life on the round-up and trail," the professor fairly leaped from his chair with enthusiasm.

Encouraged by Wendell and Professor George Lyman Kittredge, the leading authority on Anglo-American folk song at the time, Lomax resumed his collecting efforts, and the following year he wrote letters to the editors of 1,000 newspapers in the West, asking readers who knew of any old songs and ballads to please send texts to him. Responses poured in for years; even twenty years later, letters were still trickling in. Eventually this material, supplemented by what he gathered on three collecting trips in the Southwest, resulted in the 1910 publication of *Cowboy Songs and Other Frontier Ballads*. In the next two decades, Lomax sang and lectured at more than 200 colleges in forty-five states. A lecture hall favorite was "Buffalo Skinners," a cowboy ballad he first heard in Abilene, Texas. From twenty-one separate versions from all over the West, he collated a coherent text (see Chapter 6). Lomax was much more a popularizer than a scholar; his mission was to preserve the dying elements of American folk music and make them available to the people who had forgotten them. In this capacity, he played a key role in the beginnings of the folk song revival and defined one of its goals.

In the 1920s and 1930s, Lomax was joined by several other artists who sought to offer folk music on the concert stage. Their backgrounds and approaches were varied. Richard Dyer-Bennet (1913–1991) treated folk song like art song, singing ballads and songs to his own lute accompaniment, an instrument that certainly wasn't part of the American folk tradition. Burl Ives (1909–1995) learned folk songs in his youth. He had a simple, homey approach, accompanying his singing with his own guitar. Kentucky-born John Jacob Niles (1892–1980) and the great populist poet Carl Sandburg (1878–1967) both developed unusually idiosyncratic musical mannerisms that defied stylistic classification and certainly were not traditional. Niles, who had a rural background and may actually have done some song collecting in his youth, sang to the accompaniment of his own homemade—and very unusual—lute-like dulcimers. Sandburg used to perform folk song sets between readings of his own poetry on lecture tours.

Soon, two musicians with rural roots and much stronger backgrounds as traditional folksingers and composers (that is, they grew up steeped in a folk tradition and created new songs using the language, the images, and the musical vocabulary of that tradition) became involved in the folk song revival and helped broaden its aesthetic standards considerably. The first was Huddie Ledbetter, better known as "Leadbelly" (circa 1888–1949), an African American born in the Deep South near the Louisiana-Texas border. John Lomax and his son Alan had met Leadbelly in 1933 in a Louisiana prison on one of their song collecting trips through the South, shortly before his sentence was commuted by the governor. Leadbelly awed the Lomaxes with his extensive repertoire of African American folk songs, his powerful voice, and his driving twelve-string guitar playing. Once freed from the Angola State Penitentiary in August of 1934, he accompanied the Lomaxes on some of their trips as their chauffeur. Through the Lomaxes, Leadbelly met Pete Seeger, Burl Ives, and the rest of the small circle of singers who were presenting folk songs, often for liberal causes in the New York area.

The second was Woody Guthrie, another important "folk composer." Guthrie (1912–1967) was born in Oklahoma and at age fourteen, during the Dust Bowl, made his way to California. In 1941 Guthrie relocated to New York and became one of the central figures in the New York folk song revival, focusing his literary activities on liberal causes and gradually moving away from traditional songs of the Southwest that he had grown up with. By the 1960s, owing to a hereditary degenerative disease, his career was effectively terminated.

For a number of complex reasons, this flowering folk song revival became intertwined with a number of liberal social causes: support of labor unions—in particular unionization of the coal-mining industry—anti-fascism (first in Spain, then in Germany), and civil rights. This is not to suggest that all the folk song performers were social activists, but a significant number were. As a result, the folk song revival and its leaders became embroiled in headline-grabbing congressional investigations in the 1950s into the alleged infiltration of communist spies into American institutions, an episode that had a stultifying effect not only on folk music but also on many artistic media at the time. Nevertheless, although a few careers were damaged, the revival as a whole continued to grow.

Leadbelly and Woody Guthrie were the two most important influences on the musical development of another of the architects of the folk song revival: Pete Seeger. Seeger spent his early school years in New England boarding schools. Through his family and their friends, the Lomaxes, his exposure to folk music broadened. In 1936 Seeger and his father drove to Asheville, North Carolina, and attended the 9th Annual Mountain Song and Dance Festival. There, Seeger heard the five-string banjo and fell in love with it. In about 1938 Alan Lomax introduced him to Leadbelly.

In 1940 Seeger struck up a friendship with Lee Hays (1914–1981), formerly a song leader at a radical labor college in Commonwealth, Arkansas, and they performed together that December in a New York City restaurant. They were soon joined by Millard Lampell, Hays's roommate, and they began to fashion a career of sorts singing union and political songs. They called themselves The Almanac Singers, and soon more singers joined them, including Woody Guthrie, Bess Lomax Hawes (Alan Lomax's sister), and, occasionally, blues singer Josh White and others. Their aim was to write and perform topical songs for labor and political rallies. A successful concert in May 1941 in Madison Square Garden for the striking Transport Workers' Union paved the way for a national tour of CIO affiliates and a modicum of celebrity. They rented a loft in Greenwich Village that soon became known as Almanac House.

Influenced by the Paris writers' movement called "Anonymous," in which each writer's identity was known only to his publisher and cashier, the Almanacs wrote their songs jointly and credited themselves jointly. The Almanac Singers' collective career was short lived, terminated mainly by World War II for which Seeger, Guthrie, and others either volunteered or were drafted.

The Peak: The 1950s and 1960s

After the end of the war, Seeger and Hays, veterans of The Almanac Singers, and two younger artists, Ronnie Gilbert, a CBS secretary with a power-packed voice, and Fred Hellerman, Brooklyn College graduate, baritone, and guitar and banjo player, joined together to form a quartet called The Weavers. During Christmas week of 1949, they debuted at the Village Vanguard, a popular New York City nightclub. Response was lukewarm until Alan Lomax brought Carl Sandburg to hear them. Newspapers carried Sandburg's effusive praise, and soon crowds packed the club to hear the new singing sensation.

Their success at the Vanguard resulted in a contract with Decca Records, and in May 1950, they cut their first two recordings: a Hebrew version of "Tzena" and "Around the World." Three weeks later they recorded "Tzena" with English lyrics, backed with "Goodnight Irene," a song written by Leadbelly. The record, crediting Gordon Jenkins and Orchestra as primary artists with the Weavers as vocalists, skyrocketed to instant success, with sales rapidly passing the two million mark. Trade journals and disc jockeys had difficulty categorizing these novelty hits; they defied the standard classifications of pop, country and western, and rhythm and blues that had served the industry so faithfully since the Depression years.

In February of 1951, the Weavers, joined by singer Terry Gilkyson and supported by chorus and orchestra, recorded their second million seller, "On Top of Old Smokey," backed by "The Wide Missouri" (also sometimes called "Shenandoah," the text of which can be found in Chapter 3). Seventeen weeks on *Cashbox*'s bestseller list, the disc peaked at the number two position. In the next two years, the Weavers recorded twenty-eight more songs for the Decca label, the last of which was released in February 1953. In commercial terms, these recordings—especially the two million sellers, represented the peak of the Weavers' career. Compared to pop vocal styles of the day, they were lively and engaging. Although the Weavers were happy to sing for political causes, they kept their Decca material noncontroversial. The success of the Decca records led to cross-country tours, appearances at the flashiest nightclubs in Hollywood, Las Vegas, and New York, radio spots, and television appearances.

The reasons for this type of music suddenly attracting a much bigger audience in the 1950s than previously are not simple. A contributing factor may have been the state of mainstream popular music at the time. Never a genre for confronting important issues, it had become particularly bland musically and insipid lyrically. A generation of college-age youth, having experienced a decade of cold-war politics, may have been receptive to a musical genre that offered a repertoire of old songs and ballads that dealt with a wide range of social and personal issues in a very different manner, and certainly in a less superficial one, than pop songs did. Also significant was the presentation style of the new folk revival music. Based on easy-to-learn instruments like the guitar and banjo, it invited listeners to learn to play and sing the songs themselves. Pop music, on the other hand, had been designed around the format of a professional singer accompanied by a small combo or even full orchestra and did not lend itself to performance around the living room fireplace. Then, too, the sudden emergence of rock-and-roll music at about the same time, which so thoroughly captured the interest of the teenage group, may initially have dissatisfied college students. There were, of course, the positive aspects of the folk revival performers. Artists like the Weavers and Harry Belafonte were enormously dynamic and appealing: the former to those who liked their entertainment tinged with politics, and the latter to those who didn't.

Even at the peak of its success in the 1960s, the revival did not exclude genuinely traditional folk artists from performance events at college campuses and folk song festivals, and some traditional performers contributed significantly to it. Jean Ritchie and Buell Kazee were both born in traditional Kentucky communities and learned a wealth of songs as they grew up. Both received college educations and were able to see their music from the perspective of outsiders as well as from the inside. Merle Travis, another traditional Kentucky musician, went to Hollywood and became a successful country western songwriter and was also able to look at folk music from both sides. In fact, he composed two coalmining songs ("Sixteen Tons" and "Dark as a Dungeon") that are sometimes assumed to be traditional folk songs. Nevertheless, when the broad spectrum of the revival is examined, from the festival stage to the top forty charts, the dominant contributions were from the urban singers of folk song, not the traditional folksingers themselves.

The artists gathering attention in the late 1950s and early 1960s initially took their material from the few recordings of the earlier generation of artists that were available, but soon broadened their repertoires by looking to published collections of folk songs and the small number of published field recordings available from the Library of Congress Archive of Folk Song and elsewhere. Although written transcriptions of recordings, even if accurate, give a good account of words and music, they don't give a satisfactory idea of what the music was supposed to sound like. On the other hand, if performers had tried to sound like the traditional musicians of field recordings, most novice audiences would have been completely put off by the unfamiliar singing styles and the difficult-to-understand dialects. As a result the city artists of the revival modified traditional material to suit their own (and their audiences') aesthetic standards. While this left listeners with an inaccurate impression of what traditional music sounded like, it had the positive result of opening the door to a much wider audience than would otherwise have been drawn in.

Other musicians, notably a trio of young men—Mike Seeger, John Cohen, and Tom Paley—from the East Coast, who called themselves the New Lost City Ramblers (NLCR), provided an alternative aesthetic by having presentation styles scrupulously close to those of the traditional artists from whom they learned. The styles they initially chose to copy were those of early commercial hillbilly artists, which were indeed traditional but consisted primarily of lively instrumentals or vocals with instrumental accompaniment; they mostly avoided the drier sounds of the unaccompanied traditional singers of Library of Congress field recordings. Even so, the NLCR implicitly introduced the notion that folk music consisted not only of text and tune but also of style.

Folk Song Hits

Gradually, the appreciation for traditional performances grew to the point where there were two audiences for the folk revival: those who preferred the smoother, more polished presentations of the urban revivalists, and those who insisted on their music unadulterated. The wide appeal of the smoother "folk music" pushed it into the pop music charts, where it continued to thrive until the "British invasion" of rock and folk rock music edged it aside.

For various reasons, in the 1950s and 1960s, the musical styles that the revival favored were specifically those of the South. The influence of the musical preferences of the New Lost City Ramblers and their imitators certainly contributed to this. Also pertinent was that the Southeastern style, with banjo and guitar as the basis for musical accompaniment and a tendency to more swinging rhythms, was easier for fans to learn to play themselves and more adaptable to group singing than the drier Northern style. Furthermore, the traditional artists most likely to be heard in revival venues were from the South or the Southwest, like Woody Guthrie, the Lomaxes, Sam Hinton, Jean Ritchie, John Jacob Niles, or the Carter Family. Later in the 1960s bluegrass music, largely based on the traditional music of the Appalachians, was warmly received on Northern college campuses and at folk festivals, something that didn't happen with the parallel Southwestern genres of Western or western swing music.

As the folk song revival matured and artists sought to broaden their repertoires, they turned from the re-creation of the traditional songs of an older,
primarily rural culture to the composition of their own songs in the style of
those older folk songs. By the 1980s the commercial use of the term "folk music"
was applied primarily to this genre of music. Older Anglo-American folk music
was categorized as "traditional," "old-timey," or (still later) "roots" music. The
success of the folk revival contributed to a continuing disagreement over what
constituted "folk music." To some 1960s fans and critics at the time, this was
the juncture at which the Bob Dylans and Tom Paxtons of the world ceased to
be folksingers and became popular song singer/writers. Others argued that they
were never folksingers in the first place but only interpreters or revivers of folk
song. Inevitably, such discussions depended on the definition of a "folk song,"
as discussed in the Introduction.

Untroubled by the question of whether they were genuine folksingers or not,
some artists were beginning to find that, charming as the old ballads and songs
were, they were not addressing issues that were meaningful in the lives of young
Americans in the 1960s, nor were pop (adult audience) or rock music (teen
audience). Consequently, they filled an empty niche with their own original
material. Plenty of issues were available, most significantly the increasingly
futile war in Vietnam and the escalating conflicts over civil rights.

In Menlo Park, California, three college students, Nick Reynolds, Bob
Shane, and Dave Guard, liked to get together and sing and play calypso and
folk music. After polishing their act carefully, they debuted in San Francisco's
Purple Onion, where they remained for seven months. Since calypso music
constituted an early important component of their repertoire, they took the
name Kingston Trio, after the Jamaican port city and place name in several
calypso songs. In 1958, Capitol Records issued their first album, which eventually rose to the number one position on *Billboard*'s charts. Among its songs was
a traditional American ballad about a North Carolina murder committed in
1866 called "Tom Dooley."

"Tom Dooley" was probably never sung outside of North Carolina before the
late 1920s and only rarely after that until 1958. In 1959, it was played on phonographs in nearly 10 percent of the homes around the country and heard on
the radio in the others. Its popularizers were not traditional North Carolina
folksingers, nor were they long-haired, sandaled imitators of traditional singers.
They were business administration students from elite college campuses who
sported neat crew cuts and button-down shirts. They demonstrated overnight
that one didn't have to be either a political leftist or a counterculture rebel to
sing folk songs. Very likely it was the latter revelation that folk song enthusiasts
of 1959–1960 found so difficult to accept. Nevertheless, the Kingston Trio
opened up the world of folk music to an audience well beyond the political
activists and social rebels and created the possibility for suitably polished,
edited, and refined folk songs to become pop hits. From 1960 to 1963, most of
the folk songs that hit the pop charts were done by clean-cut collegiate groups

like the Kingston Trio: the Brothers Four, the Fenderman, the Highwaymen, the Cumberland Three, and the Greenwood County Singers.

Peter, Paul and Mary were, in the wake of the Kingston Trio, among the groups most responsible for broadening the appeal of folk music to large, nation-wide audiences. The three began coffeehouse appearances in 1961 and secured a recording contract the following year. Their first album, *Peter, Paul & Mary*, swept the country, becoming the top LP for seven weeks beginning in June 1962. From this album, their rendition of Lee Hays's "If I Had a Hammer" was released as a single and lasted for twelve weeks on the charts, scoring as high as number ten. Their third album, *In the Wind*, became their biggest success: number one for five weeks in the fall of 1963. During those years, Peter, Paul and Mary were one of the most popular "folk acts" in the country. By the time the trio broke up in 1970, they had released ten albums, five of which sold over a million copies.

Theme	Title and Songwriter*
General protest song	"Blowin' in the Wind" (Dylan, 1962)
Loss of individualism among those living in suburbia	"Little Boxes" (Reynolds, 1963)
Nuclear weapons	"What Have They Done to the Rain?" (Reynolds, 1962) "Eve of Destruction" (Sloan and Barri, 1965) "Hard Rain's A-Gonna Fall" (Dylan, 1963),
Native Americans	"Ballad of Ira Hayes" (LaFarge, 1962) "Now That the Buffalo's Gone" (Sainte-Marie, 1964) "My Country 'Tis of Thy People You're Dying" (Sainte-Marie, 1966),
War protest songs	"Where Have All the Flowers Gone" (Seeger, 1961) "Universal Soldier" (Sainte-Marie, 1964) "Last Night I Had the Strangest Dream" (McCurdy, 1950) "Draft Dodger Rag" (Ochs, 1964) "I Ain't Marchin' Anymore" (Ochs, 1964) "I-Feel-Like-I'm-Fixin'-to-Die Rag" (McDonald, 1965)

*The songwriters were not in all cases the artists who popularized the songs.

Apart from their musical success, Peter, Paul and Mary broke new ground by being among the first folk/pop artists to take outspoken stands on controversial issues—in particular, the Civil Rights movement and Vietnam War protests.

Another giant of this era was Bob Dylan. Born in 1941 in Duluth, Minnesota, he headed east for New York's Greenwich Village in 1962. After six months of informal apprenticeship listening to other singers, including Woody Guthrie, Cisco Houston, and Pete Seeger, Dylan was signed on for a gig at Gerde's Folk City. Dylan impressed most of his audience favorably. His first album, *Bob Dylan*, released in 1962, consisted of ten traditional songs or older compositions by traditional bluesmen, and the remaining three were his own compositions. Dylan rapidly became one of the most influential performers of the folk revival and, in the process, changed its very direction away from traditional material and toward original compositions of a topical nature, sometimes with elements of protest. His "Blowin' in the Wind," almost as much as "We Shall Overcome," became an anthem for the Civil Rights movement of the 1960s. With his fourth album, *Another Side of Bob Dylan*, protest material had practically disappeared, to be replaced by more introspective themes. Of course, there were also non-protest hit songs, like:

- "Circle Game" (Mitchell, 1966)
- "Both Sides Now" (Mitchell, 1967)
- "Sounds of Silence" (Simon & Garfunkel, 1965)
- "Turn, Turn, Turn" (Seeger, 1965)
- "Bridge over Troubled Waters" (Simon & Garfunkel, 1968)
- "The Night They Drove Old Dixie Down" (Baez, 1971)

And there were a few major hits based on traditional songs:

- "Scarborough Fair/Canticle" (Simon & Garfunkel's rendition of the Anglo-American ballad, 1968)
- "Mockingbird" (Carly Simon and James Taylor's reworking of a Deep South lullabye,1974)
- "Amazing Grace" (Judy Collins, 1971)
- "House of the Rising Sun" (the British group the Animals' rendition of a New Orleans folk song, 1964)

In the late 1950s and early 1960s, the principal venues for presenting folk music by revival performers were small coffeehouses in large cities or folk festivals on college campuses or near large cities. The festivals consisted of multi-event programs that included large audience concerts, as well as more intimate workshops or lecture-demonstrations, and sought to provide something of interest to attendees no matter what their degree of exposure to folk music. Coffeehouses drew hardcore, experienced enthusiasts, allowing acts of more limited appeal—generally the more traditional performers.

Large-Scale Folk Festivals

The folk revival movement culminated (at least, in terms of audience size and recording sales) with a pair of annual events that drew tens of thousands of spectators and participants to Newport, Rhode Island, and The National Mall in Washington, D.C.

In the summer of 1959, Newport, already famous as the site of an annual jazz festival, hosted the first Newport Folk Festival. In this and the following year, the producers sought out big names of the folk revival, but both festivals were financial failures. Attendance at the 1959 event was pegged at only 13,000. The performers were mostly city musicians, or at least musicians who were well accepted by the urban connoisseurs.

At the 1959 Newport Folk Festival, Bob Gibson, a popular Chicago folk music entertainer who just missed out on lasting fame, brought out on stage with him a young Joan Baez, who dazzled the audience with the brilliance and clarity of her singing. Traditional Anglo-American folk balladry captivated her and constituted a major component of her repertoire during her early years. Not until her second album *Joan Baez, Volume 2* appeared on the charts in late 1961 did she attract much attention. During 1961 and 1962, extensive appearances across the country at colleges, concert halls, and coffeehouses made her one of the preeminent folk revival performers.

The Newport Folk Festivals were discontinued after the second disappointing year in 1960 and would have been forgotten but for Pete Seeger's conviction that the event could be a success if it were done differently. Seeger proposed the establishment of a nonprofit foundation as the festival's basis, and minimum payment for performers so that the big name "drawing cards" could underwrite the lesser-known, traditional artists. Workshops and other events—regular features at the college festivals—could contribute to making the event educational as well as entertaining. With strong support from singer and actor Theo Bikel, Seeger convinced one of the original producers of the merits of his proposal, and the Newport Folk Foundation was established.

The 1963 festival, the first under the new management, attracted 40,000, a great improvement over previous years. Attendance in 1965 was double that. The largest audience at a single performance approached 18,000. That year, there were 228 performers spread over three days and four evenings of events. With the profits from the festivals (the largest from a single year was $70,000), the foundation sponsored fieldwork, supported local festival productions, purchased new guitars for traditional blues musicians and recording equipment for university folklore departments, and provided grants to other organizations and individuals. Seven annual festivals were held from 1963 to 1969. Then, in response to increasing pressure by the Newport City Council on behalf of residents complaining about crowds, noise, and disruption, the board of directors cancelled the festival. Reasons for the event's demise also included declining attendance and increasing expenses to satisfy municipal requirements (such as additional police protection).

During its peak years, the Newport Folk Festival epitomized the folk revival. As the revival itself changed orientation somewhat during the 1960s, so did Newport. In the 1963 event, urban performers outnumbered traditional/ethnic artists by about two to one; the ratio was reversed by 1967. At Newport hundreds of thousands of fans saw and heard traditional artists for the first time, and thanks to Vanguard Recording Society's extensive taping of the concerts, thousands more could hear the cream of the performances on LP discs (which since have been converted to compact disc). Nevertheless, the festival terminated for want of sufficient attendance. The explanation probably lays in the shifting direction of the revival in the late 1960s: young singer/songwriters such as Bob Dylan, Phil Ochs, and Tom Paxton, who had started their careers singing traditional songs and ballads, turned increasingly to writing their own material. Dylan also spearheaded a trend from acoustic instruments to electrified—a move that initially had him booed off the Newport stage in 1965. Together, these developments gradually drew much of the audience away from traditional folk music.

As Newport's folk festival declined, it was eclipsed by a larger event held a few hundred miles to the south on The Mall in Washington, D.C. In 1967, the Smithsonian Institution inaugurated its own Festival of American Folklife, an extensive presentation of American culture that embraced not only musical forms but also dance, traditional arts and crafts, occupational lore, and ethnic costume and celebrations. Newport paled beside the American Folklife event, which during its peak years occupied almost the entire summer and filled The Mall between the two rows of Smithsonian museums and art galleries with a dazzling variety of traditional and ethnic music, lore, and culture. Though a product of the folk revival, the Festival of American Folklife soon moved outside and beyond it, as its directors early evolved a policy of presenting only traditional performers and artisans rather than interpreters or imitators.

Folk festivals as large audience events peaked in 1978–1980 and declined quickly; audience attendance dropped by one-half in most cases, and many festivals were discontinued. The big events like Newport and Washington exposed city audiences to live performances by artists they had never had the opportunity to see before and perhaps had not even heard of. The Newport Folk Festival was resurrected in 1986 after a fifteen-year hiatus. Its nature changed somewhat, now focusing largely on up-and-coming urban folk groups, with just a small proportion of traditional acts. The National Folk Festival, begun in 1934 and held at Wolf Trap, Virginia, through the 1970s, is now held in a different venue each year. The Smithsonian's American Folklife Festival has become the largest annual cultural event in Washington, D.C., and lasts for ten days each summer. It is one of the top tourist attractions of the country.

Into the Next Generation

By the 1980s the folk revival was spoken of in the past tense, as if it had died out. It's certainly true that it no longer occupies the center of the America's musical stage, nor did it command the same commercial clout that it once did. The traditional music component of the folk revival had all but disappeared, but it had left an indelible mark. A new generation of singers and songwriters borrowed the simple musical style—solo or duet singing to uncluttered acoustic instrumental accompaniment, usually a single guitar or banjo—and wrote their own fresh compositions that ranged over a variety of topics, but mostly of current social significance: environmentalism, civil and women's rights, social justice, labor unionism, war, and so on. When one walks down the aisles of the record and music stores today, this is the music that is marketed as "folk." What used to be called folk needs a different term now to avoid confusion. "Traditional" or "traditional folk" are useful labels; becoming more common is the rubric "roots" music, which stresses the music as a source for other genres, whereas "traditional" stresses the community continuity of the music itself.

RECOMMENDED RECORDINGS

In Country: Folk Songs of Americans in the Vietnam War, Flying Fish, FF 70552.
Cretan Song in America, 1945–1953. Greek Archives, CD 958.
Don't Mourn—Organize!—Songs of Labor Songwriter Joe Hill, Smithsonian/Folkways, SF 40026.
The Early Minstrel Show. New World Records, LP NW 338.
Folk Music at Newport, Part 1. Vanguard, CD 77007-2.
Folk Song America: A 20th Century Revival. Smithsonian Collection of Recordings, 4 CDs.
Greatest Folksingers of the 'Sixties. Vanguard, VCD 17/18.
Irish in America. Folk-Legacy, CD-129.
Mike, Peggy, Barbara, and Penny Seeger. *Animal Folk Songs for Children.* Rounder, CD 8023/24.
Minstrels and Tunesmiths: The Commercial Roots of Early Country Music. John Edwards Memorial Foundation, LP 109.
The Music of Arab Americans: A Retrospective Collection. Rounder, CD 1122.
Old-Country Music in a New Land: Folk Music of Immigrants from Europe and the Near East. New World Records, LP NW 264.
Old Mother Hippletoe: Rural and Urban Children's Songs. New World Records, LP NW 291.
Pete Seeger, Woody Guthrie, Leadbelly. *Folkways: A Vision Revisited.* Legacy International, CD-300.
Polish Village Music: Historical Polish-American Recordings, Chicago and New York, 1927–1933. Arhoolie/Folklyric, CD 7031.
Roots N' Blues—The Retrospective, 1925–1950. Columbia/Legacy, CD C4K 47911.
Roots of Folk. Vanguard, 203/05-2, 3 CDs.
Sing for Freedom—The Story of the Civil Rights Movement through Its Songs. Smithsonian Folkways, CD SF 40032.

Songs of the Civil War, CMH, CD 8028.

Songs for Political Action: Folk music, Topical Songs and the American Left, 1926–1953. Bear Family, BCD 15720 JL; 10 CD plus book box.

'Spiew Juchasa/Song of the Shepherd: Songs of the Slavic Americans. New World Records, LP NW 283.

The Story That the Crow Told Me: Early American Rural Children's Songs, Vols. 1/2. Yazoo, 2051/52; reissues from commercial 78-rpm recordings of the 1920s and 1930s.

Texas-Czech, Bohemian, & Moravian Bands: Historic Recordings, 1929–1959. Arhoolie/ Folklyric, CD 7026.

Ukrainian Village Music: Historic Recordings, 1928–1933. Arhoolie/Folklyric, CD 7030.

White Country Blues (1926–1938): A Lighter Shade of Blue. Columbia/Legacy, CD C2K 47466, 2 CDs.

The Yiddish Dream: A Heritage of Jewish Song. Vanguard, VCD 715/16.

RECOMMENDED VIEWING

On the Road Again: Down Home Blues, Jazz, Gospel and More. Video featuring Buster Pickens, Lightnin' Hopkins, Hop Wilson, Whistlin' Alex Moore, Black Ace (B. K. Turner), Lowell Fulsom, King Louis H. Narcisse, Blind James Campbell String Band, J. E. Mainer Family Band, George Lewis, Sweet Emma Barrett, Eureka Brass Band (video, Yazoo, 520).

Times Ain't Like They Used To Be: Early Rural and Popular American Music from Rare Original Film Masters (1928–1935). Featuring Jimmie Rodgers, Bob Wills's Texas Play-boys, Whistler's Jug Band, Jack Johnson's Jazz Band, Ted Weems and His Orchestra, Otto Gray's Oklahoma Cowboys, Bela Lam, Bascom Lamar Lunsford, Jules Allen, Elder Lightfoot Solomon Michaux, Cumberland Ridge Runners, Uncle John Scruggs, Eddie Thomas and Carl Scott, Georgia Field Hands, Bun Wright's Fiddle Band, Estudiantina Invencibal, Duke Davis Banjo Band, Lemire Twins, Fran Westphal's Orchestra, anony-mous musicians at Old Time Fiddlers' Convention, Square Dances (dvd and video, Yazoo, 512).

NOTES

1. "Shinbone Alley," in Henry M. Belden and Arthur Palmer Hudson, eds., *The Frank C. Brown Collection of North Carolina Folklore*, Vol. 3: *Folk Songs* (Durham, NC: Duke University Press, 1952), p. 508.

2. "Barbara Allen," in James W. Raine, *The Land of Saddlebags: A Study of the Moun-tain People of Appalachia* (1924; repr., Detroit: Singing Tree Press, 1969), p. 115.

3. Collected anonymously in Auburn, Alabama, 1915–1916. Published in Newman I. White, *American Negro Folk-Songs* (1928; repr., Folklore Associates, 1965), p. 105.

Biographical Sketches

This chapter includes short biographical sketches of one hundred important figures in the story of American folk music. With few exceptions, all the singers whose recordings are quoted are mentioned. Most are traditional artists, but some representative revival musicians and singers and also major folk song collectors are included.

Almanac Singers. A group of singers and musicians was organized in New York City in 1940, centered around key members PETE SEEGER (see separate entry), Lee Hays (formerly a song leader at a radical labor college in Commonwealth, Arkansas), and Millard Lampell, who performed primarily labor union and political songs for leftist political causes. Their first major public appearance, a successful concert in May of 1941 in Madison Square Garden for the striking Transport Workers' Union, paved the way for a national tour of Congress of Industrial Organizations (CIO) affiliates and a modicum of celebrity. In 1941 the Almanac Singers recorded four albums: one of anti-war songs, *Songs for John Doe* one of union songs, *Talking Union*; and two of traditional songs, *Sod Buster Ballads* and *Deep Sea Chanteys and Whaling Ballads*. During their active period, other singers drifted in and out of the Almanacs, including, at one time or another, "Sis" Cunningham, Gordon Friesen, Baldwin "Butch" Hawes, CISCO HOUSTON, Bess Lomax, BROWNIE MCGHEE AND SONNY TERRY, Charley Polachek, Earl Robinson, Arthur Stern, and Josh White. The Almanac

Singers' collective career was short lived, terminated mainly by World War II, for which Seeger and others volunteered or were drafted.

Recordings: Various artists, *Secular Vocal Groups in Chronological Order—Vol. 4 (1926–1947)* (Document, DOCD 5615), includes nine selections by the Almanac Singers; The Almanac Singers, *Their Complete General Recordings* (MCA, CD MCAD-11499)

Ashley, Clarence (ca. 1895–1967). Clarence Earl "Tom" Ashley born in Bristol, Virginia, had enjoyed a successful recording career during the late 1920s and early 1930s as a solo artist and in various groups, especially the Carolina Tar Heels. When Ralph Rinzler met him at the Union Grove Old Time Fiddlers' Convention in April of 1960, Ashley was sixty-five and hadn't played banjo in years. With Rinzler's encouragement, Ashley brushed up his playing and singing and put together a band, which made its first appearance in New York in March 1961. The band, consisting of Ashley on vocals and banjo, Clint Howard (b. 1930), a first-rate lead singer and back-up guitarist, Fred Price (b. 1915), an outstanding old-time fiddler, and Doc Watson, was recorded at various locations in the next two years, from which two albums on the Folkways label were assembled. These recordings, reissued on CD, rank as among the best of old-time string band music to be recorded since the 1940s.

Recordings: Doc Watson and Clarence Ashley, *The Original Folkways Recordings: 1960–62* (Smithsonian Folkways, SF-40029/30); *The Carolina Tar Heels* (Old Homestead, OHCD 4113), reissues from 1920s/30s

Bâby, Stanley. Bâby was born in the late 1800s in Port Huron, Michigan, but lived most of his life in Ontario, Canada. He was the son of a sea captain who began a career at sea in 1871 and sang many maritime ballads and songs when he was home during the winter months. Stanley learned many of his songs from his father that way. He was already a retired seaman when folklorist Edith Fowke visited him in 1956 and began recording his repertoire.

Recording: Various artists, *Songs of the Great Lakes* (Folkways, LP/Cass FM 4018), includes seven songs by Bâby

Baez, Joan (1940–). Born in Staten Island, New York, she attended high school in California, where she listened to records of Harry Belafonte and Odetta and learned to play the guitar and sing folk songs. Her family moved to Boston in 1958, and she soon became part of the music scene in Cambridge, Massachusetts, one of the country's most active folk revival communities. Soon Baez was performing at Cambridge's best known folk music coffeehouse, Club 47. Traditional Anglo-American folk balladry captivated her and constituted a major component of her repertoire during those early years. Her first album, *Joan Baez*, issued in 1961, consisted entirely of traditional folk ballads and songs. Extensive appearances across the country at colleges, concert halls, and coffeehouses in the 1960s made her one of the preeminent folk revival performers. Later in her career, she broadened her repertoire to include more contemporary songs and her own compositions. By the mid-1970s, her albums contained few of the traditional ballads that earlier had underpinned her reputation.

Recordings: Joan Baez, *The First 10 Years* (Vanguard, VCD-6560/1); *The Joan Baez Country Music Album* (Vanguard, VCD-105/6); *Joan Baez in Concert* (Vanguard, VCD-113/14)

Bailey, Green (1900–ca. 1980). Green Bailey was born in Owsley County, Kentucky. After completing high school, he began his teaching career in a one-room school in Clark County. Later, he attended Eastern Normal in Richmond, Kentucky, the University of Kentucky in Lexington, and Kentucky Wesleyan in Winchester until his graduation in 1938. While a paraplegic most of his life, Bailey was passionate about old ballads and songs, learning them from friends and neighbors. In 1928 to 1929, accompanied by Doc Roberts and ASA MARTIN (Bailey played guitar only occasionally), he made a handful of recordings for the Gennett label, most of which were never issued. Bailey lived his last years in Trapp, Kentucky, bedridden by a stroke and unable to communicate except to his wife.

Recording: Various artists, *Kentucky Mountain Music* (Yazoo, 2200, 7 CDs), includes Bailey's "Shut Up in Coal Creek Mine"

Ball, Estil (1913–1978), and Orna (1907–2000). Estil C. Ball, born practically on the Virginia–North Carolina border, was first recorded by John A. Lomax for the Library of Congress in 1941 and had begun playing professionally at about that time. In the 1960s and 1970s, he and his wife, Orna Reedy Ball, played primarily gospel music in public performances and weekly local radio broadcasts. LP albums featuring him and his wife showed that his repertoire was considerably broader, including humorous secular songs, guitar instrumentals, and ballads sung to his own guitar or banjo accompaniment. Although religious material was the backbone of the Balls's performances, Estil's not-flashy-but-rock-solid guitar picking fitted equally well on the secular tunes—some of his own compositions.

Recordings: E. C. *Ball with Orna Ball & the Friendly Gospel Singers* (Rounder, CD 11577); E. C. and Orna Ball, *Through the Years: 1937–1975* (Copper Creek, CCCD-0141)

Barker, Horton (1889–1973). Sightless from early childhood as the result of an accident, Barker was born in Laurel Bloomery, northeast Tennessee, but he lived most of his life in Virginia. In the 1930s, he came to the attention of folk song collectors and made his first public singing appearance at Virginia's White Top Mountain Folk Festival in 1933. He sang at numerous festivals in the next three decades and learned many of his songs from other performers at such gatherings. He was recorded in the 1930s by Annabel Buchanan at White Top and by Sarah Gertrude Knott and later Alan Lomax in Washington, D.C. Collector Sandy Paton visited him around 1961, and the opportunity to document Barker's wonderful singing with decent recording equipment resulted in a full LP on the Folkways label. Barker had a sweet, gentle tenor voice and sang in an unornamented style.

Recording: Horton Barker—Traditional Singer (Folkways, LP/Cass FA 2362)

Barry, Phillips (1880–1937). One of the first and most important folk song scholars in the generation after Francis J. Child, Phillips Barry collected extensively in New England, though his interests included all of traditional songlore. He founded and edited the *Bulletin of the Folk-Song Society of the Northeast* (1930–1934) and coauthored several important volumes on New England folk songs. He wrote extensively about the theoretical aspects of oral tradition and traditional songs, and he was instrumental in developing the theory that songs are not communally written by an anonymous community but may be continually rewritten by a succession of singers, thus blurring with time the contributions of the original authors.

Belafonte, Harry (1927–). Belafonte was born in New York City of Jamaican and Martiniquan parents, was educated in his early years in Jamaica, and then moved back to New York. After leaving college, he pursued various careers, finally deciding in 1950 to specialize in folk songs. In early 1956, a succession of albums for RCA Victor catapulted him to fame as a folk song performer: *"Mark Twain" and Other Favorites, Belafonte,* and a few months later *Calypso,* the latter two both becoming number one albums. One song from the latter album, "Banana Boat Song," became a million-selling single, and "Jamaica Farewell" also made the charts. Although Belafonte had some legitimate claims to knowing Jamaican music from his youth, most of these calypso numbers he learned from Irving Burgie ("Lord Burgess"), a successful Julliard-trained calypsonian who had arranged many older traditional Jamaican folk songs.

Recordings: Harry Belafonte, *Calypso* (RCA, CD 53801); *Very Best of Harry Belafonte* (RCA, CD 68097)

Blake, Norman (1938–). Born in Chattanooga, Tennessee, but reared in Georgia, Blake became adept at several instruments, including guitar, mandolin, and fiddle, as he was growing up. His first band, formed while still in his teens, was the Dixie Drifters, who performed on various radio stations in the 1950s. Later he joined Bob Johnson and then Walter Forbes to perform as The Lonesome Travelers. In the 1960s and 1970s, he performed on the Johnny Cash show and worked with BOB DYLAN, Kris Kristofferson, JOAN BAEZ, and John Hartford. Since 1974 he has performed mainly with his wife, Nancy, who plays mandolin, fiddle, guitar, and cello, and also with fiddler James Bryan. The trio performs traditional music as well as Blake's own compositions in traditional styles, influenced by other types of contemporary music.

Recordings: Norman and Nancy Blake, *Just Gimme Somethin' I'm Used To* (Shanachie, CD 6001); Norman and Nancy Blake, *While Passing along This Way* (Shanachie, CD 6012); Norman and Nancy Blake, *The Hobo's Last Ride* (Shanachie, CD 6020); Norman Blake, *Chattanooga Sugar Babe* (Shanachie, CD 6027)

Boggs, Dock (1897–1971). Moran Lee "Dock" Boggs, a Virginia-born collier, was a minor hillbilly artist who made a dozen recordings in 1927 and 1929. Boggs's unique combination of vocal and banjo styles produced an intense musical experience that no listener can ever forget. Though he learned to play banjo in a frailing style, as his father and other relatives played while he was young, he chose to develop a picking style based on the playing of an African American banjoist who deeply impressed him in his youth. Relatively unimportant in terms of the history of commercially recorded hillbilly music, Boggs virtually disappeared from public view with the coming of the Depression. After his "rediscovery" by MIKE SEEGER, three Folkways albums were issued: one consisting mostly of interviews and the others, of his music. Boggs's style was an almost anomalous blend of black and white influences, unique in the 1920s; in the 1960s he still sounded much as he had four decades earlier.

Recordings: Dock Boggs, *Country Blues: Complete Early Recordings (1927–29)* (Revenant, CD 705); Dock Boggs, *His Folkways Years, 1963–1968* (Smithsonian Folkways, SF-CD-40108), reissues from Folkways, FA 2351, Folkways, FA 2392, and Asch, AH 3903

Bolick, Bill (1917–), and Earl (1919–1998). Among the many old-time hillbilly artists of the 1930s and 1940s who were brought back to the concert stage by the folk revival were North Carolinians Bill and Earl Bolick, the Blue Sky Boys. They had enjoyed great popularity on both the radio, starting in 1935, and on record, beginning in 1936. After the hiatus in their careers caused by World War II, they resumed activity until 1951, making records for several labels; Earl then chose to quit the profession for family reasons. In 1963 Archie Green and Ed Kahn located Bill Bolick in Greensboro, North Carolina, and Earl in Atlanta, and they persuaded the brothers to reunite for a concert at the University of Illinois in October 1964, the first of several campus appearances. While in Los Angeles to play at the 1965 UCLA Folk Festival, they recorded an album for Capitol Records. Perceiving the different interests of their folk festival audiences from those of their Southern rural fans, the Bolicks stressed the older numbers in their repertoires for these recordings, including many selections they had not previously recorded.

Recording: Blue Sky Boys, *The Sunny Side of Life* (Bear Family, BCD 15951 EK)

Brand, Oscar (1920–). Singer, guitarist, songwriter, actor, author, and radio emcee, Oscar Brand was born in Winnipeg, Ontario, Canada, but received most of his schooling in Brooklyn. After graduating from high school in 1937, he worked his way across the country as a farm hand with his banjo, learning folk songs as he went. In 1945 he got a job as folk music coordinator for the New York City radio station WNYC, where he started his own radio program, *Folk Song Festival*, which ran for several decades. In the 1960s he produced another radio program, *The World of Folk Music*, which was broadcast weekly over more than 1,800 stations and was government sponsored. His first, and perhaps best remembered, recordings were a series of bawdy song albums starting in the late 1950s on the Audio Fidelity label.

Recordings: Oscar Brand, *Presidential Campaign Songs, 1789–1996* (Smithsonian/ Folkways, SFW CD 45051); Oscar Brand, *Pie in the Sky* (Tradition, CD 1021)

Bronson, Bertrand Harris (1902–1986). Bertrand Bronson was a professor of English at the University of California at Berkeley for most of his academic career from 1927 to 1970. Although he authored many articles on particular ballads, his primary contribution was in the study of the music of the traditional ballads—their variety, their relationships, and, in particular, how tune and text are related to each other. His most cited work is his monumental four-volume study, *The Traditional Tunes of the Child Ballads*. While Child's aim was to publish every extant version of each of the 305 ballads he considered "popular," Bronson's goal was to publish each one with its tune and to group them according to tune families. Unlike Child's catalog, many of Bronson's sources are from the United States and Canada.

Broonzy, Big Bill (1898–1958). Bill Broonzy grew up in poverty; his large family moved back and forth between Mississippi, where he was born, and Arkansas. During those difficult years, he built a homemade fiddle and guitar and taught himself to play both instruments, learning spirituals, folk songs, and blues songs. In 1919 he moved to Chicago, got a job with the Pullman Company, and polished his guitar playing. In the late 1920s and 1930s, he established himself as one of the leading figures in Chicago's vibrant blues scene, which drew both performers and audiences from the large numbers of African Americans who emigrated northward from the Mississippi delta region in search of better economic opportunities and social justice. In the 1940s his musical career waned, and he made his living at menial jobs. In the 1950s he enjoyed a second successful career as a musician in the folk revival, which lasted almost until his death from cancer. In this period his repertoire shifted from the electric urban blues of the 1940s back to the older blues and songs of his childhood. In either genre, his singing and outstanding guitar playing represented the best in African American traditional music.

Recordings: Trouble in Mind (Smithsonian/Folkways, 40131); *Big Bill Broonzy Sings Folk Songs* (Smithsonian/Folkways, 40023)

Carson, "Fiddling" John (1868 or 1874–1949). One of the first Anglo-American folk artists to make commercial recordings, Carson was born in Fannin County, Georgia, and lived all his life in north Georgia. Carson made the first of his more than 170 commercial recordings for the OKeh label in 1923 and his last for RCA Bluebird in 1934. A housepainter by trade, Carson was a local fixture at fairs, fiddle conventions, and political rallies in his community. Never a flashy fiddler, he was an exceptional personality nevertheless, whose archaic singing and playing were more impressive in person than on record.

Recording: Fiddlin' John Carson, Vols. 1–7 (Document, DOCD-8014-8020)

Carter Family. One of the most influential hillbilly groups of the decades before World War II—they recorded 250 songs from 1927 to 1941—the original Carter Family consisted of Alvin Pleasant ("A. P.") Delaney Carter (1891–1960), his wife Sara Elizabeth Dougherty (1898–1979), and Sara's cousin, Maybelle Addington (1909–1978), all from Scott or Wise counties, Virginia, in the Clinch Mountain region. The trio's musical career initially was rather informal, but it became more professional after some recording auditions in 1927 for the Victor Talking Machine Company's talent scout, Ralph Peer, in Bristol, Virginia. Sara and Maybelle both sang and played either guitar or autoharp; A. P. occasionally sang but contributed mainly to the group by making bookings and gathering songs for their repertoire, often by traveling through the mountains and collecting them from friends and neighbors. Their repertoire, mainly sentimental, moralistic, and religious songs and ballads, as well as (especially later in their careers) some original compositions, did much to shape the repertoire of early commercial country music in general. Maybelle, an outstanding instrumentalist, developed a guitar-playing style that became standard among country guitarists for decades.

Recording: Carter Family, *In the Shadow of Clinch Mountain* (Bear Family, BCD 15865 KL, 12 CDs and book set)

Chandler, Dillard (1907–1992). Madison County, North Carolina, has maintained one of the richest traditions of ballads and songs to be found in the Appalachians. Dillard Chandler, recorded by John Cohen in 1963 to 1968, was an outstanding singer with a highly ornamented, melismatic vocal style whose repertoire included many old imported ballads and songs.

Recordings: Dillard Chandler, *The End of an Old Song* (Folkways, LP/Cass FA 2418); Various artists, *Old Love Songs & Ballads from the Big Laurel, North Carolina* (Folkways, LP/Cass FA 2309)

Video: John Cohen, *The End of an Old Song* (Video: Shanachie, 1404)

Child, Francis James (1825–1896). Son of a Boston sailmaker, Francis James Child became Harvard's first professor of English in 1876, where he remained until his death. While he wrote extensively on Shakespeare and medieval English literature, he is known primarily for his five-volume compilation, *The English and Scottish Popular Ballads* (written from 1882 to 1898, with later reprints), the major source for anyone seriously interested in the older ballads. This work includes all the texts that Child could find of the 305 ballads that he considered "popular," with his copious annotations and references to versions in other languages and cultures.

Cleveland, Sara (1905–1987). Unaccompanied ballad singer Cleveland born in Hartford, New York, was hailed by folklorist Kenneth Goldstein as our "best living traditional female singer." Cleveland had a repertoire of 200 ballads and songs, all learned from a relatively small circle of relatives and friends, and remarkable for its breadth: unusual ballads of British origins, American ballads from the West as well as from the Northeast, homiletic and sentimental pieces from Tin Pan Alley, religious pieces, and hillbilly songs. Her distinctiveness lies in the extent of her repertoire and the completeness of her texts.

Recordings: Sara Cleveland, *Ballads & Songs of the Upper Hudson Valley* (Folk Legacy, LP FSA-33); *Sara Cleveland* (Philo, LP 1020)

Collins, Judy (1939–). Judith Margorie Collins studied classical piano from the age of four but became interested in folk music in her teens. She learned to play guitar and began her professional career in clubs in the Denver area. Her earliest album, issued in 1962, consisted mostly of traditional material sung in her clear, beautiful voice, but by her fourth and fifth albums she included mostly contemporary songs by Tom Paxton, Phil Ochs, and others. By 1967 she was writing her own material as well.

Recording: Judy Collins, *A Maid of Constant Sorrow & Golden Apples of the Sun* (Elektra, CD 8122)

Cotten, Elizabeth (1895–1987). North Carolina–born Elizabeth Cotten worked as a domestic for the Charles Seeger household during the years when young Mike and Peggy Seeger were first exploring folk music. An accomplished musician, she would surreptitiously take up one of the Seeger guitars and pick out tunes she had not played since her youth. Impressed by her talents, the Seegers encouraged her to perform in public. Through the 1960s and later, she was a popular figure at folk festivals. Her composition "Freight Train" became a widely copied standard.

Recordings: Elizabeth Cotton, *Live!* (Arhoolie, CD 477); Elizabeth Cotton, *Freight Train and Other North Carolina Folk Songs and Tunes* (Smithsonian/Folkways, CD SF 40009)

Video: Elizabeth Cotten (Video and DVD: Vestapol, 13019)

Crockett Family. The musical Crocketts of Kentucky consisted of John "Dad" Crockett (1877–1972) and six of his children, George, Alan, Albert, Clarence, John Jr., and Elnora. In 1919 they moved to California's Central Valley and had a radio program on a Fresno station, one of the first country acts to broadcast in the Far West. They made a series of 78-rpm recordings for the Brunswick label in 1929 and for Crown in 1931.

Recordings: Crockett's Kentucky Mountaineers, *Classic Old Time String Band Music* (British Archive of Country Music, BACM CD D 023)

Davis, Gary (1896–1972). Born in Laurens County, South Carolina, Davis was ordained a Baptist minister when he was thirty-three years old. He made his first recordings in 1935 as Blind Gary, and until very late in life, he recorded almost exclusively religious songs to his own guitar accompaniment. After moving to New York in about 1940, he sang on street corners, developing a hoarse, powerful singing voice with an astonishing guitar virtuosity. He remained in New York until his death, after which a considerable number of records and compact discs were issued from concert tapes.

Recordings: Blind Gary Davis, *Harlem Street Singer* (Biograph, BCD 123); Rev. Gary Davis, *Blues and Ragtime* (Shanachie, CD 97024); Rev. Gary Davis, *Demons and Angels*

(Shanachie, CD 6117); Rev. Gary Davis, *Pure Religion and Bad Company* (Smithsonian Folkways, CD SF 40035; Folklyric, FL 125 and 77 LA 12/14)

Dickens, Hazel (1935–). Born in Mercer County, West Virginia, where mining was the principal occupation, Hazel Jane Dickens came from a family with coal dust in its blood (one brother died of black lung disease). After moving to Baltimore at age nineteen, she began to sing and perform in public. Later she met Alice Gerrard, and they formed a partnership that resulted in four albums of traditional and contemporary songs. Dickens performed or sang in three films about the coal mining industry, *Harlan County, USA, Coal Mining Women* (1984), and *Matewan* (1987). Her own compositions, highlighting the hardships of life in poverty-stricken Appalachia, are formed by her long familiarity with traditional music of the region.

Recordings: Hazel Dickens, *Hard Hitting Songs for Hard Hit People* (Rounder, CD 126); Hazel Dickens and Alice Gerrard, *Hazel and Alice* (Rounder, CD 27)

Dixon Brothers. Dorsey (1897–1968) and Howard Dixon (1903–1961) were both born in Darlington, South Carolina, and worked all their lives in the cotton mills. In the 1930s they performed as a duet on local radio stations and made a series of 78-rpm recordings for the RCA Bluebird label with Dorsey playing steel guitar and Howard, straight guitar. Dorsey was also a prolific composer for whom songwriting was not a commercial venture but an act of personal catharsis. His best known song, "Wreck of the Highway," popularized by Roy Acuff (unaware of Dixon's authorship at the time he recorded it), is an example of just that.

Recordings: Nancy Dorsey and Howard Dixon, *Babies in the Mill* (High Tone, HMG 2502; from Testament, LP T-3301); Dixon Brothers, *Weave Room Blues* (Old Homestead, OHCD 4151); Dixon Brothers, *Spinning Room Blues* (OHCD 4164)

Dyer-Bennet, Richard (1913–1991). Of mixed American and British parentage, Richard Dyer-Bennet studied English and music at the University of California at Berkeley. In 1935 he went to Sweden, where he learned to sing European art and folk songs and accompany himself first on lute, then on guitar. Since 1944 he made the concert presentation of folk and art songs his primary vocation. His first recordings appeared in the 1940s on 78-rpm albums on a variety of labels, and in the mid-1950s he started his own label, Dyer-Bennet, to distribute his recordings. His high tenor voice and classical guitar style were popular before the folk revival was influenced by more traditional styles of presentation.

Recording: *Richard Dyer-Bennet 1* (Smithsonian Folkways, CD 40078)

Dylan, Bob (1931–). Bob Dylan, born Robert Zimmerman in Duluth, Minnesota, exhibited an interest in music while still in elementary school. In 1962 after one year in Minneapolis attending the University of Minnesota and frequenting local coffeehouses, he headed east for New York City's Greenwich Village. There he visited clubs and called on other singers, including Woody Guthrie, whose style he learned to imitate with astonishing accuracy. His first album, *Bob Dylan* (Columbia, CL 1779/CS 8579), released in March 1962, included ten pieces that were either traditional songs or older compositions by traditional bluesmen, plus three pieces of his own composition. On following albums, Dylan struck out more on his own, discarding the Guthriesque style and stressing increasingly his original compositions. Dylan rapidly became one of the most influential performers of the urban folk revival; and in the process, twice changed its very direction. His first redirection lured the revival away from traditional material and toward original compositions of a topical nature—sometimes with sharp elements of protest. "Blowin' in the Wind," from his second album, became an anthem for the Civil Rights movement of the 1960s. His "Talking John Birch Society Blues" was so trenchant that Columbia Records, fearing adverse Birch Society reaction, remastered the album without it. With his fourth album, *Another Side of Bob Dylan* (Columbia, KCS 8993), the protest material had practically disappeared, replaced by more introspective themes. Dylan's style underwent several further changes in the following decades, from acoustic folk to electric folk rock, to country rock, to religious. By the end of the century, he had more than thirty albums to his credit, many of which made the top forty charts.

Recordings: The Essential Bob Dylan (Sony, CD 85168); *Bob Dylan* (Sony, CD 8579), reissue of first LP

Gilbert, Ollie (1913–1991). Aunt Ollie Gilbert was born in the Arkansas Ozarks and started amassing her huge repertoire (reputedly over 500 songs) from her mother's singing. Little is available of her music, though in the 1960s she did travel about and appear at various folk festivals. On her one solo LP, recorded at age eighty-three, her voice is somewhat scratchy, and she sings in a plain, almost casual style, as if she were just singing to herself. Most of her recordings consist of unaccompanied singing, but on a few selections she also plays banjo.

Recordings: Aunt Ollie Gilbert Sings Old Folk Songs to Her Friends (Rimrock, Rlp-495); Various artists, *Lomax Collection, Vol. 7: Ozark Frontier—Ballads and Old-Timey Music from Arkansas* (Rounder, CD 1707, includes five selections by Gilbert)

Gladden, Texas Anna Smith (1895–1966). Born in Saltville, Virginia, Texas Gladden first came to public attention at the White Top Festival in southern Virginia in the 1930s with her singing of old ballads and songs. Eleanor Roosevelt heard her and her brother, HOBART SMITH, there and invited them to perform at the White House. In 1938 she appeared at the National Folk Festival in Washington, D.C. Alan Lomax first recorded her in 1941 for the Library of Congress and several times again over the next two decades. She had an extensive repertoire that included comic songs, hillbilly songs, and play party songs as well as older ballads. The Rounder album cited below includes recordings made in 1941 and 1946 for other studios.

Recording: Texas Gladden, Ballad Legacy (Rounder, CD 1800)

Gordon, Robert W. (1895–1967). Maine native Robert Gordon parlayed an early interest in folk song with a fellowship from Harvard that funded him to travel around the country and record on a portable cylinder machine traditional music in the early 1920s, one of the first folklorists to undertake such fieldwork. Between 1923 and 1927, he wrote the column "Old Songs Men Have Sung" in *Adventure* magazine and developed an extensive correspondence with hundreds of individuals who regularly sent him song texts. In 1928 he was named the first head of the Archive of American Folk Song at the Library of Congress, a position he held until 1933.

Grayson, G. B. (1888–1930). Gilliam Banmon Grayson and his guitar accompanist, Henry Whitter, recorded a series of remarkably influential ballads, songs, and tunes for RCA Victor from 1927 to 1929 that were copied in the next half century by many country and city musicians. Born in Ashe County, North Carolina, Grayson was nearly blind from infancy. He was an outstanding old-time fiddler with an archaic playing style and an excellent singer as well. He died in an automobile accident in 1930. Henry Whitter was one of the first hillbilly musicians to make commercial recordings (1923), but he made no more recordings after Grayson's death. The duo's complete works have been reissued on compact disc.

Recordings: G. B. Grayson and Henry Whitter, *Complete Recorded Works in Chronological Order—Vol. 1* (Document, DOCD 8054); G. B. Grayson and Henry Whitter and others, *Complete Recorded Works in Chronological Order—Vols. 2* (Document, DOCD 8055)

Greenbriar Boys. At the University of Wisconsin, John Herald, Bob Yellin, and Eric Weissberg formed the Greenbriar Boys in 1958, one of the first urban bands to attempt bluegrass music with fidelity to the Monroe tradition. In 1959 mandolinist Ralph Rinzler replaced Weissberg; and thus the group remained until 1964, when Rinzler left to work for the Newport Folk Festival.

Recordings: Greenbriar Boys, *The Best of the Vanguard Years* (Vanguard, CD 206-07/2); *The Best of the Greenbriar Boys Featuring John Herald* (Vanguard, CD VMD 79317)

Grover, Carrie (ca. 1878–1959). Carrie Grover was born in Nova Scotia into a family that had brought a considerable number of British ballads and songs to the New World in the early 1800s. When she was twelve, her family moved to Maine, where she attended Gould Academy and later taught music there. She recorded some songs for Alan Lomax and the Library of Congress and later compiled and privately published a large collection of songs and ballads from her family's tradition.

Recording: Various artists, *Anglo-American Songs and Ballads* (Library of Congress, LP AFS L 21, includes "Loss of the *New Columbia*," "Wild Barbaree," and "Lowlands of Holland" by Grover)

Gunning, Sarah Ogan (1910–1983). Sarah Gunning is perhaps best known as the sister of AUNT MOLLY JACKSON and Jim Garland and, like them, for her involvement in the folk song/protest song movement in New York in the late 1930s. She composed several bitter pieces reflecting her experiences from when she grew up in the coalfields of southeastern Kentucky in the 1920s. Her repertoire, a mixture of older traditional folk songs and protest material, is sampled on two albums recorded a decade apart. Her harsh, biting voice lends itself well to the themes of her own protest song material.

Recordings: Sarah Ogan Gunning, *Girl of Constant Sorrow* (Folk Legacy, LP FSA 26); Sarah Ogan Gunning, *The Silver Dagger* (Rounder, LP 0051)

Guthrie, Woody (1912–1967). Woody Guthrie was born into an Oklahoma family that truly experienced hardship. At age fourteen, after a succession of family disasters, he left home and rambled on his own. Oklahoma's dust bowl disaster in the 1930s sent thousands of "Okies" west to California, and in 1937 he hoboed his way to the Golden State. Off and on between 1937 and 1940, Guthrie had a radio show on the Los Angeles station KFVD with an audience comprised mainly of Okie migrants and other transients, for whom he sang old hillbilly and folk songs, told tales, and offered homespun philosophy much in the vein of his fellow Oklahoman, Will Rogers. During those years, Guthrie wrote some of his best songs about the Dust Bowl disaster: "Dusty Old Dust" (a.k.a. "So Long, It's Been Good to Know You"), "Talking Dust Bowl Blues," and "I Ain't Got No Home in This World Anymore." During the difficult Depression years, he met many unionists and political activists and soon was writing a daily newspaper column titled "Woody Sez" for the West Coast Communist daily, *People's World*. At KFVD, he met CISCO HOUSTON, who became a constant friend and singing partner and one of the first folksingers to disseminate Guthrie's rapidly growing bag of compositions. In 1941 Woody relocated to New York and became one of the central figures in the New York City folk song revival, focusing his literary activities on liberal causes and gradually moving away from traditional songs of the Southwest that he had grown up with. By the 1960s the hereditary degenerative disease that he was suffering from, Huntington's chorea, had become so severe that he checked himself into a hospital, and his career was effectively terminated. At the end of the twentieth century, long after his death in 1967, Guthrie's songs and style could still be discerned in American music.

Recordings: Woody Guthrie Sings Folk Songs (Smithsonian Folkways, CD SF 40007; Folkways, LP FA 2483); Woody Guthrie, *Struggle* (Smithsonian Folkways, CD SF 40025); Woody Guthrie, *The Asch Recordings, Vols. 1–4* (Smithsonian Folkways, SFW CD 40112); Woody Guthrie, *Cowboy Songs/Southern Mountain Hoedowns* (Stinson, CD SLP 32)

Hall, Vera Ward (ca. 1906–1964). Collector John A. Lomax considered Vera Ward Hall and her cousin, Doc Reed, as his greatest "finds" as traditional folksingers. (Actually, Lomax was introduced to them by Alabama writer and collector Ruby Pickens Tartt.) Born into a poor African American farming family in southern Alabama, Hall earned her living doing menial work.

The few dozen of her songs that have been recorded include children's songs, work songs, spirituals, and blues ballads. No complete records or compact discs have been issued of her music, but the two CDs cited include a representative selection.

Recordings: Various artists, *Deep River of Song* (Rounder, CD 1829, includes seven selections by Hall recorded by John A. Lomax in 1939 and 1940); Various artists, *Sounds of the South* (Atlantic, CD 7-82496-2, includes four selections by Hall recorded by Alan Lomax in 1959)

Hammons Family. The Hammons family, currently living in Pocahontas County, West Virginia, had a rich family tradition of fiddle and banjo tunes, ballads, play party songs, riddles, ghost and witch tales, and family anecdotes. They were recorded by folklorists Carl Fleischhauer and Alan Jabbour from 1970 to 1972, from which material two documents were issued. The Library of Congress double disc features three members of the family: Maggie Hammons Parker (1899–1987), Sherman Hammons (1903–1988), and Burl Hammons (1908–1993). Mrs. Parker was a fine traditional ballad singer, with a moderately decorated *rubato parlando* style.

Recordings: The Hammons Family, *Shaking Down the Acorns: Traditional Music and Stories from Pocahontas & Greenbrier Counties, West Virginia* (Rounder, LP 0018); *The Hammons Family* (Rounder, CD 1504/05; from Library of Congress AFS L65 and AFS L66)

Hicks, Dee and Delta. Between the two of them, Dee Hicks and his wife Delta contributed 400 songs and tunes to the Library of Congress Archive of Folk Culture. Folklorist Bobby Fulcher worked extensively with them and edited an LP album of recordings made in the late 1970s featuring primarily Dee (1906–1983), with two selections by Delta (1910–1996). Other recordings were published in 1982 by the Tennessee Folklore Society. The couple set a high premium on the old, established traditions with which they grew up—what they described approvingly as "old-fashioned." Until late in life, the Hickses had little public exposure and were not commercially oriented. Dee himself was particularly shy on stage.

Recordings: Dee and Delta Hicks, *Ballads & Banjo Music from Tennessee Cumberland Plateau* (County, LP 789); The Hicks Family, *A Cumberland Singing Tradition* (Tennessee Folklore Society, LP TFS 104)

Video: Chase the Devil: Religious Music of the Appalachians (Film features Dee and Delta Hicks, Nimrod Workman, and others)

Hinton, Sam (1917–). Born in Tulsa, Hinton grew up in Oklahoma and Texas, interested in both biology and singing. He earned a B.S. in zoology from UCLA in 1940 and eventually joined the staff of the Scripps Oceanographic Institute in La Jolla, California, where he remained until he retired in 1980. His earliest recordings, consisting of songs from his youth in East Texas, were made for the Library of Congress in 1947. He made his first commercial LP in 1952: *Folk Songs of California and the Old West* (Bowmar Records).

Two of his LPs were models of folk song presentation in an educational context: *A Family Tree of Folk Songs* (Decca, 1956) and *The Wandering Folk Song* (Folkways, 1967). His large repertoire, extensive knowledge of American folk songs, pleasing voice, and facile guitar playing made him a concert and festival favorite for many years.

Recording: Library of Congress Recordings, March 25, 1947 (Bear Family, CD 16383)

Holcomb, Roscoe (ca. 1912–1981). One of folk song collector John Cohen's most important finds during his fieldwork in Kentucky was Roscoe Holcomb, a singer of incredible emotional intensity who projected that emotion and so overwhelmed himself while singing that performing was often an ordeal for him. He lived his entire life near Hazard, Kentucky. By the time he was in his teens, he played both banjo and guitar, often accompanying a fiddler at local dances. He worked in coalmines as long as the mines were active. He appeared at the Newport Folk Festival, University of Chicago festival, UCLA, University of California at Berkley, and elsewhere. He also toured Europe from 1965 to 1966. The first album devoted entirely to him (Folkways, FA 2368, selections since reissued on the CDs cited below) demonstrated his ability to adapt material from old Anglo-American ballads and African American blues to his inimitable style. Accompanying himself on either guitar or banjo, his high, shrill, piercing voice is the essence of what is called the Kentucky "high lonesome" style.

Recordings: Roscoe Holcomb, *The High Lonesome Sound* (Smithsonian Folkways, SF-CD-40104; from Folkways, FA 2368); Roscoe Holcomb, *An Untamed Sense of Control* (Smithsonian Folkways, SF-CD-40144)

Video: John Cohen, *The High Lonesome Sound* (Video: Shanachie, 1404)

Hopkins, Doc (ca. 1899–1988). Doctor Howard Hopkins, born in Harlan County, Kentucky, was named Doctor because he was the seventh son, which in some communities was believed to promote healing powers. He enjoyed great popularity on Chicago's WLS and various other radio stations through the 1930s and 1940s. His success on radio and in person was not matched in recordings: a handful of scarce records on the Broadway label in 1931, another batch in 1936 for the American Record Corp. with the Cumberland Ridge Runners, and a few more in 1941 for Decca constituted the extent of his recordings during the period. Hopkins left show business in 1949 and worked as a machinist in Chicago for many years, then in Los Angeles. There, he performed at two UCLA folk festivals, at which time he also recorded the material for an LP album. In 1965, he sounded much as he did three decades earlier: competent, intricate banjo and guitar accompaniment, and a bland but pleasant vocal style.

Recording: Doc Hopkins (Birch, LP 1945)

Houston, Cisco (1918–1961). Gilbert Houston was born in Wilmington, Delaware, and was first exposed to folk songs from his grandmother, whose family was from Virginia and the Carolinas. Houston grew up in Los Angeles and learned to play guitar while in high school. After graduating, he took his guitar on the road, traveling about and picking up odd jobs, occasionally sing-ing at local clubs and on radio stations. In the early 1940s, he and WOODY GUTHRIE toured together. He had a rich, strong voice and was an important exponent in the beginnings of the folk song revival in the 1950s.

Recordings: Cisco Houston, *Best of the Vanguard Years* (Vanguard, CD 79574); Cisco Houston, *The Folkways Years, 1944–1961* (Smithsonian Folkways, CD 40059)

Mississippi John Hurt (1960s). *Photographer unknown; author's collection.*

Hurt, John (1898–1966). "Mississippi" John Hurt enjoyed a brief professional fling in 1928 when he recorded a dozen or so ballads and blues songs to his own guitar accompaniment for OKeh records, but he then slipped back into obscurity. He repre-sents an older generation of "songsters"— African American singers whose repertoires largely predated the era of the blues. He was "rediscovered" in 1963 and enjoyed a few years of adulation at festivals and cof-feehouses before his death.

Recordings: Mississippi John Hurt, *Legend* (Rounder, CD 1100); Mississippi John Hurt, *Avalon Blues: Complete 1928 OKeh Recordings* (Sony, 64986)

Ives, Burl (1909–1995). Born in Hunt, Illinois, into a singing family, Ives was exposed early to folk music from his family members, in particular his grandmother. In 1929 and 1930, he bummed across the country, playing guitar and banjo and learning songs everywhere he went. Though intent on an act-ing career, he continued his musical activities. In Washington in 1938, he made his first recordings for ALAN LOMAX at the Library of Congress; then, in 1940, CBS radio offered him a regular radio program, *The Wayfaring Stranger.* His commercial recording career began in 1941 with a 78-rpm album of American folk songs for Columbia Records, but it was then interrupted by World War II, during which he spent much of his time entertaining service-men. After the war, a series of folk song albums on the Decca and Asch labels made his name almost synonymous with "folksinger." He popularized such songs as "Foggy, Foggy Dew," "The Erie Canal," "Blue-Tail Fly," and "Big Rock Candy Mountain"—performances that served to define folk music for many listeners for the next decade. In the 1950s, his career shifted to acting on stage, screen, and television.

Recordings: Burl Ives, *Greatest Hits* (MCA, CD 11439); Burl Ives, *Wayfaring Stranger* (Collectables, CD 6474)

Jackson, Aunt Molly (1880–1960). Mary Magdalene Garland Jackson grew up in Bell and Clay counties, Kentucky, in a coalmining community. Not many years after her birth, her father went to work in the mines and soon became involved in union organizing; Aunt Molly followed his footsteps. She became an ardent activist on behalf of the suffering miners struggling to unionize and secure better working conditions. In 1931 she was essentially run out of Kentucky for her radical unionizing, and she moved to New York to raise money for the struggling miners. There she learned that her traditional songlore, augmented by her own militant topical compositions, could win the support of moneyed New York liberals. For ALAN LOMAX and Mary Elizabeth Barnacle, she recorded her store of traditional Kentucky ballads and songs, some of which have been issued on Library of Congress albums. A highly creative singer and songwriter, she composed numerous songs out of her own experiences. The Folkways album cited below includes her own wonderfully dramatic narratives and some of her songs as interpreted by John Greenway.

Recordings: The Songs and Stories of Aunt Molly Jackson (Folkways, LP/cass FH 5457); *Aunt Molly Jackson—Library of Congress Recordings* (Rounder, LP 1002)

Jackson, John (1924–). In 1964 folklorists Chuck and Nan Perdue spotted an African American man at a gas station near Fairfax, Virginia, holding a guitar. They asked for a song, and in spite of his protestations of lack of skill, he overwhelmed them with his flawless fingerpicking and singing. This was John Jackson of Rappahannock County, Virginia, son of a tenant farmer who made his living doing odd jobs. His repertoire as represented on discs includes blues songs that he learned from 78-rpm recordings as well as older traditional ballads, spirituals, and songs.

Recording: John Jackson, *Don't Let Your Deal Go Down* (Arhoolie, CD 378)

Jarrell, Tommy (1901–1985). The son of Ben Jarrell, an influential musician of the 1920s, Thomas Jefferson Jarrell absorbed a rich musical tradition from turn-of-the-century Mt. Airy, North Carolina, where he was reared. Though he rarely played for thirty-five years, retirement and the death of his wife provided incentive to return to his music, and he shared it with an eager younger generation for two decades as a steady succession of banjo and fiddle players (many of them city born and bred) made the pilgrimage to Mt. Airy to learn at the master's knee. From 1968 until his death, he was one of the most influential traditional fiddlers and was recorded extensively, often in the company of his long-time friend, banjo player Fred Cockerham.

Recordings: Tommy Jarrell and Fred Cockerham, *Tommy & Fred* (County, CD 2702); *The Legacy of Tommy Jarrell, Vol. 1: Sail Away Ladies* (County, CD 2724)

Kazee, Buell (1900–1976). Kentucky native Kazee became interested in formal folksinging in college, when he realized that the ballads in his English literature classes were still being sung in his native region. Between 1927 and 1929, he made nearly sixty recordings for the Brunswick label, one of the most memorable (and frequently reissued) of which was his version of the old Anglo-American ballad "Lady Gay" (Child, 68). At the time, Kazee was preparing for the ministry, and he made no subsequent recordings until folklorist and banjo enthusiast Gene Bluestein visited him at his home in Lexington, Kentucky, in 1956 and taped their casual conversations, in which Kazee talked about his music and career and illustrated his comments with musical examples. An LP on the June Appal label, put together after Kazee's death, was taken mostly from tapes made by Mark Wilson around 1969. His recorded repertoire consisted of songs, ballads, and religious numbers, all accompanied by his own singing with his immaculate banjo playing.

Recordings: Buell Kazee Sings and Plays (Folkways, LP FS 3810); *Buell Kazee* (June Appal, LP 009)

Kincaid, Bradley (1895–1989). Bradley Kincaid, whose long career in music was documented by Loyal Jones, made his first recordings in 1928 and his last in the early 1970s. Born in the foothills of the Cumberland Mountains of Kentucky, he learned his first songs from his parents and continued consciously to collect long after his career was well underway, until his repertoire was well over 300 songs. He was very popular on radio especially in the Midwest, where his pleasant voice and plain singing style, accompanied by his own guitar, were very appropriate. When his own store of traditional material was exhausted, he solicited songs and ballads from friends and listeners of his radio programs. In his own way, he was a folk song collector just as were the more academic collectors such as CECIL SHARP and VANCE RANDOLPH. In 1928 he issued the first of a dozen songbooks, becoming the first hillbilly performer to do so and starting a popular tradition that other entertainers continued for decades. In 1963, he recorded 162 songs for a Texas record label, many of which have since been reissued on the Old Homestead label.

Recording: Bradley Kincaid, Old-Time Songs and Hymns (Old Homestead, OHCD 4014)

Kingston Trio. In the 1950s at Menlo College in Menlo Park, California, two young business administration students, Nick Reynolds (1933–) and Bob Shane (1934–) liked to get together and sing and play calypso and folk music. They were joined by Dave Guard (1934–1991), an economics student at nearby Stanford University who had grown up with Shane in Hawaii. After polishing their act carefully, they debuted in San Francisco's Purple Onion, where they remained for seven months. Since calypso music constituted an early important component of their repertoire, they took the name Kingston Trio, after the Jamaican port city and place name in several calypso songs. Their first album was issued in 1958, eventually capturing the number one position. Among its songs was a traditional American ballad about a North Carolina murder committed in 1866 called "Tom Dooley," a performance that, in spite of its nontraditional style, inaugurated a new wave of interest in traditional folk music.

Recording: Kingston Trio, *Greatest Hits* (Curb, CD 77385)

Ledbetter, Huddie (ca. 1888–1949). One of the first African American musicians to sing extensively for urban white audiences in the folk revival, "Leadbelly," as Ledbetter came to be known, was born in Louisiana near the Texas border. He showed a keen interest in music at an early age and learned to play both the accordion and the guitar. A powerfully built and sometimes short-tempered man, Leadbelly was frequently in trouble; he was twice sentenced to the penitentiary for long terms. While he was in prison for attempted murder in 1933, John and Alan Lomax came to record prisoners who knew traditional songs. The Lomaxes obtained a commercial contract for Leadbelly with the American Record Corp. soon after his pardon in 1935, and another with the RCA Victor Co. in the 1940s. For a period he was employed by the Lomaxes as chauffer on their cross-country song-collecting trips, and he helped to break the ice with African American performers. He proved surprisingly adept at learning songs from the Lomaxes's interviewees, adding them to his own immense repertoire. He and his wife served the Lomax household as hired domestics for a brief period, then moved East and took an apartment in New York City. A dynamic singer and imposing presence who played vigorously on a twelve-string guitar (and occasionally, piano or accordion), Leadbelly awed adult audiences and delighted children with his stories and songs.

Recordings: Leadbelly, *King of the 12-String Guitar* (Columbia, CK CD 46776); Leadbelly, *Library of Congress Recordings*, Vols. 1–6 (Rounder, CD 1044/5/6, 1097/8/9); *Leadbelly Sings Folk Songs* (Smithsonian Folkways, CD SF 40010; Folkways, FTS 31006); Leadbelly, *Bourgeois Blues* (Smithsonian Folkways, SF CD 40045); *Leadbelly Sings for Children* (Smithsonian Folkways, SF CD 45047)

Ledford, Lily May (1917–1985). Together with Violet Koehler and Daisy Lange, Ledford constituted the Coon Creek Girls, an eastern Kentucky hillbilly group that was prominent at the Renfro Valley Barn Dance from 1937 to 1957. They recorded commercially for Vocalion in 1938 and performed publicly before President and Mrs. Roosevelt and the king and queen of England in 1939. Later, Daisy and Violet left the group and were replaced by Lily May's sisters, Susie and Rosie. Lily Mae Ledford (Pennington) was noted for her fine vocals and driving, frailing banjo playing in the style characteristic of Kentucky.

Recordings: *The Coon Creek Girls* (County, LP 712); Lily May Ledford, *Banjo Pickin' Girl* (Greenhays, LP GR712); Lily May Ledford, *Gems* (June Appal, CD 0078)

Limeliters, The. Glen Yarbrough (1930–) and Alex Hassilev (1932–) co-owned the Aspen, Colorado, club, The Limelite, and occasionally performed together. In Los Angeles, while performing at Cosmo Alley in 1959, they met Louis Gottlieb (1923–), who had been a member of the Gateway Singers in 1950s but left to complete his Ph.D. in musicology at UCLA. Later that year, they appeared in San Francisco's popular night spot "hungry " and were a raving success. Their first album, *The Limeliters*, was issued on RCA Victor in 1960. Their repertoire included Spanish, Mexican, Russian, and Yiddish favorites as well as American folk songs.

Recording: The Limeliters (Collector's Choice, CD 264)

Lipscomb, Mance (1895–1976). Texas sharecropper Mance Lipscomb was one of a handful of African American songsters whose repertoire represented the pre-blues tradition of the late nineteenth and early twentieth centuries. He made no recordings until he was visited by collectors Chris Strachwitz and Mack McCormick in 1960, and in the years until his death he made several LPs and appeared at numerous folk festivals and coffeehouses. A fine guitarist and singer, most of his recordings have been transferred to CDs.

Recordings: Mance Lipscomb, *Texas Blues Guitar* (Arhoolie, CD 001); Mance Lipscomb, *Texas Songster* (Arhoolie, CD 306); Mance Lipscomb, *Captain, Captain!* (Arhoolie, CD 465)

Video: Mance Lipscomb in Concert (Video and DVD: Vestapol, 13011)

Lomax, Alan (1915–2002). Alan Lomax, son and collaborator of JOHN A. LOMAX, was the individual most responsible for the resurgence of interest in traditional folk song in America in the late twentieth century. He regarded as his main strength his ability to make singers feel at ease in front of the microphone, and his legacy is an enormous collection of some of the greatest recordings of traditional American songlore ever made. His fieldwork was not confined to the United States (although he collected most extensively in the Southeast and Southwest); he also ventured into the British Isles and Italy, where Alan cooperated with local experts to produce outstanding collections. In later years, he turned from recorded audio media to visual ones and produced a number of outstanding film documentaries.

Lomax, John Avery (1867–1948). Though he was born in Mississippi, John Lomax was reared in Texas, where his family moved when he was two. He grew up hearing cowboy songs and slave hymns and took degrees at the University of Texas in Austin (1895) and at Harvard (1907). At Harvard he impressed English scholars George Lyman Kittredge and Barrett Wendell with some of the texts he had collected years earlier, and they facilitated his receiving a scholarship so he could travel through the Southwest to collect songs. His book, *Cowboy Songs and Other Frontier Ballads* (1910 and later editions) was the first fruit of that work. In the 1930s, a series of field trips with his son, ALAN LOMAX, under the auspices of the Library of Congress resulted in a collection of 10,000 recordings, which formed the basis for several published collections of American folk songs. Lomax's orientation was not so much to preserve songs in precisely the form found as to make them available to a broader public and thereby reinvigorate American singing traditions.

Lunsford, Bascom Lamar (1882–1973). Bascom Lamar Lunsford, born in Madison County, North Carolina, was a legendary figure in the Asheville,

North Carolina, area. Trained as a lawyer, his love for his native music led him to collect and learn hundreds of songs and ballads and to start the annual Mountain Dance and Folk Festival in 1928. He made his first recordings on cylinders in 1922 for Frank C. Brown of the University of North Carolina and his first commercial recordings in 1924 for the OKeh label; then in 1935, he recorded over 300 numbers at Columbia University in New York City (subsequently deposited at the Library of Congress Archive of American Folk Song). In the 1930s and 1940s, he appeared regularly at folk festivals and on college campuses; in 1939, he was invited to sing before King George V and Queen Elizabeth at the White House. Lunsford had a rather hard, abrasive voice and generally accompanied himself on banjo. He was aware of the inconsistency in his roles of tradition bearer—trying faithfully to reproduce the songs and ballads as he learned them—and of entertainer—composing, recomposing, and adapting his material to suit his audiences.

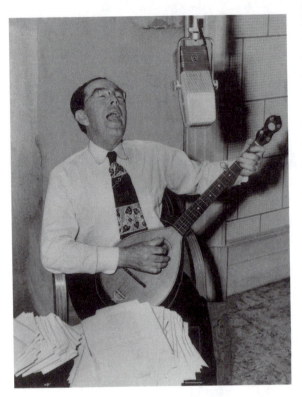

Bascom Lamar Lunsford recording at the Library of Congress Archive of Folk Song (1949). The instrument seems to be a homemade banjo-mandolin hybrid. *Copyright Washington Post, reprinted by permission of the DC Public Library.*

Recording: Bascom Lamar Lunsford, *Ballads, Banjo Tunes, and Sacred Songs of Western North Carolina* (Smithsonian Folkways, SF CD-40082)

Macon, Uncle Dave (1870–1952). David Harrison Macon was one of the greatest hillbilly stars of radio, stage, and records in the 1920s and 1930s. Born in Warren County, Tennessee, Macon was nearly fifty years old before he sought payment for his music. He made his first recordings in 1924, when the hillbilly recording industry was just beginning, and was a featured star on Grand Ole Opry almost until his death. His repertoire included some older Anglo-American traditional ballads and songs, a selection of religious songs, and a large portion of material from the late nineteenth-century minstrel and vaudeville stages. Two years before his death, folklorist Charles Faulkner Bryan taped him at his home, material which has since been issued on LP and presents a more reflective, personal side.

Recordings: Uncle Dave Macon, *Go Long Mule* (County, CD-3505); Uncle Dave Macon, *Country Music Hall of Fame Series* (MCA, MCAD-10546); *Uncle Dave Macon at Home: His Last Recordings, 1950* (Bear Family, LP BFX 15214); Uncle Dave Macon, *Keep My Skillet Good and Greasy* (Bear Family, BCD 15978 JM, 10 CDs and book set)

Martin, Asa (1900–1979). Asa Martin from Clark County, Kentucky, appeared extensively on commercial hillbilly recordings in the 1920s and 1930s and also in personal performances in his part of the state well into the 1940s. In 1972 and 1973, he was recorded again with a new band and for a new audience. His repertoire consists mainly of local songs and ballads and of pieces from the late minstrel stage and Tin Pan Alley of the early 1900s.

Recording: Asa Martin and the Cumberland Rangers, *Dr. Ginger Blue* (Rounder, 0034)

McCarn, Dave (1905–1964). David McCarn was born in Gaston County, North Carolina, and spent most of his working life in the cotton mills in Gastonia. In 1930 McCarn and his brother quit their jobs and started traveling around the country. They found themselves in Memphis at the same time that Ralph Peer's Victor recording outfit was in the city, and McCarn auditioned for a recording. An excellent guitarist, singer, and songwriter, he sang some older traditional numbers as well as some of his own witty compositions about the hardships of working in the cotton mill. Some of his recordings were picked up and copied by other artists, from both country and city, but he made no more recordings after 1930. He spent his last years as a TV repairman. No full record albums or compact discs of his recordings have been reissued.

McClintock, Harry (1882–1957). Born in Knoxville, Tennessee, Harry "Haywire Mac" McClintock had an adventure-packed youth. He ran away from home and a longtime position as choirboy to join a dog-and-pony show at the age of fourteen, but he left that after a month and hopped a west-bound freight train. He hoboed around the country for four years, paying his way by singing songs, eventually to his own banjo accompaniment. In 1897 he wrote (or revised and popularized) two songs destined to become American classics of wanderlust, "Big Rock Candy Mountain" and "Hallelujah, I'm a Bum." Between 1902 and 1903, he was a muleskinner in the Philippines and then in Portuguese East Africa, a journalist's aide in China, a railroad brakeman in Rhodesia, a seaman and stevedore, and a rugby player in Australia before returning to the United States. For the next several years, he worked for various railroads, taking time out to sing at political rallies for Jack London when he ran for mayor of Oakland, California, and singing and playing banjo or guitar whenever he had a few days in some small town. In San Francisco in 1925, he was offered a radio program telling tales of his adventures, singing songs, and playing guitar. In 1938 Mac moved to Hollywood and joined the *Happy Go Lucky* network radio show and played bit parts in several Gene Autry movies. Steeped in traditional songlore, Mac was neither the stereotypical naive rustic folksinger nor the trained citybilly who learns folk songs for the purposes of becoming a professional musician; rather, he was a natural entertainer who composed songs in the traditional style that surrounded him throughout his early life.

Recording: Haywire Mac (Folkways, LP/Cass FD 5272)

McCurdy, Ed (1919–2000). Born in Pennsylvania, Ed McCurdy began his career as a professional folksinger in 1946 on the radio with the Canadian Broadcasting Corporation, though he had sung gospel music professionally in Oklahoma City as early as 1937. He recorded traditional ballads and bawdy songs from Elizabethan England extensively in the early 1950s and wrote a celebrated antiwar song, "Last Night I Had the Strangest Dream." A paralysis interrupted his singing career between 1966 and 1970, after which he resumed recording.

Recording: Alan Lomax and Ed McCurdy, *Cowboy Songs of the Old West* (Music Digital, CD 6338)

McGhee, Brownie, and Sonny Terry. Singer and guitarist Walter Brown McGhee (1915–1996) and his longtime musical partner, singer and harmonica player Saunders Terrill (1911–1986), recorded blues songs in the early 1940s for African American patrons before becoming involved in the folk revival that popularized their music among a very different type of audience. Their repertoire balanced older traditional blues and African American ballads with contemporary blues and songs of their own composition.

Recordings: Brownie McGhee, *Brownie's Blues* (Prestige, CD OBC-505; Prestige, LP BV-1042); Sonny Terry, *Sonny Is King* (Prestige, CD OBC-521; Prestige, BV-1059); *The Complete Brownie McGhee* (CBS/Columbia, C2K 52933)

Video: Brownie McGhee and Sonny Terry, *Red River Blues* (DVD: Vestapol, 13056)

Monroe, Bill (1911–1996). Born into a poor farming family in west central Kentucky, William Smith Monroe numbered among his early musical influences his maternal uncle, Pendleton Vandiver, and a local African American musician, Arnold Shultz. In the 1930s Monroe and his brothers began performing on local radio stations, and by 1935 he had turned to music as a fulltime profession. He and his brother, Charlie, recorded a series of highly influential songs for the RCA Victor and Bluebird labels from 1936 through 1938. In the 1940s he developed a style of string band ensemble music and combined elements of older traditional southeastern string band music with influences from the commercial country music of the time. He named his band the Bluegrass Boys, after his native Kentucky, the bluegrass state, and the music—quickly emulated by other bands—soon came to be called bluegrass music.

Recordings: The Essential Bill Monroe and His Bluegrass Boys, 1945–49 (Columbia, CD C2K 42478); Bill Monroe, *Blue Grass, 1950–1958* (Bear Family, BCD 15423)

Video: High Lonesome: The Story of Bluegrass Music (Video and DVD: Shanachie, 604)

New Lost City Ramblers. The New Lost City Ramblers (NLCR) were the first folk revival performers successfully to consider style as an important element of folk music. They were also among the first to draw attention to a previously neglected aspect of Anglo-American folk music: commercial hillbilly records of the 1920s and 1930s. The trio, formed in mid-1958, initially consisted of MIKE SEEGER (1933–), Tom Paley (1928–), and John Cohen (1932–). Though all were New York City born and bred, the NLCR immersed themselves in the musical culture that they were portraying on stage and in the studio. Cohen met Paley when they were both students at Yale, and the two began playing together. A professional photographer, Cohen's musical and artistic interests took him into the mountains of Kentucky (and later, Peru) to photograph and record traditional music and musicians. Seeger met the other two when Cohen came to Maryland to visit Paley, and the three formed the NLCR. In 1962 Paley left the group and moved to England, where he resumed teaching and became involved with the British folk revival. He was replaced by Tracy Schwarz (1938–), also born in New York. Through the early 1960s, the Ramblers were regulars at college folk music festivals and coffeehouses across the country. They produced field recordings, worked with traditional artists, compiled an excellent songbook, *The New Lost City Ramblers Song Book* (Oak, 1964), wrote articles in *Sing Out!* and other periodicals, and contributed immensely to the serious aspects of the folk revival in general and the preservation and dissemination of old-time and traditional music in particular.

Recordings: New Lost City Ramblers, *The Early Years, 1958–1962* (Smithsonian Folkways, CD SF 40036); New Lost City Ramblers, *There Ain't No Way Out* (Smithsonian Folkways, SF-CD 40098); *The New Lost City Ramblers & Friends* (Vanguard, 77011-2, from the Newport Folk Festival)

Niles, John Jacob (1892–1980). John Jacob Niles was at one time called "the dean of American balladeers." Born in Louisville, Kentucky, he was steeped in traditional folk music in his youth but was classically trained in conservatories in the United States and Europe. In the late 1920s he published two song collections that resulted from his experiences in the army during World War I, and during the 1920s and 1930s, he prepared ten small folk song collections for the music publisher, G. Schirmer. From 1939 through 1941, he recorded several 78-rpm albums for RCA Victor, and a few years later, he recorded four albums for Moses Asch's new Disc label. Niles claimed to have done extensive song collecting in the Appalachians and published and/or recorded many rare ballads that were otherwise practically unknown in the United States. For this reason and also because of some lack of forthrightness in identifying his informants, some scholars have questioned the authenticity of his sources. His musical renditions are highly idiosyncratic and unlike anything anyone else has ever recorded in the field. Some songs that he performed were presented to the public as songs that he had collected; this was during a period when great prestige attached to having gone "into the field" and collected rare and unusual folk songs. Whatever the source—probably more his own creativity at work than anyone else's—Niles was responsible for some beautiful songs that became classics of the folk revival of the 1950s and 1960s, including "Go Way from My Window," "I Wonder as I Wander," "Black, Black, Black Is the Color," "Venezuela," and "Lass from the Low

Countrie." Unintentionally, he played an important role in the folk revival by drawing attention to the question of fidelity to tradition in the artistic presentation of folk songs.

Recordings: John Jacob Niles Sings Folk Songs (Folkways, FA LP/Cass 2373); John Jacob Niles, *Folk Balladeer* (RCA Victor, LP LPV-513)

Odetta (1930–). Odetta Holmes was born in Alabama but grew up in Los Angeles where she sang and acted on the stage. Singing gigs at the "hungry" club and the Tin Angel in San Francisco in 1953 and 1954 led to her first record. Her repertoire included sea shanties, Woody Guthrie compositions, and Anglo-American ballads and songs, but she excelled in African American spirituals, work songs, and blues.

Recording: Essential Odetta (Vanguard, VCD 43/44)

Ohrlin, Glenn (1926–). Born in Minneapolis, Ohrlin left home in California at the age of sixteen to ride horses in Nevada. In 1943 he started working rodeos as well as working as a cowboy. He enjoyed singing from childhood and frequently entertained friends in bars, bunkhouses, or rodeo arenas. His gravelly voice, laconic presentation, and wry wit (all true to the idiom), make him the quintessential cowboy performer; his interest in songs prompted him to collect from friends and associates whenever he could. Besides several albums to his credit, he has written an engaging book on cowboy and Western songs, *The Hell-Bound Train* (University of Illinois Press, 1973). Brochure notes to his albums often include Ohrlin's own extensive comments on his sources for most of the numbers, as well as text and tune transcriptions, biographical background information, and some of Ohrlin's own pen-and-ink sketches.

Recording: Glenn Ohrlin, A Cowboy's Life (Rounder, CD 0420)

Older, Lawrence (ca. 1913–1982). Lawrence Older, a singer and fiddler from the southern Adirondack Mountains, learned most of his songs and tunes from his family, which traces its emigration to America to British Regular Thomas Older, who arrived in 1749. Like most Northeastern singers, Older sings in a confident but undecorated style, accompanying himself competently on guitar or fiddle.

Recording: Lawrence Older, Adirondack Songs, Ballads, & Tunes (Folk Legacy, CD-15)

Peter, Paul and Mary. In the wake of the Kingston Trio, Peter, Paul and Mary (PP&M) were among the groups most responsible for broadening the appeal of folk music to large, nationwide audiences. Mary Travers (1936–), born in Louisville, Kentucky, but reared in New York, attended progressive private schools where folk music provided cultural enrichment. Noel Stookey (1937–) grew up in Baltimore and moved to New York in 1958, where he encountered folk music in Greenwich Village and decided on a career as an entertainer. He met Travers at the Village nightclub, the Gaslight, and they decided to work together. Peter Yarrow (1938–) was born in New York City and early on listened to folk music by Woody Guthrie, Burl Ives, Pete Seeger, and Josh White. While a student at Cornell University, he took to performing publicly, and upon graduation went to Greenwich Village hoping to launch a career. His manager, Albert Grossman, brought the threesome together hoping for a combination that would top the Kingston Trio, renaming Stookey "Paul" for a better group name. The three began coffeehouse appearances in 1961, and the following year, their first album, *Peter, Paul & Mary* (WB W 1449), swept the country. From this album, their rendition of Lee Hays's "If I Had a Hammer" was released as a single and lasted twelve weeks on the pop music charts. A few older traditional songs reached the pop charts from 1963 through 1966: "Stewball," "Tell It on the Mountain," and "Cruel War." During those years, PP&M were one of the most popular "folk" acts in the country. By the time the trio broke up in 1970, they had released ten albums, five of which were million sellers. Apart from their musical success, PP&M broke new ground by being among the first folk/pop artists to take outspoken stands on controversial issues, in particular, the Civil Rights movement and the opposition to the war in Vietnam.

Recording: Peter, Paul & Mary (Warner Brothers, CD 1449)

Presnell, Monroe, & Family. From 1961 to 1964, folk collector Sandy Paton found a wealth of traditional songlore in the Beech Mountain region in northwestern North Carolina. One of his best singers was Lee Monroe Presnell (ca. 1875–1963); others were Presnell's daughters, niece, and their children.

Though Presnell was well past his prime as a singer, his grand style was still apparent. Two outstanding albums were issued from this stunning material, the first of which in particular represents some of the best in traditional Anglo-American balladry.

Recordings: Traditional Music of Beech Mountain, No. Carolina, Vol. 1: The Older Ballads and Sacred Songs (Folk Legacy, CD-22); *Traditional Music of Beech Mountain, No. Carolina, Vol. 2: The Later Songs and Hymns* (Folk Legacy, CD-23)

Proffitt, Frank (1913–1965). In the pages of the history of the folk song revival, Frank Proffitt earns a footnote as the ultimate source of the Kingston Trio's highly successful "Tom Dooley." Proffitt loved old songs and ballads and consciously learned and preserved them. Born in Laurel Bloomery, North Carolina, Proffitt made his living farming tobacco and carpentering, supplementing his income by making and selling fretless banjos and dulcimers.

Frank Proffitt with a fretless banjo in Reese, North Carolina (Wautauga County, ca. 1962). *Photographer, Sandy Paton; Courtesy of Folk Legacy Records.*

Although Frank and Ann Warner collected songs from him as early as 1938, the first recordings were made in 1961 by Sandy and Caroline Paton and issued on Folkways. The following year, the Patons recorded him again and featured him on the first album on the Patons' new Folk Legacy record label, of which most of the material has been reissued recently. Most of Proffitt's songs are sung with his own banjo accompaniment.

Recordings: Frank Proffitt Sings Folk Songs (Folkways, FA LP/Cass 2360); *Frank Proffitt of Reese, NC: Traditional Songs and Ballads of Appalachia* (Folk Legacy, CD-1)

Ramsey, Obray (1913–1997). Banjo player and singer Obray Ramsey was born on the edge of the Great Smoky Mountains in western North Carolina, where he learned most of his songs from his mother and grandmother. In his early years, Ramsey sang mostly unaccompanied, but in 1953 BASCOM LAMAR LUNSFORD induced him to sing at his Asheville Folk Festival and in return gave him a banjo and urged him to learn to play it. The Riverside album was Ramsey's first, featuring his singing and banjo playing in a program of mostly well-known traditional songs. One of Ramsey's gems on Prestige 13020 is the white blues song "Rain and Snow," which was the source of a later hit by the Grateful Dead.

Recordings: Obray Ramsey, *Banjo Songs of the Blue Ridge and Great Smokies* (Riverside, LP 12-649); *Obray Ramsey Sings Folk Songs from the Three Laurels* (Prestige, LP INT 13020); Obray Ramsey, *Folk Songs from the Gateways to the Great Smokies* (Prestige, LP Int 13030)

Randolph, Vance (1892–1980). A native of Kansas, Vance Randolph moved to the Ozarks in 1920, where he spent the next six decades collecting and writing about Ozark speech, customs, folklore, and songs. His four-volume *Ozark Folk-Songs* (1946–1950) remains one of the best regional collections of traditional folk songs, partly because, unlike many of his predecessors, Randolph was not reluctant to collect and publish songs that he knew were no older than the 1920s.

Riddle, Almeda (1892–1980). Granny Riddle of Heber Springs, Arkansas, was one of America's great American ballad singers. Her extensive repertoire has been the subject of five full record albums and a book-length autobiography edited by Roger Abrahams. Riddle was an especially active tradition bearer, always seeking out better versions of songs in her repertoire and re-shaping her texts accordingly. She was first recorded in 1959 by Alan Lomax after a tip from John Quincy Wolfe, who had met her in 1952. Unlike many of the great Appalachian singers with whom she is often compared, Granny Riddle's singing style was marked by a rock-solid meter rather than a *rubato parlando*. Riddle generally had the fullest text ever recorded of any ballad that she sang, collating songs from various sources when she did not remember all the words that she had known in her youth.

Recordings: Granny Riddle's Songs and Ballads (Minstrel, CD JD-203); Various artists, *Lomax Collection, Vol. 7: Ozark Frontier—Ballads and Old-Timey Music from Arkansas*

(Rounder, CD 1707, includes seven selections by Riddle); Various artists, *Sounds of the South* (Atlantic, 7-82496-2, includes five selections by Riddle)

Ritchie, Jean (1922–). Kentucky-born Jean Ritchie went to New York in 1947, after graduating from the University of Kentucky with a degree in social work, to teach children's songs and dances at the Henry Street Settlement House summer camp. She found there an urban audience for the folk music that had been part of her life, and she began an involvement with the folk revival that has never stopped. In the half century since, she has recorded more than forty albums. Initially confining herself to her own store of Kentucky ballads, songs, and dulcimer tunes, she later developed into a songwriter of skill and sensitivity, able to fill in the lapses in her own memory or even write an entirely new composition without departing from the traditional style that is part of her cultural heritage. Ritchie sings in a beautiful high soprano voice with heavy vibrato not usually associated with the southern Appalachians. For an audience unfamiliar with traditional singing styles, Ritchie's recordings are an easy introduction to the best of older Anglo-American balladry. Ritchie often accompanies herself on the plucked dulcimer.

Recordings: Jean Ritchie, *None but One/High Hills and Mountains* (Greenhays, CD GR 70708); *The Ritchie Family of Kentucky* (Folkways, LP/Cass 02316); Jean Ritchie, *Ballads from Her Appalachian Family Tradition* (Smithsonian Folkways, SFW CD 40145)

Robeson, Paul (1898–1976). Born and reared in New Jersey, Paul Robeson distinguished himself in several fields at Rutgers University, lettering in football and earning a bachelor's degree in 1919. At Columbia University in New York City, while earning his law degree, he took up acting and also classical singing. He gave his first concert in 1925, featuring African American spirituals and folk songs. In the following decades, he continued his brilliant career on stage and was renowned for playing Othello and singing "Old Man River" in *Showboat*, as well as in concert. In the 1930s he took up the fight for civil rights for African Americans and became sympathetic to the Soviet Union, where he saw no evidence of racial prejudice. His Soviet leanings led to the revocation of his U.S. passport, and many artistic venues were closed off to him for many years. Eventually the passport, and his honor, were restored, and he enjoyed several more years of celebrity.

Recordings: Paul Robeson, *The Power and the Glory* (Columbia, CK CD 47337); Paul Robeson, *Live at Carnegie Hall* (Vanguard, VCD 72020)

Rogers, Grant (1907–1979). Grant Rogers was born in Walton, New York. He learned to play the fiddle when quite young and was already playing for dances in the Delaware River Valley by age seven. Much later, he began to play guitar and write his own songs. By 1950, he was sufficiently well known as a local performer that Norman Studer invited him to perform at Camp Woodland, where he came to the attention of other folk song enthusiasts. Rogers was a good example of a contemporary regional folk musician, who added to his repertoire of older material with songs learned from hillbilly phonograph recordings as well as his own locally based compositions as the need or mood arose.

Recordings: Grant Rogers, *Songmaker of the Catskills* (Folk Legacy, LP FSA-27); Grant Rogers, *Ballad Singer* (Kanawha, LP 308)

Sandburg, Carl (1878–1967). Though he is known primarily as a poet and novelist, Carl Sandburg collected folk songs during his wanderings about the country, and in the 1920s he began the practice of closing each of his poetry recitations with a few folk songs to his own rather unusual guitar accompaniment. In 1927 he put out *The American Songbag*, one of the first general collections of American folk songs intended primarily for singing rather than scholarly use. He made a handful of recordings for Victor in 1926 and several albums in the following decades.

Recording: *The Great Carl Sandburg: Songs of America* (Lyrichord, CD 6003)

Seeger, Mike (1933–). Michael Seeger, eldest child of musicologist Charles Seeger and musician Ruth Crawford Seeger, was born in New York City and grew up in a household where traditional music was constantly available. He learned to play numerous instruments, including banjo, fiddle, guitar, autoharp, and harmonica, and in the early 1950s, he began to travel through the Appalachians finding and recording traditional singers and musicians. In the late 1950s, Seeger began to issue an important series of albums on the Folkways label documenting Southeastern rural music—collections that constituted some of the most important fieldwork in the area since the work of JOHN LOMAX and ALAN LOMAX. In 1958 Seeger, Tom Paley, and John Cohen formed the NEW LOST CITY RAMBLERS, but Seeger also continued to make solo recordings. Years of informal study and respect for those musical traditions, together with his exceptional musical abilities, make him one of the foremost interpreters and re-creators of traditional American music of many genres.

Recordings: Mike Seeger, *Solo: Old Time Music* (Rounder, CD 0278); Mike Seeger and Paul Brown, *Way Down in North Carolina* (Rounder, CD 0383); Mike Seeger, *Southern Banjo Sounds* (Smithsonian Folkways, SFW-CD-40107); Mike Seeger, *True Vine* (Smithsonian Folkways, SFW CD 40136)

Seeger, Peggy (1935–). Peggy Seeger, sister of Mike and half-sister of Pete, was born in New York City and, growing up in the Seeger household, was early exposed to traditional American music. She went to England in 1956, where she became a member of a folk song quartet that included Scottish songwriter, playwright, and singer Ewan MacColl, whom she married two years before settling permanently in England. From the 1950s on, she made a number of albums of traditional songs and ballads, some alone, others with MacColl or other members of the Seeger family. On most of her recordings, she accompanied herself with banjo or guitar.

Recording: Peggy Seeger, *The Folkways Years, 1955–1992* (Smithsonian Folkways, CD SF 40048)

Seeger, Pete (1919–). Son of renowned musicologist, Charles Seeger, Peter was born in New York City and spent his early school years in New England boarding schools. There his interests were divided between journalism, painting, and music, and each of the three became his planned vocation at one time. In 1936 Pete and his father attended the 9th Annual Mountain Song and Dance Festival in Asheville, North Carolina. There, Pete heard the five-string banjo playing traditional Appalachian music, and it immediately captured his fancy. He entered Harvard as his father had done before him but dropped out of a chosen career in journalism before graduating. After a bicycling trip across country, he returned to New York City and looked for jobs, occasionally singing and playing the banjo on street corners for small change. In 1938 ALAN LOMAX, then assistant-in-charge of the Archive of American Folk Song, invited Seeger to come to Washington to become his assistant. In 1940 Seeger and WOODY GUTHRIE became the nucleus of a group, the ALMANAC SINGERS, whose activities centered on labor and protest songs performed for various labor and liberal organizations. After World War II ended, Seeger helped organize an informal liberal songwriters' union called People's Songs, which promoted contemporary political and protest songs and songwriters, as well as more traditional material. In addition to his work with the WEAVERS, Seeger continued his own active career on stage and in the recording studio, resulting in more than three dozen albums. Seeger's repertoire always included a mix of traditional songs, ballads, and blues along with international traditional pieces and contemporary songs written by himself and others. A dynamic personality on stage, his vigorous playing and singing never fail to warm up an audience, who he invariably induces to sing along with him.

Recordings: Pete Seeger, *Darling Corey and Goofing Off Suite* (Smithsonian Folkways, CD SF 40018); Pete Seeger, *American Industrial Ballads* (Smithsonian Folkways, SFW-CD-40058; Folkways, FA 5251); Pete Seeger, *American Favorite Ballads, Vol. 1* (Smithsonian Folkways, SFW-CD-40150); Pete Seeger, *Abiyoyo and Other Songs* (Smithsonian Folkways, CD SF 45001); *The Essential Pete Seeger* (Vanguard, VCD-97-98)

Sharp, Cecil James (1859–1924). English folk song collector and educator Cecil Sharp became interested in traditional English music as an adjunct to his music teaching. After extensive field collecting in England, he traveled to the United States where, in 1916 through 1918, he spent forty-six weeks in the southern Appalachians and collected several thousands songs and tunes, amounting to the first major collection from the region. Sharp was amazed to find that, whereas in his native England ballad singing was confined to the oldest residents, in the Appalachians people of all ages knew them.

Simon & Garfunkel. Paul Simon (b. 1941) and Art Garfunkel (b. 1941) grew up together in Queens, New York, and began singing pop songs in high school. After a brief recording career under the pseudonyms of Tom and Jerry in the mid-1950s, they abandoned their joint career for several years. They got together again in 1962 and, starting in 1964, issued a string of highly successful albums for Columbia Records. Though most of their material was written by Simon, their repertoires included material assimilated via the folk revival— most notably their hit, "Scarborough Fair/Canticle," which overlays an early Anglo-American ballad (Child, 4) with a modern anti-war lyric. Both continued to record after their musical partnership terminated in about 1970.

Recording: Simon & Garfunkel, *Parsley, Sage, Rosemary and Thyme* (Sony, CD 66001)

Smith, Hobart (1897–1965). Hobart Smith was born in Smyth County, Virginia, the seventh generation of Smiths in Virginia since his ancestors emigrated from England. He began playing banjo when seven years old and later learned guitar, fiddle, and piano, becoming remarkably adept on all of them. He was first recorded by ALAN LOMAX in 1942 for the Library of Congress and subsequently on the Disc, Tradition, Atlantic, and Prestige labels. Smith often performed locally during the 1930s and 1940s, and his repertoire included country tunes of the day. It was Alan Lomax who urged him to "pull back into the old folk music."

Recordings: Hobart Smith, *Blue Ridge Legacy* (Rounder, CD 1799); Hobart Smith, *America's Greatest Folk Instrumentalist* (Folk Legacy, LP FSA-17)

Snow, Kilby (1905–1980). Some of the best known traditional autoharp players have come from Virginia, and John Kilby Snow of Grayson County was one of the finest to be recorded. In addition to instrumental numbers, Snow's repertoire includes some older ballads, contemporary country songs, and original compositions.

Recording: Kilby Snow, *Country Songs and Tunes with Autoharp* (Asch, LP AH 3902)

Sprague, Carl T. (1895–1978). One of the first Westerners to record cowboy songs was Carl T. Sprague. During his college years at Texas A&M, Sprague had his own band, and after he joined the school's athletic department, he hosted a regular program on the college radio station. Vernon Dalhart's phenomenal success with "The Prisoner's Song" convinced Sprague to contact the Victor Talking Machine Company to see if he could record some of his cowboy songs, which he did in the summer of 1925. Sprague recorded several times for Victor in the next four years and then gave up his musical career—until the folk revival of the 1960s lured him back to college campuses to sing some of his old favorites. From 1972 through 1974, he taped a number of his old songs, which were issued in Germany by the Bear Family label and subsequently reissued.

Recordings: Carl T. Sprague, *Classic Cowboy Songs* (Bear Family, BCD 15456); Carl T. Sprague, *Cowtrails, Longhorns, and Tight Saddles* (Bear Family, BCD 15979)

Stanley, Ralph and Carter. Brothers Carter (1925–1966) and Ralph (1927–) Stanley and the Clinch Mountain Boys were one of the very first bluegrass bands to record commercially following BILL MONROE's development of the bluegrass style. Born in Stratton, Virginia, the brothers learned traditional music from their father, who sang, and from their mother, who played banjo. Throughout their professional careers, their repertoires varied from older traditional material to slick contemporary country/bluegrass. After Carter's death, Ralph continued his career with even more emphasis on the older songs and ballads. Ralph is an exceptional musician: a remarkable singer with a piercing, high-lonesome singing style, and a five-string banjo player proficient in many different styles.

Recordings: Ralph Stanley and the Clinch Mountain Boys, 1971–1973 (Rebel, REB-4001); Ralph Stanley & Clinch Mtn. Boys, *Bound to Ride—Vintage Mountain Bluegrass* (Rebel, CD-1114)

Steele, Pete (1891–1985). Pete Steele was born in Kentucky, but after several moves, he and his wife Lillie (who contributed occasional vocals) settled in Hamilton, Ohio, in 1937. ALAN LOMAX recorded them there in the following year for the Library of Congress. Two decades later, Ed Kahn and Art Rosenbaum visited the Steeles and recorded enough material for a full record on the Folkways label. Steele was a versatile banjo player and used several different styles (though always using only two fingers—thumb and forefinger), including frailing, double-thumbing, and up-picking. Steele's singing is unremarkable except for the charm of his matter-of-fact approach—in particular, in his performance of (and introduction to) "The War Is A-Ragin'," which was later recorded, reaching a much wider audience, by Peter, Paul and Mary and then Cher.

Recording: Pete Steele, *Banjo Tunes and Songs* (Folkways, LP FS 3828)

Tarlton, Jimmie (1892–1979). Johnny James "Jimmie" Rimbert Tarlton was born in Chesterfield County, South Carolina, where he learned to play banjo from his father and ballads from his mother and grandmother. After hearing traveling Hawaiian guitarists, he began playing Hawaiian-style guitar and, with his musical partner Tom Darby, recorded over seventy-five songs between 1927 and 1933. He was "rediscovered" in 1963 and for several years enjoyed a second musical career performing at folk festivals and coffeehouses during the halcyon folk song revival years, playing mostly steel-guitar style but occasionally banjo as he had in his youth. His repertoire ranged from old Child ballads to his own compositions ("Administration Blues," about Franklin D. Roosevelt's reelection) and recompositions of Tin Pan Alley songs ("My Blue Heaven"). At age seventy-one, when the solo album cited here was recorded, Tarlton was still an excellent singer, with a beautiful, high, clear voice, and an amazing guitarist, whose near-blindness did not prevent him from keeping an audience spellbound through his deft performances and stories.

Recordings: Jimmie Tarlton, *Steel Guitar Rag* (Hightone, CD HMG 2503; Testament, LP T-3302); Tom Darby and Jimmie Tarlton, *Complete Recordings* (Bear Family, BCD 15764)

Thompson, Ernest (1892–1961). Ernest Thompson of Winston-Salem, North Carolina, was one of the first traditional rural musicians to make commercial recordings, starting in 1924. In his youth various accidents left him nearly sightless and also damaged his throat, so that he sang in a raspy, high-pitched voice. He played several instruments, but on his recordings, he accompanied himself usually on guitar and sometimes on banjo.

Recording: Ernest Thompson, *Pioneer Artist from North Carolina* (British Archive of Country Music, BACM CD D 031)

Van Ronk, Dave (1936–2002). Brooklyn-born Van Ronk's early musical interests centered on jazz, which he played with various groups in New York in the 1950s, until he worked briefly with West Coast singer ODETTA and became more interested in traditional folk music and blues. He cut two albums for Folkways in 1959 and 1961 of such authentic-sounding blues that many listeners doubted that such a singer could be white. In the mid-1960s he turned more to jazz and jug band music than blues. In 1964 his group, the Ragtime Jug Stompers, put out an album of the same name on the Mercury label, and he continued to record and perform extensively through the 1970s and into the 1980s.

Recording: Dave Van Ronk, *The Folkways Years, 1959–1961* (Smithsonian Folkways, CD SF 40041)

Wallin, Doug (1919–2001). Born in ballad-rich Madison County, North Carolina, Douglas Wallin was awarded a Heritage Fellowship from the National Endowment for the Arts, which described him as "quite simply the finest living singer of unaccompanied British ballads in southern Appalachia." Coming from a family with a rich tradition of folk song and music (CECIL SHARP collected songs from his aunt and other near relatives, and DILLARD CHANDLER is his second cousin), Wallin has a large repertoire that he sings in the best Appalachian style, sometimes accompanying himself on fiddle. The Smithsonian compact disc cited here also includes a few tracks by his younger brother, Jack, who sings and accompanies himself on guitar or banjo.

Recording: Doug and Jack Wallin, *Family Songs and Stories from the North Carolina Mountains* (Smithsonian Folkways, SF CD 40013)

Ward, Fields (1911–1987). Fields Ward continued the Ward family musical tradition after the death of his father Crockett Ward and of his uncle, WADE WARD. Fields was only about fourteen when he made his first recordings playing guitar with Crockett Ward and His Boys for the OKeh label; at the time the band was dominated by Fields's father and older brothers. He then played with his father, uncle, and other in the Bogtrotters (see next entry). Several years later, the older Wards gave up playing regularly, and the Bogtrotters disbanded. Fields left the Galax, Virginia, area in 1947 and moved to Maryland, where he continued the rich Ward musical tradition for another four decades.

The Bogtrotters Band (Galax, Virginia): Doc Davis (autoharp), Uncle Alex Dunford (fiddle), Crockett Ward (fiddle), Wade Ward (banjo), and Fields Ward (guitar) (1937). *Photographer, CBS, at the time of the Alan Lomax School of the Air Broadcast in Galax (LC-USZ62-32439); from the Farm Security Administration—Office of War Information Photo Collection, Library of Congress Prints and Photographs Division.*

Recordings: Fields and Wade Ward (Biograph, LP RC-6002); Fields Ward & His Buck Mountain Band, *Early Country Music* (Historical, HLP-8001); Fields Ward, *Bury Me Not on the Prairie* (Rounder, LP 0036)

Ward, Wade; The Bogtrotters. Benjamin Wade Ward (1892–1971) is regarded as one of the finest traditional banjo players from the Southeast. He was born near Independence, in the southwest corner of Virginia not far from the North Carolina border, and lived all his life in that area. He began playing banjo at age eleven and took up fiddling five years later. In about 1922, the Grayson County Bogtrotters band formed, whose membership generally consisted of Wade Ward (banjo), his older brother Crockett Ward (fiddle), Crockett's son FIELDS (guitar), and neighbors Alec "Eck" Dunford (fiddle) and Dr. W. P. Davis (autoharp). This band made a few recordings for the OKeh label in New York in 1927. JOHN LOMAX recorded them more extensively for the Library of Congress at the Galax Old Time Fiddlers Convention in October 1937; a sampling of these recordings was issued on Biograph, LP RC-6003. A later sampling of Ward's music was issued on Folkways, FA 2380, compiled mostly from recordings made between 1958 and 1964 by Eric Davidson. The selections are banjo and fiddle tunes that date mostly from the turn of the century or earlier, many found only in Grayson and Carroll counties where Ward lived all his life.

Recordings: The Bogtrotters: 1937–1942 (Biograph, LP RC-6003, from Library of Congress recordings); *Uncle Wade: A Memorial to Wade Ward, Old Time Virginia Banjo Picker, 1892–1971* (Folkways, LP/Cass FA 2380)

Watson, Doc (1923–). The career of Doc Watson is a refreshing reminder that traditional music is not a static entity (if it were, it would still be played on skin drums and wood flutes) but that it changes in the hands of its more creative bearers. Arthel "Doc" Watson, born in Deep Gap, North Carolina, was "discovered" by folk collectors Ralph Rinzler and Eugene Earle as a musical associate of CLARENCE ASHLEY. At the time, he was playing electric guitar in a contemporary local rockabilly band. Through Rinzler's urging, he returned to his older musical roots and created a new (and far more commercially successful) career for himself. An engaging, articulate, and entertaining performer, Watson is one of the best traditional artists re-discovered by the folk revival of the 1960s and certainly the most successful in commercial terms. Fortunately, his commercial success, while providing the impetus to innovation and modification, has not enticed Doc too far from his musical roots. His first appearance on a record album was as an accompanist for Clarence Ashley's band—one of the best modern old-timey bands ever recorded. On the first Watson Family album (Folkways, FA 2366, recorded 1961–1962), he was presented as a traditional musician with a store of early hillbilly and pre-hillbilly ballads and tunes. Watson perceived what his patrons wanted and had the background and repertoire to be able to provide it. His repertoire moved forward somewhat in time with his string of Vanguard and Sugar Hill albums, occasionally venturing into the field of Broadway show tunes, jazz standards, and his (and his family's) own compositions. Watson is an intelligent and perceptive observer as well as performer, with a warm and ingratiating style that cannot but win over his audience, and his recordings show it.

Recordings: Doc Watson Family, *Tradition* (Rounder, CD 0129; Topic, LP 12TS336); *The Watson Family* (Smithsonian Folkways, CD SF 40012; Folkways, LP FA 2366); Doc Watson, *My Dear Old Southern Home* (Sugar Hill, SH-CD-3795); Doc Watson Family, *Songs from the Southern Mountains* (Sugar Hill, SH-CD-3929); Doc Watson, *The Vanguard Years* (Vanguard, 155/58-2, 4 CDs); Doc Watson & Family, *Treasures Untold* (Vanguard, VCD 77001)

Videos: Doc Watson: Rare Performances, 1963–1981 (Video and DVD: Vestapol, 13023); *Doc Watson: Rare Performances, 1982–1993* (Video and DVD: Vestapol, 13024)

Weavers. The Weavers, formed in 1948 in New York City, consisted of PETE SEEGER and Lee Hays (1914–1981), veterans of the ALMANAC SINGERS, and two younger members, Ronnie Gilbert, a secretary at CBS, and Fred Hellerman, a Brooklyn College graduate, baritone, and guitar and banjo player. The group made its first radio appearance on Oscar Brand's weekly folk music show on WNYC. The Weavers campaigned that fall for Vito Marcantonio,

American Labor Party candidate for the House of Representatives; made their first recordings for two small labels, Charter and Hootenanny; and during Christmas week of 1949, debuted at the nightclub, the Village Vanguard. As a result of that successful appearance, they were offered a contract with Decca. On May 4, 1950, they cut their first two records: a Hebrew version of "Tzena" and "Around the World." Three weeks later they recorded the single "Tzena" with English lyrics, backed with "Goodnight, Irene," and the disc sales shot rapidly past the two million mark. In 1951 the Weavers recorded their second million seller, "On Top of Old Smokey," backed by "The Wide Missouri" ("Shenandoah"). In the next two years, the Weavers recorded twenty-eight more songs for Decca, the last of which was released in February of 1953. In commercial terms, these recordings represented the peak of the Weavers' career. The success of the Decca records led to cross-country tours, appearances at the flashiest nightclubs in Hollywood, Las Vegas, and New York, radio spots, and television appearances. Success soured in 1951, as McCarthyism led to the hounding of public figures in all professions who had any alleged associations with "communist" or "communist-front" organizations. In spite of the apolitical nature of their Decca material, doors closed to the Weavers, and public appearances were cancelled. Nevertheless, they were still able to sell out two Christmas concerts that December. In February of 1952, an informant testified before the House Committee on Un-American Activities that three of the Weavers were members of the Communist Party, and consequently opportunities for public performances evaporated. Remarkably, they were still able to make six records for Decca after this debacle. They disbanded after their February 1953 recordings.

Recordings: The Weavers, *Wasn't That a Time* (Vanguard, VCD4-147/150, 4 CDs); *The Weavers at Carnegie Hall* (Vanguard, CD VMD-73101); *The Weavers at Carnegie Hall Vol. 2* (Vanguard, CD VMD 79075)

West, Hedy (1938–). Hedy West grew up in north Georgia in a poor family of hill farmers. She is the daughter of poet Don West, who taught her many of the coalmining songs he learned while he was a union organizer for the miners in the 1930s. Most of her other songs come from older family tradition. West accompanies her lovely singing with graceful banjo playing. The Bear Family release is a collection of songs "from and about farm workers, millhands, and miners," for which Hedy West drew (and continues to draw) from her own family tradition, most strongly represented by the repertoire of her grandmother. These are supplemented by selections from other sources, printed and recorded—sometimes to find alternative versions to songs and ballads West learned in her own youth. On her later albums, West has developed a conversational singing style, moving alternately between straight singing and almost talking.

Recordings: Hedy West, *Love, Hell, and Biscuits* (Bear Family, LP 15003); Hedy West, *Old Times and Hard Times* (Folk Legacy, LP FSA-32; Topic, LP 12T117); Hedy West, *Pretty Saro* (Topic, LP 12T146)

Workman, Nimrod (1895–1994). Born in Martin County, Kentucky, Workman grew up in a musical environment heavily influenced by the hardships of work in Kentucky and West Virginia's coalfields. His repertoire harbors some scarce old gems as well as more modern original compositions, many dealing with his own life experiences. He sings in a penetrating, stark voice, with the metrical freedom of the best *rubato parlando* style, sometimes joined by his daughter, Phyllis Boyens. Workman's own compositions often address with bitterness the problems of his fellow coalminers. He retired from forty-two years of mining in 1952, afflicted with black lung disease.

Recordings: Nimrod Workman and Phyllis Boyens, *Passing Thru the Garden* (June Appal, LP JA 001); Nimrod Workman, *Mother Jones' Will* (Rounder, LP 0076)

Appendix:
Plot Synopses of Traditional Ballads Most Commonly Found in the United States and Canada

POPULAR ("CHILD") BALLADS

Altogether about 125 of the 305 ballads listed in Child's compendium, *The English and Scottish Popular Ballads*, have been recovered in North America. The following are the ballads most often found. The number given represents the number assigned to them by Child in his book. After the title, the region and frequency is noted, as follows in this key:

Region Abbreviations:[1]	Frequency of Recovery:
SE = Southeast	+++ = collected more than 100 times
NE = Northeast	++ = collected 50 to 99 times
MW = Midwest	+ = 10 to 49 times
NW = Northwest	
C = Canada	

These indicators can be somewhat misleading because there has been so much more collecting activity in the Southeast than elsewhere; therefore, there are many marked as being collected over 100 times in the Southeast, but none for other regions. The synopses given are only for the most common versions; there can be many variant details and sometimes important additions to the story.

1   "Riddles Wisely Expounded," "The Devil's Nine Questions" (SE: +)
A stranger (sometimes demonic) challenges a maid or young boy with a series of questions that must be answered to escape his clutches.

2   "The Elfin Knight," "Scarborough Fair," "A True Lover of Mine," "Cambric Shirt," "Every Rose Grows Merry in Time" (NE: +, MW: +, SE: +)
Two would-be lovers challenge each other with impossible tasks.

4   "Lady Isabel and the Elf-Knight," "The False Knight," "Seven (Six) King's Daughters," "Pretty Polly" (SE: +++, NE: +, MW: +, C: +)
A knight (or would-be suitor) entices a maid to ride off with him; he threatens to drown her, but she must first remove her expensive clothes. She tells him to turn his back on account of her modesty, but she then pushes him in instead, and he drowns.

7   "Earl Brand," "Sweet William" (SE: ++)
A maid is carried off by her lover; her father and brothers pursue them but the lover slays them all in combat.

10   "The Two Sisters," "Lord by the North Sea," "The Miller's Two Daughters" (SE: +++, NE: +, MW: +)
A gentleman prefers the younger of two sisters; the jealous older sister drowns the younger, whose body is fished out of the stream by a miller. He makes a musical instrument out of part of her body, and it reveals the murderer.

11   "The Cruel Brother," "Lily O" (SE: +)
One of three suitors wins a girl's favor; he asks her parents for her hand but neglects to ask her brother. The brother slays the sister on the way to the wedding.

12   "Lord Randal," "Jimmy Randall," "Johnny Randolph" (NE: ++, SE: +++, MW: +, SW: +)
In a dialog between mother and son, the son reveals that he has visited his sweetheart and she has poisoned him; the dialog ends with the son's instructions to his mother for the distribution of his possessions (oral last will and testament).

13   "Edward," "The Little Yellow Dog," "Son David," "How Came That Blood on Your Shirt Sleeve" (SE: ++)
In a dialog between mother and son, the son reveals that he has slain his brother (sometimes father) in a dispute, the nature of which is at the most only hinted, and vows to leave, never to return.

18   "Sir Lionel," "(Old) Bangum and the Boar," "The Wild Hog (in the Woods)," "Jobal Hunter" (SE: +)
The hunter and his lady are in the woods, which are frequented by a wild boar. He blows his horn, the boar appears, and he slays it. In some versions, she first rejects his proposal, then accepts.

20   "The Cruel Mother," "Down by the Greenwood Side," "The Three Babes" (SE: ++, NE: +, C: +)
A woman bears the illegitimate children fathered by her husband's clerk, then slays them. Later she sees some children at play; they reveal that they are her own (in the form of spirits, or revenants) and foretell her fate in hell.

26   "The Three Ravens," "Two Corbies," "The Crow Song" (SE: ++, MW: +, NE: +)
Two or three raven-like birds wonder what they will dine upon, then see the corpse of some animal in the field, on which they feast.

46   "Captain Wedderburn's Courtship," "Captain Woodstock" (SE: +, NE: +)
A maid's suitor would lie with her, but she insists he answer several riddles first. In some versions, they marry.

49   "The Two Brothers," "The Little Schoolboy" (SE: ++)
One brother slays the other after a dispute, the cause of which is not always clear.

53   "Young Beichan," "Young Beham," "Lord Bateman (and the Turkish Lady)," "The Jailer's Daughter" (NE: +, SE +, C: ++)
The nobleman Bateman is captured by Turks while at sea; in prison, the Turkish jailer's daughter frees him after a mutual pact of fidelity for seven years. Back in England, he is about to wed when the daughter appears at his wedding, and he pledges to marry her instead (or in addition).

54   "The Cherry Tree Carol," "Joseph and Mary" (SE: ++)
Joseph and the pregnant Mary are en route to Jerusalem; Mary asks Joseph to pull down some cherries from a tree; he retorts that the father of her child should feed her. The unborn Christ then commands the tree to bow down and let Mary eat.

68   "Young Hunting," "Lord Barnet," "Love Henry," "Henry Lee," "Lowe Bonnie," "Song of a Lost Hunter" (SE: +++)
Returning from his hunt, Lord Henry is asked by his sweetheart to spend the night. He refuses, saying he loves another; she stabs him.

73   "Lord Thomas and Fair Annet (Eleanor)," "The Brown Girl," "Fair Eleanor (Ellender)" (SE: +++, NE: +, MW: +)
Thomas asks his mother whether he should wed the fair Ellen or the wealthy brown girl; she advises the latter. He invites Ellen to the wedding; she insults the bride, who stabs her. Thomas slays the bride and impales himself on his sword.

74   "Fair Margaret and Sweet William," "False William," "Lady Margaret's Ghost," "Little Margaret" (SE: +++, NE: +, MW: +)
Margaret sees William and his new bride from her window and is grief-stricken. That night her spirit appears at the bridal bed and asks whom he loves best. In the morning, he goes to her father's house, learns she is dead, and asks to see, then kiss, her corpse, after which he dies also.

75   "Lord Lovel," "Lady Nancy (Bell)" (SE: +++, NE: +, MW: +)
Lovel bids farewell to Nancy before riding off for distant parts. When he returns he learns she has died; he too dies of grief.

76   "The Lass of Roch Royal," "Who Will Shoe My Pretty Little Feet," "Lord Gregory" (SE: ++)
A girl with newborn babe sets off in a boat to seek her true love. When she reaches his house, his mother denies her entrance. After the girl sails off, the man returns, learns what happened, and hastens after the girl, just in time to see her drown.

79   "The Wife of Usher's Well," "The Lady Gay," "The Three Babes" (SE: +++)
A mother sends her sons off to learn their grammery (i.e., magic; the root for the words "grammar" and "glamour"). After they die there, their spirits return to her at Christmas time. They decline the food and drink she offers them and request her not to mourn them because her tears wet their winding sheets (burial shrouds).

81   "Little Musgrave and Lady Barnard," "Lord Banner," "Lord Daniel," "Matty Groves," "Mathy Grove" (SE: +++, NE: +, C: +)
While the lord is off hunting, his wife entices Matty Groves to spend the night with her. Her servant rides off to warn the lord, who races back and finds the two lovers in bed. He offers Matty the better of his swords before slaying him and then his wife.

84   "Bonny Barbara Allen," "Barbara Allen's Cruelty" (SE: +++, NE: +, MW: +, SW: +, C: ++)
After Barbara and William declare their mutual love, he slights her in the tavern; she is offended and ignores him. Despondent and dying, he begs her to come to him. She scorns him. After he dies, she has a change of heart and dies of grief as well.

85   "Lady Alice," "George Collins," "Giles Collins," "The Dying Hobo," "One Cold December Day" (SE: +++)
Collins rides home (sometimes after an encounter with a fairy love), takes sick, and dies. His sweetheart opens his coffin, kisses him, and dies, too.

93   "Lamkin," "Bold Lamkin," "Bolakin," "Cruel Lincoln" (SE: ++, NE: +, MW: +)
The mason Lamkin is not paid for the work he performs for a lord; he gains entrance to the house in the lord's absence and with the collusion of a nurse first stabs the baby, then murders the lady of the house. The lord returns; usually Lamkin and the nurse are executed.

95   "The Maid Freed from the Gallows," "Hangman (Slack the Rope)," "The Gallows Pole," "The Golden Ball," "Prickley Bush" (SE: +++)
A woman (or man), about to be hanged, pleads a delay in hopes that her parents will bring the gold (or fee) to secure release. Her parents and relatives in turn say they have not brought her fee but have come to see her hang; a sweetheart finally brings her fee.

105   "The Bailiff's Daughter (of Islington)," "There Was a Youth" (SE: +, NE: +, C: +)
The bailiff's daughter and her true love have been parted for seven years, usually after she had spurned him. She sets off (in disguise) in search of him and finds him. Not recognizing her, she asks if he knows his true love. She says the true love has died; he expresses his grief, then she reveals herself, and they agree to marry.

155   "Sir Hugh, or, The Jew's Daughter," "The Jeweler's Daughter," "It Rained a Mist," "The Fatal Flower Garden" (SE: ++, NE: +, MW: +)
A little boy's ball goes into the Jew(eler)'s garden; he follows and asks for it. The woman invites him in, then murders him. In some versions, he asks that his mother be told he is asleep and his playmates, that he is

dead. In some versions, the body is thrown into a well. (The ballad is based on the death of Hugh of Lincoln, England, in 1255.)

167 "Sir Andrew Barton," "Andrew Batan," "Elder Bordee" (NE: +)
Three Scottish brothers cast lots to determine which shall become a pirate and support the family. The lot falls to the youngest, who robs a rich merchant ship. The king sends his captain out to catch the robbers, who are caught and hanged (or sometimes drown).

173 "Mary Hamilton," "The Four Maries" (SE: +, C: +)
Mary Hamilton, one of the Scottish queen's serving women, is with child by a member of the court. She throws the baby into the sea when it is born. When the truth is discovered, she is condemned to death. (The ballad seems to mix a scandal in the court of Mary Queen of Scots, in the 1560s, with another incident during the reign of the Russian Czar Peter in the 1710s.)

200 "The Gypsy Laddie," "Gypsy Davy," "Blackjack David," "The Three Gypsies" (SE: +++, NE: +, SW: +, SW: +, C: ++)
The lord's wife espies a band of roving gypsies, falls in love with the leader, and rides off with them after renouncing her wealth and children. The lord returns, learns what happened, and rides off after them. Overtaking them, he asks whom she loves best, and she declares her love for the gypsy. In some versions, she ultimately repents, is discarded by the gypsy, or is slain by the lord.

209 "Geordie," "Georgie," "As I Walked Over London's Bridge" (SE: +)
Geordie/Georgie is in prison awaiting execution for a capital offence, pardonable only by a large ransom. His sweetheart brings the money, but in most versions, it is too late—he is hanged.

243 "James Harris," "The Demon Lover," "House Carpenter," "Well Met" (SE: +++, NE: +, MW: +)
A seaman and his love exchange vows before he sails off. After a long absence, she marries a carpenter. The seaman (or his spirit) returns and lures her off in his ship with the promise of great wealth. After kissing her babes farewell, she runs off with him, and ultimately the ship sinks at sea.

272 "The Suffolk Miracle" (SE: +)
After a young girl is sent away by her father, her lover dies. His spirit appears later, riding her father's horse, to take her home. On the ride, he complains of a headache, and she binds his head in her kerchief. Arriving at her home, the lover vanishes; her astonished father opens his grave, and they find the corpse with her kerchief about its head.

274 "Our Goodman," "Three (Four/Five/Six) Nights Drunk (Experience)," "Cabbage Head (Blues)" (SE: +++, NE: +)
A drunkard returns home to find the horse, coat, head, etc. of another man in the place where his should be. Demanding explanations of his wife, she castigates him and gives ridiculous explanations (the horse is a milk-horse, the coat is a bed quilt, the head is a cabbage head, and so on). Puzzled, he declares he has never seen a milk-horse with a saddle, a bed quilt with pockets, a cabbage head with a moustache, and so on.

277 "The Wife Wrapt in Wether's Skin," "Dandoo," "Gentle Fair Jenny," "Old Man Who Lived in the West" (SE: ++, NE: +, SW: +)

A man marries a woman who refuses to work or make his supper. He wraps her in a sheepskin and beats her. When she protests, he declares he is only tanning the hide. In the end, she reforms.

278 "The Farmer's Curst Wife," "Devil and the Farmer's Wife," "Old Woman and the Devil," "Randy Riley," "Little Devils" (SE: +++, NE: +)

The devil accosts the farmer one day and demands his wife. He carts her back to hell where she proceeds to beat or kick the little demons one by one. They plead with the devil to take her back to her home. In some versions, she beats her husband upon her return.

286 "The Sweet Trinity," "The Golden Vanity," "Turkish Revelee," "(Golden) Willow Tree," "Lowlands Low," "Merry Golden Tree" (SE: +++, NE: ++)

The ship's captain offers gold and his daughter's hand in marriage to the sailor who will jump overboard and bore a hole in the hull of the marauding pirates' ship. A cabin boy accepts the offer, sinks the ship, and pleads to be pulled up on deck. The captain refuses to honor his pledge. Rather than take revenge by sinking his own ship (and endangering his crewmates), the cabin boy drowns (or dies of exhaustion after his mates haul him on board).

289 "The Mermaid," "Waves on the Sea," "The Raging Sea" (SE: ++)

A ship's crew espies a mermaid, a sign of bad luck. The ship goes down.

295 "The Brown Girl" (in America, the ballad designated by this name is usually the derivative ballad, "Rich Irish Lady" [Laws P 9])

A woman spurns her former love and then falls ill. When she sends for him, he mocks her, reminding her how she treated him, and promises to dance on her grave.

BALLADS FROM BRITISH BROADSIDES

The following list is categorized and numbered as in Laws's, *American Balladry from British Broadsides*. Hardly any of the older ballads listed previously have known historical antecedents; with the broadsides, it is easier to associate a date. A place preceding the synopsis indicates the setting; a date indicates either when it supposedly took place or when it was composed.

J War Ballads

J 10 "The Heights of Alma" (C: +)

1854–1856, Crimea: British soldiers force the Russians to retreat back to Sebastopol; thousands die in the bloody battle.

J 12 "Donald Monroe" (C: +)

1770s, America: Monroe emigrates to America but can't afford passage for his two sons. Seven years later, they enlist in the British army and sail to America; one is killed by American rebels (including their father), and the other is fatally wounded. The son forgives his father, who is stricken with grief and remorse.

K Ballads of Sailors and the Sea

K 9 "Lady Franklin's Lament," "The Sailor's Dream" (C: +)
1845, Arctic: Two ships and the crew of Sir John Franklin, Arctic explorer, vanish.

K 10 "The Sailor and His Bride" (SE: +)
Bride's husband goes to sea three months after marriage and is lost.

K 12 "The Sailor Boy" (SE: +++, MW: +)
Girl asks father to build a boat, so she can search for her sailor boy, who was lost at sea. Failing to find him, she commits suicide in her grief.

K 13 "The Faithful Sailor Boy" (C: +)
Sailor dies at sea; his comrades give his girl his farewell note.

K 16 "A Gay Spanish Maid" (C: +)
Linnete bids farewell to her lover about to set sail; all of crew save him are lost in storm. She dies of grief before he reaches home.

K 27 "The Maid on the Shore" (C: +)
Captain invites maid on board; she sings crew to sleep, then robs him.

K 28 "The *Flying Cloud*" (C: +)
Mid-1700s: Edward Halloran joins the *Flying Cloud* crew, which hauls slaves, then turns to piracy. It is finally captured by a warship. The crew is taken to Newgate and sentenced to death.

K 29 "The Bold *Princess Royal*" (C: +)
Captain safely outraces a pirate ship that threatens them en route from England to Newfoundland.

K 36 "Johnny the Sailor," "Green Beds" (SE: +)
Innkeeper's daughter Nancy spurns Johnny until she sees his gold, then he spurns her.

L Ballads of Crime and Criminals

L 1 "The Yorkshire Bite" (NE: +, C: +)
His master sends John to the fair to sell a cow; he foils a highwayman by scattering his money on the road. When the robber tries to retrieve it, he seizes the robber's horse and rides home with robber's money-laden saddlebags.

L 9 "My Bonny Black Bess II" (C: +)
1739, England: English highwayman Dick Turpin praises his horse; shoots her to keep justice's bloodhounds from getting her.

L 12 "The Rambling Boy," "Wild and Wicked Youth," "Rake and Rambling Boy" (SE: ++)
1770s, England: Narrator, about to be hanged, laments his life of crime.

L 16B "Boston Burglar" (SE: ++, NE: +, MW: +)

> Wayward youth, about to be sent to jail, laments his fate and remembers his aged, grieving parents.

L 20 "The Wild Colonial Boy" (C: +)

> 1870s, Australia: Jack Dolan (Dowling) leaves Ireland for Australia, where he robs wealthy squires but helps the poor. Three troopers pursue him, and he is shot dead.

M Ballads of Family Opposition to Lovers

M 1 "Early, Early in the Spring" (SE: ++)

> A sailor gets no reply from his fiancée, who he learns has married another because her father withheld his letters from her.

M 2 "Johnny Doyle" (C: +)

> The mother of a girl about to elope with Johnny finds out and forces her to wed another. The mother reconsiders, but too late, and the girl dies of grief.

M 3 "Charming Beauty Bright" (SE: ++, MW: +)

> Learning of her love, a girl's parents confine her to her room. The lover goes to sea (or joins the army) for seven years, returns, and learns she died of grief.

M 4 "The Drowsy Sleeper," "Awake, Awake, You Drowsy Sleeper" (SE: ++, MW: +)

> A girl tells her lover rapping at the window to leave because of parental opposition. She either expects to die of grief, to leave her parents, or to join lover in mutual suicide.

M 6 "Erin's Lovely Home" (C: +)

> A servant falls in love with his employer's daughter. They plan to elope, but her father has him arrested and transported (to Australia); she promises to wait for him.

M 8 "Riley's Farewell," "Riley to America" (C: +)

> To escape his lover's father, her mother helps Riley to flee Ireland for America. He later returns; the two sail together, and both die in a shipwreck.

M 13 "Locks and Bolts," "I Dreamed of My True Love" (SE: ++)

> Disapproving parents lock girl in uncle's house; lover breaks in and escapes with her.

M 25 "The Banks of Dundee," "Undaunted Mary" (C: +)

> Mary's uncle has a press gang abduct her lover. In a violent fight, she kills her uncle and the squire he wanted her to marry.

M 26 "The New (Red) River Shore" (C: +)

> The narrator is forced to flee his lover; on his return, her father dispatches an armed band of twenty or more, who fail to kill him. He wins the girl.

M 27 "The Bold Soldier" (SE: ++, NE: +)

> A father threatens his daughter who insists on marrying a soldier. He sends seven armed men to kill him, but the soldier fights so fiercely that the father

recants and offers daughter dowry. She demands still more; the father makes the soldier the heir to all his lands and money.

M 31B   "Villikins and His Dinah" (SE: +)

When Dinah's father insists she marry someone she doesn't love, she writes a suicide note, takes poison, and dies. Villikins (William) finds her and also takes the poison.

M 32   "The Bramble Briar," "In Bruton (Seaport) Town," "The Merchant's Daughter" (SE: ++, NE: +)

The merchant's daughter's brothers murder her servant lover, who then appears to her in a dream. She finds his corpse.

M 34   "Edwin in the Lowlands Low" (SE: +, C: +)

Edward returns from sea, shows his lover his gold; her father robs and murders him. She informs on her father.

M 35   "Lovely Willie" (C: +)

A girl falls in love with Willie, of low degree; her father murders him, and she grieves.

N   Ballads of Lovers' Disguises and Tricks

N 2   "The Paisley Officer," "India's Burning Sands" (C: +)

India: Henry and Mary marry; she disguises herself as a recruit and goes with his regiment to India, where both die.

N 5   "The 'Lady Leroy'" (C: +)

A girl disguises herself as a man, buys a ship, and sails away with her lover. The angry father sends a ship in pursuit; a fight ensues, and the girl is victorious.

N 7   "Jack Monroe," "Jackie Frazier," "The Wars of Germany" (SE: +++, MW: +)

Polly's father has her suitor, Jackie Frazier, sent to the wars in Germany; she follows in disguise as Jack Monroe. She finds her wounded lover, cares for him, and they marry.

N 8   "William and Nancy," "Lisbon," "Men's Clothing I'll Put On" (C: +)

William is called off to war; Nancy begs to disguise herself and go, too. They marry and sail off together.

N 9   "The Banks of the Nile," "Men's Clothing I'll Put On" (C: +)

1801, Egypt: Williams is sent off to Egypt; Molly begs to go, too, but he refuses to let her.

N 11   "William Taylor" (C: +)

Willie is pressed to sea; his true love dresses as a man and follows. During battle, her bosom is revealed. The captain tells her Willie has been unfaithful; she pursues him and kills him and his new love. The captain rewards (or marries) her.

N 14   "Polly Oliver" (C: +)

Polly dresses as a man to follow her lover captain; she meets him at an inn (in disguise) but declines to share his bed. She reveals herself in the morning; they marry.

N 20   "The Golden Glove," "Dog and Gun" (SE: ++)

    A lady falls in love with a farmer, who is to take part in her wedding to a squire. She contrives to give the farmer her glove, then announces its loss, and says she'll wed whoever finds it.

N 31   "Waterloo II" (C: +)

    1815, Belgium: The narrator informs a girl her lover, Willie, died of bayonet wounds. She faints in his arms; he then reveals himself as Willie.

N 32   "The Plains of Waterloo" (C: +)

    1815, Belgium: A soldier tells Sally he brings message from her lover, William, who died at Waterloo. He then shows her a broken token that proves he is William.

N 35   "The Dark-Eyed Sailor," "Fair Phoebe and Her Dark-Eyed Sailor" (C: +)

    A sailor tries to woo a maid, but she remains faithful to her dark-eyed sailor, William. He shows her his half of a broken ring; marriage follows.

N 36   "John (George) Riley" (SE: +)

    A sailor tells a maid her lover, Riley, was his messmate and was killed by a French cannon ball, then reveals himself as Riley.

N 38   "The Mantle So Green" (C: +)

    1815: William O'Reilly meets a girl, proposes marriage, tells the girl her love died at Waterloo, then reveals himself as her lover.

N 39   "MacDonald's Return to Glencoe," "The Pride of Glencoe" (C: +)

    After being rejected, MacDonald shows the girl the glove she had given him as a love token and reveals himself.

N 40   "The Banks of Claudy" (C: +)

    The narrator tells a dejected girl on the banks of Claudy that her love Johnny is false, then that he died in shipwreck off the coast of Spain. He then reveals himself as Johnny.

N 42   "Pretty Fair Maid (in the Garden)," "The Broken Token" (SE: +++, C: +)

    A sailor woos a maid who expresses devotion to her lover who has been at sea for seven years; he shows her a broken token (or ring), revealing himself as her love. She swoons, and a happy reunion follows.

O   Ballads of Faithful Lovers

O 3   "The Foggy Dew," "The Bugaboo" (SE: +)

    The narrator beds a pretty girl to keep her from the foggy dew (or bugaboo); he departs in the morning, and later she has a child. In some versions they marry.

O 6   "The Lass of Glenshee" (C: +)

    The narrator woos a Scottish shepherdess with an offer of a carriage and servants. She prefers her crook and herd but agrees to join him; happy marriage follows.

O 13   "The Jolly Young Sailor and the Beautiful Queen" (C: +)

    A rich girl is smitten by a handsome sailor. She says he should stay ashore and marry some nice rich girl. At first reluctant to give up the sea, he agrees when she offers him land and wealth.

O 15   "The Green Mossy Banks of the Lea" (C: +)
   An American lad sails to Ireland, where he meets and falls in love with a girl; he tells her father he has a fortune and asks for her hand. They marry and go to America to live on the banks of the Lea.

O 17   "Seventeen Come Sunday" (SE: +)
   The narrator meets a pretty girl on an errand for her mother. He asks her age. She lets him visit that night. Either the mother doesn't hear him or she does and gives the girl a beating.

O 23   "When Will Ye Gang Away" (C: +)
   Jamie brings Janie gifts, then teases her saying he is already married with three children. Seeing her discomfort, he relents and promises marriage.

O 25   "The Lady of Carlisle," "The Lion's Den" (SE: +)
   To choose between two rival suitors, a lady throws her glove into a lion's den and promises her hand to the one who is brave enough to retrieve it. The lieutenant declines; the brave sea captain gets it, and they marry.

O 34   "Burns and His Highland Mary" (C: +)
   Burns meets Mary by the banks of the Ayr, and they pledge fidelity. She must return to the Highlands; then she dies of sadness and is buried on the banks of the Clyde.

O 36   "Molly Bawn," "Polly Vaughan," "The Shooting of His Dear" (SE: ++)
   Jimmy goes hunting at dusk and mistakenly takes his sweetheart, wearing a white apron, for a swan and shoots her. At the trial, Polly's spirit appears and pleads on his behalf.

O 39   "The Sheffield Apprentice" (SE: +, C: +)
   An apprentice runs away from his London master to Holland to serve a lady who later proposes marriage. He spurns her because he loves her chambermaid. Angered, she plants her gold ring in his pocket and has him arrested and condemned as a thief.

P   Unfaithful Lovers

P 1   "The Girl I Left Behind" (SE: ++, MW:.+, C: +)
   The narrator leaves his sweetheart to go west to seek his fortune, after they pledge to be true. Later, he receives a letter (sometimes after meeting another girl) saying his sweetheart has married another, and he regrets not marrying her while he had the chance.

P 7   "The Foot of the Mountain Brow" (C: +)
   Jimmy woos Polly and promises to work hard for her, but she criticizes his frivolous habits. He leaves her, and she regrets her words.

P 8   "The Gray Mare," "Roger the Miller" (C: +)
   The miller won't accept Kate's hand and dowry unless her father throws in his mare; the angry father turns him out. Later, he meets Kate, and she describes him as the man who came courting her father's mare.

P 14   "The Nightingale," "One Morning in May" (SE: ++)
   A soldier meets a pretty girl; they converse, and he takes out his fiddle and plays her a tune. When she asks him to marry her, he says he has

a wife and children in London. The ballad ends with warning against such deceivers.

P 21   "Mary of the Wild Moor" (SE: +, MW: +, C: +)
Mary's father doesn't hear her pounding at the door with her babe in the storm, and she dies in the night. He dies of grief and the babe dies, too, leaving the empty cottage.

P 24   "The Butcher Boy" (SE: +++, MW: +, C: +)
When the butcher boy leaves his sweetheart for another girl with more gold, she hangs herself in her bedroom, leaving a suicide note that her father discovers.

P 27   "Caroline of Edinburgh Town" (SE: +)
Caroline goes to London with a Highland suitor, and they wed, in spite of her parents' objections. He treats her harshly and goes to sea, telling her to go back to Edinburgh; after wandering about, she plunges to her death in the sea.

P 29   "The Lily of the West" (SE: +)
The narrator woos handsome Flora (or Mary), who loves another. He stabs the rival to death and is sentenced for his crime.

P 31   "The Nobleman's Wedding," "The Faultless Bride," "The Love Token" (C: +)
A man returns home in time to attend, in disguise, the wedding of his former sweetheart. He shows her the gold token of her love pledge and chastises her. She dies with remorse that night at her mother's house.

P 34   "The Sailor's Tragedy," "The Sailor and the Ghost" (C: +)
Deserted by her lover, a pregnant girl hangs herself in a grove. He goes to sea; her spirit follows and demands to see him. The captain says he has died, but she threatens to cause a storm unless he is brought forth. The captain complies; she denounces her lover and sinks the boat in flames.

P 35   "The Wexford (Knoxville/Oxford/Lexington) Girl," "The Cruel Miller" (SE: +++, MW: +, C: +)
1700s: After seducing his sweetheart and getting her pregnant, the miller's apprentice lures her for walk in the woods and murders her. Returning home, he explains his bloody clothes as caused by a nose bleed. The truth is discovered, and he is condemned to hang.

P 36   "The Cruel Ship's Carpenter," "The Gosport Tragedy," "Pretty Polly" (SE: +++, C: +)
ca. 1737: After seducing Polly and getting her pregnant, Willie, a carpenter, lures her for a walk in the woods and murders her (Laws, P 36 A). In some versions (Laws, P 36 B), her spirit appears on the ship and accuses him, after which he confesses and dies raving; her parents find her body and give it proper burial.

P 37   "The Old Oak Tree" (C: +)
After Betty leaves home to meet her lover and fails to return, her mother dies of grief. During a foxhunt, the hounds find her grave by an oak tree. Her wounds bleed afresh in the presence of the squire whose knife is found by her body. He confesses and commits suicide.

Q   Humorous and Miscellaneous

Q 1   "Father Grumble" (SE: +, MW: +)

After the old man criticizes his wife, she offers to exchange tasks with him. He bungles the household chores and eventually acknowledges her superiority.

Q 2   "The Old Woman of Slapsadam" (SE: +, C: +)

The old woman, in love with another, feeds her husband marrow bones to make him blind. He says he will drown himself and asks her to push him in. At the last minute, he steps aside, and she falls in the water. When she pleads for help, he reminds her that he is blind and can't help her.

Q 3   "Johnny Sands" (SE: +, C: +)

Johnny announces he is tired of life and plans to drown himself. He asks his wife to tie his hands and push him in. At the last minute, he steps aside, and she falls in the water. When she pleads for help, he reminds her that his hands are tied, and he can't help her.

Q 4   "Devilish Mary" (SE: +)

The narrator marries shrewish Mary, who torments and abuses him. He suggests they part ways, and she leaves; he swears next time to wed a woman who won't wear the breeches. (Most collected American versions have too little narrative to qualify as ballads.)

Q 9   "Will the Weaver" (SE: +)

John comes home unexpectedly while his wife is making love to the weaver, who hides up the chimney. The cuckolded husband spies him, builds a fire to smoke him out, and beats him. In some American versions, he beats his wife as well.

Q 19   "Doran's Ass" (C: +)

On his way to meet his Biddy, drunken Pat lies down to sleep, and an ass lies down by him. Thinking he is caressing his girl, Pat is startled when he is awakened by braying and runs to Biddy, who comforts him.

Q 21   "The Miller's Will" (SE: +++)

Preparing his will, the miller tests his three sons and asks each what they would charge for grinding grain. The eldest son says he would take a peck, the second son says a half, and the youngest says all (or most) of the grain. Satisfied, the miller wills everything to the third son.

Q 26   "The Bad Girl's Lament," "Unfortunate Rake," "St. James's Hospital" (SE: ++, SW, +, C: +)

The wayward girl (or soldier), dying from debauchery (or venereal disease), gives instructions for her funeral and regrets a life of sin.

Q 27   "Erin's Green Shore" (C: +)

The narrator dreams of a beautiful girl bedecked in shamrocks and roses who has come to awaken her countrymen asleep on Erin's green shore. He awakens and wishes success to this goddess of freedom.

Q 30   "The Farmer's Boy" (C: +)

A farmer's wife and daughter urge him to take in a homeless lad who seeks shelter or employment. The boy proves to be a faithful worker, and when the farmer dies, he wills his estate to the boy.

INDIGENOUS POPULAR BALLADS

The following list is categorized and numbered as in Laws's, *Native American Balladry*. A place preceding the synopsis indicates the setting; a date indicates either when it supposedly took place or when it was composed.

A   War

A 5   "James Bird" (by Charles Miner) (NE: +, MW: +)
    1814: After fighting bravely with Commodore Perry in the Battle of Lake Erie, Bird deserts from guard duty, is tried, convicted, and executed.

A 8   "The Texas Rangers" (SE: ++, C: +)
    Probably from Texas, 1830s: The narrator's band of Texas Rangers fights with Native Indians, and many of the Rangers are killed.

A 14   "The Dying Ranger" (SE: +)
    The cowboy (or soldier) talks about his sister at home in Texas (or New England); his comrades promise to be brothers for her.

A 17   "The Last Fierce Charge" (SE: +, C: +)
    Battle of Fredericksburg, 1860s: Two soldiers, a young boy and a married man, about to ride into battle, promise that the survivor will write a letter for the other should he die. Both are killed.

A 18   "The *Cumberland*'s Crew" (NE: +, MW: +)
    1862: In a battle with the ironclad *Merrimac* in Chesapeake Bay, the *Cumberland* is rammed and sinks, sending many of the crew to their deaths.

B   Cowboys and Pioneers

B 1   "The Cowboy's Lament" (by Francis H. Maynard, based on "The Unfortunate Rake" [Laws, Q 26]) (SE: +)
    1876, Southwest: A wounded and dying cowboy, lamenting a life of sin, gives detailed instructions for his funeral and dies.

B 2   "The Dying Cowboy" (by H. Clemons [?]) (SE: +, SW: +)
    1872, Southwest: Dying cowboy pleas to be taken home to be buried near his father in the churchyard rather than out on the prairie, but his request is unheeded.

B 3   "When the Work's All Done This Fall" (by D. J. O'Malley, originally called "After the Roundup") (SE: +)
    1893, Southwest: A cowboy dies in a stampede and regrets that he won't see his mother again.

B 4   "Utah Carroll" (SE: +)
    Southwest, 1880s: Carroll leads stampeding herd away from his boss's daughter by waving a red blanket; he dies under their hooves.

B 8   "A Fair Lady of the Plains," "Death of a Maiden Fair" (SE: +)
    The lady, who drinks red liquor and handles a six-shooter, is killed by Native Indians while camping with her husband near a herd of wild steers. He rides out to avenge her.

B 9   "Sweet Betsy from Pike" (by John A. Stone) (SE: +)
        1858: Betsy and her lover, Ike, from Pike County, Missouri, travel by wagon
        to California.

B 10 "The Buffalo Skinners" (SW: +)
        1870s, Texas: After a difficult summer, the buffalo skinners kill Crego, their
        employer, who has refused to pay them fairly.

B 11 "The Sioux Indians" (SE: +)
        A group of pioneers crossing the plains is attacked by Sioux Indians, whom
        they defeat though they are outnumbered.

B 14 "Joe Bowers" (by John Woodward or John A. Stone) (SE: +)
        1850s: Joe leaves Pike County, Missouri, for California to make his fortune.
        He learns from his brother that his sweetheart has married a red-haired
        butcher, and she now has a red-haired baby.

B 18 "The Strawberry Roan" (by Curley Fletcher) (SW: +)
        1915: The overconfident cowboy agrees to ride the untamed roan for ten
        dollars, and in most versions, fails.

B 25 "The Rolling Stone" (SE +)
        Based on the English ballad "Dialogue for a Clown and His Wife" (1695):
        Wife counters all of her husband's arguments for going West, noting that a
        rolling stone gathers no moss; her warning that she and the children might
        be murdered by Native Indians convinces him to stay.

C Lumberjacks

C 1   "The Jam on Gerry's Rock" (NE: +, MW: +, C: +)
        Maine or Michigan: The leader of a logging crew is killed when a logjam
        breaks; his sweetheart Clara dies of grief and is buried beside him.

C 4   "Jimmie Judd," "The Beau Shai River" (C: +)
        Ontario (?): Jimmie drowns trying to break up a logjam; his body is recov-
        ered the next day by a fisherman's boy.

C 5   "The Wild Mustard River," "Johnny Stile" (MW: +, C: +)
        Michigan (?): Johnny gets his foot caught while trying to break a logjam
        and is swept downstream when the jam gives way. His comrades recover
        and bury his mangled body.

C 7   "James Whalen" (C: +)
        ca. 1878, Ontario: James Whalen drowned at King's Chute in Frontenac
        County while trying to break up a logjam.

C 8   "Lost Jimmie Whalen" (C: +)
        ca. 1878, Ontario: Though based on same incident as the preceding ballad,
        this is a romantic tale about the grieving girl calling forth the spirit of her
        drowned sweetheart from the grave.

C 13 "Harry Bale" (by Charles Bahel) (MW: +)
        1879, Michigan: Orphaned Harry Bahel, aged 19 (author's brother),
        is fatally injured in mill accident; he dies a day later, and his siblings
        grieve.

C 14   "Harry Dunn," "The Hanging Limb" (C: +)
Michigan: Dunn goes to work in the woods, despite his mother's advice to stay home. He has a premonitory dream one night, and the next day is crushed to death by a falling limb. When his body is sent home, his parents die of shock.

C 16   "The Little Brown Bulls" (MW: +)
1872–1873, northwestern Wisconsin: McClusky bets twenty-five dollars that his steers can skid more logs than Gordon's little brown bulls, and loses.

C 17   "Canaday I-O" (by Ephraim Braley, adaptation of "Canada-I-O") (MW: +)
1854: After a brutally cold winter in the woods in Canada (or Michigan or Pennsylvania), the lumbermen are glad to return home.

C 25   "Jack Haggerty" (by Dan McGinnis) (MW: +)
1872, Michigan: Jack expects to marry Anna, a blacksmith's daughter. When she suddenly writes that she plans to wed another, he blames her mother and loses all faith in women.

C 27   "Peter Amberley" (by John Calhoun) (NE: +, C: +)
1881, New Brunswick: Peter is fatally injured in the woods of New Brunswick and sends farewell messages to his parents and sweetheart.

D   Sailors and the Sea

D 24   "The *Titanic* I" (SE: +)
1912: The *Titanic*, believed to be unsinkable, hits an iceberg and sinks on her maiden voyage out of Southampton, England, en route to New York, with a loss of 1,513 lives.

D 27   "The Ship That Never Returned" (by Henry C. Work) (SE: +)
1865: A young man sets sail on a voyage for his health; the captain plans to retire after this last trip. The ship is never heard from again.

E   Criminals and Outlaws

E 1   "Jesse James I" (SE: ++)
1882, Missouri: Jesse James is treacherously killed by gang member Robert Ford for the $10,000 reward on his head.

E 3   "Cole Younger" (SE: +)
1876: The Younger Brothers, Cole and Bob, and the James Brothers, Frank and Jesse, are foiled in an attempt to rob bank in Northville, Minnesota.

E 4   "Sam Bass" (by John Denton [?]) (SE: +)
1879: Indiana-born Bass turns from raising cattle to train robbing and is killed at Round Rock, Texas, in 1878 by a Texas Ranger.

E 6   "Claude Allen" (SE: +)
1912, Hillsville, Virginia: Allen killed the sheriff in a courthouse shootout during his brother Sidney's trial. This ballad is a lament for Claude, who is to be executed because of the governor's indifference.

E 10   "Wild Bill Jones" (SE: +)
        The narrator shoots Wild Bill because Bill has taken his girl, Lula.

E 11   "Charles Guiteau" (SE: +, MW: +)
        1881, based on an 1870s ballad: Guiteau assassinates President James A.
        Garfield and is condemned to be hanged; he laments his life of crime.

E 15   "Young Companions," "Bad Companions" (SE: +)
        A young man, about to be executed, relates how he left his home for Chicago,
        where he sinned constantly and finally murdered a young woman.

E 16   "Twenty-One Years" (by Bob Miller) (SE +)
        1930: A man is sentenced for his crimes and pleads with his girlfriend to ask
        the governor to pardon him.

E 20   "The Rowan County Crew," "Tolliver-Martin Feud" (by James W. Day)
        (SE: +)
        1884, Kentucky: This ballad relates the details of a family feud that left
        several men dead and no satisfactory resolution.

F   Murders and Murderers

F 1   "The Jealous Lover," "Fair Florella (Floella)" (SE: ++, MW: +)
        Edward lures Florella into the woods on the pretext of making wedding
        plans, but instead he murders her. Some versions are localized to the events
        surrounding the death of Pearl Bryan (Greencastle, Indiana, 1896).

F 4   "Poor Omie" (SE: +++)
        1808, North Carolina: John Lewis murders pregnant Omie (Naomi) Wise
        rather than marry her. The body is discovered, and he goes to jail.

F 5   "On the Banks of the Ohio" (SE: +)
        A young man drowns the girl he loves because she wouldn't marry him.

F 6   "Rose Connoley," "Down in the Willow Garden" (SE: +)
        Possibly Irish: The narrator, on the scaffold about to be executed, relates
        how he murdered Rose by first poisoning her with wine, then stabbing her—
        all because his father promised him that they could pay to set him free.

F 11   "(Poor) Ellen Smith" (SE: ++)
        1893, North Carolina: Peter Degraph protests that he did not shoot Ellen
        near Mt. Airy but is sentenced to hang.

F 13   "McAfee's Confession" (SE: +)
        1825, Ohio: McAfee poisons his wife after falling in love with another
        woman, Hettie Stout, and is sentenced to be hanged.

F 16   "Fuller and Warren" (by Moses Whitecotton [?]) (SE: +, MW: +)
        1820, Indiana: Amasa Fuller shoots Palmer Warren at Lawrenceburg be-
        cause his fiancée announces her intention to marry Warren; he is hanged
        for the crime.

F 20   "Mary Phagan," "Leo Frank and Mary Phagan" (SE: +)
        1913, Atlanta: Little Mary is beaten to death in the pencil factory by Leo
        Frank, who is tried and condemned to death. (Though Frank was found
        guilty, many believed him innocent, and the governor commuted his death

sentence. In August 1915, he was lynched by an enraged mob, who kidnapped him from the Georgia State Prison Farm.)

F 22   "Poor Goins" (by Gabriel Church) (SE: +)

1844, Virginia: Pretending to help Goins, a horse trader, escape from bandits, Boggs leads him into their hands; Goins is clubbed to death.

F 24   "The Peddler and His Wife" (by Charles Oaks [?]) (SE: +)

ca. 1906, Kentucky: While riding in their wagon, a peddler and his wife are ambushed, robbed, and murdered.

F 35   "The Lawson Murder" (by Walter "Kid" Smith) (SE: +)

1929, North Carolina: Charles Lawson goes berserk and shoots his wife and six children on December 26th, closes their eyes, then commitssuicide.

G   Tragedies and Disasters

G 1   "Casey Jones" (SE: +)

Based on engineer John Luther Jones's death on the Illinois Central's "Cannonball" in 1900 near Vaughan, Mississippi. Casey bids his wife farewell, tells his fireman to shovel in more coal, and is killed in a collision with another train standing on the track.

G 2   "The Wreck of the Old 97" (by Fred Jackson Lewey and others) (SE: +)

1903, Virginia: Engineer Steve Broady misses a fast curve driving the Southern's mail train from Washington, D.C., to Atlanta. The train flies off the track between Lynchburg and Danville, Virginia.

G 3   "The Wreck on the C&O" (SE: +)

1890, West Virginia: Engineer George Alley is killed on the C&O railroad line when his engine overturns because of a landslide.

G 9   "The Cross Mountain Explosion" (by Thomas Evans[?]) (SE: +)

1911: 150 miners die in mine explosion at Coal Creek, Tennessee.

G 16   "Springfield Mountain" (NE: ++, SE: +, MW: +)

1761, Farmington, Connecticut: Timothy Mirick dies of a snakebite while working in his field.

G 17   "Young Charlotte" (by Seba Smith, originally "A Corpse Going to a Ball") (SE: ++, MW: +, NE: +, C: +)

1843: Charlotte's vanity keeps her from wrapping herself in blankets, and she freezes during the sleigh ride to the ball. (The ballad is based on a newspaper account of a girl who froze to death in a sleigh on the way to a New Year's Eve ball in 1840.)

G 19   "Willie Down by the Pond," "Sinful to Flirt" (SE: +)

The girl loves Willie, but she teasingly says she won't marry him; he drowns himself in the mill pond, where he is found with a rose from her hair pressed to his lips.

G 21   "The Silver Dagger" (SE: +)

A young man's father opposes his marriage to a girl on account of her poverty. The girl stabs herself and is found by her lover, who in turn stabs himself with the same dagger.

G 22   "(Death of) Floyd Collins" (by Andrew Jenkins) (SE: +)
        1925, Kentucky: Collins tells his parents of a premonitory dream he had,
        then dies in a sandstone cave that he was exploring.

G 26   "The Wreck of the Number Nine" (by Carson J. Robison, 1927) (SE: +)
        An engineer, to be married the following day, bids his fiancée farewell and
        is killed in a head-on collision with another train.

H   Miscellaneous Subjects

H 1   "An Arkansas Traveller" (SE: +)
        Bill Stafford is overwhelmed by the misery of Arkansas, where he has come
        for employment. When he leaves, he vows never to return.

H 2   "Ten Thousand Miles from Home," "Danville Girl," "Standing on the Plat-
        form" (SE: +)
        A hobo cannot resist the urge to wander, in spite of the kind people who
        try to help him.

H 3   "The Dying Hobo" (SE: +)
        The dying hobo tells his partner about the hobo paradise that awaits him; he
        dies, and the partner swipes his shoes and hat and catches the next train.

H 4   "The Roving Gambler" (SE: +)
        The gambler falls in love with a pretty girl, who takes him in her parlor; she
        decides to leave home and go with him.

H 6   "Wicked Polly" (by Rev. J. H. Lewis, originally titled "The Dying Girl
        Unprepared to Meet Her God") (SE: +)
        1830s, Rhode Island: Sinful Polly plans to repent before too long, but she
        takes sick and dies before she has a chance, knowing her soul is condemned
        to hell.

H 7   "The Little Family" (SE: +)
        Lazarus becomes ill and Jesus prays for him; Lazarus rises from the grave.
        (This ballad is based on the Biblical story of Mary, Martha, and Lazarus.)

H 8   "The Little Mohea" (SE: +++, MW: +, C: +)
        The Native Indian girl invites the stranger to live with her, but he says he
        must return to his true love in his own country. When he does return to her,
        she proves untrue, and he longs for the Indian maid. (This is an American
        recomposition of the British broadside ballad, "The Indian Lass.")

H 9   "The Lake of Ponchartrain" (C: +)
        ca. 1886: A traveler meets a Creole girl, and she takes him to her father's
        house. He proposes, but she refuses, saying she is awaiting a lover who is
        at sea.

H 10   "The Chippewa Girl" (C: +)
        A rover proposes to the Native Indian girl he meets, but she refuses, saying
        she is too young and her parents would disapprove.

H 11   "On the Banks of the Pamanaw" (C: +)
        An Native Indian maid, bereft of her family and deserted by her lover,
        refuses the white man's offer to take her to safety.

H 12   "The Lonesome Scenes of Winter" (SE: +, C: +)
 A girl refuses the narrator's proposal, saying she has another suitor. He reprimands her for her snobbery and plans to go away. In some versions, she changes her mind, but too late.

H 13   "The Young Man Who Wouldn't Hoe Corn" (SE: +)
 A lazy young man does not tend his corn and loses the entire crop; the girl to whom he proposes turns him down because of his indolent ways.

H 17   "The Plain Golden Band" (by Joe Scott) (C: +)
 1890s, Maine: A girl, momentarily believing tales about her fiancé's lack of devotion, asks him to take back the engagement ring because she has been unfaithful to him.

H 22   "I Wonder Where's the Gambler" (SE: +)
 A sinning gambler is helped home by friends and staggers to bed; his mother prays for his forgiveness, but he says it's too late to pray.

H 23   "The Old Maid and the Burglar" (by E. S. Thilp, originally "Burglar Man") (SE: +)
 1897: Surprised by a returning old maid, a burglar slips under the bed and watches her remove her glass eye, wig, wooden leg, and so on. She hauls him out and threatens to shoot him if he doesn't marry her; he begs her to shoot.

H 27   "Ten Broeck and Mollie," "Molly and Tenbrooks" (SE: +)
 1878, Kentucky: Kentucky thoroughbred Ten Broeck beats Mollie after telling his jockey not to hold him back.

BLUES BALLADS

 The following list is categorized and numbered as in Laws's, *Native American Balladry*. A place preceding the synopsis indicates the setting; a date indicates either when it supposedly took place or when it was composed.

I 1   "John Henry" (SE: ++)
 1870 or 1872, West Virginia, or 1880s, Alabama: Steel driver John Henry outperforms a mechanical drill in a contest but dies afterward from exhaustion.

I 2   "John Hardy" (SE: ++)
 1894, West Virginia: Hardy threatens and kills the first man who beats him in a gambling game. He is arrested, sentenced, and hanged.

I 3   "Frankie and Albert," "Frankie and Johnny" (SE: ++)
 1899, St. Louis: Frankie shoots her lover, Johnny, because he two-timed her. (This ballad is based on the murder of Allen Britt by Frankie Baker.)

I 4   "Coon Can Game" (SE: +)
 The narrator goes to the depot, sees his woman, who ran away with another man, on a train and shoots her. He is arrested, sentenced, and jailed.

I 8   "Bad Lee Brown," "Little Sadie" (SE: +)
 After killing Little Sadie, the bully flees, is apprehended, arrested, tried, and sentenced to ninety-nine years.

I 9   "Brady," "Duncan and Brady" (SE: +)
  1890, St. Louis: Duncan murders the policeman Brady, who has tried to arrest him in his saloon. (Based on a true event: Harry Duncan shot the policeman James Brady in a saloon on October 6, 1890.)

I 13   "Railroad Bill" (SE: +)
  1894–1897, Florida/Alabama: Bill terrorizes the region for several years before being caught and shot by the local sheriff. (This is based on Morris Slater, nicknamed "Railroad.")

I 15   "Stagolee" (SE: +)
  1895, St. Louis: Stagolee shoots his friend, Billy Lyons, because he has beaten him in a gambling game and/or taken his brand new Stetson hat. (Based on a true event: "Stag" Lee Shelton shot William Lyons in a St. Louis bar.)

I 17   "The Boll Weevil" (SE: +)
  The weevil eats farmer's cotton and his wife's dress and resists the farmer's attempt to stop him; he's just looking for a home. (Boll weevils crossed the Rio Grande into Texas ca. 1900.)

I 19   "The Blue-Tail Fly," "Jim Crack Corn" (by Daniel D. Emmett) (SE: +)
  ca. 1846: The slave's master is pitched from his horse and dies after the horse is bitten by a blue-tail fly.

I 23   "Ida Red" (SE: +)
  A negro thief regrets that a jail term will keep him from his Ida. (Most versions of this title are an unrelated banjo song.)

SENTIMENTAL BALLADS AND
BALLAD-LIKE PIECES

"The Drunkard's Dream" (SE: +, MW: +, C: +)
 Prior to 1850: The reformed drunkard tells the narrator that he reformed because of a warning dream that foretold what tragedy would befall his family if he continued on his path.

"Gypsy's Warning" (Arr. by H. A. Coard) (SE: +, MW: +, C: +)
 1864: A gypsy fortuneteller warns a young girl not to trust her lover, because he previously proved unfaithful to another woman (the gypsy's daughter), who died of grief as a result.

"Father, Dear Father," "Come Home with Me Now" (by H. C. Work) (SE: +)
 1864: A lad pleads with his father at the saloon to come home to his sick sister and anguished mother.

"When You and I Were Young, Maggie" (by G. W. Johnson and J. A. Butterfield) (SE: +)
 1866: A widower visits the spot that he and his late wife of many years used to frequent and reminisces on the happy past.

"Package of Old Letters," "Little Rosewood Casket" (by C. A. White and L. P. Goullaud) (SE: ++, C: +)
 1870: A dying woman asks her sister to bring her the packet of old love letters her faithless sweetheart had written, promising to die as she hears them read one last time.

"Little Old Log Cabin in the Lane" (by W. S. Hays) (SE: +)
>   1870: A traveler returns to the old cabin where he grew up, sees the state of disrepair, learns everyone he used to know has died, and recalls his happy past.

"Put My Little Shoes Away" (by S. N. Mitchell & C. Pratt) (SE: +)
>   1873: A feverish, dying girl tells her mother to put her little shoes away and save them for her infant brother.

"I'll Be All Smiles Tonight" (by T. B. Ransom) (SE: +, C: +)
>   1879: The old love vows to attend her former sweetheart's wedding and to be all smiles, though her heart is secretly breaking.

"Grandma's Old Arm Chair" (by J. Read and F. S. Carr) (C: +)
>   1878: At the reading of his grandmother's will, a young man is ridiculed because all she left him was her arm chair. Later, the chair breaks, and he finds two thousand pounds in bills in the cushion stuffing.

"May I Sleep in Your Barn Tonight, Mister?" (SE: +)
>   1890s: A tramp, searching for his wife who ran away with a stranger, asks if he can spend the night and tells his story.

"After the Ball" (by C. K. Harris) (SE: +)
>   1892: An old man explains to his grandniece why he never married; at a ball, after seeing his sweetheart in the arms of another man, he left without speaking a word to her. Years later, he learned the other man was her brother and that she died of grief.

"The Fatal Wedding" (by W. H. Windom and G. L. Davis) (SE: +, MW: +)
>   1893: A mother and her child appear at the door to the church as the wedding is about to start and exclaims that the groom is her child's father; the child dies, the groom commits suicide, and the would-be bride's parents take in the mother and care for her.

"Two Little Girls in Blue" (by C. Graham) (SE: +)
>   1893: An old man explains to his nephew the cause for his tears on viewing an old photograph: he and his brother (the nephew's father) married two schoolgirl friends in blue. Later, mistakenly believing his wife unfaithful, he left her.

"The Blind Child," "The Blind Girl's Prayer" (SE: +)
>   Prior to 1894: The blind child, whose widowed father is about to wed again, explains why her stepmother can never take her real mother's place in her heart and dies that night.

"Give My Love to Nell," "Jack and Joe" (by W. B. Gray) (SE: +)
>   1894: As Jack and Joe set sail to make their fortunes, Joe tells his brother to give his love to his sweetheart Nell; when Joe returns he finds that Jack and Nell have wed.

"In the Baggage Coach Ahead" (by G. L. Davis) (SE: +)
>   1896: Passengers on a train complain when a man's young infant cries and keeps them awake at night; in response to suggestions to fetch the infant's mother, he says she lies dead in the baggage car.

"Engineer's Dying Child," "Red and Green Signal Lights," "Just Set a Light" (by H. Neil and G. L. Davis) (SE: +)

1896: An engineer, whose child is very ill, asks his wife to set in the window that his train passes a green light if the child is better and, if she's dead, to show the red. As he passes by, he is relieved to see the green light.

"My Mother Was a Lady," "If Brother Jack Was Here" (by E. B. Marks) (SE: +)
1896: Two drummers (salesmen) tease the waitress in a café. She bursts into tears saying they wouldn't do that if her brother Jack were there. One drummer says he knows Jack and asks her to marry him.

"The Letter Edged in Black" (by H. Nevada) (SE: +, C: +)
1897: Standing by the window one morning, Jack sees the postman coming down the path with a letter for him from his estranged father telling him his dear mother has died.

"The Lightning Express," "Please Mr. Conductor, Don't Put Me Off the Train" (by J. Fred Helf and E. P. Moran) (SE: +)
1898: The passengers on a train take up a collection for a young boy going to see his dying mother one last time but has no money to pay his fare.

"The Express Office," "He's Coming to Us Dead" (by G. L. Davis) (SE: +)
1899: An old man comes to the freight train station to meet his son. The agent directs him to the passenger station across the way, but the man explains that he's come for the body of his son, who died in the war.

NOTE

1. The West and Southwest are not noted because too little collecting has been done there to give any ballad a frequency above 10. The main source is the electronic database, *Folksong Index*, 2002, compiled and distributed by folklorist Steve Roud of Sussex, England, supplemented by the author's own collection of recordings.

Glossary

Antiphonal singing. Singing in alternating choruses. Also refers to polyphonic music composed for two or more alternating groups.

Appoggiatura. A rhythmically strong dissonant note occurring in place of a harmonic note (a second above or below), played on the beat.

Archaism of the fringe. The tendency for older customs and styles to continue at the fringes of a culture area, while new customs and styles are developed at the (usually urban) cultural centers.

Ballad. A poem set to music that tells a story, is divided into stanzas of consistent length and rhyme scheme, and is sung to a repeating melody.

Ballet. Term used by traditional singers in some regions to denote a handwritten or printed song text. A *ballet-book* is a collection of texts, such as a notebook.

Bar. Same as measure.

Bel canto. (Italian for beautiful song or singing). The vocal technique developed in eighteenth-century Italy that emphasizes beautiful sounds and brilliance of performance; still used by singers of Italian and Mozartian opera.

Blackface, blackface minstrelsy. The stage presentation, generally by Anglo-American performers, with faces blackened with burnt cork, of music, dances, and humorous patter; derived from, or believed to be derived from, the culture of African and African American slaves and former slaves.

Blue notes. Deviations from standard Western pitch—that is, slightly flattened 3rd, 7th, and occasionally 5th notes of the scale that vary between the standard (European) pitch and the flattened note. Instrumentally, this is achieved on the guitar by bending the strings; on the piano, it is simulated by trilling back and forth between the two adjacent notes or by playing the minor 3rd or 7th with a major chord accompaniment. These pitches may represent survivals from non-Western musical scales common in Africa.

Broadside. Single sheets, printed on one side, sold or handed out on the street or posted on walls, containing anything from political messages to advertisements, to songs, to announcements of the coming end of the world. In this book, the term "broadside" will refer specifically to sheets with song texts. They consisted of one or several song texts arranged on a page, often with decorative woodcut illustrations and/or borders, publisher's name and address, and perhaps a price. Only occasionally was an author acknowledged. Rarely was music included; more usual was a brief notation, "To the tune of . . ." Also called song sheet, ballet, stall ballad, vulgar ballad, or "come-all-ye." Broadsheets are similar but printed on both sides of the paper.

Broken token ballad. A ballad about two lovers who, before parting, break some token (generally a ring) and each keep half as a means of identifying the other when next they meet.

Burden. Musical equivalent of a refrain.

Chapbook. A small booklet of songs, poems, short stories, sermons, or lectures distributed on the streets to the common folk.

Child ballad. One of the 305 ballads collected and published by Francis James Child in his five-volume work, *The English and Scottish Popular Ballads* (1882 to 1898). Throughout this book, the number Child assigned to a ballad is given in parentheses.

Children's song. A song sung by (and sometimes composed by) children, typically among themselves.

Chorus. A section of a song or ballad set to a melody different from the verses and often sung repeatedly between them. Sometimes successive choruses have different words.

Chromatic scale. A musical scale that adds some notes produced by the black keys of the piano (sharp and flat notes) to a diatonic scale.

Commonplace. A formulaic phrase (for example, "milk white steed") in a ballad or song, ranging from a few words to a stanza, that is often used in a particular genre of folk literature, including ballads and songs.

(Criminal's) last goodnight. A ballad or song supposedly written and sung by a criminal facing execution. It generally recounts his life of crime and repents his wicked deeds.

Cumulative song. A song in which elements added in each stanza are retained and accumulate in successive stanzas.

Declamando. A passage of a ballad or song that is spoken rather than sung; often the last few words in New England and Irish singing styles.

Diatonic scale. A succession of seven different musical notes playable on seven adjacent white keys of a piano. A diatonic scale played on white keys beginning with C is the major scale.

Feathering. A sharply rising break in the voice at the end of phrases of a song or ballad; sometimes (formerly) called "goosing."

Full step. See the entry for *Half step*.

Gospel song, gospel music. A Christian religious song or genre with lively rhythm and simple harmony, generally imitating the secular music style of the day, developed in the United States after the Civil War.

Grace note. A note printed in small type to indicate that its time value is not counted in the rhythm of the bar and must be subtracted from that of an adjacent note.

Half step. In a musical scale, the interval between two adjacent notes on the piano keyboard, whether they are white keys or black. A full step is the interval between two keys that have another key between them. For example, the intervals from C to C♯ or E to F are half steps; the intervals from C to D or E to F♯ are full steps.

Hillbilly. Term applied (sometimes pejoratively) to the Anglo-American culture of the rural Southeastern United States. Hillbilly music is the commercialized folk or folk-derived music developed out of the traditional music of that culture, especially as recorded after 1923. In the 1940s, it evolved into what was called "country and western" or "country" music.

Holler. A brief musical phrase consisting of either words or vocables (syllables) sung loudly and characterized by highly stylized ornaments: yodels, portamento, *staccato*, blue notes, or other devices. It can be used as an emotional expression, as a means of calling domestic animals, or for communicating over long distances with other individuals.

Incipit. A beginning phrase of a ballad requesting the audience's attention, such as "Come all you good people . . ." or "Boys and girls, come and listen . . ." It was common in minstrel and broadside ballads.

Incremental repetition. A term introduced by early students of Child balladry to denote repetition of verses but with minor modifications that advance the plot dramatically.

Leaping and lingering. A term introduced by early students of Child balladry to denote the trait of lingering on one scene and then jumping over details that must have occurred to linger on to the next scene.

Legato. See *Staccato*.

Measure. A series of musical beats, the first of which is usually accented. In printed or written music, measures are separated by vertical bar lines; hence measures are sometimes also called bars.

Melisma. A series of musical notes sung on a single syllable of text.

Mode. One of seven different possible diatonic musical octave scales. They differ in the placement of the half steps and full steps. Note that it is not necessary to start these scales on C: each one can be played (or transposed so it can be played) on the piano, regardless of whether it starts on a different note. As long as the sequences of half steps and full steps remains the same, the scale sounds the same to our ears. Musical modes are what gives a piece of music its recognizable character for most modern listeners. A Hungarian folk tune suggests "gypsy" because of the scale employed (C, D♭, E, F, G, A♭, B, C). Some songs may sound sad because they are in a minor scale (C, D, E♭, F, G, A♭, B♭, C), and in most Western music contexts listeners associate a minor scale with sadness. Four modes are commonly used in American folk music and can be played successively on the white keys of the piano but starting at different notes: Ionian, from C to C; Dorian, from D to D; Mixolydian, from G to G, and Aeolian, from A to A.

- *Ionian mode.* Another name for the modern major scale. The half steps occur between the 3rd and 4th and between the 7th and 8th notes.
- *Aeolian mode.* The mode with the same notes as the modern natural minor scale. The half steps occur between the 2nd and 3rd notes and between the 5th and 6th notes.
- *Mixolydian mode.* A scale with half steps between the 3rd and 4th and between the 6th and 7th notes. For example, "Old Joe Clark," or the Tim Hardin's pop song, "If I Were a Carpenter."
- *Dorian mode.* A scale with the half steps between the 2nd and 3rd notes and between the 6th and 7th notes. "Greensleeves" as originally written was in this mode, though there is a tendency to play it now in the minor mode because we are no longer used to Dorian.

Mordent. A musical ornament consisting of the alternation of the written note with the note immediately below it.

Nuncupative testament. Oral last will and testament; common when a ballad hero dies. Found in early Anglo-American ballads ("Edward") and indigenous ones as well ("When the Work's All Done This Fall").

Nursery song. A song sung for the entertainment of young children.

Occupational song. A song in which descriptions of work, work conditions, or attitudes toward work form a significant textual element.

Passing tone. Rhythmically weak note occurring between two successive melody notes.

Pentatonic scale. A musical scale consisting of only five notes. In Anglo-American folk music, the important pentatonic scales are those that can (by transposition, if necessary) be played entirely on the black keys of the piano.

Play party song. A combination of game, dance, and song developed in American frontier communities, often employing dance figures, generally without instrumental accompaniment. Play parties were social gatherings primarily for young adults.

Polyphony, polyphonic music. Two or more simultaneous, independent lines of melody, unlike harmony in which one line is subordinate to the other.

Portamento. Sliding from one note of the melody to the next by passing through all the intermediate pitches.

Ragtime. A strongly syncopated form of American popular instrumental music that developed in the early 1900s, heavily influenced by older African American folk music.

Refrain. In poetry, one or two identical lines recurring at the end of each stanza (external refrain) or between the lines of a stanza (internal refrain) of a poem that is divided into stanzas.

Responsorial singing. Sung by a soloist in alternation with a chorus, as opposed to two alternating half choruses, known as antiphonal singing.

Rhythm. The rhythm is signified in sheet music by a sign that looks like a fraction: 2/4, 3/4, and so on. These notations can be interpreted as follows for each rhythm (count repeatedly the numbers shown and clap on the underlined numbers): 4/4, 1-2-3-4; 2/4, 1-2; 3/4, 1-2-3; 6/8, 1-2-3-4-5-6; and 9/8, 1-2-3-4-5-6-7-8-9. Some examples: the reel (2/4 or 4/4 time, fairly fast), jig (6/8 or 9/8, fast), hornpipe (2/4 or 4/4, slower than the reel), march (2/4, 4/4, or 6/8), quadrille (2/4 or 6/8), waltz (3/4), and schottische (4/4, slower than the reel).

Ring dance. Also called ring shout, this is an old African-derived tradition. It is a circle dance in which dancers move counterclockwise in a circle, singing or chanting in call-and-response fashion. Sometimes these were carried out in a religious context after prayer meeting and church service. In a secular context, the same type of activity can become a children's play game.

Rubato. An elastic, flexible tempo involving slight accelerandos (increases in tempo) and ritardandos (decreases in tempo). *Rubato parlando* mimics ordinary speaking tempo.

Shanty (Chantey). A maritime work song in which a leader (shantyman) usually sings a solo part and is answered by the men in a chorus, accented in synchrony with the task being performed.

Shape notes. A system of musical notation developed in America early in the nineteenth century in which the notes are indicated by different shapes (rather than all elliptical, as is the common practice of uniform notes since the late Middle Ages). There were four-shape and seven-shape systems used. Some early American traveling teachers found shape notes more effective—using a series of four shaped notes, one for fa, another for sol, and so on (different writers used different sets of shapes) rather than teaching the usual uniform notes. This method was frequently used for teaching religious songs. A song would first be sung with the solmization, then with the words. The common use of the four-syllable fa-sol-la-fa-sol-la-mi, originating before Shakespeare's time, rather than the now familiar seven-syllable (do-re-mi-fa-sol-la-ti) method gave the name "fasola music" to the genre. This method is also called "Sacred Harp singing" after one of the earliest (first published in 1844) four-note songbooks, although some practitioners prefer to restrict the term to the repertoire of that particular publication. After the Civil War, most of the songbooks gradually switched from the four-note to the seven-note system, but some very popular songbooks published late in the twentieth century continued using the four-note pattern. Most shape-note songs are written in four independent parts (soprano-alto-tenor-bass), though some are three part, with the intent of making all parts melodically interesting. The result is more polyphony or counterpoint than our modern notion of a single melody line with three lines of subordinate harmony.

Solmization. System for designating the degrees of the scale by syllables instead of letters. Syllables used today are: do(h), re, mi, fa, sol, la, ti(si), do(h). Currently, there are two methods: In the "fixed do" system, the syllables are applied to "fixed" notes, that is, "do" always refers to C. In the "movable do," "do" is always the tonic note, regardless of key.

Song folio. An inexpensively produced booklet of words and music to songs, often published by professional and semiprofessional musicians, sometimes including a biographical sketch as well as popular pieces from their repertoires. Sold by the musicians on the streets or advertised in the mass media.

Songster. (1) A booklet, usually pocket sized (four by six inches or smaller), that contained the texts of music hall, patriotic, religious, and sometimes traditional songs. They were cheaply printed and distributed in large quantities, often (especially after the Civil War) by manufacturers of medicines, tonics, or elixirs, by distributors of other consumable goods, or by popular stage entertainers. They often contained advertisements, testimonials, and short homilies in support of the company's wares. Like the broadsides, they rarely included musical notations. They ranged from a few dozen pages to several hundreds. (2) An African American folksinger whose repertoire consists mainly of ballads and songs that predate the blues genre (that is, from ca. 1880 to ca. 1920).

Spiritual. A simple religious song of Anglo-American or, more particularly, African American folk communities.

Staccato. A performance style that shortens notes slightly and leaves a very short rest between them, as opposed to "*legato*" in which the notes are smoothly connected.

Swing rhythm, shuffle rhythm. A style, common in popular and folk music, in which a melody written as a sequence of notes of even length (such as all eighth notes) is sung or played as if it were an alternating sequence of longer and shorter notes: these sound like triplets where the first two notes are tied together (the "long" note) and the next note is the remaining third of the triplet (the "short" note). Sometimes these are written as dotted eighth notes followed by a sixteenth, but they are still performed with the triplet rhythm so that the longer notes are approximately twice the length of the shorter ones.

Syncopation. Shifting of the musical note or accent before or after the normal position.

Tin Pan Alley. The commercial popular songwriting establishment centered in New York City in the neighborhood around 28th Avenue from the 1890s to the 1930s.

Tonic note. The tonic note is the central note of a melody in the sense that the melody keeps coming back to it and ends on it. In a major scale, the tonic note is the "do" of the scale, for example, the note C in the C scale.

Transposition. Moving a musical scale to a different starting note but preserving the intervals (half steps and full steps) in proper sequence. For example, the ordinary C major scale is C-D-E-F-G-A-B-C; transposed to the key of D, it becomes D-E-F♯-G-A-B-C♯-D. In each case, the intervals between the third and fourth notes and between the seventh and eighth notes are half steps; the other intervals are full steps. To most ears, a transposed scale has the same sound and feeling of the original scale, though it starts on a higher or lower note.

Trill. An alternation between a note and the next higher note in the scale (for example, in the key of C, from C to D or E to F).

Version, variant. Versions are significantly different texts or melodies of the same ballad or song. Variants are slightly different texts or melodies. The distinction is not clear-cut, and sometimes the terms are used interchangeably.

Vibrato. (1) In stringed instruments, a slight fluctuation of pitch on sustained notes produced by an oscillating motion of the hand that stops the strings. (2) In singing, the term is ambiguous. According to some, vocal vibrato is the quick reiteration (usually eight times per second) of the same pitch produced by a quickly intermittent stream of breath with fixed vocal chords. This effect corresponds to what string players call "tremolo." Most singers use the term to define a scarcely noticeable wavering of the tone (corresponding to a violinist's moderate vibrato).

Work song. A song sung during the work process.

Bibliography

Abernethy, Francis Edward. *Singin' Texas*. Dallas: E-Heart Press, 1983.

Abraham, Edward J. *When the Moonbeams Gently Fall Songster*. New York: n.d. (ca. 1882).

Abrahams, Roger D., ed. *A Singer and Her Songs: Alameda Riddle's Book of Ballads*. Baton Rouge, LA: Louisiana State University Press, 1970.

Abrahams, Roger D., and George Foss. *Anglo-American Folksong Style*. Englewood Cliffs, NJ: Prentice-Hall, 1968.

Alderson, William. "Notes and Queries." *California Folklore Quarterly* 1 (October 1942): 375–376.

Allen, Jules Verne. *Cowboy Lore*. San Antonio: Naylor, 1933.

Allen, Ray, and Lois Wilcken, eds. *Island Sounds in the Global City: Caribbean Popular Music & Identity in New York*. Urbana, IL: University of Illinois Press, 2001.

Allen, William Francis, Charles Pickard Ware, and Lucy McKim Garrison. *Slave Songs of the United States*. 1867. Reprint, New York: Dover, 1995.

Alloy, Evelyn. *Working Women's Music: Songs and Struggles of Women in the Cotton Mills, Textile Plants and Needle Trades*. Hatboro, PA: Legacy Books, 1976.

Ancelet, Barry Jean. *Musiciens Cadiens et Créoles: The Makers of Cajun Music*. Austin, TX: University Texas Press, 1984.

Anonymous. *The Forget-Me-Not Songster*. 1848. Reprint, Norwood, PA: Norwood Editions, 1974.

Arnold, Byron. *Folksongs of Alabama*. University, AL: University of Alabama, 1950.

Atkins, John. "The Carter Family." In *Stars of Country Music*, ed. Bill C. Malone and Judith McCulloh. Urbana, IL: University of Illinois Press, 1975.

Barry, Phillips, ed. *The Maine Woods Songster*. Cambridge, MA: Powell Printing, 1939.

Barry, Phillips, Fannie Hardy Eckstorm, and Mary Winslow Smyth. *British Ballads from Maine*. New Haven, CT: Yale University Press, 1929.

Bastin, Bruce. *Red River Blues: The Blues Tradition in the Southeast*. Urbana, IL: University of Illinois Press, 1986.

Bayard, Samuel P., ed. *Dance to the Fiddle, March to the Fife: Instrumental Folk Tunes in Pennsylvania*. University Park, PA: Pennsylvania State University Press, 1982.

Bayard, Samuel Preston. *Hill Country Tunes: Instrumental Folk Music of Southwestern Pennsylvania*. New York: Kraus, 1940.

Bean, Annemarie, James V. Hatch, and Brooks McNamara, eds. *Inside the Minstrel Mask: Readings in Nineteenth-Century Blackface Minstrelsy*. Hanover & London: University Press of New England, 1996.

Beck, Earl Clifton. *Lore of the Lumber Camps*. Ann Arbor, MI: University of Michigan Press, 1948. (Revision of *Songs of the Michigan Lumberjacks*, 1941)

Belden, Henry M. *Ballads and Songs Collected by the Missouri Folk-Lore Society*. Columbia, MO: University of Missouri, 1940.

Belden, Henry M., and Arthur Palmer Hudson, eds. *Frank C. Brown Collection of North Carolina Folklore*, Vol. 2: *Folk Ballads* and Vol. 3: *Folk Songs*. Durham, NC: Duke University Press, 1952.

Bethke, Robert D. *Adirondack Voices: Woodsmen and Woods Lore*. Urbana, IL: University of Illinois Press, 1981.

Blegen, Theodore C., and Martin B. Ruud. *Norwegian Emigrant Songs and Ballads*. Minneapolis: University of Minnesota Press, 1936.

Boatright, Mody C., Wilson M. Hudson, and Allen Maxwell, eds. *Folk Travelers: Ballads, Tales and Talk*. Austin, TX: Publication of the Texas Folklore Society, 1953.

Botkin, B. A. *The American Play-Party Song*. New York: Ungar, 1937.

Boyer, Walter E., Albert F. Buffington, and Don Yoder. *Songs along the Mahantongo: Pennsylvania Dutch Folksongs*. 1941. Reprint, Hatboro, PA: Folklore Associates, 1964.

Brewster, Paul G. *Ballads and Songs of Indiana*. New York: Folklorica Press, 1940.

Bronner, Simon J. *Old-Time Music Makers of New York State*. Syracuse, NY: Syracuse University Press, 1987.

Bronson, Bertrand Harris. *The Traditional Tunes of the Child Ballads*. 4 Vols. Princeton, NJ: Princeton University Press, 1959–1972.

Browne, Ray B. *Alabama Folk Lyric: A Study in Origins and Media of Dissemination*. Bowling Green, KY: Bowling Green University, 1979.

Brunvand, Jan Harold, ed. *American Folklore: An Encyclopedia*. New York: Garland, 1996.

Brunvand, Jan Harold, ed. *The Study of American Folklore*. New York: W. W. Norton, 1986.

Bruynoghe, Yannick. *Big Bill Blues*. New York: DaCapo, 1964.

Bumgardner, Georgia B., ed. *American Broadsides: 60 facsimiles dated 1680 to 1800 Reproduced from Originals in the American Antiquarian Society*. Barre, ME: Imprint Society, 1971.

Burton, Thomas G., ed. *Tennessee Traditional Singers: Tom Ashley, Sam McGee, Bukka White*. Knoxville: University of Tennessee Press, 1981.

Cantwell, Robert. *When We Were Good: The Folk Revival*. Cambridge, MA: Harvard University Press, 1996.

Carawan, Guy, and Candie Carawan, eds. and comp. *Sing for Freedom: The Story of the Civil Rights Movement through Its Songs*. Bethlehem, PA: Sing Out, 1990.

Carawan, Guy, and Candie Carawan. *We Shall Overcome!—Songs of the Southern Freedom Movement*. New York: Oak, 1963.

Cauthen, Joyce. *With Fiddle and Well-Rosined Bow: Old Time Fiddling in Alabama*. Tuscaloosa, AL: University of Alabama Press, 1989.

Cazden, Norman, Herbert Haufrecht, and Norman Studer. *Folk Songs of the Catskills*. Albany: SUNY, 1982.

Chalmers, Wilma Grand. *$2 at the Door: Folk, Ethnic, and Bluegrass Music in the Northwest*. McMinnville, OR: Broadsheet Publications, 1981.

Chase, Gilbert. *America's Music: From the Pilgrims to the Present*. 3rd ed. Urbana, IL: University of Illinois Press, 1987.

Chase, Richard. *Singing Games and Playparty Games*. New York: Dover, 1949.

Cheney, Thomas E. *Mormon Songs from the Rocky Mountains*. Austin, TX: University of Texas, Publications of the American Folklore Society #53, 1968.

Child, Francis James. *The English and Scottish Popular Ballads*. 5 Vols. 1882–1898. Reprint, New York: Cooper Square Publishers, 1965. Also available on CD-ROM from Heritage Muse.

Cochran, Robert. *Vance Randolph: An Ozark Life*. Urbana, IL: University of Illinois Press, 1985.

Cockrell, Dale. *Demons of Disorder: Early Blackface Minstrels and Their World*. Cambridge, UK: Cambridge University Press, 1997.

Coffin, Tristram P. *The British Traditional Ballad in North America*. Rev. ed. Philadelphia: American Folklore Society, 1977.

Cohen, Anne. *Poor Pearl, Poor Girl!: The Murdered-Girl Stereotype in Ballad and Newspaper*. Austin, TX, and London: University of Texas Press for the American Folklore Society, 1973.

Cohen, John, and Mike Seeger, eds. *The New Lost City Ramblers Song Book*. New York: Oak, 1964.

Cohen, Norm. *A Finding List of American Secular Songsters Published between 1860 and 1899*. Murfreesboro, TN: Center for Popular Music, MTSU, 2002.

Cohen, Norm. Insert for *Folksong America: The Folk Revival*. Washington, DC: Smithsonian Institution Press, 1991.

Cohen, Norm. *Long Steel Rail: The Railroad in American Folksong*. 2nd ed. Urbana, IL: University of Illinois Press, 2000.

Cohen, Norm. "'The Persian's Crew'—The Ballad, Its Author, and the Incident." *New York Folklore Quarterly* (December 1969): 289–296.

Cohen, Norm. "The Sinking of the *Titanic* and the Floundering of American Folksong Scholarship," *Southern Folklore* 56 (1999): 3–26.

Cohen, Norm. *Traditional Anglo-American Folk Music: An Annotated Discography of Published Sound Recordings*. New York: Garland, 1994.

Cohen, Ronald D. *Rainbow Quest: The Folk Music Revival and American Society, 1940–1970*. Amherst, MA: University of Massachusetts, 2002.

Cohen, Ronald D., ed. *"Wasn't That a Time!" Firsthand Accounts of the Folk Music Revival*. Metuchen, NJ: Scarecrow Press, 1995.

Cohn, Lawrence, ed. *Nothing but the Blues: The Music and the Musicians*. New York: Abbeville, 1993.

Colcord, Joanna C. *Songs of American Sailormen*. New York: Bramhall House, 1938.

Combs, Josiah H. *Folk-Songs of the Southern United States,* ed. D. K. Wilgus. Austin, TX: University of Texas Press for American Folklore Society, 1967.

Conway, Cecilia. *African Banjo Echoes in Appalachia: A Study of Folk Traditions*. Knoxville, TN: University of Tennessee Press, 1995.

Courlander, Harold. *Negro Folk Music USA*. New York: Columbia University Press, 1963.

Cox, John Harrington. *Folk-Songs of the South*. Cambridge, MA: Harvard University Press, 1925.

Crawford, Richard. *America's Musical Life: A History*. New York & London: W. W. Norton, 2001.

Cray, Ed. *The Erotic Muse*. 2nd ed. Urbana, IL: University of Illinois Press, 1992.

Cray, Ed. *Ramblin' Man: The Life and Times of Woody Guthrie*. New York: W. W. Norton, 2004.

Creswell, Nicholas. *The Journal of Nicholas Creswell 1774–1777*. New York: Dial Press, 1924.

Dane, Barbara, and Irwin Silber. *The Vietnam Songbook*. Guardian Books, n.d.

Davis, Arthur Kyle Jr. *Traditional Ballads of Virginia*. Charlottesville, VA: University Press of Virginia, 1929.

Dean, Michael C. *The Flying Cloud*. 1922. Reprint, Norwood, PA: Norwood Editions, 1973.

Denisoff, R. Serge. *Great Day Coming: Folk Music and the American Left*. Urbana, IL: University of Illinois Press, 1971.

Dickey, Dan William. *The Kennedy Corridos: A Study of the Ballads of a Mexican American Hero.* Austin, TX: University of Texas at Austin Center for Mexican American Studies, 1978.

Doerflinger, William. *Shantymen and Shantyboys: Songs of the Sailor and Lumberman.* New York: Macmillan, 1951.

Dolph, Edward Arthur. *"Sound Off!": Soldier Songs from Yankee Doodle to Parley Voo.* New York: Cosmopolitan Book Corp., 1929.

Driggs, Frank, and Harris Lewine. *Black Beauty, White Heat: A Pictorial History of Classic Jazz.* New York: William Morrow and Company, 1982.

Eckstorm, Fanny Hardy, and Mary Winslow Smyth. *Minstrelsy of Maine: Folk-Songs and Ballads of Woods and Coast.* Boston and New York: Houghton Mifflin, 1927.

Eddy, Mary O. *Ballads and Songs from Ohio.* 1939. Reprint, Hatboro, PA: Folklore Associates, 1964.

Emrich, Duncan. "Mining Songs." *Southern Folklore Quarterly* 6 (1942).

Emrich, Duncan. "Songs of the Western Miners." *California Folklore Quarterly* 1 (July 1942).

Epstein, Dena J. *Sinful Tunes & Spirituals: Black Folk Music to the Civil War.* Urbana, IL: University of Illinois Press, 1977.

Everest, Allan S. *Rum across the Border: The Prohibition Era in Northern New York.* Syracuse, NY: Syracuse University Press, 1978.

Fife, Austin E., and Alta S. Fife. *Cowboy and Western Songs.* New York: Clarkson Potter, 1969.

Filene, Benjamin. *Romancing the Folk: Public Memory & American Roots Music.* Chapel Hill, NC: University of North Carolina Press, 2000.

Fischer, David Hackett. *Albion's Seed: Four British Folkways in America.* New York and Oxford: Oxford University Press, 1989.

Flanders, Helen Hartness. *Ancient Ballads Traditionally Sung in New England.* 4 Vols. Philadelphia: University of Pennsylvania Press, 1960–1965.

Flanders, Helen Hartness, Elizabeth F. Ballard, George Brown, and Phillips Barry. *The New Green Mountain Songster: Traditional Folk Songs of Vermont.* 1939. Reprint, Hatboro, PA: Folklore Associates, 1966.

Flanders, Helen Hartness, and George Brown. *Vermont Folk-Songs & Ballads.* 1931. Reprint, Hatboro, PA: Folklore Associates, 1968.

Flanders, Helen Hartness, and Marguerite Olney. *Ballads Migrant in New England.* 1953. Reprint, Hatboro, PA: Folklore Associates, 1968.

Foner, Philip S. *American Labor Songs of the Nineteenth Century.* Urbana, IL: University of Illinois Press, 1975.

Force, Robert, and Albert d'Ossche. *In Search of the Wild Dulcimer.* New York: Amsco Music Publishing Co., 1974–1975.

Fowke, Edith. *Lumbering Songs from the Northern Woods.* Austin, TX: University of Texas Press for American Folklore Society, 1970.

Frank, Stuart M. *The Book of Pirate Songs.* Sharon, MA: Kendall Whaling Museum, 1998.

Friedman, Albert B. *Viking Book of Folk Ballads of the English-Speaking World.* New York: Viking, 1956. Reprinted as the *Penguin Book of Folk Ballads of the English-Speaking World.*

Gardner, Emelyn Elizabeth, and Geraldine Jencks Chickering. *Ballads and Songs of Southern Michigan.* 1939. Reprint, Hatboro, PA: Folklore Associates, 1967.

Garst, John. "Chasing John Henry in Alabama and Mississippi." *Tributaries: Journal of the Alabama Folklife Association* 5 (2002).

Gellert, Lawrence. *Negro Songs of Protest.* New York: American Music League, 1936.

Gifford, Paul M. *The Hammered Dulcimer: A History.* Lanham, MD, and London: Scarecrow Press, 2001.

Gilbert, Douglas. *American Vaudeville: Its Life & Times.* 1940. Reprint, New York: Dover, 1963.

Gilliam, Dorothy Butler. *Paul Robeson: All-American.* Washington, DC: New Republic Book Co., 1976.

Gordon, Robert W. "Folk-Songs of America, XI: Fiddle Songs." *New York Times Magazine,* November 27, 1927.

Gordon, Robert W. "Folk Songs of America, XIV: Songs of the Pioneers." *New York Times Magazine,* January 15, 1928.

Grame, Theodore C. *America's Ethnic Music.* Tarpon Springs, PA: Cultural Maintenance Associates, 1976.

Gray, Roland Palmer. *Songs and Ballads of the Maine Lumberjacks.* Cambridge, MA: Harvard University Press, 1925.

Green, Archie. *Only a Miner.* Urbana, IL: University of Illinois Press, 1972.

Green, J. W. "Notes and Queries: 'Sing Ha-Ha, Come from China.'" *Western Folklore* 6(3) (July 1947): 278.

Greenway, John. *American Folksongs of Protest.* New York: Perpetua Books, 1960.

Grover, Carrie B. *A Heritage of Songs.* 1953. Reprint, Norwood, PA: Norwood Editions,1973.

Gura, Philip F., and James F. Bollman. *America's Instrument: The Banjo in the Nineteenth Century.* Chapel Hill, NC: University of North Carolina Press, 1999.

Hamm, Charles. *Yesterdays: Popular Song in America.* New York and London: W. W. Norton, 1979.

Hand, Wayland D., Charles Cutts, Robert C. Wylder, and Betty Wylder. "Songs of the Butte Miners." *Western Folklore* 9 (January 1950).

Handy, W. C. *Father of the Blues.* New York: Macmillan, 1941.

Hansen, Barry. *Rhino's Cruise through the Blues.* San Francisco: Miller Freeman Books, 2000.

Harris, Joseph, ed. *The Ballad and Oral Literature.* Cambridge, MA: Harvard University Press, 1991.

Herrera-Sobek, Maria. *Northward Bound: The Ethnic Immigrant Experience in Ballad and Song.* Bloomington, IN: Indiana University Press, 1993.

Herzog, George. "Song: Folk Song and the Music of Folk Song." In *Standard Dictionary of Folklore*, ed. Maria Leach. New York: Funk & Wagnalls, 1950.

Hodgart, M. J. C. *The Ballads*. 2nd ed. London: Hutchison University Library, 1962.

Hubbard, Lester A. *Ballads and Songs from Utah*. Salt Lake City, UT: University of Utah, 1961.

Huber, Patrick. "Cain't Make a Living at a Cotton Mill: The Life and Hillbilly Songs of Dave McCarn." *North Carolina Historical Review* 70 (July 2003): 297–333.

Hudson, Arthur Palmer. *Folksongs of Mississippi*. 1936. Reprint, New York and Philadelphia: Folklorica, 1981.

Hugill, Stan. *Shanties from the Seven Seas*. New York: E. P. Dutton & Co., 1966.

Hugill, Stan. *Songs of the Sea*. New York: McGraw-Hill, 1977.

Hull, Kenneth C. *Lily May: A Legend in Our Time*. New York: Carlton Press, 1975.

Hullfish, William. *The Canaller's Songbook*. Brockport, NY: Bravo Productions, 1994.

Huntington, Gale. *Songs the Whalemen Sang*. Barre, MA: Barre, 1964.

Hustvedt, Sigurd Bernhard. *Ballad Books and Ballad Men*. Cambridge, MA: Harvard University Press, 1930.

Ives, Burl. *The Wayfaring Stranger's Notebook*. New York: Bobbs-Merrill, 1962.

Jackson, Bruce, ed. *The Negro and His Folklore in Nineteenth-Century Periodicals*. Austin, TX: University of Texas Press, 1967.

Jasen, David A., and Gene Jones. *That American Rag: The Story of Ragtime from Coast to Coast*. New York: Schirmer, 2000.

Jones, Loyal. *Minstrel of the Appalachians: The Story of Bascom Lamar Lunsford*. Boone, NC: Appalachian Consortium Press, 1984.

Jones, Loyal. *Radio's "Kentucky Mountain Boy": Bradley Kincaid*. Rev. ed. Berea, KY: Berea College, 1988.

Karpeles, Maude. *Cecil Sharp: His Life and Work*. Chicago: University of Chicago Press, 1967.

Kincaid, Bradley. *Favorite Old-Time Songs and Mountain Ballads, Book 2*, 1929.

Korson, George. *Coal Dust on the Fiddle*. 1943. Reprint, Hatboro, PA: Folklore Associates, 1965.

Korson, George. *Minstrels of the Mine Patch*. 1938. Reprint, Hatboro, PA: Folklore Associates, 1964.

Krehbiel, Henry Edward. *Afro-American Folksongs: A Study in Racial and National Music*. New York: Ungar, 1962.

Larkin, Margaret. *Singing Cowboy: A Book of Western Songs*. 1931. Reprint, New York: Oak Publications, 1963.

Latham, Robert, ed. *Catalogue of the Pepys Library at Magdalene College, Cambridge. The Pepys Ballads, Facsimile Volume I*. Cambridge, UK: D. S. Brewer, 1987.

Laws, G. Malcolm Jr. *American Balladry from British Broadsides: A Guide for Students and Collectors*. Philadelphia: American Folklore Society, 1957.

Laws, G. Malcolm Jr. *Native American Balladry: A Descriptive Study and a Bibliographical Syllabus*. Rev. ed. Philadelphia: American Folklore Society, 1964.

Leach, MacEdward. *Folk Ballads and Songs of the Lower Labrador Coast*. Ottawa, ON: National Museum of Canada, 1965.

Lieberman, Robbie. *"My Song Is My Weapon": People's Songs, American Communism, and the Politics of Culture, 1930–50*. Urbana, IL: University of Illinois Press, 1989.

Lingenfelter, Richard E., Richard A. Dwyer, and David Cohen. *Songs of the American West*. Berkeley and Los Angeles: University of California Press, 1968.

Linscott, Eloise Hubbard. *Folk Songs of Old New England*. Hamden, CT: Archon, 1939 (reprint 1962).

List, George. *Singing about It: Folk Song in Southern Indiana*. Indianapolis: Indiana Historical Society, 1991, includes cassette.

Logsdon, Guy. *"The Whorehouse Bells Were Ringing" and Other Songs Cowboys Sing*. Urbana, IL: University of Illinois Press, 1989.

Lomax, John A. *Cowboy Songs and Other Frontier Ballads*. New York: Macmillan, 1931.

Lomax, John A., and Alan Lomax. *American Ballads and Folk Songs*. New York: Macmillan, 1934.

Lomax, John A., and Alan Lomax. *Best Loved American Folksongs*. New York: Grosset & Dunlap, 1947.

Longhi, Jim. *Woody, Cisco & Me: Seamen Three in the Merchant Marine*. Urbana, IL: University of Illinois Press, 1997.

Lott, Eric. *Love and Theft: Blackface Minstrelsy and the American Working Class*. Oxford University Press, 1993.

Loza, Steven. *Barrio Rhythm: Mexican-American Music in Los Angeles*. Urbana, IL: University of Illinois Press, 1993.

MacDonell, Margaret. *The Emigrant Experience: Songs of Highland Emigrants in North America*. Toronto, ON: University of Toronto Press, 1982.

MacLeod, R. R. *Document Blues 2*. Edinburgh, Scotland: PAT Publications, 1995.

Malone, Bill C. *Country Music, U.S.A.: A Fifty Year History*. Rev ed. Austin, TX, and London: University of Texas Press, 1985.

Malone, Bill C. *Singing Cowboys and Musical Mountaineers: Southern Culture and the Roots of Country Music*. Athens: University of Georgia Press, 1993.

Malone, Bill C., and Judith McCulloh, eds. *Stars of Country Music: Uncle Dave Macon to Johnny Rodriguez*. Urbana, IL: University of Illinois Press, 1975.

Malone, Henry H., S. J. Sackett, and William E. Koch. *Kansas Folklore*. Lincoln: University of Nebraska Press, 1961.

Marshall, Charles. *Cowboy Songs as Sung by Charles Marshall, the "Singing Cowboy" in Death Valley Days*. Wilmington, CA, 1934.

Martin, Philip. *Farmhouse Fiddlers: Music & Dance Traditions in the Rural Midwest*. Mt. Horeb, WI: Midwest Traditions, 1994.

McCloud, Barry, et al. *Definitive Country: The Ultimate Encyclopedia of Country Music and Its Performers*. New York: Perigee, 1995.

McGill, Josephine. *Folk-Songs of the Kentucky Mountains*. New York: Boosey, 1917.

Mellinger, E. Henry. *Folk-Songs from the Southern Highlands*. New York: J. J. Augustin, 1938.

Moloney, Mick. *Far from the Shamrock Shore: The Story of Irish-American Immigration through Song*. New York: Crown Publishing, 2002, includes CD.

Moore, Ethel, and Chauncey O. Moore. *Ballads and Folk Songs of the Southwest*. Norman, OK: University of Oklahoma, 1964.

Morris, Alton C. *Folksongs of Florida*. 1950. Reprint, New York and Philadelphia: Folklorica, 1981.

Nathan, Hans. *Dan Emmett and the Rise of Early Negro Minstrelsy*. Norman, OK: University of Oklahoma Press, 1962.

Newell, William Wells. *Games and Songs of American Children*. 2nd ed. 1903. Reprint, New York: Dover, 1963.

Odum, Howard W. "Folk-Song and Folk-Poetry as Found in the Secular Songs of the Southern Negroes—Concluded." *Journal of American Folklore* 24 (October–December 1911).

Odum, Howard W., and Guy B. Johnson. *The Negro and His Songs: A Study of Typical Negro Songs in the South*. 1925. Reprint, Hatboro, PA: Folklore Associates, 1964.

Odum, Howard W., and Guy B. Johnson. *Negro Workaday Songs*. Chapel Hill, NC: University of North Carolina Press, 1926.

Ohrlin, Glenn. *The Hell-Bound Train: A Cowboy Songbook*. Urbana, IL: University of Illinois, 1973.

Oliver, Paul. *Songsters & Saints: Vocal Traditions on Race Records*. Cambridge, UK: Cambridge University, 1984.

Owens, William A. *Texas Folk Songs*. Dallas, TX: Southern Methodist University, Publications of Texas Folklore Society #23, 1950.

Paredes, Américo. *A Texas-Mexican Cancionero*. Urbana, IL: University of Illinois Press, 1976.

Paredes, Américo. *"With His Pistol in His Hand": A Border Ballad and Its Hero*. Austin, TX: University of Texas Press, 1958.

Parker, Paul. "Notes and Queries: A Monterey County Song." *California Folklore Quarterly* 1:4 (October 1942): 378.

Parrish, Lydia. *Slave Songs of the Georgia Sea Islands*. 1942. Reprint, Hatboro, PA: Folklore Associates, 1965.

Pawlowska, Harriet M. *Merrily We Sing: 105 Polish Folksongs*. Detroit: Wayne State University Press, 1961.

Peña, Manuel. *Texas-Mexican Conjunto: The History of a Working-Class Music*. Austin, TX: University of Texas, 1985.

Peters, Harry B. *Folk Songs Out of Wisconsin*. Madison, WI: State Historical Society of Wisconsin, 1977.

Pinker, Steven. *The Language Instinct*. New York: William Morrow and Co., 1994.

Porter, Susan L., and John Graziano, eds. *Vistas of American Music: Essays and Compositions in Honor of William K. Kearns*. Warren, MI: Harmonie Park Press, 1999.

Porterfield, Nolan. *Last Cavalier: The Life and Times of John A. Lomax*. Urbana, IL: University of Illinois Press, 1996.

Pound, Louise. *American Ballads and Songs*. 1922. Reprint, New York: Charles Scribners Sons, 1972.

Pound, Louise. *Folk-Song of Nebraska and the Central West*. Lincoln, NE: Nebraska Academy of Sciences, ca. 1916.

Raine, James W. *The Land of Saddlebags*. New York: Council of Women for Home Missions, 1924.

Randolph, Vance. *Ozark Folklore*, 2 Vols. Columbia, MO: University of Missouri Press, 1972–1987.

Randolph, Vance. *Roll Me in Your Arms: "Unprintable" Ozark Folksongs and Folklore*, Vol. 1: *Folksongs and Music*. Ed. and with an introduction by G. Legman. Fayetteville, AR: University of Arkansas Press, 1992.

Renwick, Roger deV. "Ballad" and "Folksong." In *American Folklore: An Encyclopedia*, ed. Jan Harold Brunvand. New York: Garland, 1996.

Rickaby, Franz. *Ballads and Songs of the Shanty-Boy*. Cambridge, MA: Harvard University Press, 1926.

Ritchie, Jean. *The Dulcimer Book*. New York: Oak, 1974.

Ritchie, Jean. *Singing Family of the Cumberlands*. New York: Oak, 1955.

Roderick, B. H. A., Sr., ed. *Panhandler Songbook*, Vol. 1: *Folksongs of Southeast Alaska and the Yukon*. Juneau, AK: By the people of Southeast Alaska and the Yukon, 1979.

Romalis, Shelly. *Pistol-Packin' Mama: Aunt Molly Jackson and the Politics of Folk Song*. Urbana: University of Illinois Press, 1998.

Rooney, James. *Bossmen: Bill Monroe and Muddy Waters*. New York: Da Capo, 1971.

Rosenbaum, Art, and Margo Rosenbaum. *Folk Visions and Voices: Traditional Music and Song in North Georgia*. Athens, GA: University of Georgia, 1983.

Rosenberg, Neil V. "American Folksong Scholarship: A Response to Norm Cohen." *Southern Folklore* 56 (1999): 27–33.

Roud, Steve. *Folksong Index*. Electronic database. Sussex, England, UK, 2002.

Sackett, S. J., and William E. Koch, eds. *Kansas Folklore*. Lincoln, NE: University of Nebraska, 1961.

Sandburg, Carl. *The American Songbag*. New York: Harcourt-Brace, 1927.

Savoy, Ann Allen. *Cajun Music: A Reflection of a People*. Vol. 1. Rev. ed. Eunice, LA: Bluebird Press, 1986.

Scarborough, Dorothy, assisted by Ola Lee Gulledge. *On the Trail of Negro Folk-Songs*. 1925. Reprint, Hatboro, PA: Folklore Associates, 1963.

Schuller, Gunther. *Early Jazz: Its Roots and Musical Development*. New York: Oxford University Press, 1968.

Scott, John Anthony. *The Ballad of America: The History of the United States in Song and Story*. New York: Bantam, 1966.

Seeger, Pete, and Bob Reiser. *Carry It On!: A History in Song & Picture of Working Men & Women of America*. New York: Simon and Schuster, 1985.

Seeger, Pete, and Bob Reiser. *Everybody Says Freedom: A History of the Civil Rights Movement in Songs and Pictures*. New York: Norton, 1989.

Sharp, Cecil J. *English Folk Song: Some Conclusions*. 4th rev. ed. East Ardsley, UK: EP Publishing, 1972.

Sharp, Cecil J. *English Folk Songs from the Southern Appalachians*, prepared by Maud Karpeles. 4th rev. ed. 1965. Reprint, Wakefield: E.P. Pub., 1972.

Shelton, Robert. *No Direction Home: The Life and Music of Bob Dylan*. New York: Beech Tree Books/Wm. Morrow, 1986.

Shepard, Leslie. *The Broadside Ballad*. London: Herbert Jenkins, 1962.

Silber, Irwin, ed. *Soldier Songs and Home-Front Ballads of the Civil War*. New York: Oak, 1964.

Silber, Irwin, ed. *Songs America Voted By*. Harrisburg, PA: Stackpole Books, 1971.

Silber, Irwin. *Songs of the Civil War*. New York: Columbia University, 1960.

Silber, Irwin. *Songs of the Great American West*. 1967. Reprint, New York: Dover, 1995.

Silber, Irwin. *Songs of Independence*. New York: Stackpole Books, 1973.

Silverman, Jerry. *Mel Bay's Immigrant Songs*. Pacific, MO: Mel Bay, 1992.

Slobin, Mark. *Tenement Songs: The Popular Music of the Jewish Immigrants*. Urbana, IL: University of Illinois Press, 1982.

Solomon, Olivia, and Jack Solomon, eds. *"Honey in the Rock": The Ruby Pickens Tartt Collection of Religious Folk Songs from Sumter County, Alabama*. Macon, GA: Mercer University Press, 1991.

Sorrels, Rosalie. *Way Out in Idaho*. Lewiston, ID: Confluence Press, 1991.

Stambler, Irwin, and Grelun Landon. *The Encyclopedia of Folk, Country & Western Music*. 2nd ed. New York: St. Martin's Press, 1983.

Stearns, Marshall. *The Story of Jazz*. New York: Oxford University Press, 1956.

Stout, Earl J. *Folklore from Iowa*. New York: G. E. Stechert for the American Folklore Society, 1936.

Talley, Thomas W., and Charles K. Wolfe, ed. *Negro Folk Rhymes*. Knoxville, TN: University of Tennessee Press, 1949 (revised edition with music, 1991).

Thomas, Cloea, ed. and transcriber. *Scenes & Songs of the Ohio-Erie Canal*. Columbus, OH: Ohio Historical Society, 1971.

Thomas, Philip J. *Songs of the Pacific Northwest*. Saanichton, BC: Hancock House, 1979.

Thorp, N. Howard "Jack." *Songs of the Cowboys*. 1921. Reprint, Lincoln: University of Nebraska Press, 1984.

Thorp, N. Howard "Jack," Austin E. Fife, and Alta S. Fife, eds. *Songs of the Cowboys*. New York: Clarkson Potter, 1966.

Tinsley, Jim Bob. *He Was Singin' This Song*. Orlando, FL: University Presses of Florida, 1981.

Titon, Jeff Todd. *Old-Time Kentucky Fiddle Tunes*. Lexington, KY: University Press of Kentucky, 2001, includes CD.

Toelken, Barre. *Morning Dew and Roses: Nuance, Metaphor, and Meaning in Folksongs*. Urbana, IL: University of Illinois Press, 1995.

Toll, Robert C. *Blacking Up*. New York: Oxford University Press, 1974.

Tuso, Joseph F. *Singing the Vietnam Blues: Songs of the Air Force in Southeast Asia*. College Station, TX: Texas A&M University Press, 1990.

Walton, Ivan H., and Joe Grimm. *Windjammers: Songs of the Great Lakes Sailors*. Detroit: Wayne State University Press, 2002, includes CD.

Wells, Evelyn. *The Ballad Tree*. New York: Ronald Press Co., 1953.

Welsch, Roger L. *A Treasury of Nebraska Pioneer Folklore*. 1939. Reprint, Lincoln, NE: University of Nebraska Press, 1966.

Whall, W. B. *Sea Songs and Shanties*. 6th ed. Glasgow: Brown, Son & Ferguson, 1927.

Wheeler, Mary. *Roustabout Songs: A Collection of Ohio River Valley Songs*. New York: Remick Music Corp., 1939.

Wheeler, Mary. *Steamboatin' Days*. Baton Rouge, LA: Louisiana State University Press, 1944.

White, B. F., and E. J. King. *The Sacred Harp*. 3rd ed. 1859. Reprint, Nashville: Broadville Press, 1968.

White, John I. *Git Along, Little Dogies: Songs and Songmakers of the American West*. Urbana, IL: University of Illinois, 1975.

White, Newman I. *American Negro Folk Songs*. 1925. Reprint, Hatboro, PA: Folklore Associates, 1965.

Wiggins, Gene. *Fiddlin' Georgia Crazy: Fiddlin' John Carson, His Real World, and the World of His Songs*. Urbana, IL: University of Illinois Press, 1987.

Wilgus, D. K. *Anglo-American Folksong Scholarship since 1898*. New Brunswick, NJ: Rutgers, 1959.

Willens, Doris. *Lonesome Traveler: The Life of Lee Hays*. New York: W. W. Norton, 1988.

Wolfe, Charles K., ed. *Folk Songs of Middle Tennessee: The George Boswell Collection*. Knoxville, TN: University of Tennessee Press, 1997.

Wolfe, Charles, and Kip Lornell. *The Life and Legend of Leadbelly*. New York: Harper Collins, 1992.

Wolff, Francie. *Give the Ballot to the Mothers: Songs of the Suffragists—A History in Song*. Springfield, MO: Denlinger's Publishers, Ltd., 1998.

Wolford, Leah Jackson. *The Play-Party in Indiana*. Indianapolis, IN: Indiana Historical Commission, 1916.

Wright, John. *Traveling the High Way Home: Ralph Stanley and the World of Traditional Bluegrass Music*. Urbana, IL: University of Illinois Press, 1993.

Wright, Rochelle, and Wright, Robert L. *Danish Emigrant Ballads and Songs.* Carbondale and Edwardsville, IL: Southern Illinois University Press, 1983.

Wyman, Loraine. *Lonesome Tunes: Folk Songs from the Kentucky Mountains.* New York: H. W. Gray, 1916.

Yanow, Scott. *Jazz: A Regional Exploration.* Westport, CT: Greenwood Press, 2005.

Young, Henry. *"Haywire Mac" and "The Big Rock Candy Mountain."* Stillhouse Hollow Publishers, 1981.

Index

Folksongs: bawdy, erotic, 56; collecting, xxxvi–xxxvii; lyric, 52; meaning of, xxx
"Fond du Lac Jail," 153–154
Ford, Charlie, 160
Ford, Robert, 160
Forsyth, Nelson, 181
Foster, Stephen C., 106, 185, 212, 223
Franco-Americans, 139–140
"Frankie (and Johnny)" (Laws, I 3), 27, 124
Fraternity songs, xxx
"Free Nigger," 119
"Freight Train," 248
French, Frank, 172
French Canadians, 84, 139–140
French harp. See Harmonica
"Frog Cam to the Myl Dur, The" ("The Frog Came to the Mill Door"), 36
"Froggie Went a-Courtin'," 36
"Fuller and Warren" (Laws, F 16), 150
Fur trappers, 167

Garfunkel, Art, 6
"George Collins" (Child, 85), 7
"Georgia Buck," 110
Gibson, Bob, 237
Gilbert, Ronnie, 231
Gilkyson, Terry, 231
"Girl I Left Behind, The" (Laws, P 1b), 15, 20 111, 150
"Girl I Left Behind Me, The," 39
"Go in and out the Window," 39
"Go Tell Aunt Rhody," 37
"Go Way from My Window," 263
"Going Down the Road Feeling Bad," 109
Gold, discovery of: in California, 169, 182, 185–187; in Northwest, 169, 172
"Golden Slippers," 218
"Golden Vanity, The" (Child, 286), 9, 85
"Goober Peas," 223, 225
"Goodbye Old Paint," 201, 203
"Goodnight Irene," 175, 231, 275

Gordon, Robert W., xxxv
Gorman, Larry, 24
Gospel music, 48
"Gosport Tragedy, The" (Laws, P 36a), 112–115
Grand Coulee Dam, 174
"Grand Hotel, The," 172–173
Grayson, G. B., 117
Great Awakening, 44
Great Depression, 174
Great Lakes, songs of, 149
"Great Titanic, The" (Laws, D 24), 104
Green, Archie, 137
"Green Grass Grew All Around," 222
Green Grow the Lilacs, (play) 181
"Green Grows the Laurel," 181
"Greenland Whale (Fisheries), The" (Laws, K 21), 102–103
Grover, Carrie, 112
Guard, Dave, 234
Guitar: English (cetra), 70; Hawaiian or steel, 71; Spanish, 70
Guiteau, Charles, xxvi
"Gunpowder Tea," 86–88
Guthrie, Woody, 175, 220, 230–231
"Gypsy Davy, The" (Child, 200), 9, 85, 111

"Half Hitch, The" (Laws, N 23), 85
"Hallelujah, I'm a Bum," 260
Hampton Institute, 47
Hanby, Benjamin R., 213
Hand, Wayland, 169
Handy, William C., 51, 219
"Hangman" (Child, 95), 9
"Happy Birthday," xxxviii
"Hard Rain's A-Gonna Fall," 235
Harmonica, 73
Harris, Charles K., 195
"Haul the Bowline," 97
Hawes, Bess Lomax, 231
Hays, Lee, 231
Hays, Will S., 156
Helf, J. Fred, 217
"Hell-Bound Train, The," 29
Hellerman, Fred, 231

"Poor Omie" (F 4). *See* "(Little) Omie
    Wise"
"Poor Tramp Has to Live, The," 216
"Pop Goes the Weasel," 35, 92
"Pretty Fair Maid in the Garden"
    (Laws, N 37/N 42), 15, 111
"Pretty Polly" (Laws, P 36b), 15,
    111–115
Price, Laurence, 8, 9
"Prisoner's Song, The," 270
Prohibition, songs about, 94–96
Psalms, 44

Quantrill, William Clarke, 157

Race music, 141
Radio, hillbilly music on, 142
Ragtime, 140
"Ragtime Annie," 140
Rail travel, early, 175
"Railroad Bill" (Laws, I 13), 27
Railroads: attitudes toward, 176; link
    to Northwest, 172; songs about,
    174–178
"Rain and Snow," 266
"Rake and a Rambling Boy" (Laws,
    L 12), 15
Randolph, Vance, xxxviii, 76, 79, 111
Redwine, Judge, 117
"Redwing," 220
Religious songs, 42
Revolutionary War, songs from,
    86, 88
Rexford, Eben E., 217
Reynolds, Malvina, 235
Reynolds, Nick, 234
Rice, Thomas D. "Daddy," 208
"Rich Irish Lady" (Laws, P 9), 15, 111
Riddle, Almeda, xxxiii, 24, 25, 80
Riggs, Lynn, 181
Riley the Bum, 176
"Ring around a Rosie," 35
Ring dance/ring shout, 128
Ritchie, Jean, 72, 232–33
River boatsmen, songs about, 102
Roberts, Dock Phil, 121
Robin Hood, 158

"Robin Hood and the Beggar II"
    (Child, 134), 2
"Robin Hood Newly Revived" (Child,
    128), 2
"Robin Hood's Birth, Breeding, Valor,
    and Marriage" (Child, 149), 3
Robison, Carson J., xxxii–xxxiii
"Rock-a-Bye Baby," 37
"Rock the Cradle Lucy," 209
Rodgers, Jimmie, 143
"Roll on, Columbia," 175
"Roll on Little Dogies," 196, 199
"Rosie," 131–132
Rousseau, Jean-Jacques, 37
"Rousseau's Dream," 37
"Roving Gambler, The" (Laws, H 4),
    24
"Row, Row, Row Your Boat," 35
"Rumrunner's Song," 96
Rutherford, Leonard, 121

Sacred Harp, The, 45
"Sailor Boy, The" (Laws, K 12), 15,
    111, 150
"Sailor's alphabet, The," 162
"St. Louis Blues," 52, 219
"St. Louis Tickle," 140
Sainte-Marie, Buffie, 235
"Sally Goodin'" ("Possum Up a Gum
    Stump, Coony in the Hollow"),
    39, 43
Samson, song about, 132–133
Sandburg, Carl, 228–229, 231
Sankey, Ira, 47
Santa Anna, General, 182
Sa(u)nders, Wash, xxxix
"Says the Miner to the Mucker,"
    170–171
Scales, 77
"Scarborough Fair/Canticle" (Child,
    4), 236
"Schloof, Bobbeli, Schloof," ("Sleep,
    My Baby, Sleep"), 105–106
Scopes, John T., xxxii
Scott, James, 140
Scott, Joe, 24
Scott, Sir Walter, 8, 76

About the Author

NORM COHEN is the author of *Long Steel Rail: The Railroad in American Folksong*, 2nd ed. (2001) and *Traditional Anglo-American Folk Music: An Annotated Discography of Published Recordings* (1994). He has edited and/or annotated two dozen albums and written extensively on various aspects of folk, country, and popular music. He is a retired chemist and currently teaches college science in Portland, Oregon.